COULTER LIBRARY ONONDAGA COMM.
E185.96.B536 1982
Black leaders of the

3 0418 00022356 8

BLACKS IN THE NEW WORLD: *August Meier, Series Editor*

A list of books in the series appears at the end of this book.

Black Leaders of the Twentieth Century

The Sidney B. Coulter Library
Onondaga Community College
Rte. 173, Onondaga Hill
Syracuse, New York 13215

Black Leaders
of the Twentieth Century

Edited by John Hope Franklin
and August Meier

UNIVERSITY OF ILLINOIS PRESS
Urbana Chicago London

*All illustrations courtesy of Moorland-Spingarn Research Center
at Howard University, Washington, D.C.*

© 1982 by the Board of Trustees of the University of Illinois
Manufactured in the United States of America

3   4   5   6   C

This book is printed on acid-free paper.

LIBRARY OF CONGRESS CATALOGING IN PUBLICATION DATA

Main entry under title:

Black leaders of the twentieth century.

  (Blacks in the new world)
  Includes index.
  1. Afro-Americans—Biography.   I. Franklin, John Hope,
1915–   .   II. Meier, August, 1923–   .   III. Series.
E185.96.B536   920′.009296073 [B]   81–11454
ISBN 0–252–00870–7 (cloth)   AACR2
ISBN 0–252–00939–8 (paper)

Contents

INTRODUCTION   ix

1. BOOKER T. WASHINGTON AND THE POLITICS OF ACCOMMODATION
   Louis R. Harlan   1

2. T. THOMAS FORTUNE: MILITANT EDITOR IN THE AGE OF ACCOMMODATION
   Emma Lou Thornbrough   19

3. THE LONELY WARRIOR: IDA B. WELLS-BARNETT AND THE STRUGGLE FOR BLACK LEADERSHIP
   Thomas C. Holt   39

4. W. E. B. DU BOIS: PROTAGONIST OF THE AFRO-AMERICAN PROTEST
   Elliott Rudwick   63

5. JAMES WELDON JOHNSON AND THE DEVELOPMENT OF THE NAACP
   Eugene Levy   85

6. MARCUS GARVEY AND THE POLITICS OF REVITALIZATION
   Lawrence W. Levine   105

7. A. PHILIP RANDOLPH: LABOR LEADER AT LARGE
   Benjamin Quarles   139

8. CHARLES CLINTON SPAULDING: MIDDLE-CLASS LEADERSHIP IN THE AGE OF SEGREGATION
   Walter Weare   167

9. MARY MCLEOD BETHUNE AND THE NATIONAL YOUTH ADMINISTRATION: A CASE STUDY OF POWER RELATIONSHIPS IN THE BLACK CABINET OF FRANKLIN D. ROOSEVELT
   B. Joyce Ross   191

10. CHARLES HAMILTON HOUSTON: SOCIAL ENGINEER FOR CIVIL RIGHTS
    Genna Rae McNeil   221

11. MABEL K. STAUPERS AND THE INTEGRATION OF BLACK NURSES INTO THE ARMED FORCES
    Darlene Clark Hine   241

12. ADAM CLAYTON POWELL, JR.: THE MILITANT AS POLITICIAN
    Martin Kilson   259

13. MARTIN LUTHER KING, JR., AND THE PROMISE OF NONVIOLENT POPULISM
    David Levering Lewis   277

14. MALCOLM X: WITNESS FOR THE PROSECUTION
    Peter Goldman   305

15. WHITNEY M. YOUNG, JR.: COMMITTING THE POWER STRUCTURE TO THE CAUSE OF CIVIL RIGHTS
    Nancy J. Weiss   331

NOTES ON CONTRIBUTORS   359

INDEX   361

Introduction

THIS VOLUME analyzes the careers of fifteen nationally known twentieth-century American black leaders who sought in diverse ways to advance the race and overcome the racial barriers and oppression that pervaded American society. Essentially the book presents the current state of our knowledge in the field and thus prepares the way for deeper and more systematic study of the subject of twentieth-century Negro leadership.

While a few of the essays are based upon new research, we have largely chosen as authors individuals who are recognized authorities on the people they write about; for the remaining studies we have enlisted scholars who are well known for the breadth of their knowledge and teaching experience in American Negro history. All but one of the essays were written expressly for this anthology.

Of course, it has not been possible to include all the leaders of national stature who would be appropriate subjects for essays in this book. We decided at the outset that in order to achieve a better perspective, it would be wise to exclude from treatment persons still alive, although we made an exception for Mabel K. Staupers, who is now over ninety years old and whose public career had ended by 1950. In addition, space limitations and the state of current research have helped shape our choices. Obvious omissions are people like William H. Hastie, the civil rights leader, New Deal official, and first black on the federal judiciary; Paul Robeson, the radical intellectual; Mary Church Terrell, a central figure in the black women's club movement; William Monroe Trotter, an outspoken and acerbic critic of Booker T. Washington at the turn of the century; Walter White, who headed the National Association for the Advancement of Colored People for a quarter of a century; college presidents like John Hope and Mordecai W. Johnson; and Ralph Bunche, the political scientist and United Nations undersecretary. Nor have we been able to include any leaders of fraternal organizations; ministers whose influence was exercised principally through their religious and denominational roles; religious cult leaders like Daddy Grace, Elder Solomon Lightfoot Micheaux, and

Father Divine; or typical machine political leaders like the succession of Chicago congressmen—Oscar DePriest, Arthur Mitchell, and William Dawson.

On the other hand, we have striven to represent a broad variety of leaders—men and women; nationalists and integrationists; leaders whose principal base was their organizational affiliation; leaders who exercised influence mainly through their personal charisma; politicians, civic leaders, and government bureaucrats; and individuals who came to prominence through the labor movement, business, the arts, and the professions.

The leaders examined here also represent a wide diversity of styles, programs, and strategies. Three were important officials in the NAACP—as befits the central role played by that organization in efforts to advance blacks during the twentieth century—but all three people exhibit striking differences in styles and methods, and they functioned in very different roles. Yet all of the individuals discussed here were propagandists, in that they sought through their speeches, writings, and other activities to mobilize blacks to struggle harder for racial advancement and freedom and—except for the nationalists Marcus Garvey and Malcom X—to win white allies and support in the crusade for Negro rights. We have asked each of the contributors to examine the kind of role played by his or her subject in the struggle for black advancement and how the person functioned as a leader of blacks and—where relevant—as a mobilizer of white support. Beyond this, on the other hand, given the diversity among the leaders discussed, the authors were encouraged to develop their essays as seemed most appropriate to them. In view of the interrelationships among a number of the leaders treated, there is inevitably a certain degree of overlapping among some of the essays; yet in such cases each author approaches the matter from the perspective of the subject.

We hope that future research will pursue the questions raised explicitly and implicitly in the various essays. How much power did the various leaders actually have, what were the sources and limits of that power, and how did they use that power or influence in seeking to attain their goals? To what extent was this power derived from black support, to what extent from white support, and to what extent from an organizational base or from a position in government? What tactics did individual leaders use to appeal to blacks and/or whites to achieve their aims? To what extent did the leaders cooperate with each other, to what extent were they competing with each other, to what extent were their relationships marked by conflict, and how in turn did such patterns of cooperation, competition, and conflict shape the course of their careers and the degree to which the cause of black advancement was hindered or promoted? What were the different ways in which the style and strategies of the individual leaders were shaped by their personal backgrounds and by the differing social contexts in which they operated? Finally, to what extent were any of them able to move beyond their role as leaders in the cause of black advancement, to become leaders prominent in other broader and predominantly white social movements as well?

We wish to thank Richard L. Wentworth of the University of Illinois Press for first proposing this anthology to us, and for his unfailing support and helpful suggestions durings its preparation.

Black Leaders of the Twentieth Century

Louis R. Harlan   **1**

Booker T. Washington and the
Politics of Accommodation

*During the final decades of the nineteenth century after the collapse of
Radical or Black Reconstruction, the status of Negroes, especially in the
South, deteriorated sharply, reaching its "nadir" (as historian Rayford
Logan has phrased it) at the turn of the century. Most blacks were rural
tenant farmers, exploited by a sharecropping system that at its worst de-
scended into peonage. Those in the cities were ordinarily relegated to the
least skilled and most menial jobs, and by the 1890s were incurring the
rising hostility of organized white labor. First through intimidation and
legal subterfuge and finally by constitutional amendment, Negroes in the
southern states were systematically deprived of the franchise. Segregation in schools and in public accommodations, first developed on a de
facto basis, was the law throughout the South by the early part of the
twentieth century. Undergirding this racial system was a pattern of mob
violence—lynchings and race riots—that effectively kept blacks in a subordinate place. In the North blacks were permitted to vote, but they
faced economic discrimination and increasing segregation. On the other
hand, even in the face of these obstacles, a few blacks through hard work
and good fortune were able to maintain themselves as a relatively well-
to-do group.*

*In this context of worsening conditions there developed a marked ten-
dency for many Afro-American leaders, especially in the South, to
adopt an accommodating stance that tolerated, for the present, segregation and discrimination, believing it best not to protest against the obvious oppression. Instead, they would appeal skillfully for aid from
prosperous whites and northern philanthropists, while insisting that
blacks could, through a program of self-help, lift themselves by their
bootstraps. This meant securing an education and achieving an economic competence that would win the respect of whites and the recognition of blacks' own constitutional rights. The most conspicuous and
influential of these spokesmen was Booker T. Washington, who suddenly achieved international prominence in 1895. Washington, as Louis
Harlan's essay indicates, was in effect chosen by white elites to represent
blacks, yet just because of his prominence and his achievements, he also
had a loyal following in the black community, both among ordinary
people and, with great enthusiasm, among the tiny black entrepreneurial
elite.*

It is ironic that Booker T. Washington, the most powerful black American of his time and perhaps of all time, should be the black leader whose claim to the title is most often dismissed by the lay public. Blacks often question his legitimacy because of the role that favor by whites played in Washington's assumption of power, and whites often remember him only as an educator or, confusing him with George Washington Carver, as "that great Negro scientist." This irony is something that Washington will have to live with in history, for he himself deliberately created the ambiguity about his role and purposes that has haunted his image. And yet, Washington was a genuine black leader, with a substantial black following and with virtually the same long-range goals for Afro-Americans as his rivals. This presentation is concerned with Washington's social philosophy, such as it was, but it also addresses his methods of leadership, both his Delphic public utterances that meant one thing to whites and another to blacks and his adroit private movements through the brier patch of American race relations. It does not try to solve the ultimate riddle of his character.

Washington's own view of himself was that he was the Negro of the hour, whose career and racial program epitomized what blacks needed to maintain themselves against white encroachments and to make progress toward equality in America. The facts of his life certainly fitted his self-image. He was the last of the major black leaders to be born in slavery, on a small farm in western Virginia in 1856. Growing up during the Reconstruction era in West Virginia, he believed that one of the lessons he learned was that the Reconstruction experiment in racial democracy failed because it began at the wrong end, emphasizing political means and civil rights acts rather than economic means and self-determination. Washington learned this lesson not so much through experience as a child worker in the salt works and coal mines as by what he was taught as a houseboy for the leading family of Malden, West Virginia, and later as a student at Hampton Institute in Virginia. Hampton applied the missionary method to black education and made its peace with the white South.

After teaching school in his home town, Washington briefly studied in a Baptist seminary and in a lawyer's office. But he soon abandoned these alternative careers, perhaps sensing that disfranchisement and the secularization of society would weaken these occupations as bases for racial leadership. He returned to Hampton Institute as a teacher for two years and then founded Tuskegee Normal and Industrial Institute in Alabama in 1881. Over the next quarter of a century, using

2

Hampton's methods but with greater emphasis on the skilled trades, Washington built up Tuskegee Institute to be an equal of Hampton.

Washington's bid for leadership went beyond education and institution-building, however. Symbolic of his fresh approach to black-white relations were a speech he gave in 1895 before a commercial exposition, known as the Atlanta Compromise Address, and his autobiography, *Up from Slavery* (1901). As Washington saw it, blacks were toiling upward from slavery by their own efforts into the American middle class and needed chiefly social peace to continue in this steady social evolution. Thus, in the Atlanta Compromise he sought to disarm the white South by declaring agitation of the social equality question "the merest folly" and proclaiming that in "purely social" matters "we can be as separate as the fingers, yet one as the hand in all things essential to mutual progress." These concessions came to haunt Washington as southerners used segregation as a means of systematizing discrimination, and northerners followed suit. And they did not stop at the "purely social."

Washington's concessions to the white South, however, were only half of a bargain. In return for downgrading civil and political rights in the black list of priorities, Washington asked whites to place no barriers to black economic advancement and even to become partners of their black neighbors "in all things essential to mutual progress." Washington saw his own role as the axis between the races, the only leader who could negotiate and keep the peace by holding extremists on both sides in check. He was always conscious that his unique influence could be destroyed in an instant of self-indulgent flamboyance.

Washington sought to influence whites, but he never forgot that it was the blacks that he undertook to lead. He offered blacks not the empty promises of the demagogue but a solid program of economic and educational progress through struggle. It was less important "just now," he said, for a black person to seek admission to an opera house than to have the money for the ticket. Mediating diplomacy with whites was only half of Washington's strategy; the other half was black solidarity, mutual aid, and institution-building. He thought outspoken complaint against injustice was necessary but insufficient, and he thought factional dissent among black leaders was self-defeating and should be suppressed.

Washington brought to his role as a black leader the talents and outlook of a machine boss. He made Tuskegee Institute the largest and best-supported black educational institution of his day, and it spawned a large network of other industrial schools. Tuskegee's educational function is an important and debatable subject, of course, but the central concern here is Washington's use of the school as the base of operations of what came to be known as the Tuskegee Machine. It was an all-black school with an all-black faculty at a time when most black colleges were still run by white missionaries. Tuskegee taught self-determination. It also taught trades designed for economic independence in a region dominated by sharecrop agriculture. At the same time, by verbal juggling tricks, Washington convinced the southern whites that Tuskegee was not educating black youth away from the farms. Tuskegee also functioned as a model black community, not only by acquainting its students with a middle-class way of life, but by buying up the surrounding farmland and selling it at low rates of interest to create a community of small landowners and homeowners. The Institute became larger than the town.

Washington built a regional constituency of farmers, artisans, country teachers, and small businessmen; he expanded the Tuskegee Machine nationwide after the Atlanta Compromise seemed acceptable to blacks all over the country, even by many who later denounced it. His first northern black ally was T. Thomas Fortune, editor of the militant and influential New York *Age* and founder of the Afro-American Council, the leading forum of black thought at the time. Washington was not a member, but he usually spoke at the annual meetings, and his lieutenants so tightly controlled the council that it never passed an action or resolution not in Washington's interest. Seeking more direct allies, Washington founded in 1900 the National Negro Business League, of which he was president for life. The league was important not so much for what it did for black business, which was little, but because the local branch of the league was a stronghold of Washington men in every substantial black population center.

Other classes of influential blacks did not agree with Washington's stated philosophy but were beholden to him for the favors he did them or offered to do for them. He was not called the Wizard for nothing. White philanthropists who approved of him for their own reasons gave him the money to help black colleges by providing for a Carnegie library here, a dormitory there. Through Washington Andrew Carnegie alone gave buildings to twenty-nine black schools. Not only college administrators owed him for favors, but so did church leaders, YMCA directors, and many others. Though never much of a joiner, he became a power in the Baptist church, and he schemed through lieutenants to control the secret black fraternal orders and make his friends the high potentates of the Pythians, Odd Fellows, and so on. Like any boss, he turned every favor into a bond of obligation.

It was in politics, however, that Washington built the most elaborate tentacle of the octopus-like Tuskegee Machine. In politics as in everything else, Washington cultivated ambiguity. He downgraded politics as a solution of black problems, did not recommend politics to the ambitious young black man, and never held office. But when Theodore Roosevelt became president in 1901 and asked for Washington's advice on black and southern appointments, Washington consented with alacrity. He became the chief black adviser of both Presidents Roosevelt and William Howard Taft. He failed in his efforts to liberalize Republican policy on voting rights, lynching, and racial discrimination, however, and relations between the Republican party and black voters reached a low ebb.

In patronage politics, however, Washington found his opportunity. For a man who minimized the importance of politics, Washington devoted an inordinate amount of his time and tremendous energy to securing federal jobs for his machine lieutenants. These men played a certain role in the politics of the period, but their first obligation was to the Tuskegean. Washington advised the presidents to replace the old venal officeholding class of blacks with men who had proven themselves in the independent world of business, but in practice it took only loyalty to Washington to cleanse miraculously an old-time political hack.

Washington also used high political office in the North to win the loyalty of key figures in the legal profession whose ideology and natural bent were usually in the direction of more outspoken protest. A notable example was William H. Lewis of Boston, a graduate of Amherst College and Harvard University Law School, who had been an outspoken critic of Washington. President Roosevelt had long admired Lewis's all-American prowess on the football field as much as his professional attainments, and when Washington began talking of raising the quality of the black civil service, Roosevelt brought up Lewis. Washington was skeptical, but as soon as possible he met with Lewis and made a deal with him. As Lewis wrote, there were "many things about which we might differ, but that we had the same aims and the same end in view." Lewis became, with Washington's blessing, the assistant U.S. district attorney in Boston, and a few years later Taft appointed him assistant attorney general of the United States, the highest

5

appointive federal post held by a black man up to that time—and for decades afterward.

In another sphere also Washington spread the web of his Tuskegee Machine over the several hundred black weekly newspapers and half-dozen magazines through which the black community communicated with itself. W. E. B. Du Bois tried in 1903 to prove that Washington's "hush money" controlled the black press through subsidies and outright ownership. Challenged, Du Bois could not prove his case, but when Washington's papers were opened forty years later, they revealed the essential accuracy of the charge. The question of how *much* control is complicated, however, by the willing complicity of the editors in this domination. The editors were themselves small businessmen who generally agreed with Washington's economic orientation and the conventional wisdom of a commercial age. Furthermore, Washington's small subsidies, except in a few instances, were only a minor part of the operating funds of these newspapers.

Washington's outright critics and enemies were called "radicals" because they challenged Washington's conservatism and bossism, though their tactics of verbal protest would seem moderate indeed to a later generation of activists. They were the college-educated blacks, engaged in professional pursuits, and proud of their membership in an elite class—what one of them called the Talented Tenth. The strongholds of the radicals were the northern cities and southern black colleges. They stood for full political and civil rights, liberal education, free expression, and aspiration. They dreamed of a better world and believed Booker T. Washington was a menace to its achievement.

The first to challenge Washington and all his works was a young Harvard graduate, William Monroe Trotter, who founded in 1900 a newspaper, the Boston *Guardian*. Trotter not only differed with the Tuskegean on every conceivable subject but engaged in personal abuse. He spoke of Washington's "crime of race ridicule and belittlement." He called him Pope Washington, the Black Boss, the Benedict Arnold of the Negro race, the Exploiter of Exploiters, the Great Traitor, and the Great Divider. In reporting a speech by Washington in Boston in 1902 Trotter described him thus: "His features were harsh in the extreme. His vast leonine jaws into which vast mastiff-like rows of teeth were set clinched together like a vise. His forehead shot up to a great cone; his chin was massive and square; his eyes were dull and absolutely characterless, and with a glance that would leave you uneasy and restless during the night if you had failed to report to the police such a man around before you went to bed." That this yellow journalism was far from an accurate description of Washington's modest and reassuring appearance was beside the point. In Trotter's vendetta against Washington no charge, true or false, was too big or too petty to use.

Trotter seized the chance to confront Washington directly when the black leader spoke at a Boston church in 1903 under sponsorship of the local branch of the National Negro Business League. Trotter stood on a chair to interrupt Washington's speech with nine questions that were actually challenges. Quoting from a Washington speech, for example, Trotter asked: "When you said: 'It was not so important whether the Negro was in the inferior car as whether there was in that car a superior man not a beast,' did you not minimize the outrage of the insulting Jim-crow car discrimination and justify it by the 'bestiality' of the Negro?" The final provocative question was: "Are the rope and the torch all the race is to get under your leadership?"

The police moved through the crowd to arrest Trotter for disorderly conduct, and Washington proceeded with his speech as though nothing had happened, but Trotter had achieved his purpose. The incident appeared next day in all the newspapers as the Boston Riot, penetrating Washington's news screen to show that not all blacks approved of Washington's leadership. Washington publicly ignored the affair, but his Boston lieutenants made a martyr of Trotter by vigorous prosecution of his case, forcing him to serve thirty days in jail.

Perhaps the most important effect of the Boston Riot was that it forced Du Bois, the leading black intellectual and now the leading civil rights champion of his generation, off the fence. A Harvard Ph.D. with German university training, Du Bois was never even considered for tenure in any leading American university, and in 1903 he was a professor at Atlanta University. In *The Souls of Black Folk*, published before the Boston Riot, he had criticized Washington in a searching but moderate way, in no way comparable with Trotter's cry that the emperor had no clothes. Believing that Trotter was being victimized, Du Bois wrote Trotter a private letter of sympathy, which Trotter promptly published, and this started Du Bois's movement out of academe into the arena of racial politics.

Washington had a chance in January 1904 to heal the wounds of dissidence that the Boston Riot had opened. With the consent and cooperation of Du Bois, Washington convened the Carnegie Hall Conference, a three-day secret meeting of about thirty black leaders, excluding Trotter. But Washington with his penchant for bossism torpedoed his own effort at rapprochement by packing the meeting with his own lieutenants to such a degree that Du Bois and his adherents resigned from the organization that was created at the conference.

The following year, Du Bois and Trotter formed their own organization, the Niagara Movement, dedicated to "persistent manly agitation" for civil rights, voting rights, job opportunities, equal educational opportunities, and human rights in general. The Niagara Movement is an important link in the historical development of the civil rights movement, but here we are concerned with its role in the minority-group leadership struggle with Washington. This small band of intellectuals, hurling their manifestos, was no match for the political skill and marshaled power of the Wizard of Tuskegee. They themselves limited their membership to the small black professional class, insisted on an ideological "likemindedness" that few could achieve, and had no white allies. By contrast, Washington had a broader base and a commoner touch. Though Washington proposed the leadership of another elite class, the black businessmen, he kept in close touch with the black masses and directed his program to their immediate needs. Furthermore, he fished for allies wherever he could find them, among whites and even among the professional men who would ordinarily be expected in the Niagara Movement. He cared little about the ideology of a lieutenant, as long as the man did what Washington wanted done.

The Niagara Movement called Washington, in effect, a puppet of the whites, who thrust him into prominence because he did not challenge their wrongdoing. According to the Niagarites, Washington needed to mollify the whites in behalf of his school to such an extent that he was rendered unfit for black leadership, that instead of leadership he gave them cowardice and apology. Furthermore, his critics charged that Washington was a half-educated southerner whose control over black affairs was stifling an emergent black educated elite, the Talented Tenth, the logical leaders. Because of his own class orientation he was trying to change the social position of blacks through the acquisitive propensities and the leadership of businessmen instead of through political and civil rights agitation, which the Niagara men saw as the need of the hour. Extremists among them called Washington an instrument of white indirect rule, like the slave drivers of the old days. Even the moderate Kelly Miller of Howard University observed in 1903 that Washington was "not a leader of the people's own choosing." Though they might accept his gifts, said Miller, "few thoughtful colored men espouse what passes as Mr. Washington's policy without apology or reserve."

Washington dismissed his black critics by questioning their motives, their claim to superior wisdom, and—the politician's ultimate argument—their numbers. Washington understood, if his critics did not, that his leadership of the black community largely depended on his recognition by whites as the black leader. If he did not meet some minimal standards of satisfactoriness to whites, another Washington would be created. He obviously could not lead the whites; he could not even divide the whites. He could only, in a limited way, exploit the class divisions that whites created among themselves. He could work in the cracks of their social structure, move like Brer Rabbit through the brier patch, and thus outwit the more numerous and powerful whites.

While Washington recognized the centrality of black-white relations in his efforts to lead blacks, he was severely restricted by the historical context of his leadership. It was an age of polarization of black and white. The overheated atmosphere of the South at the turn of the century resembled that of a crisis center on the eve of war. Lynching became a more than weekly occurrence; discrimination and humiliation of blacks were constant and pervasive and bred a whole literature and behavioral science of self-justification. Race riots terrorized blacks in many cities, and not only in the South. It would have required not courage but foolhardiness for Washington, standing with both feet in Alabama, to have challenged this raging white aggression openly and directly. Even unqualified verbal protest would have brought him little support from either southern blacks or white well-wishers. Du Bois took higher ground and perhaps a better vision of the future when he urged forthright protest against every white injustice, on the assumption that whites were rational beings and would respond dialectically to black protest. But few white racists of the early twentieth century cared anything for the facts. And when Du Bois in his Atlanta years undertook to implement his protest with action, he was driven to the negative means of refusing to pay his poll tax or refusing to ride segregated streetcars and elevators.

Instead of either confronting all of white America or admitting that his Faustian bargain for leadership had created a systemic weakness in his program, Washington simply met each day as it came, pragmatically, seeking what white allies he could against avowed white enemies. A serious fault of this policy was that Washington usually appealed for white support on a basis of a vaguely conceived mutual

9

interest rather than on ideological agreement. For example, in both the South and the North Washington allied himself with the white upper class against the masses. In the South he joined with the planter class and when possible with the coal barons and railroad officials against the Populists and other small white farmer groups who seemed to him to harbor the most virulent anti-black attitudes born of labor competition. Similarly, in the North, Washington admired and bargained with the big business class. The bigger the businessman, the more Washington admired him, as the avatar and arbiter of American society. At the pinnacle in his measure of men were the industrialists Carnegie, John D. Rockefeller, and Henry H. Rogers and the merchant princes Robert C. Ogden and Julius Rosenwald. To be fair to Washington, he appreciated their philanthropic generosity at least as much as he admired their worldly success, but his lips were sealed against criticism of even the more rapacious and ungenerous members of the business elite.

Washington made constructive use of his philanthropic allies to aid not only Tuskegee but black education and black society as a whole. He guided the generous impulse of a Quaker millionairess into the Anna T. Jeanes Foundation to improve the teaching in black public schools. He persuaded the Jewish philanthropist Julius Rosenwald to begin a program that lasted for decades for building more adequate black schoolhouses all over the South. Washington's influence on Carnegie, Rockefeller, Jacob Schiff, and other rich men also transcended immediate Tuskegee interests to endow other black institutions. In short, Washington did play a role in educational statesmanship. There were limits, however, to his power to advance black interests through philanthropy. When his northern benefactors became involved in the Southern Education Board to improve the southern public school systems, for example, he worked repeatedly but without success to get this board to redress the imbalance of public expenditures or even to halt the rapid increase of discrimination against black schools and black children. He had to shrug off his failure and get from these so-called philanthropists whatever they were willing to give.

Having committed himself to the business elite, Washington took a dim view of the leaders of the working class. Immigrants represented to him, as to many blacks, labor competitors; Jews were the exception here, as he held them up to ambitious blacks as models of the work-ethic and group solidarity. He claimed in his autobiography that his disillusionment with labor unions went back to his youthful membership in the Knights of Labor and stemmed from observation of their disruption of the natural laws of economics. In his heyday, however, which was also the age of Samuel Gompers, Washington's anti-union attitudes were explained by the widespread exclusion of blacks from membership in many unions and hence from employment in many trades. There is no evidence that Washington ever actively supported black strikebreaking, but his refusal to intervene in behalf of all-white unions is understandable. It was more often white employees rather than employers who excluded blacks, or so Washington believed. He worked hard to introduce black labor into the non-union, white-only cotton mills in the South, even to the extent of interesting northern capitalists in investing in black cotton mills and similar enterprises.

Washington was a conservative by just about any measure. Though he flourished in the Progressive era it was not he, but his opponents who were the men of good hope, full of reform proposals and faith in the common man. Washington's vision of the common man included the southern poor white full of rancor against blacks, the foreign-born anarchist ready to pull down the temple of American business, and the black sharecropper unqualified by education or economic freedom for the ballot. Though Washington opposed the grandfather clause and every other southern device to exclude the black man from voting solely on account of his color, Washington did not favor universal suffrage. He believed in literacy and property tests, fairly enforced. He was no democrat. And he did not believe in woman suffrage, either.

In his eagerness to establish common ground with whites, that is, with some whites, Washington often overstepped his purpose in public speeches by telling chicken-thief, mule, and other dialect stories intended to appeal to white stereotypes of blacks, and he occasionally spoke of the Afro-American as "a child race." No doubt his intent was to disarm his listeners, and before mixed audiences he often alternately addressed the two groups, reassuring whites that blacks should cooperate with their white neighbors in all constructive efforts, but saying to blacks that in their cooperation there should be "no unmanly cowering or stooping." At the cost of some forcefulness of presentation, Washington did have a remarkable capacity to convince whites as well as blacks that he not only understood them but agreed with them. It is one of Washington's intangible qualities as a black leader that he could influence, if not lead, so many whites. The agreement that whites sensed in him was more in his manner than in his program or goals, which always included human rights as well as material advancement for blacks.

In his constant effort to influence public opinion, Washington relied on the uncertain instruments of the press and the public platform. A flood of books and articles appeared over his name, largely written by his private secretary and a stable of ghostwriters, because he was too busy to do much writing. His ghostwriters were able and faithful, but they could not put new words or new ideas out over his signature, so for the crucial twenty years after 1895, Washington's writings showed no fresh creativity or real response to events, only a steady flood of platitudes. Washington's speeches generally suffered from an opposite handicap, that he was the only one who could deliver them. But he was too busy making two or three speeches a day to write a new one for each occasion, so the audiences rather than the speeches changed. But everywhere he went, North, South, or West, he drew large crowds ready to hear or rehear his platitudes.

Washington did try to change his world by other means. Some forms of racial injustice, such as lynching, disfranchisement, and unequal facilities in education and transportation, Washington dealt with publicly and directly. Early in his career as a leader he tried to sidestep the lynching question by saying that, deplorable though it was, he was too busy working for the education of black youth to divide his energies by dealing with other public questions. Friends and critics alike sharply told him that if he proposed to be a leader of blacks, he was going to have to deal with this subject. So he began an annual letter on lynching that he sent to all the southern white dailies, and he made Tuskegee Institute the center of statistical and news information on lynching. He always took a moderate tone, deplored rape and crime by blacks, but always denied that the crime blacks committed was either the cause of or justification for the crime of lynching. He tried to make up for his moderation by persistence, factual accuracy, and persuasive logic. Disfranchisement of black voters swept through the South from Texas to Virginia during Washington's day. He publicly protested in letters to the constitutional conventions and legislatures in Alabama, Georgia, and Louisiana and aided similar efforts in several other states. He failed to stop lynching, to prevent the loss of voting rights, and to clean up the Jim Crow cars or bring about even minimal standards of fairness in the public schools. But he did try.

As for social segregation, Washington abided by southern customs while in the South but forthrightly declared it unreasonable for white southerners to dictate his behavior outside of the South. His celebrated dinner at the White House in 1901, therefore, though it caused consternation and protest among white southerners, was consistent

12

with his lifetime practice. Tuskegee Institute underwent an elaborate ritual of segregation with every white visitor, but the man who came to dinner at the White House, had tea with the queen of England, and attended hundreds of banquets and private meals with whites outside the South certainly never internalized the attitudes of the segregators.

What Washington could not do publicly to achieve equal rights, he sought to accomplish secretly. He spent four years in cooperation with the Afro-American Council on a court case to test the constitutionality of the Louisiana grandfather clause, providing funds from his own pocket and from northern white liberal friends. In his own state of Alabama, Washington secretly directed the efforts of his personal lawyer to carry two grandfather-clause cases all the way to the U.S. Supreme Court, where they were lost on technicalities. He took the extra precaution of using code names in all the correspondence on the Alabama cases. Through private pressure on railroad officials and congressmen, Washington tried to bring about improvement in the Jim Crow cars and railroad waiting rooms. He had more success in the Dan Rogers case, which overturned a criminal verdict against a black man because blacks were excluded from the jury. He also secretly collaborated with two southern white attorneys to defend Alonzo Bailey, a farm laborer held in peonage for debt; the outcome here was also successful, for the Alabama peonage law was declared unconstitutional. These and other secret actions were certainly not enough to tear down the legal structure of white supremacy, but they show that Washington's role in Afro-American history was not always that of the accommodationist "heavy." He was working, at several levels and in imaginative ways, and always with vigor, toward goals similar to those of his critics. If his methods did not work, the same could be said of theirs. And he did not take these civil rights actions as a means of answering criticism, because he kept his part in the court cases a secret except to a handful of confidants, a secret not revealed until his papers were opened to historians in recent decades.

There was another, uglier side of Washington's secret behavior, however—his ruthless spying and sabotage against his leading black critics. Washington never articulated a justification for these actions, perhaps because, being secret, they did not require defense. And yet Washington and Emmett Scott left the evidence of his secret machinations undestroyed in his papers, apparently in the faith that history would vindicate him when all the facts were known. Then, too, Washington was not given to explaining himself.

Espionage became an important instrument of Washington's black

13

leadership—or bossism—a few days before the Boston Riot in 1903, when he hired a young black man, Melvin J. Chisum, to infiltrate the inner councils of Trotter's anti-Washington organization in Boston. Chisum later spied on the Niagara Movement's Brooklyn branch, arranged to bribe an opposition newspaper editor in Washington, D.C., and reported these and other clandestine actions to the Wizard on a park bench in New York City. Washington also used Pinkerton detectives and other paid and unpaid secret agents on a variety of errands, to infiltrate the inner councils of the Niagara Movement, to repress newspaper reporting of Niagara meetings, to find out if Trotter's wife worked as a domestic, to research the tax records of Atlanta to get evidence that Du Bois, a champion of black political action, had not paid his poll tax. When a young black magazine editor, J. Max Barber, began to criticize him, Washington tried to muzzle Barber through his publisher and advertisers, then hounded Barber not only out of his magazine but out of job after job until Barber retired from race work to become a dentist. Even the white liberals who joined with the Niagara Movement to form the interracial National Association for the Advancement of Colored People in 1909 were not immune from Washington's secret attacks. Washington arranged with the racially biased New York newspaper reporters to cover—in a sensational fashion—a dinner meeting of the Cosmopolitan Club, an interracial social group to which a number of the NAACP leaders belonged. Even they never guessed that Washington had done this in collusion with white racists.

The Booker T. Washington who emerges into the light of history from his private papers is a complex, Faustian character quite different from the paragon of self-uplift and Christian forbearance that Washington projected in his autobiography. On the other hand, there is little evidence for and much evidence against the charge of some of his contemporaries that he was simply an accommodationist who bargained away his race's birthright for a mess of pottage. Nor does he fit some historians' single-factor explanations of his career: that he offered "education for the new slavery," that he was a proto-black-nationalist, that he was or must have been psychologically crippled by the constraints and guilt feelings of his social role.

Washington's complexity should not be overstressed, however, for the more we know about anybody the more complex that person seems. And through the complexity of Washington's life, its busyness and its multiple levels, two main themes stand out, his true belief in his program for black progress and his great skill in and appetite for politics, broadly defined, serving both his goals and his personal power.

First, let us look closely at Washington's industrial education and small business program. It may have been anachronistic preparation for the age of mass production and corporate gigantism then coming into being, but it had considerable social realism for a black population which was, until long after Washington's death, predominantly rural and southern. Furthermore, it was well attuned to the growth and changing character of black business in his day. Increasingly, the nineteenth-century black businesses catering to white clients surrendered predominance to ghetto businesses such as banks, insurance companies, undertakers, and barbers catering to black customers. These new businessmen, with a vested interest in black solidarity, were the backbone of Washington's National Negro Business League. Washington clearly found congenial the prospect of an elite class of self-made businessmen as leaders and models for the struggling masses. There was also room for the Talented Tenth of professional men in the Tuskegee Machine, however. Washington welcomed every college-educated recruit he could secure. Directly or through agents, he was the largest employer in the country of black college graduates.

Second, let us consider Washington as a powerful politician. Though he warned young men away from politics as a dead-end career, what distinguished Washington's career was not his rather conventional goals, which in public or private he shared with almost every other black spokesmen, but his consummate political skill, his wheeling and dealing.

Du Bois spent much of his long life puzzling over the phenomenon of Washington, a man who did not seem to have an abstraction about him. But toward the end of his life, in 1954 in an oral history memoir at Columbia University, Du Bois said of his old rival dead almost forty years: "Oh, Washington was a politician. He was a man who believed that we should get what we could get." Du Bois, who himself found the political part of his race work the least agreeable, went on to say of Washington: "It wasn't a matter of ideals or anything of that sort. . . . With everybody that Washington met, he evidently had the idea: 'Now, what's your racket? What are you out for?' " Du Bois was a shrewd observer, but what he saw in Washington as a lack—of ideals, of principles, of vision—was his great and almost unique gift as a black political leader. Washington could almost immediately, intuitively, and without formal questioning see through the masks and intellectual superstructure of men to the mainsprings of their behavior. Then he imaginatively sought to bend their purposes to his own. Du Bois said that Washington had no faith in white people but that he was very popular among them because, whenever he met a white man, he listened to him until he figured out what that man wanted him to say, and then as soon as possible he said it. Washington did not always get his way, of course, but he always understood, as his more doctrinaire critics did not, that politics was the art of the possible. What was surprising about Washington was the number and diversity of those he enlisted in his coalition.

Washington's program was not consensus politics, for he always sought change, and there was always vocal opposition to him on both sides that he never tried to mollify. Denounced on the one hand by the Niagara Movement and the NAACP for not protesting enough, he was also distrusted and denounced by white supremacists for bringing the wooden horse within the walls of Troy. All of the racist demagogues of his time—Benjamin Tillman, James Vardaman, Theodore Bilbo, Thomas Dixon, and J. Thomas Heflin, to name a few—called Washington their insidious enemy. One descriptive label for Washington might be centrist coalition politics. The Tuskegee Machine had the middle and undecided majority of white and black people behind it. Washington was a rallying point for the southern moderates, the northern publicists and makers of opinion, and the thousands who read his autobiography or crowded into halls to hear him. Among blacks he had the businessmen solidly behind him, and even, as August Meier has shown, a majority of the Talented Tenth of professional men, so great was his power to reward and punish, to make or break careers. He had access to the wellsprings of philanthropy, political preferment, and other white sources of black opportunity. For blacks at the bottom of the ladder, Washington's program offered education, a self-help formula, and, importantly for a group demoralized by the white aggression of that period, a social philosophy that gave dignity and purpose to lives of daily toil.

It could be said with some justification that the Tuskegee Machine was a stationary machine, that it went nowhere. Because the machine was held together by the glue of self-interest, Washington was frequently disappointed by the inadequate response of his allies. The southern upper class did not effectively resist disfranchisement as he had hoped and never gave blacks the equal economic chance that he considered an integral part of the Atlanta Compromise. Washington's philanthropist-friends never stood up for equal opportunity in public education. Black businessmen frequently found their own vested interest in a captive market rather than a more open society. And Washington himself often took the view that whatever was good for Tuskegee and himself was good for the Negro.

To the charge that he accomplished nothing, it can only be imagined what Washington would have answered, since he did not have the years of hindsight and self-justification that some of his critics enjoyed. He would probably have stressed how much worse the southern racial reaction would have been without his coalition of moderates, his soothing syrup, and his practical message to blacks of self-improvement and progress along the lines of least resistance. Washington's power over his following, and hence his power to bring about change, have probably been exaggerated. It was the breadth rather than the depth of his coalition that was unique. Perhaps one Booker T. Washington was enough. But even today, in a very different society, Washington's autobiography is still in print. It still has some impalpable power to bridge the racial gap, to move new readers to take the first steps across the color line. Many of his ideas of self-help and racial solidarity still have currency in the black community. But he was an important leader because, like Frederick Douglass before him and Martin Luther King after him, he had the program and strategy and skill to influence the behavior of not only the Afro-American one-tenth, but the white nine-tenths of the American people. He was a political realist.

Note on Sources

The Booker T. Washington Papers, edited by Louis R. Harlan and Raymond W. Smock (Urbana: University of Illinois Press, 1972–), a fourteen-volume series now nearing completion, includes Washington's autobiographical writings and reveals Washington's private thoughts and the secret stratagems that made his leadership style unique. Among the biographies that contribute to an understanding of the Tuskegean are Samuel R. Spencer, Jr., *Booker T. Washington and the Negro's Place in American Life* (Boston: Little, Brown and Co., 1955), and Louis R. Harlan, *Booker T. Washington: The Making of a Black Leader, 1856–1901* (New York: Oxford University Press, 1972), the first volume of a two-volume study. August Meier, *Negro Thought in America, 1880–1915* (Ann Arbor: University of Michigan Press, 1963), though not biographical, provides the best analysis of Washington's relationship with the black ideologies and race movements of his day.

For some of the themes developed in this essay, readers may find further details in my articles, especially "The Secret Life of Booker T. Washington," *Journal of Southern History*, 37 (Aug. 1971): 393–416, and "Booker T. Washington and the *Voice of the Negro*, 1904–1907," *Journal of Southern History*, 45 (Feb. 1979): 45–62. Several studies of Washington's contemporaries cast light on his career, particularly Elliott Rudwick, *W. E. B. Du Bois: A Study in Minority Group Leadership* (Philadelphia: University of Pennsylvania Press, 1960), Stephen R. Fox, *The Guardian of Boston: William Monroe Trotter* (New York: Atheneum, 1970); Emma Lou Thornbrough, *T. Thomas Fortune: Militant Journalist* (Chicago: University of Chicago Press, 1972); and Hugh Hawkins, ed., *Booker T. Washington and His Critics*, 2nd ed. (Lexington, Mass.: D. C. Heath and Co., 1974).

T. Thomas Fortune:
Militant Editor in the Age of Accommodation

Especially in the North black protest retained considerable vigor, and one of the leading spokesmen for this tradition was New York City's T. Thomas Fortune, the leading Negro editor and journalist of the late nineteenth and early twentieth centuries. Yet like many prominent black intellectuals who retained militant leanings, Fortune became intimately involved with the Wizard of Tuskegee. While his career was erratic and ended more tragically than that of most other prominent Negro intellectuals who were his contemporaries, it is an excellent illustration both of the breadth of Booker T. Washington's power and the complexities in the actions of black leaders and spokesmen in the heyday of Washington's career.

B<small>EFORE</small> he was thirty years old Timothy Thomas Fortune was widely acclaimed as the most able and influential black journalist of his times and was seen by some as a possible successor to Frederick Douglass. As an editor in New York toward the end of the nineteenth century, he sought to use the press as a vehicle for mobilizing black public opinion to support his militant ideology and for establishing himself as spokesman for and defender of the rights of Afro-Americans in the South as well as in the North. He viewed political action as necessary for achieving his ideological goals as well as an instrument for fulfilling his own personal aspirations. He also conceived of a national organization as a means of carrying out his aims and led in the formation of the National Afro-American League. His political ambitions were thwarted as were his hopes for the league, and in later years his reputation as a militant and uncompromising champion of the rights of blacks was compromised by his ties with Booker T. Washington, with whom his career became inextricably linked. This seemingly paradoxical relationship between the two men grew out of the interest that each had in furthering his own career as well as out of mutual respect and affection. But as Washington's prestige and power grew, Fortune's influence and reputation declined.

Fortune was born in Marianna, Florida, in 1856, also the year of

Washington's birth, and, like Washington, he was born a slave. During his boyhood he was introduced to politics and journalism—the two interests that dominated his later career. In Florida he was exposed to the realities of white racism and to the politics of the Reconstruction era. Jackson County, his birthplace, became the scene of some of the worst outrages of the Ku Klux Klan. Threats of reprisals by the Klan because of his political activities forced Fortune's father, Emanuel, to move to Jacksonville. The elder Fortune, a former slave, early recognized as a leader, was a member of the Florida constitutional convention of 1868 and the state House of Representatives. In Jacksonville he continued to be active in politics until the 1890s. From his father and from certain white political leaders who had come to Florida as agents of the Freedmen's Bureau, young Fortune early developed an interest in politics. As a page in the state Senate he observed some of the sordid aspects of Reconstruction politics and developed a lasting suspicion of white politicians who posed as friends of blacks, while using them for selfish purposes. As a boy Tim also spent many hours in the offices of various local newspapers, where he learned the printer's trade and developed a fascination with newspapers.

His formal education was meager. He attended schools sponsored by the Freedmen's Bureau for a few months, and as a young man he spent a year as a student in the preparatory department of Howard University in Washington, D.C. During that year he worked in the printshop of the *People's Advocate*, an early Negro newspaper. Somehow he found books to read, and he read voraciously in literature, history, government, and law. Largely self-taught, he developed a distinctive literary style and an eloquence in oratory that few could match.

In 1881 Fortune left Florida permanently and went to New York City. He found the racial atmosphere of the post-Reconstruction South intolerable and never lived there again, but he always retained his love for the region, and as a journalist he waged an unceasing campaign to make the public aware of the plight of southern blacks. While in Washington Fortune had married his Florida sweetheart, Carrie C. Smiley. During the early years in New York three children were born to the couple—Jessie, Stewart, who died in infancy, and Fred.

Fortune came to New York to earn his living as a printer, working for a time on a white-owned publication, but almost as soon as he arrived he began his career in black journalism as editor and owner or co-owner of the paper named first the *Globe*, then the New York *Free-*

man, and finally in 1887 the New York *Age*. Like all the contemporary black newspapers Fortune's publications had meager financial resources and faced recurring crises. In order to support himself and a growing family and to keep the *Age* in operation Fortune was compelled to seek additional employment. For years he wrote for the New York *Sun*. During the 1890s he traveled extensively in the South, reporting on conditions there for the *Sun*. Editorials written by Fortune were frequently published in the Boston *Transcript*, and he did freelance writing for other newspapers and periodicals. Within a few years after his arrival in New York, Fortune was recognized as the most brilliant and influential black journalist in the United States, a reputation he continued to enjoy until he sold his interest in the *Age* in 1907. The prestige of Fortune's papers was due in part to their high literary quality and to meticulous editing, but more to Fortune's talents as a writer of editorials, and it was as editor that Fortune made his most significant contribution as a race leader. In an early essay on "The Editor's Mission" he said that blacks must have a voice in working out their own destiny. They could not trust whites, however well intentioned, to define their "place." Most of the white press in the North as well as the South was arrayed against the Negro and his rights. Blacks had to counter this influence through their own papers. Race was the *raison d'être* of black journalism. "The mark of color," he said, made its possessor "a social pariah, to be robbed, beaten, and lynched," and one who "has got his own salvation to work out, of equality before the laws, with almost the entire population of the country arrayed against him." It was the special mission of the black editor to lead the fight.

Although he was a "race" man, Fortune was also an American, an *Afro-American citizen*. "As an American citizen," he declared in *Black and White* (1884), "I feel it born in my nature to share in the fullest measure all that is American . . . feeling the full force of the fact that while we are classed as Africans, just as the Germans are classed as Germans, we are in all things American citizens, American freemen." As American citizens blacks were entitled to all of the rights guaranteed by the U.S. Constitution, and the government had the obligation to protect those rights. "We do not ask the American government or people for charity. . . ," he said in an editorial in 1883, "we do not ask any special favor from the American government or people. But we do demand that impartial justice which is the standard reciprocity between equals."

He excoriated the U.S. Supreme Court editorially for its decision in the Civil Rights Cases in 1883 and for other decisions in which it failed to protect the rights of black citizens. "We are declared to be created equal, and entitled to certain rights," he said, but as the result of Supreme Court interpretation, "there is no law to protect us in the enjoyment of them. We are aliens in our own land." To claim that states would protect the rights of blacks, if left free from interference by the federal government, was fatuous. He heaped scorn upon spokesmen of the "New South," particularly Henry W. Grady of the Atlanta *Constitution*, who appealed to the North to leave the race question to "us." The *we* Grady had in mind, said Fortune in response, in an article in the *A.M.E. Church Review*, would not be permitted to settle the issue alone. "Not only the white *we*, but the colored *we* as well, will demand a share in that settlement. . . . We protest against the current treatment of this momentous question by which we are completely counted out, or regarded as . . . passive or acquiescent factors."

Blacks must use their political rights to protect themselves and determine their own destiny. Fortune wavered in allegiance to political parties, but his insistence on the importance of the vote and his fight against limitations on suffrage were unwavering. As the disfranchisement movement gained momentum in the South, he remained uncompromising. He strongly supported the Lodge Federal Elections bill in 1890 and was bitterly critical of white Republicans and blacks who did not fight for its adoption. Black men, he said, could not afford to sit back and fail to protest over erosion of their constitutional rights. In 1903 in an editorial he declared: "Our view of the matter is that the suffrage question is the basic principle of national citizenship; that it should, therefore, be controlled absolutely by the federal Government, in a fundamental act mandatory upon all the States and from which no state could deviate in the uniform and absolute equality of its conditions." If there were illiterate citizens, unqualified to vote, the answer lay in improving educational opportunities, not in property or educational qualifications for voting.

Frustrated and disillusioned over politics, and bitter over the failure of government to protect black citizens, Fortune sometimes urged blacks to use physical force to defend themselves and retaliate for outrages. In an early editorial in the *Globe* he warned that if blacks became convinced that neither state or federal government would protect them, they would "show the very same disposition to fight for their rights as any other people." Black men, he said, tended to be too servile and docile. "We do not counsel violence," he said, "we counsel manly retaliation. We do not counsel a breach of the law, but in the absence of law . . . we maintain that the individual has every right . . . to . . . protect himself." Sometimes it might be necessary for blacks to use force "to assert their manhood and citizenship."

Expressions of this sort, especially if he made them extemporaneously in a speech, alarmed white politicians and more cautious blacks and gave Fortune the reputation of being a dangerous agitator. Sometimes he admitted that his language was intemperate, but he continued to insist, as in a letter to the Brooklyn *Eagle* in 1900, that if the black race allowed itself "to be robbed of its manhood and womanhood rights, to be lynched and . . . degraded . . . if it continues . . . without protest . . . then it will fall into contempt."

On the matter of segregation and race relations in general, Fortune was as outspoken in denouncing any kind of racial distinction as he was in denouncing efforts to circumvent political rights. On the subject of separate coach laws, he said in the *Age* in 1891: "There are some laws which no self-respecting persons should be expected to obey. . . . No man is compelled to obey a law which degrades his manhood and defrauds him of what he paid for." He caustically denied that blacks who defended their civil and political rights sought "social equality" with whites. In an article "Civil Rights and Social Privileges," written in part as a reply to Grady, he pointed out that civil rights and social privileges were not synonymous. Protection of civil rights was the duty of government. Social privileges were a private matter, depending on the tastes of individuals. Elsewhere in the *Globe* he denied that blacks wanted to force themselves on whites who did not want to associate with them. What blacks wanted and demanded was "the concession of every right given to the white man under the laws of the United States. . . . Call this social equality if you will."

Fortune defended, without advocating, the right of persons of different racial backgrounds to intermarry. He pointed out that Afro-Americans were already a mixed race and bitterly denounced antimiscegenation laws as evidences of white hypocrisy, designed not to insure racial purity but to protect white men from responsibility toward their Afro-American common-law mates and children. His barbs at "racial purity" and his defense of interracial marriage offended some blacks as well as whites. Dark-skinned Alexander Crummell, who organized the American Negro Academy in 1897, had a low opinion of light-skinned Fortune, and Fortune in turn expressed doubts about the avowed aim of the academy to emphasize "the integrity and perpetuity of the black race as such." He warned against the possibly divisive effects of a "color line within a color line," by which distinctions were made between persons of clearly mixed ancestry and those of darker color.

In his earlier years, Fortune used the terms "colored," "negro" [*sic*], and "black" more or less indiscriminately. He later became the leading advocate of the term "Afro-American." He considered the term "Negro" a misnomer since only a minority of persons of African descent were all-black, and "negro" was an invidious term of contempt. "Colored" he considered "a cowardly subterfuge," which suggested that a person had no race that he wanted to acknowledge. "We are African in origin and American in birth," he said, and therefore logically Afro-Americans. Fortune was unsuccessful in persuading Washington to use the term, and W. E. B. Du Bois also chose to use "Negro," but Fortune had considerable success in popularizing "Afro-American."

Believing in Afro-*Americanism*, Fortune had no sympathy with back-to-Africa movements as a solution to racial problems in the United States. He regarded emigration schemes as delusions and the men who promoted them as, at best, misguided. Edward Wilmot Blyden, the West Indian–born agent of the American Colonization Society, and Bishop Henry M. Turner of the African Methodist Episcopal Church, the foremost American advocate of back-to-Africa, were both targets of his journalistic attacks. Fortune denounced Turner, who continued to live in the United States, for calling Afro-Americans who did not choose expatriation to Africa "scullions" and "cowards."

While holding these views on expatriation, Fortune was not indifferent to Africa and sometimes wrote scathing editorials on the exploitation of black Africa by white colonial powers. He was sympathetic to missionary work by the African Methodist Episcopal Church. As early as 1896 in an editorial in the *Age* he suggested that the time was ripe for an "association of Africans and the descendents of Africa from all parts of the world."

Fortune saw his work as editor and journalist as his most important mission, but he regarded political activity as indispensable to the attainment of his goals, and he himself was politically active and ambitious. Disillusionment with existing political parties and personal ambition and frustration caused him to follow a tortuous and inconsistent course. Basically he was skeptical of white politicians and political parties dominated by whites. He resented white politicians who manipulated and duped blacks while wooing their votes. As a very young man Fortune became disillusioned with the Republican party and its claims

24

that blacks owed a special allegiance to the party of Abraham Lincoln. When nearly all black newspapers were avowedly partisan, the *Globe* proclaimed its independence. *Globe* editorials bitterly assailed the Republican party for betraying black voters in the South by the Compromise of 1877 and the Republican-dominated Supreme Court for failure to protect constitutional rights. As early as 1882 Fortune joined a small group of northern blacks who were urging political independence, which put him in opposition to the venerable Douglass and most black leaders. In a speech in Douglass's home territory of Oswego in western New York state in 1886 he declared that the party had deserted its black supporters. "You are simply a political cipher in the South and a voting machine in the North," he told one black audience. He urged them to put race above party and cease to be Republicans and become "Negrowumps." In a pamphlet *The Negro in Politics*, published the same year, he inveighed against the "sentimental politics" that tied Negroes to the Republicans, their "sense of infinite obligation [to the party] for the God-given right to be free and the constitutional right to vote—or, oftener to be shot in attempting to vote."

In 1884 Fortune wavered between support of Republican presidential candidate James G. Blaine and Grover Cleveland, his Democratic opponent. By 1888 he had openly swung his support to Cleveland and actively campaigned for his reelection. After Cleveland's defeat he returned to the Republican party and remained nominally a member during the remainder of his active career. He acknowledged that the Democratic party, dominated by white southerners, was hopelessly racist and that the Republican party was the lesser of the two evils.

Fortune's political shifts and tergiversations were motivated in part by personal expedience. He was brilliant and ambitious and hoped for a distinguished political appointment and for political subsidies for his newspaper that might relieve chronic financial problems. Therefore after 1890 he grudgingly supported Republican candidates and was active in Republican campaigns as an orator. But he found his role galling. "I have never met a white in the North or South," he said in *The Negro in Politics*, "who did not talk and act as if I belonged to his party, body and soul, simply because my face was colored, and just in proportion as this spirit had obtruded itself upon me I have felt indignant and disgusted and rebellious." His "rebellious spirit" was evident to white politicians, most of whom distrusted him because of his militance and impetuosity. Fortune could not refrain from excoriating President William McKinley for his efforts to woo the white South and his failure to denounce increasing outrages against southern blacks. Fortune always distrusted President Theodore Roosevelt, and Roosevelt did not like Fortune and the type of Negro whom Fortune symbolized to him. Fortune cultivated his ties with Washington in part in the vain hope that Washington would exert his influence with Republican leaders, especially Roosevelt, to secure a political appointment for him. Fortune's reputation for inconsistency and his sometimes abrasive and arrogant personality alienated black political leaders as well as white. Nevertheless, the Republican National Committee and local Republican organizations used Fortune's talents as a writer and speaker.

Fortune's reputation as an orator was second only to his reputation as a journalist. Sometimes his speeches were carefully prepared, at other times they were extemporaneous. He was particularly eloquent in denouncing denial of political rights and mob violence. A description of one of his performances in 1900 was reported in the *Washington Colored American*. At the conclusion of a dinner Fortune was called upon to respond to a toast, "supremest moments." Standing gaunt and erect, "his hair standing straight up like a bush, his eyes spitting fire, and his bony index finger beating time to his impassioned eloquence," he said that his "supremest moments" came whenever he had an opportunity to strike a blow in defense of the rights of his people. He then launched into a speech in which he denounced southern whites and disfranchisement. When he finished, he sat down to tremendous applause, "trembling and much overwrought from his effort."

In addition to using the black press and political action as instruments to arouse blacks to assert their rights and to fulfill his personal ambitions, Fortune sought to mobilize them through a national race organization. But his vision proved to be premature. In 1887 in the columns of the *Freeman* he proposed a National Afro-American League, which would incorporate local and state organizations from all parts of the United States. The principal grievances that the league would combat would be the suppression of voting rights, lynch and mob law, the convict lease and chain gang system, discrimination and indignities in public transportation, and denial of accommodations in public places. Fortune recognized the difficulties and dangers involved in organizing blacks in the South; nevertheless, since grievances were most acute in the South, he thought the South must be the stronghold of the proposed league. In the North the principal work would be to arouse public opinion and exert political pressure.

In December 1889 in response to Fortune's call, delegates from twenty-three states met in Chicago, plans for a meeting in Nashville having been abandoned because of lack of suitable hotel accommodations and the hostility of local whites. Delegates were present from six states in the South. In a speech that he made as temporary chairman Fortune said that the convention met to form an organization to attain for Afro-Americans every right guaranteed by the Constitution. "We shall no longer accept in silence," he said, "a condition which degrades manhood and makes a mockery of our citizenship." He insisted that the national organization must be nonpartisan and not identified with either of the two major political parties, which was probably the reason that no major political figures attended the convention. A constitution was adopted which declared that the purpose of the league was attainment of full citizenship and equality. These objectives were to be sought by mobilizing public opinion through the press, the pulpit, and public meetings and by appeals to courts of law, "the purpose of the league being to secure the ends desired through legal and peaceable means." It is probable that Fortune expected to be elected president of the organization, but some delegates undoubtedly regarded him as too controversial a figure. Instead, an able but conciliatory man, Joseph C. Price, president of Livingstone College in North Carolina, was chosen president, and Fortune secretary.

In spite of Fortune's strenuous efforts to organize local chapters and to raise funds, the league showed little vitality. At a second convention in Knoxville, Tennessee, in 1891 delegates came from only seven states, largely because local leagues lacked funds. Hopes for a significant court case to publicize the league and win support were thwarted. A projected suit against a southern railroad that had compelled a black passenger to ride in a Jim Crow car, even though he had bought a first-class ticket, was dropped because, as Fortune remarked, it was "simply tomfoolery to institute [a] suit against a railroad without money to prosecute it." In 1893 he announced that the league was defunct because of lack of funds and mass support. He expressed himself as disillusioned and of the opinion that the race was not yet ready for such an organization.

Nevertheless, the league idea did not die, and deteriorating conditions in the South led to calls for its revival. In 1898 the organization was reconstituted as the National Afro-American Council, with objectives similar to those of the defunct league. Fortune had doubts about the attempt to form a national organization and refused to accept the presidency in 1898. Nevertheless, he was always a guiding force in the council and was elected president in 1902. The council attracted more attention than the league, partly because after 1902 Washington was prominently identified with it, but its achievements were meager.

While seeking with little success to encourage blacks to organize to secure constitutional rights, Fortune fought the battle personally by resisting discriminatory treatment to himself and by assisting individuals in resisting discrimination. He himself was involved in at least two court cases in New York that arose out of denial of service—once when he was arrested for demanding service in a saloon, and another time when he protested the refusal of a theater to sell him tickets for orchestra seats. When the young anti-lynching crusader, Ida Wells, was forced to flee from Memphis, Fortune befriended her, gave her a job on the *Age*, and helped her to carry on her campaign against lynching. Fortune tried to help other women and to enlist them in the fight against racial discrimination. He urged the participation of women in the Afro-American League. "In the League," he said, "a woman is just as good as a man. Out of it she is usually much better." He was one of three men who participated in the convention in Boston in 1895 at which delegates from women's clubs all over the country organized the National Federation of Afro-American Women.

At the turn of the century, after the death of Douglass in 1895, Fortune was the best known militant black spokesman in the North. Du Bois, who was at Atlanta University, had not yet become the activist in behalf of civil and political rights he became in later years. Critics sometimes denounced Fortune as an "Afro-American agitator," a term apparently coined by Grady. Fortune welcomed the appellation. In an editorial he praised the "new creature" whose appearance spelled the demise of the timid, cringing black, who for more than two centuries had deferred to the white man. The mission of the agitator was to compel the concession of absolute justice under state and federal constitutions.

The white press sometimes contrasted Fortune, "the agitator," with the "sound" and "safe" Washington, always to the detriment of the former. A typical example from a Syracuse paper said, "According[ly] as the T. Thomas Fortune type, with its loud insistence upon rights, is forced to subside, and the Booker T. Washington type, with its earnest effort in the direction of quiet self-improvement, gains ascendancy, progress for the race may be expected."

Ironically, while the white press portrayed Fortune as the antithesis of Washington, Washington's black critics were denouncing Fortune as Washington's collaborator and tool. Few whites were aware of the long-standing friendship between Fortune and Washington. It appears that the two men first met during the 1880s when Washington was as yet the unknown principal of a struggling school in Alabama who came

North seeking funds. During his travels in the South in the 1890s Fortune frequently visited Tuskegee, and the two men became close friends. By the latter part of the decade they were on terms of such intimacy that they wrote to each other almost daily, and sometimes twice a day. After Emmett Scott came to Tuskegee as Washington's confidential secretary, he and Fortune also became close friends. The friendship of the editor and the Tuskegee principal, in part the result of mutual self-interest, nevertheless was grounded on mutual affection and admiration. The two, both born slaves in the same year, had similar backgrounds. Both had grown to manhood in the South during Reconstruction. Both loved their native region and felt a deep obligation to improve the condition of southern blacks.

In an article, "The Quick and the Dead," published soon after Washington's death, Fortune gave his own version of their relationship. From 1895 until 1915, he said, Washington had been the leader of the "Negro people," but "without their selection or election, and because white men labeled him leader after the Atlanta address in 1895, and gave him plenty of money to carry out the purpose of his leadership." Fortune said that he had helped make Washington a leader and had continued to support him because he agreed with Washington that education and economic progress were necessary for the attainment of recognition of black citizenship and manhood. But while defending his support of Washington, he insisted that he had "nothing in common with the policies of Dr. Washington, especially his personal and political ones."

In appearance and personality the two men presented a sharp contrast. Fortune was intense, impetuous, hot-tempered, and probably overly sensitive to racial slights; Washington possessed remarkable self-control and ability to disguise his feelings. In spite of a carefully maintained facade of guileless simplicity he was an adroit and subtle diplomat. Fortune had deep respect for the other man's self-control and skill.

Their rhetoric, methods, and priorities differed, but for years the two worked together because they thought that they shared the same ultimate goals for their race. During the first years in New York Fortune had been influenced by the economic theories of Henry George, originator of the single-tax proposal. In early writings he stressed class solidarity and mutual interests of poor blacks and poor whites, sympathized with the Knights of Labor, and opposed blacks acting as strikebreakers. In contrast, Washington was critical of labor unions and opposed to strikes. In later years Fortune showed little interest in the labor movement and was no longer critical of capitalists. But even in the 1880s in *Black and White* and editorials in the *Globe* he enunciated a doctrine of progress through thrift, hard work, and acquisition of land that anticipated views later widely publicized by Washington. Like Washington, Fortune emphasized the importance of education. He defended the right of blacks to pursue an education on exactly the same terms as whites. He did not disparage academic education but thought that practical vocational training was the greatest need of the black masses at their present state of emergence from slavery. Like Washington he said that any system of education was "false" that was not suited to the condition and need of the student.

Although Fortune and Washington played different roles and presented contrasting images to the public, each found the association useful to his purposes. As the editor of the leading black newspaper, Fortune was valuable to Washington. In the columns of the *Age* Fortune publicized the work of Tuskegee and interpreted and defended Washington's ideology and methods. He also wrote articles and editorials favorable to the Tuskegean in the Boston *Transcript* and other white publications. In private Fortune was often critical of Washington's overly conciliatory attitudes toward southern whites and his persistent optimism in the face of deteriorating conditions. He disagreed with Washington's willingness to endorse educational and literacy requirements for voting. But he applauded Washington's leadership because he was from the South, where the mass of blacks lived. Publicly he praised Washington's cordial relations with the leaders of the white South and refuted black critics who charged that Washington was merely an apologist for that section of the country. Fortune asserted that the future of southern blacks would be bleak indeed if they did not have the sympathy and good will of whites, and he insisted that Washington was able to cultivate friendly relations "without sacrificing any interest or dignity of the race." He recognized the limitations that living in the South and the necessity for raising funds for Tuskegee imposed on Washington and said that northern critics, who had not lived in the South, could not understand the realities under which he must operate.

Fortune's editorials were valuable to Washington in answering black critics, the more so because of Fortune's own reputation as an uncompromising champion of rights of black citizens. The editor's record as a militant was useful in other ways. Fortune, the Afro-American agitator, dared to say things with which Washington secretly agreed but could not say. At the same time Fortune's militancy furnished a useful foil to his own conciliatory conservatism.

The *Age* sometimes published unsigned editorials written by Washington or Scott. Fortune helped to edit and wrote the introduction to *Black Belt Diamonds*, the first published compilation of Washington's speeches. And behind the scenes his services to the Tuskegee Wizard were much greater. In spite of the differences in style Washington's intellectual indebtedness to Fortune is apparent to anyone who carefully reads the writings and speeches of the two men. Washington frequently consulted with the editor over the content of speeches and articles. Fortune also assisted in the preparation of materials published in Washington's name. Busy with administrative and fund-raising responsibilities at Tuskegee and traveling widely on lecture tours, Washington had no time for research and little time for writing. Yet the public was eager to buy what he wrote, and invitations from publishers poured in. Consequently, he relied heavily on others to gather information, to revise what he wrote, and sometimes to do the writing. Fortune was the ghostwriter for a number of books and articles that appeared under Washington's name, among them *A New Negro for a New Century* and *The Negro in Business*.

In other ways Fortune collaborated with Washington in maintaining his image of spokesman and leader of all black Americans. He assisted in the formation of the National Negro Business League, an organization that reflected Washington's ideology and that Washington completely dominated. As president of the league Washington named Fortune as chairman of the executive committee. Fortune also allowed his friend to use him in dominating the revived Afro-American Council and silencing attempts to criticize Washington and his policies. Fortune's election to the presidency of the council in 1902 was attributed to the Tuskegean's machinations.

If Fortune served Washington's interests, he, in turn, benefited from the friendship, although in the end it proved ruinous to him. As Washington's reputation and influence grew, it was advantageous to be identified as his friend and confidant. Fortune continued to hope that Washington's behind-the-scenes influence in the Republican party would secure for him a political appointment that would ease his chronic financial difficulties. Fortune had grave misgivings about the southern policy of Roosevelt and Washington's part in the shaping of that policy, but for a long time he refrained from criticizing the president publicly. Roosevelt gave Fortune a short-term appointment on a mission to the Philippines in 1903, but Fortune's hopes that through Washington's influence he would receive an appointment suitable to his needs and talents were never realized, partly because Washington did not make the necessary effort and partly because Roosevelt disliked Fortune.

Income from the *Age* was never sufficient to furnish a living for both Fortune and his partner Jerome Peterson. Moreover, Fortune's many race activities, especially in connection with the Afro-American Council, required both time and money, and Fortune enjoyed living well. In 1901 he bought a house, Maple Hill, in Red Bank, New Jersey, from which he could commute to New York. The house brought much happiness to his entire family, but mortgage payments added to his financial burdens. He was always frantically seeking additional work to supplement income from the *Age*.

Both Fortune personally and the *Age* became increasingly dependent on aid from Washington. For much that he did for Washington he received no money, but for his work in editing and ghostwriting and for some speeches that he gave at Tuskegee, he was paid, although never generously. From time to time Fortune also borrowed money from Washington during difficult periods. As early as 1896 Washington appears to have had an account with the *Age* for publication of material on Tuskegee. Later he frequently sent items on Tuskegee, on his own activities, and on other racial matters to Fortune for publication. Sometimes he or his secretary, Scott, wrote editorials that they asked Fortune to publish anonymously. In accepting pay for both his services to Washington and "public relations" that appeared in the *Age* and in publishing Tuskegee-inspired editorials, Fortune did not feel he was compromising his integrity. But in later years, as serious differences developed between the two men, Fortune was confronted with an ethical dilemma. Nevertheless, the dependency deepened as Washington continued secretly to subsidize the *Age*, although the subsidy was never sufficient to prevent recurring deficits and crises.

Fortune continued to defend Washington, not only for reasons of personal self-interest, but because he knew, as Washington's critics did not, of Washington's clandestine efforts to fight disfranchisement and segregation. As attacks on Washington and the Tuskegee Machine mounted, Fortune, the former "Afro-American Agitator," was denounced as an apostate and a weakling and untrustworthy by Du Bois and William Monroe Trotter. Even former friends, like Ida Wells-Barnett, spoke scornfully of him. In reply Fortune felt compelled to insist that he was not Washington's tool and that the *Age* was not a subsidized mouthpiece. He pointed out the similarity between the Declaration of Principles of the Niagara Movement, founded by Washington's critics in 1905, and his own platform of the Afro-American League.

Meanwhile, behind the scenes, relations between Washington and Fortune became more and more strained. While Fortune chafed under his dependence upon Washington but could find no alternative, Washington became increasingly impatient with Fortune's impetuosity and growing addiction to alcohol—and he began to doubt Fortune's loyalty. He no longer confided in him but turned to new confidants whom he encouraged to report to him on Fortune's activities. But in spite of growing mutual distrust and Washington's doubts about Fortune's emotional stability, ties between the two men were strengthened early in 1907, when the *Age* was reorganized and was incorporated for the first time, with Washington as one of the principal stockholders. For years Washington had secretly subsidized not only the *Age* but several other publications, while vigorously denying in response to charges by Trotter and others that he had any financial interest in any publication and insisting that it would be improper for him to do so. Consequently the new arrangement with the *Age* was elaborately concealed. Nevertheless, Washington was committed to invest money to enlarge the paper and buy new equipment. Fortune at first tackled the new responsibilities that the move entailed with enthusiasm, but his financial problems were compounded rather than being resolved. Washington was slow about supplying promised funds, and deficits mounted.

During the summer of 1907 Fortune suffered what contemporaries described as a "nervous breakdown," falling into a period of acute depression and sometimes irrational behavior. The immediate causes are not clear, but his collapse was the culmination of mounting pressures and frustrations, psychological and financial, over a period of years. He was convinced that he personally was a failure and was disillusioned over his long fight in behalf of his race. Discouraged over the seeming apathy of the black masses, he had resigned the presidency of the National Afro-American Council in 1904. In 1905 he wrote to Scott: "I have reached the conclusion that the Fates have the cards stacked against me. . . . *All the way I have shaken the trees and others have gathered the fruit.*" Inner conflicts resulting from his relationship with Washington were also a factor in his collapse. In spite of his public defense of Washington, he felt ideologically drawn to members of the

Niagara group. His alienation from the Tuskegee group was intensified by the aftermath of Roosevelt's discharge of black regiments following a riot in Brownsville, Texas, in 1906. While Washington publicly continued to support Roosevelt, Fortune joined members of the Niagara group and others in denunciation of Roosevelt.

And Fortune's personal life was not happy. He and his wife, Carrie, had become less and less compatible and had separated in 1906. Fortune was in love with another woman and wanted to be free to marry her. He wanted to escape from his marriage but felt guilty about betraying a wife who was blameless and still devoted to him. In the face of problems that appeared insoluble, he sought escape in drink and was a confirmed alcoholic by 1907.

While suffering from severe depression and in an abnormal mental state, in September he agreed to sell his interest in the *Age* to Fred R. Moore. Moore was a long-time friend who was also closely identified with Washington. He held the post of organizer for the National Negro Business League and had edited the *Colored American Magazine*, which Washington had secretly subsidized. Moore agreed to pay Fortune $7,000 for his interest in the *Age*, giving him notes for that amount to be paid over a three-year period. Washington agreed to advance the necessary funds to Moore, although this fact was carefully concealed from Fortune and Peterson, his partner.

Following Fortune's departure from the *Age*, he temporarily "went over to the enemy," as Washington called his critics. He wrote a letter, published in the Boston *Guardian*, congratulating Trotter for his "brave fight" and his opposition to Roosevelt and William Howard Taft. He also wrote letters to other Negro publications refuting Washington's claim that he did not and never had owned any part of the *Age*, thereby confirming what Washington's black critics had been claiming. Fortune probably thought that by publicly defying Washington and praising his enemies he was vindicating his manhood, but his defiance and independence were short-lived. Within a few months he was again seeking the support of the Tuskegee Wizard, but Washington no longer needed him. When Fortune sold his interest in the *Age*, his influence as a race leader was ended. He lived for another two decades, but the rest of his life was anticlimactic.

For several years he was virtually a derelict, continuing to suffer from acute depression, drinking excessively, and unable to find steady employment. He spent some of the money he received for the sale of the *Age* on an ill-fated attempt to resurrect *The Freeman* as a monthly publication. The rest of Moore's notes he sold at a discount to "friends" who profited from his misfortunes. Some of this money went to support his wife and to pay installments on the mortgage on Maple Hill, but in 1910 the house was sold under court order.

It is not possible to trace in detail Fortune's life after 1907. He worked for short periods on numerous ephemeral papers and from time to time was employed as an editorial writer and correspondent on the *Age* and the Amsterdam *News.* For a few months he edited the Washington *Sun* in the nation's capital, but this paper soon collapsed. He and Washington continued to write to each other occasionally until Washington's death in 1915, but the old intimacy was never renewed. With Scott close ties continued during the years of Fortune's degradation and illness, but Scott was unable to help alleviate Fortune's financial plight.

During the rest of his life Fortune lived alone, most of the time in rooms in Trenton or Lawrenceville, New Jersey. He and his wife were never reconciled, but their relations were amicable. During his last years he appeared to have experienced a complete mental recovery and was steadily employed until he died in 1928, at the age of seventy-one. In 1919 he joined the staff of the Norfolk *Journal and Guide*, an association that continued until his death. He wrote editorials and a weekly column of opinion. From 1923 until his death he was editor of the *Negro World*, the publication of Marcus Garvey's Universal Negro Improvement Association. The Garvey ideology, with its emphasis upon racial separatism and "back-to-Africa" ideas, was inconsistent with Fortune's life-long goals. There is no evidence that Fortune ever became a Garvey convert, but he admired Garvey for his ability to arouse and mobilize the black masses as no other leader had done. He considered Garvey a maligned man and bitterly attacked Du Bois for disdaining Garvey while seeking to promote Pan-Africanism. In the spring of 1928 Fortune suffered a physical collapse and was taken to the home of his son in Philadelphia, where he died on June 2.

In "The Quick and the Dead," written as an apology for his relations with Washington, Fortune had tried to evaluate his own role as race leader. He said that there had been a period of "Afro-American" leadership, which began when he was starting his journalistic career in New York. As an editor he had led in agitation for political independence on the part of northern Negroes, civil rights, and elimination of discrimination. His efforts in behalf of the Afro-American League had also been an important step in the struggle, but the race had not supported him. In this article, as he had done on other occasions, Fortune attributed his failure as a leader and the failure of the league to apathy and a lack of support by the black community.

Fortune's life was indeed a tragedy. The promise of his youth was not fulfilled. His failure was due in part to personal weaknesses and in part to the times in which he lived. The lack of support by blacks themselves, of which he complained, was no doubt inevitable at a time when the mass of blacks lived in the rural South, with no defense against white oppression. During his most active years white racism was at its most virulent, and the legal and political status of blacks steadily deteriorated. In the climate of the times the goals that he sought were impossible of attainment, and the methods he advocated were unrealistic. In the end Fortune was unable to bridge the gap between his own ideology and the accommodationism of Washington. His efforts to promote his personal interests through his alliance with Washington ruined his career. In the end, his efforts at accommodation and his compromises destroyed his credibility as a leader.

Note on Sources

PRIMARY SOURCES

THE BOOKER T. WASHINGTON PAPERS

The Washington Papers at the Manuscript Division of the Library of Congress contain rich materials on Fortune. The correspondence between Washington and Fortune and between Scott and Fortune is voluminous, and much information about Fortune is contained in other correspondence. The Washington Papers are being published by the University of Illinois Press: Louis R. Harlan and Raymond W. Smock, eds., *The Booker T. Washington Papers* (Urbana: University of Illinois Press, 1972—).

NEWSPAPERS

The editorial pages of the papers of which Fortune was the editor—the New York *Globe*, the New York *Freeman*, and the New York *Age*—are the best sources for a study of his thought on race. The newspapers also contain biographical material. Unfortunately, except for scattered numbers, the files of the *Age* from 1892 to 1905 have disappeared. Black newspapers other than those with which Fortune was directly associated also contain valuable material; the most useful were: Washington *Bee*, Cleveland *Gazette*, Indianapolis *Freeman*, Washington *Colored American*, Richmond *Planet*, and Boston *Guardian*. The scrapbooks in the Washington Papers contain clippings by and about Fortune from both white and Negro publications.

FORTUNE'S PUBLICATIONS

Black and White: Life and Labor in the South (New York, 1884) is an exposition of his views on economics and politics at that time. *The Negro in Politics* (New York, 1886) is an analysis of political parties and the position of Negroes in relation to them. *Dreams of Life* (New York, 1905) is a book of Fortune's poems that he published privately; the poems illuminate Fortune's family relationships and private life.

SECONDARY SOURCE

Emma Lou Thornbrough, *T. Thomas Fortune: Militant Journalist* (Chicago: University of Chicago Press, 1972) is a full-scale biography.

The Lonely Warrior:
Ida B. Wells-Barnett and
the Struggle for Black Leadership

The feminist and anti-lynching spokeswoman, Ida B. Wells-Barnett, is one of the best representatives of the handful of prominent blacks who consistently espoused a strategy of protest during the ascendancy of Booker T. Washington. Yet the characteristics of her personality that gave her the courage and independence to attack so vigorously the immorality of lynching at a time when a philosophy of accommodation was in the ascendancy also limited her ability to work with other Afro-Americans. Assertive and outspoken, intolerant of those whose positions contradicted her own, Wells-Barnett proved unable to participate effectively in other organizations, even those like the National Association for the Advancement of Colored People, that shared her basic philosophy. In short, as Thomas Holt aptly describes her, she was a "lonely warrior."

Wells-Barnett was not unique. William Monroe Trotter, editor of the Boston Guardian, *and even better known than she as a militant critic of Washington, also found it difficult to work with other black leaders in an organizational framework, and to a lesser extent the same was true of W. E. B. Du Bois. Like Wells-Barnett, they were outspoken propagandists, sure of the righteousness of their position, and thus willing to brave not only the negative responses of racist white Americans, but the criticisms of their Negro colleagues as well.*

IN THE LATE 1920s a young black woman in Chicago was asked to identify the living person who most resembled Joan of Arc. It is not surprising that she named Ida B. Wells-Barnett, an important protest leader of the previous half-century and certainly the most prominent woman among civil rights champions. Even when Wells-Barnett was in her late sixties, a young political scientist studying Chicago found that her "eyes gleamed with an inner fire." "Militant," "uncompromising,"

This paper was prepared while I was a Fellow at the Center for Advanced Study in the Behavioral Sciences. I am grateful to the Center, to the National Endowment for the Humanities, and to the Andrew W. Mellon Foundation for support.

"unequivocal," "outspoken," and "fearless" are the words most often used to describe Wells-Barnett. She was an obvious choice to identify with the French warrior-heroine.

However, despite her importance and stature among black leaders, the letters and papers of major black leaders and organizations reveal a limited correspondence or personal interaction with Wells-Barnett. That she was for much of her active career at odds with many of these leaders and organizations may account for this lacuna. Perhaps the personality characteristics that made the comparison with Saint Joan apt also rendered her incapable of organizational leadership. The loneliness of her struggle emerges in her autobiography as a source of both proud independence and bitter disappointment.

On the eve of her death in 1931, Wells-Barnett could look back over a career that spanned a critical transitional era in the Afro-American experience. She was born a slave during the Civil War in 1862, reared in a politically active family during Reconstruction, and educated at schools run by northern missionaries; she came of age as the Jim Crow system evolved. She was a founder of the National Association for the Advancement of Colored People, a friend of Marcus Garvey, a social worker in Chicago's ghetto during the first wave of the great northern migration, and an activist in the initial political awakening of black northerners in the first quarter of the twentieth century. But she was best known as the champion of the turn-of-the-century anti-lynching crusade.

Wells was thirty years old when she launched that crusade, but the seeds of her militancy lay in the fertile soils of Reconstruction Mississippi and New South Memphis. Her career as an activist was determined by two traumatic events of her youth. First, the death of her parents in a yellow fever epidemic when she was barely sixteen pushed her into a premature adulthood. Second, the brutal lynching of three close friends in Memphis forced upon her a cause from which she could not retreat.

Wells's father, Jim, was a slave-born carpenter and mason hired out by his owner to a contractor in Holly Springs, Mississippi. Evidently he was a strong-willed man; after the war when his employer tried to force him to vote the Democratic ticket, Jim Wells simply quit his job and moved his family from the property. He appears to have had some local political influence. Barnett recalled evenings in her childhood when she read political news to her father and his friends. James Hill, former Mississippi legislator and secretary of state, was a close family friend. And Jim Wells himself was elected to the first board of trustees of Shaw

University (later Rust College), which was established by northern Methodist missionaries in 1866. Ida Wells was educated at this college and recalled attending religious services ministered by northern whites throughout her childhood. The yellow fever epidemic that ravaged Memphis and northern Mississippi in 1878-79 claimed both Ida's parents and a younger brother. For a short while, she took a position as a country school teacher in order to keep the family together. But in the early 1880s she placed the older children in various apprenticeships or with relatives and moved to Memphis with the two younger girls.

The Memphis that Wells found was a bustling city-on-the-make, trying to fulfill Henry Grady's dream of a modernized South. During the 1880s its seven rail lines made it a major entrepôt at which the four sections of the country converged. It was a major cotton exchange, a leading distribution point for grains and livestock in the Southwest, and, by the end of the decade, the fifth largest wholesale grocery market. Blacks made up about 44 percent of the Memphis population in the 1880s. They had been politically active during the short-lived Reconstruction period and could boast a small middle class.

It was in one of the literary societies fostered by that city's black middle class that Wells discovered her vocation. Every Friday a group of teachers met to play music, give recitations, read essays, and engage in debates. One feature of these meetings was the reading of the *Evening Star*, a kind of newspaper of current events prepared by one of the members of the group but not circulated to the general public. Wells became the "editor" of this paper and gained considerable local fame, which resulted in an invitation to write for a local church paper. Soon she was contributing to several Baptist newspapers in the South under the pen name "Iola." As her fame spread, she began to attend conventions of the newly organized Colored Press Association (later the Afro-American Press Association). At the association's District of Columbia meeting in 1889 she was elected secretary. It was probably through the association that, sometime during the late 1880s, she met T. Thomas Fortune, editor of the New York *Age* and confidant of Booker T. Washington. And it was probably through Fortune that she became involved in the Afro-American League, which Fortune organized in Chicago in 1890, a short-lived national protest organization generally considered a precursor to the NAACP.

Apparently racial protest was a key theme in Wells's reporting from the very beginning of her journalistic career, although she was also noted for little sermons on self-improvement (which fits her later career as a settlement house worker). Many of her early stories involved her own experience fighting Jim Crow laws, such as her suit against the Chesapeake, Ohio, and Southwestern Railroad during the 1880s. In May 1884, while on her way to her country school to teach, Wells was physically thrown off the train because she refused to leave the "ladies" car. Her suit was initially successful, and she was awarded $500 damages by a lower court. But in April 1887 the state Supreme Court, insisting that the railroad had satisfied the statutory requirement to provide "like accommodations" and charging that Wells's actions constituted harassment, reversed the lower court.

In 1889 Wells was invited to become editor and partner of the *Free Speech and Headlight*, a small Baptist weekly in Memphis. Always a controversialist, she wrote some particularly scathing articles about the black clergy, which did not endear her to that segment of the Memphis black elite. But she also gained a reputation for fearlessness because of the militancy of her editorials. One in 1891 openly praised blacks in Georgetown, Kentucky, who had retaliated for a lynching by setting fire to the town: "Not until the Negro rises in his might and takes a hand in resenting such cold-blooded murders, if he has to burn up whole towns, will a halt be called in wholesale lynching." The Memphis school board fired her in 1891 when she wrote an article critical of conditions in the local black schools.

The turning point in her career occurred on March 9, 1892. Three of her friends, Thomas Moss, Calvin McDowell, and William Stewart, had opened on the outskirts of Memphis a store they called the People's Grocery. The store's successful competition with a white grocer directly across the street aroused animosities that eventually exploded in a minor riot. Subsequently, a deputized mob sent to arrest the store owners was fired on by a group of blacks determined to defend them, and one of the deputies was wounded seriously. Following that altercation scores of blacks were jailed, and the Tennessee Rifles, a black militia company that tried to protect the prisoners, was disarmed. Shortly thereafter, a mob took the three proprietors of the People's Grocery from the jail and killed them. The black community retaliated by encouraging all who could to migrate and those who remained to boycott the newly opened streetcar line. Spurred on by angry editorials in *Free Speech*, an estimated 2,000 blacks left the city, and the streetcar company tottered on the verge of bankruptcy. Conditions remained tense throughout the spring.

In May, Wells attended the African Methodist Episcopal Church convention in Philadelphia, but left behind an editorial to be published in the May 21st issue of the paper. Reacting angrily to a fresh wave of lynchings throughout the South, she struck at the jugular of southern white male fears: "Nobody in this section of the country believes the old thread bare lie that Negro men rape white women. If Southern white men are not careful, they will over-reach themselves and public sentiment will have a reaction; a conclusion will then be reached which will be very damaging to the moral reputation of their women."

The local press openly called for a lynching. The only cure for the scoundrel who wrote that article, according to the *Evening Scimitar*, was to "brand him in the forehead with a hot iron and perform upon him a surgical operation with a pair of tailor's shears." The more restrained *Daily Commercial* thought that "wonderful patience" had been displayed in allowing the writer to live so long, but this was the limit: "There are some things that the Southern white man will not tolerate. . . . We hope we have said enough."

They had. That evening a group of leading citizens gathered at the cotton exchange and resolved to protect southern womanhood—white womanhood, that is. The *Free Speech* presses were destroyed, and Wells was warned that her return would set off a general bloodbath.

Wells was in New York at the time, and Fortune invited her to stay and write for the New York *Age*. She exchanged the circulation list of the *Free Speech* for a one-fourth interest in the *Age* and began to write a series on lynching. The most dramatic of these was a full seven-column page on June 7, 1892, giving detailed statistics on lynchings and exploding the myth that they were intended to protect white women against rape. Ten thousand copies of the paper were distributed; with the addition of new material, the article became the basis of two pamphlets: *Southern Horrors*, published in 1892, and *A Red Record*, published in 1895.

With Fortune's aid Wells began a lecture tour of the Northeast. In 1892 and again in 1894 she lectured in England, where she helped organize the British Anti-Lynching Society. For the balance of 1894 and 1895 she toured the northern and western states, organizing similar local societies in America. Thoroughly exhausted and somewhat discouraged at the level of support from American blacks for her campaign, she ended this tour in the spring of 1895, settling into domestic life with her new husband, Ferdinand L. Barnett of Chicago.

Domesticity did not turn Wells-Barnett into a political recluse, however. She continued to contribute articles to the Chicago *Conservator*, which she and Barnett owned, the New York *Age*, and other journals, commenting on the racial issues of the day. She was also active in the Afro-American Council when it was reorganized in 1898 and for several years thereafter. As her children grew older, she was again to be found at the scenes of lynchings and race riots, as in Cairo and Springfield, Illinois, in 1908, in East St. Louis, Illinois, in 1917, and at Elaine, Arkansas in 1919. But her work became increasingly restricted to the Midwest, particularly Chicago. She campaigned for the Republican party in Illinois and Missouri, was active in Chicago's mayoral elections, worked with a variety of community centers, and eventually established a settlement house, modeled after her friend Jane Addams's Hull House, to serve the exploding black migrant population of Chicago.

Even though her daily activities were now predominantly local in scope, Wells-Barnett continued to be a prominent national spokeswoman in the struggle for racial justice. She was a major figure in the great ideological conflict between the accommodationist philosophy of Washington and the protest tradition represented by W. E. B. Du Bois. She clearly adhered to the anti-Washington camp, yet her own ideology embraced ideas not dissimilar to Washington's. The Tuskegean insisted that political action must be subordinated to economic self-help and that restraint and frugality lead ultimately to "real" power. "The opportunity to earn a dollar in a factory just now is worth infinitely more than the opportunity to spend a dollar in an opera house," Washington lectured. Writing in the November 19, 1892, issue of the New York *Age*, Wells had voiced similar sentiments: "Let the Afro-American depend on no party, but on himself for his salvation. Let him continue to education, character, and above all, put money in his purse. When he has a dollar in his pocket and many more in the bank, he can move from injustice and oppression and no one to say him nay. When he has money, and plenty of it, parties and races will become his servants."

But while Wells-Barnett's emphasis on economic accumulation and self-help had much in common with Washington's views, there was a fundamental difference; for Wells-Barnett, economic power was not a reward achieved by accommodating to the status quo, but a weapon to use against it. Washington held that the economic success of blacks would overcome the legitimate class prejudices of whites and gain their respect and acceptance; Wells-Barnett saw economic success as muscle to be used to force changes in white behavior.

She had little patience with accommodation and conciliation. In her view, recent Afro-American history had proved that approach wrong. After the violence of the Reconstruction years, "thoughtful" Afro-Americans had conceded the contest for civil and political rights and turned inward to self-help and money-making, but this had not abated the violent onslaught. "The more the Afro-American yields and cringes and begs, the more he has to do so, the more he is insulted, outraged and lynched." Indeed, her personal experience of tragedy demonstrated the fallacy of concession. Her good friends Moss, McDowell, and Stewart were among those "thoughtful" black leaders who "believed the [race] problem was to be solved by eschewing politics and putting money in the purse." But economic success and Puritan virtue did not save them from the lynch mob. Indeed, it was their material success that provoked the original assault.

Wells-Barnett's analysis of mob violence suggested that it abated where blacks exercised manly self-defense. In *Southern Horrors* she advised that "a Winchester rifle should have a place of honor in every black home." Her first action after the Memphis lynching was to buy a pistol. But the most important lesson she drew from the Memphis lynchings was that blacks were the "industrial factor in the South" and must retaliate with their economic power. Thus *Free Speech* had urged Memphis blacks to migrate to Oklahoma and to boycott the streetcar line. The migration had caused consternation among Memphis whites, and the boycott had brought the managers of the streetcar company to Wells's office to plead for mercy before her departure in May 1892. She always believed that the effectiveness of *Free Speech* in exerting this economic pressure was the real reason for its destruction, especially since "leading businessmen" were at the head of the mob.

Undoubtedly, Wells-Barnett's economic thought was rooted in those early years in Memphis. It was a New South city, intent on attracting northern and foreign capital investment and therefore dependent on an image of peace, stability, and growth. "To Northern capital and Afro-American labor the South owes its rehabilitation," she wrote in 1892. "If labor is withdrawn capital will not remain. The Afro-American is thus the backbone of the South. A thorough knowledge and judicious exercise of this power in lynching localities could many times effect a bloodless revolution. The white man's dollar is his god, and to stop this will be to stop outrages in many localities." She was confident that one of the effects of her English tour had been to curtail British investment in the South.

Again like Washington, Wells-Barnett saw ruling-class whites as the key to social change. But she was less concerned about gaining their good favor than with manipulating their self-interest. Appeals to law and conscience were useless; her own unsuccessful suit against the Chesapeake, Ohio, and Southwestern Railroad in 1884 had proved that. "I have firmly believed all along that the law was on our side and would, when we appealed to it, give us justice," she wrote in her diary following the suit. "I feel shorn of that belief and utterly discouraged, and just now, if it were possible, would gather my race in my arms and fly away with them." White legislators and judges made the laws and would interpret them according to their prejudices "and in deference to the greater financial power." It was clear that the "appeal to the white man's pocket has ever been more effectual than all the appeals ever made to his conscience."

The boycott was one such appeal, and if it were faithfully and persistently used, the "railroad corporations would be so effected [sic] they would in self-defense lobby to have the separate car law repealed." But even in the absence of direct economic pressure, protest and unfavorable publicity could create an image of instability that would frighten investors. For example, mob violence in New Orleans in 1900 was ended because it began to depress the stock market; to save the city's credit "the strong arm of the good white people of the South asserts itself and order is quickly brought out of chaos."

Of course, the anomaly in Wells-Barnett's thought was that ultimately her strategy did rely on appeals to conscience and law. The inconsistency is only apparent, however, when one realizes that the appeals were directed at powerful groups outside the benighted South, groups that possessed moral and economic authority. Therefore, one should not be misled by her advocacy of black self-help and solidarity. In the end the mobilization of blacks would serve to arouse those whites who held the balance of power. For example, following the 1898 riot in Wilmington, North Carolina, there was an emergency meeting of the newly organized Afro-American Council, at which she declared: "If this gathering means anything, it means that we have at last come to a point in our race history where we must do something for ourselves, and do it now." But this plea for racial solidarity and self-help was not a call for racial separation, as her next sentence made clear: "We must educate the white people out of their 250 years of slave history."

The struggle then was a propaganda war to win the minds and hearts of powerful non-southern whites in the American North and abroad. When the Chicago *Tribune* began a campaign in 1900 to segregate the city's schools, Wells-Barnett asked her friend Jane Addams to call a meeting of Chicago's leading citizens at Hull House. After a delegation from that meeting expressed its displeasure to the editor of the *Tribune*, the demands for segregated schools ceased. While touring Great Britain Wells was asked repeatedly why she had brought her anti-lynching campaign abroad rather than concentrate on America, where the problem was, and what could Britons do about it. Her reply was always that they must exert their moral influence on prominent American whites, just as their ancestors had done in the antislavery campaign.

Since white support was important to her strategy of protest, Wells-Barnett was disappointed that Fortune's "pugnacious" manners had turned away prominent whites from the Afro-American Council in 1898. She was disappointed, too, that her pamphlets and articles on lynching had not been picked up by the northern white press. The black press was critical to the struggle, but the white press was essential, "since it was the medium through which I hoped to reach the white people of the country, who alone could mold public sentiment." For that same reason, when she traveled through the country in 1894-95 speaking against lynching, she spoke mainly to white audiences and made special personal appeals to "[white] newspapers and to [white] ministers of leading congregations."

Like her Progressive friends, Wells-Barnett believed that research and fact-gathering were the first steps in preparing for the battle: "The people must know before they can act." When people asked her what they could do about lynching, she had always replied, "Tell the world the facts. A factual appeal to Christian conscience would ultimately stop these crimes." It was also important that the facts be accurate and reliable. Her statistics on lynching were compiled from the *Tribune*'s annual summary; it was a vast underestimate, she thought, but the general public accepted it as reliable. She quoted extensively from southern newspapers that defended lynchings in order to damn them with evidence from their own pens. On several occasions when she could not go herself to the scene of a riot, she hired a private detective to gather firsthand evidence.

The facts provided her with a different interpretation of lynching than the one generally accepted. Before her friends were killed in Memphis, Wells-Barnett admitted that she had accepted the idea that lynching was a spontaneous and irrational action that, though "irregular and contrary to law and order," was intended to defend the honor of southern white women. But it was gentlemen of property and standing who instigated the deaths of her friends, destroyed her press, and drove her into exile. Clearly the southern rape fantasy was merely "an excuse to get rid of Negroes who were acquiring wealth and property and thus keep the race terrorized and 'keep the nigger down.' " The statistics she gathered showed consistently that less than one-fifth of the victims of lynch mobs were even *accused* of rape by their killers, much less been charged with that crime in a court. The "red record" revealed that blacks were lynched for a variety of putative misdemeanors, from violating labor contracts to "shooting rabbits." They were obviously victims of southern race prejudice.

In crying "rape" southern whites screened their real motives. Their victims were branded as "moral monsters" and placed "beyond the pale of human sympathy." Weak condemnations of mob rule were "tempered with a plea for the lyncher—that human nature gives way under such awful provocation and that the mob, insane for the moment, must be pitied as well as condemned." The rape fiction made cowards of otherwise courageous men who failed to see that their actions lent "tacit encouragement" to the lynchers. "Even to the better class of Afro-Americans the crime of rape is so revolting they have too often taken the white man's word and given lynch law neither the investigation nor condemnation it deserved."

But to attack the rape fantasy required a general unmasking of southern sexual mores. For southern white men any liaison between a black man and a white women was by definition involuntary on the woman's part. The fact was, Wells-Barnett insisted, that while black men may have betrayed weakness and stupidity in contracting such alliances, the women were very often willing participants. She cited numerous examples from her own experience as well as from southern newspapers. Meanwhile, white men seduced and raped black women with impunity. The same lynch mob that killed a Nashville black man accused of *visiting* a white woman left unharmed a white man convicted of *raping* an eight-year-old black girl. With scarcely suppressed rage, Wells-Barnett observed: "The outrage upon helpless childhood needed no avenging in this case; she was black."

Such discussions were central to Wells-Barnett's counterattack on the defenders of lynching, but they aroused controversy with whites and uneasiness among some blacks. In 1894 a delegation of blacks asked her to soften her attack on the South's double sexual standard. She refused, arguing that the lynch-law defenders' major propaganda ploy was that "black men were wild beasts after white women," and this could only be controverted by exposing the hypocrisy of southern mores.

It was to be expected that Wells-Barnett's insistence on militant, aggressive exposure of injustice, especially on the sensitive subject of interracial sexual relations, would eventually bring her into conflict with Washington's strategy of quiet racial diplomacy. After all, the famous simile in Washington's Atlanta Exposition speech of 1895 that blacks and whites could be as separate socially as the fingers of the hand but joined in forging the South's economic progress was intended to reassure southern white men that their wives and daughters were safe. Wells-Barnett, on the other hand, insisted that southern hypocrisy on this subject be exposed. Yet it was slightly over four years after Washington had gained national prominence with his Atlanta speech that their differences became public and antagonistic.

Ida Wells made her first contact with Washington in November 1890, when she wrote to commend his "manly criticism of our corrupt and ignorant ministry." Throughout the 1890s Wells-Barnett and her husband continued to have amicable relations with Washington's close friend and ally, Fortune. It would appear that the turning point in the Barnetts' relationship with Washington came in mid-1899, before Washington achieved the height of his power, and before William Monroe Trotter and Du Bois had emerged as important critics of Tuskegee policy. Evidently Washington's address to the Birmingham, Alabama, Lyceum on March 30, 1899, offended some of the Chicago black elite. Washington's Chicago operative, S. Laing Williams, reported that a number of them were incensed by the Birmingham speech and by "what they seem to think is a surrender on your part to all the meaner forces in the South that are just now aiming at our disfranchisement."

In addition to southern disfranchisement of black voters, the late 1890s witnessed several well-publicized lynchings and anti-black mob violence. On several occasions, Washington issued statements that appeared to excuse these atrocities. After seven tough years of anti-lynching agitation, Wells-Barnett could hardly be expected to swallow her rage at Washington's pusillanimity. Indeed, the situation was so bad in Chicago that Fortune advised Washington not to attend the annual convention of the Afro-American Council held there in August 1899. Fortune himself did not attend for health reasons, and Washington was vilified in a raucous session.

Undoubtedly, the Barnetts were among the Chicago cabal that was forming in 1899. Fortune wrote Washington in September, informing him that a "disparaging reference" to the Tuskegean had been excised from an article Wells-Barnett sought to publish in the *Age*. Fortune described his former protégée as "a sort of bull in a china shop." But since the Barnetts had access to the editorial pages of the *Conservator*, such censorship was ultimately ineffectual and probably counterproductive. In 1900 Washington launched the National Negro Business

League, the first meeting of which was scheduled to compete with that year's meeting of the Afro-American Council in Indianapolis. Wells-Barnett wrote an editorial in the *Conservator* complaining about both the timing of the meeting and that the new organization would draw resources away from the business bureau established within the council in 1899 and headed by Du Bois. This lack of cooperation, she felt, suggested that Washington "will not go anywhere or do anything unless he is 'the whole Thing.' He can't be 'all in all' in the Council for there are others who are as anxious as he is to find the right, and equally anxious to do it." Obviously Washington preferred to form a new organization, where he would be "president, moderator and dictator."

Washington was not pleased. "Miss Wells is fast making herself so ridiculous that everybody is getting tired of her," he snorted. He *was* pleased to note that other papers had come to his defense, but evidently this was not sufficient. For some time Washington had been working to influence or directly control the black press. Through advertising, loans, direct subsidies, and outright purchase, he gained control of several papers. In July 1903 Fortune, whom an August editorial in the *Conservator* scorned as "a weak man who seems to grow more so as age tells on him," urged Washington to try to buy the paper. Evidently the Barnetts had relinquished their proprietary interests in the paper, because the following December Washington asked Williams to find out who the owners were. By 1908 Washington had gained control of the *Conservator*.

Wells-Barnett belonged to the Du Bois-NAACP camp ideologically, but in the end her relations with her allies were not much better than were her relations with Washington. She proudly claimed some of the credit for elevating Du Bois to a position of national leadership. She had urged the board of directors of the Afro-American Council to have him named director of the business bureau in 1899 to "encourage him and give him the opportunity to take hold in the work." It is ironic then that neither of the Barnetts appears to have been prominent activists in the Niagara Movement, organized by Du Bois in 1905 to oppose Washington's policies. But the singular irony of her career is that Wells-Barnett, the most prominent voice opposing lynching over the preceding decade and the most persistent advocate of a national organization to combat racial oppression, was not among the leaders of NAACP, which was organized in 1909 in response to two days of racial violence in Springfield, Illinois, in August 1908.

A national organization to mobilize white resistance to racial violence and support for black civil rights was a goal Wells-Barnett had worked toward for more than a decade. The type of organization required was one that "was really national in character, and which was numerically and financially strong enough to do the work which was so badly needed for making an organized fight upon this growing calamity." She had tried unsuccessfully to form a national protest group among blacks after her second trip to England, where she had inspired the organization of the British Anti-Lynching Society. She had taken charge of the anti-lynching bureau of the Afro-American Council, but that organization soon became defunct, a victim of the struggle between Washington and his opponents. So in 1909 she was among the sixty persons, including two black women, who signed the "Call" to the conference held in New York City on May 31, 1909, for the purpose of creating such an organization.

Although she was not on the key committees that shaped the resolutions and plans for organization, Wells-Barnett was very active in the floor deliberations of the conference, delivering one of the major speeches during the public sessions. After years of struggle against lynching, she concluded: "Agitation, though helpful, will not alone stop the crime." Although public opinion "does measurably decrease the sway of mob law," it was clear to her that the "only certain remedy" was to make lynching a federal crime. She urged support for an anti-lynching bill that had been introduced in Congress in 1902. She also urged the establishment of a bureau to publicize and investigate every lynching. Clearly then, although she now advocated federal protection against lynching, she still felt that information and propaganda were critical to the success of any anti-lynching campaign. Very early in her struggle she had realized that "it was the white people of the country who had to mold the public sentiment necessary to put a stop to lynching." Her primary strategy had always been to involve prominent whites in the struggle, and the new NAACP offered a vehicle for achieving that goal.

Those historians who have grouped Wells-Barnett with Trotter, the militant editor of the Boston *Guardian* who reputedly distrusted the NAACP because of its white leadership, have misinterpreted the source of her disaffection. In her memoirs she recalled the origin of the conflict differently. Because the chief organizer of the founding conference, Oswald Garrison Villard, had long been associated with Washington, the dissidents at the meeting were fearful that ultimate control would pass to the Tuskegee Machine. They could not know that Villard himself was aware of this problem and was seeking to re-

51

duce Washington's input while maintaining his friendship. The issue crystallized around the membership of the Committee of 40, which would plan and implement the organization of the association. Wells-Barnett recalled that she played a conciliatory role, assuaging the fears of her friends that Washington's supporters would control the executive committee. She had been assured by members of the nominating committee, of which Du Bois was a member, that she would be among the forty. But when the list was presented to the conference for approval, her name and those of many other prominent anti-Washington leaders were missing. Villard, already upset by the numerous amendments offered to resolutions passed earlier, blocked attempts to amend the list from the floor. The list was approved, and the convention adjourned.

Wells-Barnett blamed Du Bois and Mary White Ovington for this slight. After the session she was called back to discuss possible remedies for what John Milholland, the head of the Constitution League, called "a stupendous error." Milholland offered to resign so that Wells-Barnett could take his place on the committee, but she refused, insisting that his membership was essential. Meanwhile, Du Bois admitted responsibility for deleting her name and substituting that of Dr. Charles E. Bentley, also of Chicago, to represent the Niagara Movement. Du Bois said he felt she would be represented by virtue of her organizational affiliation with the Frederick Douglass Center, a black settlement house in Chicago. Presumably he was referring to the presence on the committee of Celia Woolley, the founder of the Frederick Douglass Center, of which Wells-Barnett was vice-president. Of course, he could not have known that Wells-Barnett's relations with Woolley and the Douglass Center were already quite strained and perfunctory, but it was in any case a very weak excuse, and Wells-Barnett was "furiously indignant" with him. She felt it was the white men on the committee who recognized her worth and did what they could to correct Du Bois's "deliberate intention" to ignore her.

The white women were another story. She recalled that after the session Ovington had "swept by me with an air of triumph and a very pleased look on her face." She offered no specific evidence of why or how Ovington might have opposed her, but given Du Bois's friendship with Ovington, Wells-Barnett might well have concluded that she had influenced his decision to delete her name. Ovington's memoirs, written in 1947, indicate her approval of the subsequent insertion of Wells-Barnett's name on the committee list, though she disapproved of the maneuver's illegality. It may be that she did not relish the idea of working closely with the volatile and sharp-tongued Wells-Barnett. She described Trotter and Wells-Barnett as "powerful personalities who had gone their own ways, fitted for courageous work, but perhaps not fitted to accept the restraint of organization." She found black women in general to be "ambitious for power, often jealous, very sensitive," although she added quickly that "they get things done," and she credited the women for whatever success the NAACP branches had enjoyed. Nevertheless, although she respected men like Du Bois, Ovington confessed to Villard shortly after the first NAACP conference that she occasionally forgot "that Negroes aren't poor people for whom I must kindly do something." Such a confession is evidence of her sensitivity to the problem, but even "occasional" paternalism would be galling to a proud woman like Wells-Barnett, who had had very few successful working relationships with white women in the past. Wells-Barnett was placed on the executive committee shortly after the conference adjourned and continued to serve on it and the NAACP national board that replaced it for a few years thereafter, but she was never very active in directing either the national organization or the Chicago branch.

Though it never succeeded in getting a federal anti-lynching law passed, the NAACP achieved some important legal victories and significant organizational expansion during its first decade. But in 1928, Wells-Barnett was disappointed with its development. She disparaged the NAACP's handling of the legal suit in Chicago to ban *Birth of a Nation* in 1915, and she clashed with NAACP field representatives on several occasions while investigating lynchings and mob violence in Illinois and Arkansas. She had little use for most of the national leaders, including Du Bois and Villard. About the only ones she admired were Joel Spingarn and William English Walling. But the chief cause of the organization's failure to live up to its potential, she felt, was Ovington, chairman of the board of directors from 1917 to 1932. "Miss Ovington's heart is in this work, but her experience has been confined solely to New York City and Brooklyn, and a few minor incidents along the color line," she wrote. As a result she lacked a national perspective and the executive ability "to seize any of the given situations which have occurred in a truly big way." Basking in the adoration of a few college-bred Negroes, she has "made little effort to know the soul of the black woman; and to that extent she has fallen far short of helping a race which has suffered as no white woman has ever been called upon to suffer or to understand." With hindsight she regretted not taking a more active role in the NAACP despite the insult she had received at its founding. "I cannot resist the conclusion that, had I not been so hurt over the treatment I received at the hands of the men of my own race and thus blinded to the realization that I should have taken the place which the white men of the committee felt I should have, the NAACP would now be a live, active force in the lives of our people all over this country."

Wells-Barnett's bitter protest notwithstanding, her general eclipse as a national leader over the next decade had more to do with Washington than with Ovington. Villard, aware of the Tuskegean's influence with powerful philanthropists, sought to neutralize his opposition to the NAACP even if he could not secure his support. In the main he failed, because Washington tried to undermine the NAACP as he had all other competitors for race leadership. But there were some anomalous successes, such as the Chicago branch of the NAACP.

Wells-Barnett felt slighted when Villard and Du Bois chose Addams to chair the Chicago branch. Of course that decision was undoubtedly dictated by Villard's desire for Julius Rosenwald's financial support of the Chicago branch. Rosenwald was on the Tuskegee Board of Trustees and had long been an admirer of Washington. He was not likely to underwrite any organization that Wells-Barnett directed; indeed, he had already refused to contribute to her settlement house project. On the other hand, he was a major contributor to Hull House and an admirer of Addams. Consequently, the Chicago NAACP fell under Tuskegee's influence. Indeed, Rosenwald frequently carried board members with him on his annual pilgrimage to the Tuskegee graduation, a trip Bentley thought cast a "hypnotic spell" over the visitors. It was unlikely that Wells-Barnett would find much to praise about the Chicago NAACP under the circumstances, and she did not. Thus it is probable that her disappointment with the national NAACP was very much affected by her experience with the local branch.

The fight with Washington was costly to the Barnetts in other spheres as well. In all her chosen roles—clubwoman, settlement house worker, and protest leader—Wells-Barnett was thwarted by the long shadow of Tuskegee. After some initial successes in Chicago politics, the Barnetts' influence declined while that of Washington's supporters increased.

The same Springfield riots that had inspired the eventual formation of the NAACP led Wells-Barnett to create a local group, from participants in her Sunday school class, called the Negro Fellowship League. They began with informal discussions in her home on Sunday afternoons, but shortly before the national NAACP was launched in May 1910, they established a settlement house in Chicago's expanding ghetto. The house was supported almost totally by funds secured from Victor F. Lawson, owner and editor of the *Daily News*. The center provided low-cost lodgings upstairs, a reading room and social center downstairs, and an employment service. Wells-Barnett had secured Lawson's support by demonstrating that the YMCA did not provide services to the black migrants pouring into the city. When a black branch of the YMCA was opened on Wabash Avenue in 1913, Lawson cut off his contributions. The center was moved to smaller quarters, and Wells-Barnett's political contacts enabled her to secure a job as adult probation officer, working out of the center and contributing to its budget.

But in 1915 Eugene Kinckle Jones, associate director of the National Urban League, came to Chicago to organize a local branch. Speaking with small groups of whites and blacks throughout the city in 1916, he and the local organizer T. Arnold Hill soon secured broad-based support for the league. Wells-Barnett looked on bitterly as her friends flocked to support the new group, "taking hold of the new to the detriment of the old." Robert S. Abbott, editor of the Chicago *Defender*, endorsed the league and used his news columns and editorial pages to publicize it. Woolley gave them rent-free use of the Frederick Douglass Center, which Barnett had helped to found. Her friends, the Bentleys, supported the league. So did Addams, who joined the executive board in 1918. Lawson, who had withdrawn support from Wells-Barnett's settlement house, contributed funds to the league's initial year of operation. Perhaps worst of all, the women's clubs she had organized, one of which bore her name, were among the first to endorse her new competitor, with members actively soliciting contributions for it and volunteering their time to make home visits on the league's behalf to instruct migrants in personal hygiene, deportment, and thrift—services they had never offered to Wells-Barnett's settlement house.

But more important was that the league, both locally and nationally, was strongly influenced by Washington and his philosophy. Rosenwald was the major contributor to the Chicago Urban League, supplying from one-third to one-half of its budget over several years. His personal secretary, William Graves, sat on the executive board. Several of Washington's Chicago friends and operatives were key leaders in the organization; Dr. Grover Cleveland Hall of Provident Hospital and his friend Alexander L. Jackson, head of the black branch of the YMCA, were among its directors.

Thus in one of the major areas in which she had exercised leadership, Wells-Barnett was soon eclipsed by an organization controlled by her principal political antagonists. She struggled along for three years after the league opened its settlement house, but was hampered by her declining political influence. Despite her support of William "Big Bill" Thompson in his election as mayor, she lost her job as probation officer and with it a source of support for the center. Thompson also reneged on his promise to funnel city jobs through the center's employment service. Apparently, the Chicago Urban League did a much better job of placement, claiming 8,000 jobs in 1917-18 alone. Furthermore, the league placed women in industrial jobs, while many of Wells-Barnett's female clients appear to have been placed in domestic work. Wells-Barnett had never succeeded in developing a competent staff, so while she was hospitalized in 1920 after a gallstone operation the center declined even further. After her recovery, she closed it down for good.

The sharpest blow for Wells-Barnett was her loss of status among the black women's clubs she had helped to found. She recalled that the clubs in New York City and Boston had been organized in response to speeches she had given in those cities. She was directly responsible for the Chicago club named after her. We may discount the liberty she takes in claiming direct responsibility for the organization of the National Association of Colored Women, but certainly she contributed to its creation. In 1895 Florence Belgarnie, secretary of the British Anti-Lynching Society that Wells had helped organize, sent a letter to Josephine St. Pierre Ruffin, editor of *Women's Era* and head of the Boston colored women's club. Enclosed was a letter from James Jacks, president of the Missouri Press Association, stating that the blacks in this country were wholly devoid of morality, the women were prostitutes, and all were natural thieves and liars. Wells-Barnett recalled the insult as being directed specifically at her, but evidently this was not the case. Ruffin seized upon the letter as the occasion for calling a national conference of black women's clubs. The conference established the National Federation of Afro-American Women, which eventually merged in 1896 with two other groups to form the National Association of Colored Women (NACW), with Mary Church Terrell as president.

Over the next decade Wells-Barnett reported a number of personal slights and embarrassing situations within the club movement she had helped develop. In her memoirs she attributed these to personality conflicts and ingratitude, but a closer examination suggests much more. All of the instances she cites dated from the Barnetts' emergence as critics of Washington. In 1899 the NACW met in Chicago, but Wells-Barnett was not included in the arrangements committee or on the program. Terrell confessed that Wells-Barnett had been deliberately ignored because some members of the Chicago club refused to participate if she were included. In retrospect Wells-Barnett was certain Terrell's action was motivated by her desire to be reelected to the presidency and her fear of Wells-Barnett as a rival for that post. In fact, Terrell had a number of rivals, including Ruffin of Boston and, more important, Fannie Barrier Williams of Chicago. Fannie's husband was none other than S. Laing Williams, Washington's close personal friend and Chicago agent. Despite the fact that her husband Robert received Tuskegee patronage, Terrell charted an independent course between Washington and his critics. Nevertheless, Washington and his wife, Margaret, enjoyed strong support within the NACW. Thus Terrell was probably less afraid of Wells-Barnett as a rival for the presidency than she was wary of embracing someone who had become *persona non grata* to the Tuskegee camp.

Wells-Barnett never attained high office in the national club organization. Tuskegee sympathizers controlled the organization for several years after 1903; indeed, Margaret Washington was president from 1914 to 1918. But even after Tuskegee influence declined, Wells-Barnett was unable to secure a leadership role; Mary McLeod Bethune defeated her in the presidential election of 1924.

In her memoir Wells-Barnett recalled one emotional incident that graphically demonstrated her changed relationship with the women's group. After absenting herself from NACW annual conventions for almost a decade, Wells-Barnett went to the 1909 convention in Louisville, Kentucky, only to find humiliating evidence of her loss of status and power. Entering a floor discussion on the disposition of the editorship of *National News*, the organization's newspaper heretofore published at Tuskegee by Margaret Washington, Wells-Barnett was dismayed to discover that her remarks were interpreted as a veiled attack on Washington. "The women hissed me from the floor. I went home and went to bed instead of appearing at the big banquet which was given to the delegates that night. . . . Always the personal element. It seems disheartening to think that every single move for progress and race advancement has to be blocked in this way."

The second and third decades of the twentieth century were disheartening indeed to the champion of the anti-lynching cause. Deprived of a signficant role in the national protest organization for which she had helped lay the groundwork, rebuffed by the club movement that her campaign had indirectly spawned, bereft of the settlement house she had struggled so long to maintain, shorn of any genuine political power in Chicago after Thompson's ascendancy in 1915, Wells-

Barnett wrote a bitter assessment of her life's work three years before her death. "All at once the realization came to me that I had nothing to show for all those years of toil and labor."

The most persistent themes in Wells-Barnett's memoir are the loneliness of her struggle and the ingratitude of her people. When she sued the Chesapeake, Ohio, and Southwestern Railroad in 1884, she had expected support from the black community; she did not receive it. Indeed, she claimed, the black lawyer she had hired to plead her case had been bribed by the railroad. When she lost her job for criticizing the inferior education black children received in Memphis schools, she had hoped that their parents would back her; they did not. "Up to that time I had felt that any fight made in the interest of the race would have its support. I learned then that I could not count on that." When, after her triumphal tour of Britain, African Methodist Episcopal Church ministers in Philadelphia hesitated to endorse her work, she retorted angrily: "Why, gentlemen, . . . I cannot see why I need your endorsement. Under God I have done work without any assistance from my own people." Lobbying for an anti-lynching bill introduced by Chicago Congressman William E. Lorimer in 1898, she worked to defeat a weaker bill sponsored by North Carolina Congressman George White. She was severely criticized by blacks for thus embarrassing the only black member of the Congress. "Here again was an illustration of how our own people seem to stand in the way of any accomplishment of federal intervention against lynching." Investigating lynchings in Cairo, Illinois, campaigning for the Republican party in Missouri, lobbying to get black representation on important boards and commissions, she always saw herself as a lonely warrior, battling racist forces on one front and jealous, short-sighted blacks on the other.

One could dismiss Wells-Barnett's bitter assessment of her career as the carpings of a disappointed sexagenarian, except that the rejections she described were real enough even though her interpretations of them were not necessarily valid. Possibly there is some truth in Ovington's assessment that Wells-Barnett was cut out for "courageous work" but not the discipline of organization. She repeatedly encountered difficulties—with her own local women's clubs, with the Chicago branch of Trotter's Equal Rights League, and others—because she took unilateral action without consulting her co-workers. In her assessment Ovington coupled Wells-Barnett with Trotter, and one suspects that Stephen Fox's description of Trotter could easily be applied to Barnett's relationship with the Negro Fellowship League: "In the NERL [National Equal Rights League] he was the generally acknowledged spokesman for lesser men; after himself there was no one to compare with Du Bois, Villard, Milholland, Storey, and Mary White Ovington." There were no debates over policy; "Trotter as corresponding secretary would simply issue a statement in the NERL's name, and that would stand as the group's position. The NERL was his personal fief." Likewise, Wells-Barnett herself conceded that the fellowship members were not major figures in Chicago's black community. None of them emerged as significant personalities in her memoirs; indeed, they remained practically anonymous.

The conflict with Washington also contributed to Wells-Barnett's isolation as a leader, because it shaped most of the critical encounters in her life vis-à-vis the black community: the women's club movement, the settlement house, the NAACP, and the Urban League. The differences between them were not precisely ideological, for their worldviews were in many respects similar, though they differed in emphasis. Certainly they shared the same class bias: they sought to "elevate the race" to bourgeois respectability. The key differences might best be described as strategic and tactical rather than ideological or personal. They both saw economic power as the elemental force that shaped the social environment and moved the world. They both saw members of the white ruling class, the possessors of that economic power, as critical allies in the struggle for social change. They differed on the tactical question of how those allies should be mobilized. For Wells-Barnett the rising tide of racial oppression and violence in the late 1890s demanded a vigorous counterattack that would mobilize prominent whites to mold "the public sentiment." For Washington it demanded a lower profile and racial "statesmanship," that is, the quiet persuasion of men in power to restrain the white masses.

Despite her own bitter disappointment, Wells-Barnett's work was—in one important sense—a success. The tactics she advocated were the ones adopted by the NAACP in its campaign against lynching, and eventually the red tide of violence receded. Of course various efforts to push an anti-lynching bill through the Congress, the Dyer bill in 1918 and the Wagner-Costigan bill in 1934, were thwarted by southern filibusters in the U.S. Senate. But linked with the NAACP's legislative lobby was an aggressive publicity campaign that encouraged more and more prominent whites to speak out against mob law. Thus the Call to the NAACP Anti-Lynching Conference in May 1919 included among its 120 signatures those of the U.S. attorney general, a former secretary of state, a U.S. Supreme Court justice, the president of the American Bar Association, and four governors. In the 1930s southern white women, the ostensible beneficiaries of the lynch mobs, joined the crusade, organizing as the Southern Women for the Prevention of Lynching. By 1942 a Gallup Poll revealed that an overwhelming majority of Americans, North and South, favored making lynching a federal crime. Obviously, a major transformation in public sentiment had occurred.

Any claims of success depend upon the perspective of the observer, however. Ninety percent of the men *legally* executed for rape between 1934 and 1967 were black; some would insist that they were victims of racist mores as surely as those lynched by mobs in the 1890s. Moreover, the civil rights movement produced a long list of martyrs—of whom Medgar Evers, James Chaney, Andrew Goodman, and Michael Schwerner are only the most widely publicized—whose killers were aided or led by law officers and not punished by southern courts. But from the perspective of the turn of the century—Wells-Barnett's perspective—there were vital differences. These political murders were not and could not be cloaked with the fiction of protecting female virtue. These murderers could not be so certain of public approval that they could advertise their intent in advance and pose for photographs afterward as did their spiritual ancestors in Paris, Texas, in 1893. And, most important of all, in the second quarter of the twentieth century, unlike the first, such atrocities spurred rather than retarded rapid social change. In this sense, Ida B. Wells-Barnett, despite her personal disappointments, could have looked upon her life's work as a genuine, though limited, success. The crusade continued, but one significant battle was won.

Note on Sources

The best source of information on Ida Wells-Barnett's life and thought is her memoir, *Crusade for Justice: The Autobiography of Ida B. Wells* (Chicago: University of Chicago Press, 1970), edited and published posthumously by her daughter Alfreda M. Duster. However, because of Wells-Barnett's age at the time it was written and the bitter tone of her reflections, one must exercise even more than the usual caution with this source. Three of her best known pamphlets—*Southern Horrors, A Red Record,* and *Mob Rule in New Orleans*—were collected and reprinted in *On Lynching* (New York: Arno Press, 1969). Some of her additional writings can be found in Gerda Lerner, ed., *Black Women in America: A Documentary History* (New York: Vintage Books, 1973) and in Bettina Aptheker, ed., *Lynching and Rape: An Exchange of Views* (Occasional Paper no. 25, American Institute for Marxist Studies, 1977). A few letters and scattered references to Wells-Barnett are found in volumes 3, 4, 5, and 7 of Louis R. Harlan and Raymond M. Smock, eds., *The Booker T. Washington Papers* (Urbana: University of Illinois Press, 1972-   ), and in Herbert Aptheker, ed., *The Correspondence of W. E. B. Du Bois: Selections, 1877-1934* (Amherst: University of Massachusetts Press, 1973). Ironically, her antagonist Ovington is one of the few contemporaries who discusses Wells-Barnett at any length in her memoir, *The Walls Came Tumbling Down* (New York: Arno Press, 1969 [reprint of original 1947 ed.]).

Useful secondary sources are Emma Lou Thornbrough's *T. Thomas Fortune: Militant Journalist* (Chicago: University of Chicago Press, 1972); Charles Flint Kellogg's *NAACP: A History of the National Association for the Advancement of Colored People, 1909–1920* (Baltimore: John Hopkins University Press, 1967); Stephen R. Fox's *The Guardian of Boston: William Monroe Trotter* (New York: Atheneum, 1970); David M. Tucker's "Miss Ida B. Wells and Memphis Lynching," *Phylon*, 32 (Summer 1971): 112–22; and Arvarh E. Strickland's *History of the Chicago Urban League* (Urbana: University of Illinois Press, 1966).

Elliott Rudwick   **4**

W. E. B. Du Bois:
Protagonist of the Afro-American Protest

*The complex William Edward Burghardt Du Bois remains to this day a
towering figure in the pantheon of black twentieth-century leaders. Both
his thinking and the extent to which he functioned as a leader in the struggle for race advancement underwent marked transformations over the
years. Historically Du Bois's fame rests mainly on his brilliant articulation of black protest and particularly on the key role he played early in
the century, first in marshalling Booker T. Washington's critics into
unified action and then, having secured the support of a handful of
influential progressive whites, helping to create the interracial National
Association for the Advancement of Colored People. Deeply interested
in Africa and the problems of the black masses, Du Bois was also both
an early prophet of Pan-Africanism and one of the small group of black
intellectuals who became seriously interested in Socialist and Marxist
approaches to the elimination of racial oppression.*

D URING the nineteenth century and the early decades of the twentieth, when blacks were virtually powerless, propagandists like Frederick Douglass, Booker T. Washington, and W. E. B. Du Bois natu-
rally loomed large in the pantheon of black leaders. The term
propagandist—used here in its neutral meaning as denoting one who
employs symbols to influence the feelings and behavior of an audience—is a particularly apt description of the role played by Du Bois,
the leading black intellectual and the most important black protest
spokesman in the first half of the twentieth century. As platform lecturer and particularly as editor of several publications, Du Bois was a
caustic and prophetic voice, telling whites that racist social institutions
oppressed blacks and telling blacks that change in their subordinate
status was impossible unless they demanded it insistently and continu-
ously. Du Bois himself in his noted autobiographical work, *Dusk of
Dawn*, aptly evaluated his principal contribution when he wrote of
"my role as a master of propaganda."

Central to Du Bois's role as a propagandist were the ideologies that
he articulated. And Du Bois's ideas reflected most of the diverse

themes in black thinking about how to assault the bastions of prejudice and discrimination. Most important, he articulated the blacks' desire for full participation in the larger American society and demanded "the abolition of all caste distinctions based simply on race and color." On the other hand, he also exhibited a nationalist side—a strong sense of group pride, advocacy of racial unity, and a profound identification with blacks in other parts of the world. As he said in one of his oft-quoted statements,

> One ever feels his twoness—an American, a Negro; two souls, two thoughts, two unreconciled strivings; two warring ideals in one dark body, whose dogged strength alone keeps it from being torn asunder. The history of the American Negro is the history of this strife—this longing to attain self-conscious manhood, to merge his double self into a better and truer self. In this merging he wishes neither of the older selves to be lost. . . . He simply wishes to make it possible for a man to be both a Negro and an American, without being cursed and spit upon by his fellows, without having the doors of opportunity closed roughly in his face.

In addition Du Bois was both a pioneering advocate of black capitalism, and later was one of the country's most prominent black Marxists. Essentially a protest leader he was also criticized at times for enunciating tactics of accommodation. An elitist who stressed the leadership role of a college-educated Talented Tenth, he articulated a fervent commitment to the welfare of the black masses.

Given the persistent and intransigent nature of the American race system, which proved quite impervious to black attacks, Du Bois in his speeches and writings moved from one proposed solution to another, and the salience of various parts of his philosophy changed as his perceptions of the needs and strategies of black America shifted over time. Aloof and autonomous in his personality, Du Bois did not hesitate to depart markedly from whatever was the current mainstream of black thinking when he perceived that the conventional wisdom being enunciated by black spokesmen was proving inadequate to the task of advancing the race. His willingness to seek different solutions often placed him well in advance of his contemporaries, and this, combined with a strong-willed, even arrogant personality made his career as black leader essentially a series of stormy conflicts.

Thus Du Bois first achieved his role as a major black leader in the controversy that arose over the program of Booker T. Washington, the most prominent and influential black leader at the opening of the twentieth century. Amidst the wave of lynchings, disfranchisement, and segregation laws, Washington, seeking the good will of powerful whites, taught blacks not to protest against discrimination, but to elevate themselves through industrial education, hard work, and property accumulation; then, they would ultimately obtain recognition of their citizenship rights. At first Du Bois agreed with this gradualist strategy, but in 1903 with the publication of his most influential book, *Souls of Black Folk,* he became the chief leader of the onslaught against Washington that polarized the black community into two wings—the "conservative" supporters of Washington and his "radical" critics. For Du Bois, the blacks' only effective way to open the doors of opportunity was to adopt tactics of militant protest and agitation; by employing this style of propaganda, he made a key contribution to the evolution of black protest in the twentieth century—and to the civil rights movement.

Du Bois's background helps explain his divergence from the Washingtonian philosophy. From a young age, Du Bois saw himself as a future race leader, part of an elite corps of black college graduates dedicated to advancing the welfare of black people. The Tuskegean deprecated Du Bois's perspective, and although other factors were involved in the disagreement between the two men, a central issue in what became a titanic leadership struggle was Washington's denigration of the Du Boisian commitment to higher education.

Du Bois was born in Great Barrington, Massachusetts in 1868, and his sense of special mission to free black America had appeared even before his graduation at twenty from Fisk University, one of the leading black institutions of higher education. Committed to a platform of racial unity, Du Bois, while still an undergraduate, was earnestly lecturing fellow students that as "destined leaders of a noble people," they must dedicate themselves to the black masses. He declared to his classmates: "I am a Negro; and I glory in the name! . . . From all the recollections dear to my boyhood have I come here [to Fisk], . . . to join hands with this, my people." Du Bois felt that a college degree was important because it equipped black youth with knowledge and wisdom essential to serve the race.

The first application of Du Bois's ideas about the role of an educated elite took the form of scientific investigations that were intended to advance the cause of social reform. In 1895 Du Bois became the first black to receive a Ph.D. from Harvard University, and utilizing his broad training in the social sciences, he published *The Philadelphia Negro* in 1899, the first in-depth case study of a black community in the United States. By then as a professor at Atlanta University, he had begun to publish annual sociological investigations about living conditions among blacks. Du Bois at this point in his career passionately believed that social science would provide white America's leaders with the knowledge necessary to eliminate discrimination and solve the race problem. At the same time he had seen much value in Washington's program. But with his sociological publications virtually ignored by influential reformers, and with the Negroes' status deteriorating under Washington's ascendancy, Du Bois gradually came to the conclusion that only through agitation and protest could social change ever come.

The unbridgeable differences that thus appeared between Washington's accommodating stance and Du Bois's advocacy of militant protest were rooted in personality incompatibility as well as irreconcilable emphases regarding the solution of the race problem. Du Bois felt awkward and uneasy with Washington, who, in turn, considered him haughty and arrogant and who appeared jealous of highly educated blacks with Ivy League degrees and cultural advantages. But the more serious barrier to a trusting relationship lay beyond personality. Where the heart of Du Bois's solution to the race problem lay in the hopes for the Talented Tenth—the college-trained leadership cadre responsible for elevating blacks economically and culturally—Washington was the preeminent black advocate of industrial education. Beyond this and other ideological concerns lay certain very practical conflicts: that with the popularity of industrial education the needy black colleges were slighted by the philanthropists, and that the Tuskegean—while decrying black political participation—acted as a White House broker for black appointees. Increasingly, Du Bois became incensed that Washington was using connections with the powerful to build up his own Tuskegee Machine while doing little to disturb the caste barriers that were causing devastating problems for blacks.

In 1903 Du Bois took the crucial step that led to his command of a movement dedicated to reducing Washington's influence and to raising black consciousness against the caste system. For the very first time, the Atlanta professor publicly denounced the Tuskegean for condoning white racism and for shifting to blacks the major blame for their deprivation. Charging that the accommodationist Tuskegean had brought together the South, the North, and the blacks in a monumental compromise that "practically accepted the alleged inferiority of the Negro," Du Bois declared that social justice could not be achieved through flattering racist whites; that blacks could not gain their rights by voluntarily tossing them away or by constantly belittling themselves; and that what was needed was a clamorous protest against oppression. Du Bois's critical analysis of Washington's leadership was later credited by James Weldon Johnson with effecting "a coalescence of the more radical elements . . . thereby creating a split of the race into two contending camps." Yet the camps were not evenly matched; Washington had the support of most articulate blacks and among most of those whites who displayed any interest in black advancement, and in successive battles the Du Bois forces were outmaneuvered by the wily Tuskegean.

An example of Washington's maneuvering and Du Bois's impotence was the 1904 Carnegie Hall Conference, which the Tuskegean arranged with money from white philanthropists. On the surface Washington wished to convene representatives of the two contending camps to construct a mutually acceptable platform. Washington was determined that the majority of the conferees would be under his control, but made sufficient conciliatory gestures to Du Bois so that the latter agreed to help draw up the list of participants. Du Bois suspected Washington's motives, but convinced himself that if the "radicals" caucused beforehand and came armed with documented evidence against Washington, the latter would be so overwhelmed that he would accede to the adoption of a militant racial program. Thus Du Bois bombarded his associates with confidential memos, urging them to "hammer at" Washington's record and make the conference's "main issue" Washington's accommodation to white supremacists. Du Bois also circulated the platform for radical uplift that would form the basis of his activities as a protest leader during the next thirty years: "full political rights on the same terms as other Americans; higher education of selected Negro youth; industrial education for the masses; common school training for every Negro child; a stoppage to the campaign of self-depreciation; a careful study of the real conditions of the Negro; a national Negro periodical; . . . the raising of a defense fund; a judicious fight in the courts for civil rights."

But for all of his preconference planning, Du Bois had paid insufficient attention to the fact that Washington controlled more than enough votes to dominate the proceedings. And Washington's performance was clever—first backing a statement of principles that accorded with Du Bois's views and then manipulating the selection of the Committee of Twelve that was to carry on the conference's work. Subsequently, when this committee issued conciliatory statements downplaying black higher education and the importance of the franchise, Du Bois angrily resigned. Although his action was interpreted by some black editors as selfishness and immaturity and by sympathetic whites like New York *Evening Post* editor Oswald Garrison Villard as "a great mistake," the Atlanta professor had concluded that a viable coalition with the Tuskegean was impossible.

For the black "radicals" these events of 1903–4 propelled Du Bois into the limelight as a militant leader. Now he created two tasks for himself: to expose Washington's "veiled surrender" to the race's enemies and to organize a new black rights movement. More clearly than before, Du Bois perceived the enormous influence of his adversary. Washington's power within the black community—which was more than any other black man had previously possessed—derived from his popularity with influential white politicians and philanthropists. Moreover, to millions of whites he was the only bona fide interpreter of black wishes. Washington virtually controlled the major sources of philanthropy for black schools; he had influential connections in the black church, black press, and other race institutions; and ambitious blacks found it difficult to get ahead without his approval.

Nevertheless Du Bois initiated a frontal assault on this Tuskegee Machine in 1905, publicly charging that Washington was imposing thought control inside black America through payments of "hush money" to certain editors. More important, Du Bois was already meeting privately with fellow "radicals" in several cities, exploring the extent of potential support for a militant anti-Washington movement dedicated to protesting this accommodation to white supremacy and segregation. Yet Du Bois had to ponder the chances of survival for an organization that challenged Washington. Could it accomplish anything constructive if nearly all influential whites and the most powerful among the blacks opposed its ideas? Might a militant protest prove counterproductive by arousing a white backlash? And could Du Bois answer Washington's charge that black intellectuals were merely status-hungry elitists far removed from the black masses?

Responding to Du Bois's call, twenty-nine delegates, who had been carefully screened to eliminate "bought" and "hidebound" Washingtonians, met on the Canadian side of Niagara Falls in July 1905. The Niagara Movement, whose tiny membership was drawn chiefly from the ranks of northern college-educated professional men, held annual meetings for the next five years. The chief function of these gatherings was to issue declarations of protest to white America. On every basic issue the Niagara men stood in direct contrast to Washington— denouncing the inequities of the separate-but-equal doctrine, the unfairness of the disfranchisement laws, and the notion that blacks were contentedly climbing from slavery by "natural and gradual processes."

68

Niagara platforms—in whose formulation Du Bois played the most prominent role—were sharp and vigorous, clearly telling whites that they had caused the "Negro problem" and insisting that blacks should unequivocally protest. The Niagara men declared in 1905: "We repudiate the monstrous doctrine that the oppressor should be the sole authority as to the rights of the oppressed. . . . The Negro race in America, stolen, ravished, and degraded, struggling up through difficulties and oppression, needs sympathy and receives criticism, needs help and is given hindrance, needs protection and is given mob-violence, needs justice and is given charity, needs leadership and is given cowardice and apology, needs bread and is given a stone. . . . we do not hesitate to complain and to complain loudly and insistently. To ignore, overlook, or apologize for these wrongs is to prove ourselves unworthy of freedom. Persistent manly agitation is the way to liberty."

While articulating the anger of a small group of black intellectuals, the leaders of the Niagara Movement like Du Bois said they wanted to be "in close touch with the people and with intimate knowledge of their thoughts and feelings." Clearly the Atlanta professor hoped that his propaganda would both raise the consciousness of the black millions and awaken the complacent whites. And in view of the Tuskegee Machine's influence with the mass media, both black and white, not surprisingly two basic Niagara principles were "freedom of speech and criticism" and "an unfettered and unsubsidized press." As it turned out, Du Bois was very proficient at composing annual Addresses to the Nation, but powerless at removing the barriers that prevented the messages from being widely heard.

From the day of its inception Washington plotted the destruction of the Niagara Movement. He and his associates used political patronage to strengthen their hand, and they even considered the idea of having leading Niagara men fired from their federal jobs. The public speeches of key Niagara people like Du Bois were regularly monitored, and Washington, acting through his private secretary Emmett Scott, even planted spies to report what was transpiring at the organization's conventions. Yet these cloak-and-dagger operations could hardly have produced enough significant information to justify all the trouble, and the Washingtonians were far more effective in stymying the movement through their influence over the black press. Usually black editors were counseled to ignore Niagara, but for a period Scott decided that it would be more damaging if the race press would "hammer" the movement. The Tuskegean himself justified these maneuvers on the grounds that Niagara's leaders were not honest "gentlemen," and he even went so far as to subsidize key black journals in cities where his opponents were especially active.

In the large northern centers Washington had considerable contacts among white editors who easily concluded that the Niagara Movement was potentially damaging to harmonious race relations. Thus they followed the strong suggestions of Washington and his agents to ignore the activities of Du Bois and his group. Since the Tuskegean was assumed to be the blacks' only "real leader," white editors found nothing incongruous about giving the Niagara Movement the silent treatment. Indeed with the saintly image that Washington cultivated in the white media, the Niagara Movement's anti-Washington stance was beyond their comprehension. In 1906 the editor of the prominent white weekly, the *Outlook*, contrasted the pronouncements of the Tuskegean's National Negro Business League with the recent Niagara manifesto, and Washington's "pacific" group was praised because it demanded more of blacks themselves, while Du Bois's "assertive" group unreasonably demanded more of whites on behalf of blacks—to the latter's moral detriment. The Business League was lauded for focusing on achieving an "inch of progress" rather than strangling itself in a "yard of faultfinding" as the Niagara Movement was doing. Washington's supporters in the black press made even more invidious contrasts. Thus the New York *Age* asserted that blacks needed "something cheerful," which the Tuskegean offered the masses, rather than the "lugubrious" and "bitter" commentary of Niagara's jealous "aggregation of soreheads."

Despite these highly personal attacks, the Tuskegeans were correct about the lack of accomplishments of the Niagara Movement, whose local branches were usually inactive or ineffective. The Illinois unit futilely tried to mobilize when the Negrophobic *Clansman* opened at a Chicago theater, while the Massachusetts branch lobbied unsuccessfully to prevent the state legislature from appropriating tax dollars for Virginia's segregated exposition celebrating the three hundredth anniversary of the founding of Jamestown. The Niagara Movement's weakness existed less because of its leaders than because of the nation's racist social climate. Epitomizing the steady deterioration in race relations and the Niagara Movement's inability to do anything about it were the eruption in 1906 of a race riot in Atlanta, the city where Du Bois lived and worked, and later in the same year the serious miscarriage of justice at Brownsville, Texas, where despite inadequate evidence, three companies of black soldiers were dishonorably discharged on unproven charges of "shooting up" the Texas town. Helplessly the Niagara Movement issued an "Address to the World" attacking President Theodore Roosevelt (to whom enfranchised blacks had long given political allegiance) for his unfair treatment of the soldiers.

The 1907 Niagara conference was very depressing, with Du Bois himself conceding his own "inexperience" as a leader and admitting that the movement was now operating with "less momentum" and with considerable "internal strain." Indeed during the conclave he had a serious falling-out with Boston *Guardian* editor William Monroe Trotter, one of the earliest and most prominent critics of Washington. With this controversy further damaging the Movement's morale, the organization limped along; most of its 400 members even declined to pay the modest annual dues. When the fourth annual conference opened in 1908 soon after the Springfield, Illinois, race riot, the small band of black militants faced its own impotence and the powerlessness of a race that could not count on the authorities for protection even in the North. The leaders could only curse the "Negro haters of America" and remind blacks that they possessed the right to use guns against white mobs.

While the Niagara Movement was thus falling apart, Du Bois, undoubtedly to compensate for the organization's inability to obtain publicity, managed to implement his long-held dream of editing a militant "national Negro magazine" that would be a vehicle for his agitation. Although an earlier effort to publish a periodical of "new race consciousness," the *Moon*, had failed after a brief existence, Du Bois and two associates (F. H. M. Murray and L. M. Hershaw, both civil servants in Washington) had in 1907 started publishing *Horizon*, the Niagara Movement's unofficial organ. As Du Bois informed the *Horizon*'s early subscribers, "We need a journal, not as a matter of business, but as a matter of spiritual life and death." The journal enunciated the Niagara Movement's philosophy and sought to convert the slight voting power of northern Negroes into a racial asset. Preaching that blacks owed nothing to the Republicans, it condemned the GOP and hammered away at the theme that Secretary of War William Howard Taft (associated with Roosevelt in the Brownsville injustice and a veteran apologist for the southern caste system as well as a denigrator of higher education for blacks) had to be prevented from reaching the White House in 1908 as Roosevelt's successor. But the Tuskegee Machine, operating on the Republicans' behalf, flailed away at Du Bois's political defection to the Democrats; to the disappointment of the editors of *Horizon*, on election day most black voters made Washington's choice their own. Not surprisingly, Du Bois's two colleagues on the *Horizon* had placed their government jobs in jeopardy because of their service to the race. Charles W. Anderson, who as collector of Internal Revenue in New York was a prominent Republican politician in the Tuskegee Machine, tried to persuade the president to fire the pair.

Given the temper of the times and the power of the Tuskegean, Du Bois found himself frustrated. He discovered that there were not enough blacks willing and able to make the magazine self-supporting, and for a while he and his two associates underwrote the deficit. In 1910 both the *Horizon* and the Niagara Movement finally died. Although Du Bois declared himself pleased that there was now within the race "increasing spiritual unrest, sterner impatience with cowardice and deeper determination to be men at any cost," obviously much more work remained to educate blacks away from the accommodation to white supremacy that the Washingtonians preached. While there was no doubt that the Tuskegean had seriously weakened Niagara, it is important to reemphasize that the movement's basic problem was the nation's virulent racism that had catapulted a leader like Washington into power. Even if Du Bois had demonstrated superlative leadership skills, Niagara's program of uncompromising protest for equal treatment was too far ahead of white public opinion, and this fact damaged the movement's propaganda campaign. Of course, Du Bois's personality exacerbated the problem and made it difficult for him to be a successful organizational leader. As he later freely conceded, he appeared "aristocratic and aloof," and his "natural reticence" and "hatred of forwardness" were serious impediments. Although Du Bois "hated the role" of being Niagara's top leader, Washington, in contrast, thrived in his leadership position, operating facilely as a diplomat, politician, and tactician. Given Du Bois's insensitivity to interpersonal problems and his inadequacy in handling them, his signal contribution to Niagara had been as a propagandist, writing manifestos, articles, and speeches, always showing whites that racism pervaded their social institutions and showing blacks the importance of vigorous protest. Far ahead of his time, virtually a voice in the wilderness, Du Bois articulated better than any of his contemporaries the hope for equal citizenship rights that American blacks never relinquished.

With the Niagara Movement hovering near death, it was clear that the resources to make the black protest movement viable would have to be found elsewhere. Du Bois and other leading "radicals" had been in touch with the small number of prominent whites who were becoming disillusioned with Washington's accommodationist platform. Du

Bois concluded that an interracial protest movement was essential, considering the devastating problems that his black movement had experienced and the increased resources and legitimization that prominent whites could provide. It was the mob violence at Springfield in 1908 that finally convinced this group of whites of the absolute necessity of forming an interracial protest organization possessing the aims or goals of the Niagara Movement. Through publicity directed at the whole nation, through litigation in the courts and lobbying in the legislature, this new organization called the National Association for the Advancement of Colored People hoped to topple the walls of race discrimination. Du Bois became the principal black founder and the most prominent Niagara veteran connected with the NAACP.

Although the membership was overwhelmingly black, for nearly a decade the NAACP was largely white-funded and white-dominated, and Du Bois was the only black in its inner circle. He performed a very significant role in the organization—serving as the embodiment of militant protest, the link to the small band of black "radicals," and the symbol to the public of demonstrably successful interracial cooperation. Beyond these contributions lay his more significant asset to the NAACP as its chief propagandist. As director of Publicity and Research, he founded the *Crisis* in 1910 and edited this influential NAACP official organ for a quarter-century.

In many ways Du Bois was all that the white founders had hoped for. It is true that he was not intimately involved in the administrative work of the NAACP, and only on rare occasions did he even attempt to influence policy. He quite consciously confined himself to his work as *Crisis* editor and saw his role as being a molder of public opinion— chiefly among blacks. As *Crisis* editor he recorded and supported the NAACP program for constitutional rights; he stirred up intellectual controversies, commented on current events related to the race problem, and provided arguments for racial equalitarianism. His expressions of protest were clearly, sharply, and often dramatically written, in sentences sometimes so aphoristic that black readers cherished them: "*I am resolved to be quiet and law abiding, but to refuse to cringe in body or in soul, to resent deliberate insult, and to assert my just rights in the face of wanton aggression.*" "Oppression costs the oppressor too much if the oppressed stand up and protest." "Agitate, then, brother; protest, reveal the truth and refuse to be silenced." "A moment's let up, a moment's acquiescence, means a chance for the wolves of prejudice to get at our necks." The reverence that many blacks families had for the magazine was described by the writer, J. Saunders Redding, who recollected that in his boyhood home the only periodical that the children could not touch was the *Crisis*, which "was strictly inviolate until my father himself had unwrapped and read it—often . . . aloud" to the family.

At last Du Bois had fulfilled the vision that had inspired him for so many years. The *Crisis* was his opportunity to edit a national black journal of opinion to which people would listen. As early as 1913, when the NAACP could scarcely attract 3,000 members, the circulation of the *Crisis*—chiefly among blacks—reached 30,000. Clearly Du Bois was making a considerable impact. Yet given his personality and his deep-seated desire for autonomy, the public image of harmony within the NAACP was belied by the battling that erupted between Du Bois and certain key board members.

The basic problem involved how much independence Du Bois as the only board member who was also a paid NAACP executive would have in operating the organization's official magazine, and what contributions to other NAACP activities were required of him. Du Bois, who was frequently unavailable for organizational chores like writing pamphlets, regarded the *Crisis* as "the only work" in the NAACP "which attracts me." In fact, he believed that the *Crisis*, rather than serving the NAACP as its interpreter to the public, was the one vehicle—through raising the consciousness of thousands of blacks—that could "make the NAACP *possible*." Demanding "independence of action" in running the *Crisis*, Du Bois was determined "to prove the possibilities of a Negro magazine," and he clashed with two successive white board chairmen—Villard (who was dictatorial and seemed at times subtly prejudiced) and Joel Spingarn (whom Du Bois described as a "knight" untarnished by any racist tendencies). To these board chairmen, faced with the problem of stretching limited funds to cover such vital activities as branch development and legal redress, the *Crisis* did not have the same priority that it had for Du Bois. And when the *Crisis* editor published materials that the other NAACP leaders felt were tactically ill advised and even harmful to the organization, open conflict resulted.

Villard was determined that the *Crisis* editor like other paid executives should be subordinated to the board chairman. Moreover, he resented that although the magazine was the property of the NAACP, and despite its large circulation not self-supporting, Du Bois wanted to "carry it around in his pocket." In protest Villard resigned as chairman in late 1913, being replaced by Spingarn—but the board struggle with the editor continued. Spingarn was more understanding than Villard and wanted to see a black editor like Du Bois exercise maximum influence, but he also believed that Du Bois's difficult personality produced situations that damaged the organization. Indeed there were even times when the NAACP, in its drive for black support, was acutely embarrassed by the editor's attacks on black ministers, journalists, and educators. For example, in 1912 Du Bois had indicted the Negro churches: "the paths and the higher places are choked with pretentious ill-trained men . . . in far too many cases with men dishonest and otherwise immoral." Two years later at a time when the NAACP desperately needed support from the black press, Du Bois fired a volley against these weeklies, claiming that many were not "worth reprinting or even reading" because their editors were venal, emptyheaded, or ungrammatical. The barrage did not go unanswered, and Du Bois created a serious public relations problem for the NAACP.

Du Bois's original indiscretion had been precipitated by his acute sensitivity to a black newspaper's comment that the *Crisis* was financially dependent on an NAACP subsidy. Moreover the subsidy was one that the NAACP found it hard to afford, especially with a recent recession sharply reducing the organization's income. Nonetheless, Spingarn and the board reluctantly acceded to Du Bois's demands for more staff and office space—at a time when the national administrative office with fund-raising responsibilities shouldered by a small staff was forced to accept budgetary cuts. Because of such incidents, Spingarn, although having the highest respect for Du Bois, like Villard, eventually concluded that the *Crisis* editor was exercising too much autonomy and reluctantly announced his own intention to resign as chairman. Yet in the end Spingarn had too much admiration for Du Bois's contributions to make more than a gentle rebuke. In 1916 he and the board agreed that the *Crisis* under Du Bois could not simply be a house organ and that its editorials must be permitted to represent Du Bois's opinions within the framework of broad NAACP policy.

By 1916 in the wake of Washington's death, Du Bois became the nation's most prominent black leader, freed now from the heavy burden of competing with the Tuskegean. To the end the *Crisis* editor had remained Washington's most implacable foe among NAACP leaders. Even before Washington's death, a noticeable shift in sentiment had begun among leading blacks, which was reflected in the successful attempts to organize NAACP branches. This shift reflected not only the growing stature of Du Bois and the NAACP, but changing social conditions as well. With increasing urbanization and educational attainment and with more migration to the North, growing numbers of blacks by World War I were embracing Du Bois's doctrine of agitation and protest.

Ironically, with the passing of Washington from the scene and the decline of Tuskegee's influence, Du Bois and the NAACP now occupied a centrist rather than a "radical" role in the black community, and the editor of the *Crisis* even found himself on occasion attacked for conservatism and lack of militancy. To some extent Du Bois made himself vulnerable on this score, since during World War I he muted his criticism. Hopeful that with the return of peace blacks would be rewarded for their contributions to the war that was supposed "to make the world safe for democracy," he had urged blacks to "forget our special grievances" and "close ranks" with fellow white Americans in the battle against the country's European enemies. Not only did a number of black editors openly criticize Du Bois for this stand, but during the war and postwar years the young socialist A. Philip Randolph stridently condemned the NAACP spokesman as a "hand-picked, me-too-boss, hat-in-hand, sycophant, lick spittling" Negro.

For his part, Du Bois, disillusioned by the new spurt in racism and the resurgence of mob violence that followed the war, composed some of the most ringingly militant editorials of his career. Enraged when he discovered evidence that black soldiers who had risked their lives in Europe were discriminated against by the American military establishment there, Du Bois documented these facts in a special *Crisis* issue that also featured an editorial, "Returning Soldiers": "By the God of Heaven, we are cowards and jackasses if now that the war is over, we do not marshal every ounce of our brain and brawn to fight a sterner, longer, more unbending battle against the forces of hell in our own land. *We return. We return from fighting. We return fighting.* Make way for Democracy! We saved it in France, and by the Great Jehovah, we will save it in the United States of America, or know the reason why."

This particular number of the *Crisis*, which sold 100,000 copies, was not only widely discussed among blacks but created a furor outside the race. To say that certain U.S. government officials were alarmed is putting it mildly. The Post Office Department held up the copies while debating whether to allow them through the mails. Representative James Byrnes of South Carolina, epitomizing the sentiment of many in Congress, delivered a speech charging that Du Bois and other black newsmen had precipitated the postwar rioting. Although white mobs had caused most of the bloodshed, Byrnes singled out "Returning Soldiers" as the inspiration for black violence, holding that Du Bois should be indicted for having encouraged resistance to the government. Du Bois's fury continued unabated, and he warned blacks again to arm themselves against white mobs. The Justice Department, also anxious about "Returning Soldiers," investigated the *Crisis*, Randolph's *Messenger*, and other black periodicals. Noting that blacks like Du Bois had counseled retaliatory violence against white attackers, the department reported that black newsmen were actually "antagonistic to the white race and openly defiantly assertive of [their] own equality and even superiority."

As noted earlier, there had always been a strong nationalist strain in Du Bois's thinking, and in the postwar era this aspect of his propaganda became the focus of another controversy—his acrimonious struggle with the famous black separatist leader, Marcus Garvey. The most influential aspect of Du Bois's nationalism had been his pioneering advocacy of Pan-Africanism, the belief that all people of African descent had common interests and should unite in the struggle for their freedom. Moreover, he articulated both a cultural nationalism encouraging the development of black literature and art and an economic nationalism urging blacks to create a separate "group economy."

All of these themes had been expressed much earlier. Thus in an 1897 paper aptly entitled "The Conservation of Races," Du Bois enunciated the doctrine of "Pan-Negroism"—that regardless of what nation they lived in, Africans and their descendants had a common identity and should feel an emotional commitment to one another. American blacks, the vanguard of blacks the world over, should have a special attachment to Africa as the race's "greater fatherland." Arguing that "the Negro people as a race have a contribution to make to civilization and humanity, which no other race can make," he maintained that blacks possessed "a distinct mission as a race . . . to soften the whiteness" of an uninspiring materialistic Teutonic culture that seemed to dominate the world. Accordingly, Du Bois argued that Afro-Americans should maintain their group identity and institutions; for them salvation would come only from an educated elite who would chart the way to cultural and economic elevation, teaching the doctrine that blacks "MUST DO FOR THEMSELVES," by developing their own businesses, newspapers, schools, and welfare institutions.

Later Du Bois used the *Crisis* as a vehicle for cultural nationalism. Calling for the systematic cultivation of all kinds of black art forms, he proudly presented works by young black novelists, essayists, painters, and poets, and in the early 1920s he proposed an Institute of Negro Literature and Art. Determined to harness the race's creative strivings, he told defeatists, "Off with these thought-chains and inchoate

77

soul-shrinkings, and let us train ourselves to see beauty in black." Blacks were "a different kind" of people, possessing the spirit and power to build a "new and great Negro ethos." The race, armed with "group ideals," could bring forth a flood of artistic and literary creation based on themes in black life and black history. Above all, blacks could enrich themselves and America only by defining their own standards of beauty, rather than permitting whites to define them.

The *Crisis* also taught lessons in economic nationalism. Early in his life Du Bois had made bourgeois pleas for black capitalist enterprises based on the Negro market, but after coming under Socialist influences during his leadership of the Niagara Movement, he began advocating black consumers' and producers' cooperatives as a basic weapon for fighting discrimination and poverty. Du Bois devoted considerable space in the *Crisis* to stimulate readers to open cooperative stores, and in 1918 he helped form the Negro Cooperative Guild, which hoped to set up retail stores, cooperative warehouses, and even banks. Du Bois believed that white racism, by reducing the range of black incomes, had unintentionally made a socialized black economy feasible. Blacks, rather than aspiring to be rapacious millionaires, would find it satisfying to be "consecrated" workers devoted to "social service" for the race. Du Bois saw no reason why this "closed economic circle" could not encompass a complex racial manufacturing-distributive system, with profits reinvested in useful race projects like large housing developments. Moreover, a black cooperative system could be extended to race members in far off places like Africa.

Du Bois's cultural nationalism was intimately related to the stirrings among black intellectuals and artists known as the Harlem Renaissance, but his quasi-socialistic brand of economic nationalism was never widely accepted. Even his more influential Pan-Africanism was really not a central element in Afro-American thinking at that period. Du Bois had probably been the first black American to develop explicitly the concept of Pan-Africanism; certainly of all the black American intellectuals, he was the one most deeply identified with Africa itself—at a time when most Afro-Americans were embarrassed by the "primitiveness" of their ancestral societies. In 1900 Du Bois had been a leader in the first Pan-African Conference, and as chairman of its "Committee on the Address to the Nations of the World," he called for the creation of "a great central Negro State of the World" in Africa, which would raise the status of blacks wherever they lived. No sooner had World War I ended when, amidst the discussion of European imperialism and the disposition of the German colonies in Africa, Du Bois again took up the Pan-African theme and convened four Pan-African congresses in Europe and the United States between 1919 and 1927. Urging the recognition of the "absolute equality of races" and the end of imperialist exploitation of blacks everywhere, these conclaves focused on racial developments in Africa and were, in fact, a concrete application of his notion that black intellectuals should lead the race into the future.

His nationalist Pan-African Movement shared several parallels with the integrationist Niagara Movement: it was dominated by Du Bois's towering personality; it attracted only a very small segment of the Talented Tenth; it suffered from serious internal schisms; it exemplified his strength as a propagandist leader and his weakness as an organizational leader; it clashed sharply with a popular black spokesman of the period; and yet it was important as an ideological forerunner of very significant future developments among Afro-Americans.

When Du Bois revived the Pan-African Movement in 1919, he had hoped that the NAACP would be a base of grass-roots support. But neither the black middle and upper classes who were the readers of the *Crisis* and the backbone of the NAACP's supporters nor the masses of the black poor rallied to it. The NAACP contributed only token funds and considered the movement incompatible with its basic thrust. Since Du Bois largely isolated himself from the machinery of the NAACP and was not essentially an organizational leader, he did almost nothing to convince the board to adopt his cause as their own. Certainly Du Bois did not try to alter the thinking of the leadership in conferences with key officials or in board meetings. Nor did he seek to organize NAACP branch officials behind the Pan-African Movement. Characteristically, he attempted to proselytize through *Crisis* editorials and seemed satisfied to persuade the NAACP to make occasional official statements (which he wrote) supporting his views on Africa.

Like the Niagara Movement, these Pan-African congresses were beset by insuperable external and internal problems. Basically in an imperialist age Du Bois lacked bargaining power to pressure the European nations to liberate their subject peoples. Impotent, the Pan-African Movement could assume only a conciliatory stance and produce respectful petitions that obtained for Du Bois a hearing from minor officials. Still, conciliation won permission to hold the Pan-African Congress in places like London, Paris, and Brussels. Conciliation also gained the support of influential Africans like Blaise Diagne, a Senegalese representative in France's Chamber of Deputies, but such friends did not prove to be anticolonialists, and this fact precipitated a serious split within Du Bois's movement.

Yet in a period dominated by rampant imperialism a confrontational approach, such as Garvey's nationalist Universal Negro Improvement Association (UNIA), got no further than Du Bois did. But Garvey succeeded in causing considerable problems for Du Bois and his movement. Originally Du Bois had been impressed by Garvey's Black Star Steamship Line, the company founded in 1919 to link blacks in Africa and the New World. Hoping for Garvey's cooperation, he thought that the UNIA might bring to fruition his own Pan-Africanist dreams. But Du Bois soon decided that the line was being financially mismanaged and that Garvey was self-destructive in defiantly threatening the imperialist nations while being powerless to back up the threats. For their part, Garvey and his associates decided that Du Bois was merely a jealous rival, and an "aristocratic" Uncle Tom "controlled" by white money—in fact, the *Crisis* editor was pronounced "more of a white man than a Negro." Besides being subjected to this sort of criticism from the Garveyites, Du Bois was bombarded by white journalists who confused his movement with the UNIA and queried the *Crisis* editor about plans to expel whites from Africa. During the early 1920s, when the UNIA attracted hundreds of thousands of followers, the Pan-African Congress barely managed to stay alive, and as with the Niagara Movement most members did little, not even paying their annual dues. Moreover, the problem of inactivity was exacerbated by the serious split between the French and American members. Finally in futility Du Bois announced that if the Afro-American Talented Tenth did not rally around the movement he was ready to give it up, and although another Pan-African Congress was held in 1927, it was a perfunctory affair, and Du Bois's hopes were unrealized again. (As "elder statesman" of the movement, he was later associated with the post–World War II Fifth Pan-African Congress held in England in 1945.)

Regardless of his differences with the NAACP on Pan-Africa and other matters, Du Bois usually could be counted upon to defend the organization publicly. Thus in 1921 when the *Crisis* exonerated the board of charges of undemocratic domination, its editor declared, "It is foolish for us to give up this practical program." But behind the scenes, however, the potential for serious disruption was inherent in the ongoing problem of competition for scarce resources. Money difficulties became even more acute during the 1920s because the circulation of the *Crisis* fell drastically, from over 100,000 in 1919 to about

30,000 in 1930. Du Bois expected the board to cover the deficit, and the board did so, although his colleagues would undoubtedly have been more agreeable to providing additional money had Du Bois been willing to make the *Crisis* more decidedly the house organ of the NAACP and to devote more pages to the organization's national projects as well as branch activities. But Du Bois found that route unpalatable—he still insisted that he must "blaze a trail" and perform "a work of education and ideal beyond the practical steps of the N.A.A.C.P."

At the end of the 1920s the financial crunch facing the *Crisis* set the stage for a serious, in one sense fatal, conflict between Du Bois and new NAACP Executive Secretary Walter White. White disliked Du Bois intensely and believed that the *Crisis* had become the NAACP's rather superfluous tail; for Du Bois, of course, it was still the other way around. In 1929 White protested that Du Bois's requests for ever-larger subsidies were being granted only at the expense of a weakened administrative office and were becoming a luxury that could be afforded no longer. But the board managed to find the money until the Great Depression set in, when its members paid more attention to White's admonitions that scarce dollars could be better spent on anti-lynching campaigns, court cases, and legislative lobbying.

Du Bois's problem was that as the Depression deepened, White's powers grew not only in the administrative office but also in matters directly affecting the *Crisis*. Thus in 1931, after the magazine lost another several thousand dollars (although the NAACP was paying Du Bois's entire salary), the Crisis Publishing Company was organized (with White on the board of directors) as a legal maneuver to limit the NAACP's liability for the obligations of the *Crisis*. Du Bois fought back, ostensibly to overhaul the NAACP's structure but actually to strip White of much of his power. First the *Crisis* editor informed the board that its members were undemocratically chosen since the rank-and-file throughout the country had no voice in the selection process. Then in 1932 he went public with his charges and called for transferring the central office's power to the branches; simultaneously he urged that the NAACP adopt a program that would replace the "mere negative attempt to avoid segregation and discrimination." In his solution to the many problems posed by the Depression, Du Bois went beyond the NAACP's official program of protecting constitutional rights and revived his old dream for systematic "voluntary segregation" in the form of a separate black cooperative economy "That race pride and race loyalty, Negro ideals and Negro unity have a place and function today, the NAACP never has denied and never can deny!" Refusing to accept Du Bois's distinction between enforced and voluntary separation, White and Spingarn challenged the *Crisis* editor, contending that he was undermining the decades-long struggle against segregation. White declared that blacks "must, without yielding, continue the grim struggle *for* integration" and stop the damage that Du Bois was inflicting on the organization. The whole debate degenerated into bitter personal recriminations between White and the *Crisis* editor. Defeated, Du Bois resigned in 1934 and returned to his old professorship at Atlanta University.

Neither inside nor outside the NAACP had there been any groundswell of support for Du Bois's position. The Talented Tenth by and large was marching to a different drummer. Black intellectuals like the sociologist E. Franklin Frazier, the political scientist Ralph Bunche, and the former NAACP Executive Secretary James Weldon Johnson all repudiated his separatism, arguing that an all-black economy in an era of black powerlessness could easily be destroyed by "the legal and police forces of the state [which] would inevitably be aligned against them." Most critics actually viewed Du Bois's call as retrogression, a return to Washington's accommodationist apologia for segregation.

Thus Du Bois had created serious problems for himself. His "voluntary segregation" campaign put him outside the mainstream of the civil rights movement in the mid-1930s, and in severing his *Crisis* ties he had given up the platform that was essential for his role as propagandist. Although he remained a venerated symbol, he had lost his position of effective leadership. No longer was he the molder and shaper of Negro opinion that he had been since the early part of the century.

During the 1940s Du Bois downplayed the plan for a separate economy, but he gradually identified himself with pro-Russian causes, thus drifting further from the main currents of black thinking at the time. In 1951 he was tried in federal court on charges of being an unregistered agent of a foreign power, and although the judge directed an acquittal, Du Bois became so thoroughly disillusioned about the United States that in 1961 he officially joined the Communist party and moved to Ghana.

Du Bois continued to write and lecture until the end of his life, but the output of his last three decades had slight impact among his black American contemporaries. Then, ironically, shortly after his departure from the United States, Du Bois's reputation soared, and he was transformed into a prophet. In the early 1960s the militant integrationist phase of the black direct-action protest movement was building to-

The 82 idney B. Coulter Library
Onondaga Community College
Rte. 173, Onondaga Hill
Syracuse, New York 13215

ward its climax, and his enormous contributions became widely recognized and revered among young activists. Du Bois died on the very day that one-quarter of a million people gathered at the March on Washington—August 27, 1963. Moments before the mammoth march departed from the Washington Monument, the vast assemblage stood bowed in silent tribute at the announcement of his death. Later at the Lincoln Memorial Roy Wilkins, now executive secretary of the NAACP, referred to Du Bois's vast contributions to the long struggle for black freedom. Then a few years afterward, with the decline of militant integrationism and the ascendancy of the Black Power Era with its separatist thrust, the relevance of his nationalist writings became widely appreciated.

W. E. B. Du Bois, the propagandist, had now become symbol and prophet, and events both in the United States and abroad vindicated the celebrated words he had used in *Souls of Black Folk* in 1903: "The problem of the Twentieth Century is the problem of the color line."

Note on Sources

There are two book-length biographies of Du Bois: Francis L. Broderick, *W. E. B. Du Bois: Negro Leader in Time of Crisis* (Stanford, Calif.: Stanford University Press, 1959), and Elliott Rudwick, *W. E. B. Du Bois: A Study in Minority Group Leadership* (Philadelphia: University of Pennsylvania Press, 1960). In addition there are also Du Bois's own autobiographical works: *Dusk of Dawn: A Essay Toward an Autobiography of a Race Concept* (New York: Harcourt Brace, 1940), and *The Autobiography of W. E. Burghardt Du Bois: A Soliloquy on Viewing My Life from the Last Decade of Its First Century*, ed. Herbert Aptheker (New York: International Publishers, 1968). For a literary analysis of Du Bois's life and work, see Arnold Rampersad, *The Art and Imagination of W. E. B. Du Bois* (Cambridge, Mass.: Harvard University Press, 1976). Among the anthologies of Du Bois's published writings are Julius Lester, ed., *The Seventh Son: The Thought and Writings of W. E. B. Du Bois*, 2 vols. (New York: Random House, 1971), and Philip S. Foner, ed., *W. E. B. Du Bois Speaks*, 2 vols. (New York: Pathfinder Press, 1970).

Du Bois's papers, at the University of Massachusetts, Amherst, and also available on microfilm, are surprisingly incomplete, but scattered items of significance from them will be found in Herbert Aptheker, ed., *The Correspondence of W. E. B. Du Bois*, 3 vols. (Amherst: University of Massachusetts Press, 1973–78).

Other books with relevant discussions of Du Bois and his role are August Meier, *Negro Thought in America, 1880–1915: Racial Ideologies in the Age of Booker T. Washington* (Ann Arbor: University of Michigan Press, 1963); Charles F. Kellogg, *NAACP: A History of the National Association for the Advancement of Colored People. Volume 1: 1909–1920* (Baltimore, Md.: Johns Hopkins University Press, 1967); and B. Joyce Ross: *J. E. Spingarn and the Rise of the N.A.A.C.P.* (New York: Atheneum, 1972).

James Weldon Johnson
and the Development of the NAACP

The National Association for the Advancement of Colored People, in which W. E. B. Du Bois played so important a role since its founding in 1909, really came to maturity during the second decade of its existence. Much of the credit for the NAACP's expansion and growing influence was due to James Weldon Johnson, who joined the staff in 1916 and became the organization's first black executive secretary in 1920. The versatile Johnson had first achieved prominence in the field of the arts and as an American diplomat in Latin America. An individual who reflected extraordinarily well the shifts in black public opinion, he supported Booker T. Washington, becoming active in the NAACP only after Washington's death. Johnson's administration also signaled the transition of the NAACP from a white-led to a black-dominated organization. His membership drives gave the NAACP a firm base in the Negro community. With this base and with his skill as chief executive, there was a shift in power from a predominantly white active nucleus on the board of directors into the hands of the black secretariat; and Johnson's persuasive gifts made the NAACP a respectable lobbying force in the halls of Congress. Johnson's work with the NAACP thus set the stage for the quarter-century secretaryship of Walter F. White, who would bring the organization through the Depression greatly strengthened and more influential than ever and then guide the NAACP's struggle for equality until its celebrated victory in the school desegregation cases of 1954.

ONE OF THE PLEASURES—and difficulties—in understanding the role of James Weldon Johnson as a leader is that he is well known in two very different fields. Some are familiar with Johnson as the head of the National Association for the Advancement of Colored People in the 1920s, when he was a political activist and spokesman for civil rights. Others are cognizant of Johnson's role as poet, novelist, and leading black literary figure in the earlier years of the twentieth century. In both roles Johnson fought to move beyond the severe constraints set by racial prejudice and discrimination to shape the attitudes and actions of both black and white Americans.

As did other black leaders, Johnson often struggled with a lack of power, and he soon discovered that leadership without at least some power is unlikely to produce results. Motive and resource, James Mac-Gregor Burns points out in *Leadership*, are the two essentials of power. Black leaders in the nineteenth and early twentieth centuries were strongly motivated to combat segregation and discrimination, but they usually lacked the resources to win many battles.

The conflict between motives and resources affected Johnson's role in the NAACP as deeply as it affected others in the organization. The leaders of the NAACP, blacks and whites, were well motivated, highly talented, and strong-willed. What the association lacked in the years closely following its founding in 1909 was a leader who possessed not only motivation, talent, and firm conviction but also the skills necessary to knit individuals into an effective, goal-directed organization that had few resources and that operated in a largely hostile environment.

Johnson brought such skills to the NAACP when he joined it as field secretary in late 1916. When he retired as its chief executive in 1930, he had not only united the staff of the NAACP in working toward well-articulated goals, but also he had become a widely recognized spokesman for an interracial, evolutionary approach to achieving civil rights for all Americans.

To understand Johnson as a leader we must understand the circumstances of his life that gave him the will and the skill to shape the organization's activities. Johnson was born in Jacksonville, Florida, in 1871, of parents who provided him with a secure, middle-class culture within which to mature. Neither of his parents had been slaves. His father, a waiter in a leading Jacksonville hotel, had been born a freeman in Virginia and had spent most of his young adulthood in New York City. His mother, born in the Bahamas, was for many years a school teacher in Jacksonville's largest black school. James, their elder son, went to Atlanta University for both his high school and college education (B.A., 1894; M.A., 1904). At Atlanta he received the conventional education of the day, and it was here also that he developed considerable skill both as a writer and public speaker.

In 1894 Johnson returned to Jacksonville to become principal of the grammar school he had attended and in which his mother had taught. He began to assert himself, attempting to find a leadership role he felt that as a member of the black elite he was duty-bound to provide. Johnson started a daily newspaper (it only lasted six months), read law and became one of the few black lawyers in town, and generally pursued activities that made him a prominent member of Jacksonville's black community.

Johnson himself short-circuited his career as a local black leader in a Jim Crow southern community. His younger brother, Rosamond, had already achieved a start as a writer of popular music. They soon teamed up, with James writing the lyrics. What started out as an amusing hobby had led the brothers to New York shortly after the turn of the century and to fame and at least some fortune on Broadway as part of the ragtime song writing team of Cole and Johnson Brothers.

While in New York Johnson became a close friend of Collector of Internal Revenue Charles Anderson, a black Republican leader and confidant of Booker T. Washington. Anderson's friendship with Washington led to another career change for Johnson in 1906. On the recommendation of Washington, the Department of State offered Johnson the U.S. consulship in Puerto Cabello, Venezuela, a minor post but one which to Johnson seemed to offer a position of unqualified respectability and, through eventual advancement in the U.S. Foreign Service, the resources to exercise power effectively.

Johnson spent six years as a consular official, first at Puerto Cabello and then, beginning in 1909, at Corinto, Nicaragua. It was also during his years in Latin America that he wrote *The Autobiography of an Ex-Colored Man*, a novel that received little notice when published in 1912, but that quickly became a classic in black literature when republished in the 1920s. From the evidence in the State Department files Johnson handled his duties extremely well, whether he dealt with routine matters or whether he had to confront a crisis as he did in Nicaragua when revolution led the United States to send in the Marines in 1912.

Probably the most valuable benefit he received from his experience in Latin America was the honing of a group of leadership skills. In Nicaragua Johnson had to work with officials of various warring factions, U.S. military officers, and frightened civilians under unstable conditions and at worst in the midst of outright violence. Johnson's negotiating skills under these conditions brought high praise from other U.S. officials.

Johnson left the consular service in 1913, not because he had any qualms about American military intervention in Central America, but because he felt a combination of race and politics (Woodrow Wilson, a Democrat, had just been elected president) would frustrate any chance he had for career advancement. It soon became clear to him

87

that if he were to achieve any lasting measure of success it would have to be in the United States and as a part of the struggle for equal rights.

Johnson spent most of the next three years in New York. In 1914 he landed a job as an editorial writer for the important black weekly, the New York *Age*. His well-crafted column, "Views and Reviews," attacked consistently and vehemently the myriad aspects of what in many ways appeared to be an increasingly segregated society. Johnson developed in his early columns a call for action by examining such issues as residential segregation, lynching, and the need for race pride, making known to his readers that he believed in forthright, explicit protest. Johnson wrote with great feeling in 1917 that the "greatest thing the American Negro gained as a result of the Civil War and the amendments to the Constitution was the right to contend for his rights." Blacks had to assert themselves, he urged in column after column, to overcome the unjust handicaps placed on them by white Americans.

During this period Johnson remained on good terms with Emmett Scott, Fred R. Moore, editor of the *Age*, and Anderson, men who drew their influence from their connection with Washington. But Johnson also joined the New York branch of the NAACP. W. E. B. Du Bois, Oswald Garrison Villard, and others connected with the NAACP praised him highly for his editorials.

It was Johnson's skill as a spokesman *and* his ability to deal with others that brought him to the attention of NAACP leaders in 1916. The seven-year-old civil rights association needed a field secretary to organize branches throughout the country. Joel Spingarn, a white liberal who served as chairman of the NAACP board of directors, believed that Johnson's personality and skills would make him a highly effective field secretary. Spingarn agreed with Roy Nash, the association's secretary, who indicated that Johnson had a "social bent," was a "good talker," and "would offend no group or audience." Spingarn also noted, with obvious relish, that it would be a "coup d'etat" to bring into the NAACP leadership a writer for the *Age*, a paper strongly identified with the Washington camp.

When Johnson in December 1916 accepted Spingarn's offer to be field secretary, the NAACP had about seventy branches, many of them inactive and most of them in the North. It also had somewhat less than 9,000 members and an annual budget of $14,000, both figures small in comparison to the magnitude of the problem.

Over the next four years Johnson spent weeks at a time on the road, seeking to build up membership in every region of the country. In his first tour, for example, he visited established branches in Washington, D.C., and Baltimore, and then moved into the unorganized South, where he stopped at towns in Virginia, North and South Carolina, and Georgia. Later trips took him to the upper South, the Midwest, and the Pacific Coast. In each of these organizing trips Johnson spoke to individuals, small groups, and large audiences. His efforts were in good measure responsible for the tenfold (to 90,000) increase in NAACP membership between 1916 and 1920.

Johnson communicated well with a variety of people, black and white, constantly seeking to establish personal rapport to put his listeners at ease. He also had a clear-cut method to establish branches. The easiest way to organize a new NAACP branch, he explained in 1919, "is to get hold of two or three key men and women in the community, write them about the purposes of the organization and of what it has already accomplished, and point out to them the need of having a branch in their community." Once Johnson convinced these few of the need for the NAACP, they, in turn, would bring together twenty or thirty others to whom he would present the organization's program. A local branch, Johnson argued forcefully, could work for better schools for blacks, justice in the courts, and a lessening of racial discrimination. "In ninety-nine cases out of a hundred," Johnson indicated to a friend, "they will decide to organize at once."

Johnson's personal charm and organizational skill nurtured scores of new branches. It was a task that required both skill and physical endurance. On his first organizing effort on the West Coast in the spring of 1919, for example, Johnson spoke before a large group in Los Angeles, then drove more than a hundred miles to San Diego, and addressed another group there. He returned to the Los Angeles area and again met with those interested in the NAACP. Over the next few weeks he spoke to scores of groups in California, Oregon, and Washington on the work of the NAACP and its local branches. Johnson took considerable pride not only in his influence on blacks, but also on white listeners as well. He brought into the San Diego branch, he wrote, "two judges, the chief of police and the city treasurer."

Two aspects stand out in Johnson's efforts at branch organizing. One was his commitment to an interracial organization on a national and, as far as possible, on a local level. The second was his firm belief that the national office should do its very best to back up the efforts of branches to fight local discrimination. The reins of leadership in America were held by whites, he argued, and the NAACP had to work within that reality. This did not mean the association had to back off when facing a fight; a well-organized and coordinated coalition of blacks and whites, Johnson believed, could exert enough power to win a number of significant victories on the local as well as the national level.

The South, of course, was an especially difficult area in which to organize branches. Intimidation by whites was the rule rather than the exception. Where intimidation existed, Johnson wrote in 1919, "the National Office must stand strongly behind the locals. It will not do to let them feel it is their fight and not ours." The promise of national support for the efforts of local branches, Johnson felt, was an important factor in the growth of the NAACP in the South where there were 42,000 members in 1920.

Johnson's opportunity to assume leadership of the NAACP came in 1920. In August 1919 John R. Shillady, the association's chief executive, was badly beaten in Austin, Texas, by a band of whites who did not like the leader of an equal rights organization in their town. Shillady was both white and a trained social worker, but neither attribute protected him from physical harm. He recovered physically, but the incident was psychologically devastating. In April 1920 Shillady resigned, explaining in discouragement that he was "less confident than heretofore of the speedy success of the Association's full program," given "the forces opposed to Negro equality."

Johnson was under no illusion as to the possibility of "speedy success." He knew it would take time and a great deal of effort to breach the wall of segregation. Nevertheless, Johnson wanted to lead the NAACP, and he had his wish fulfilled when in November 1920 the board of directors appointed Johnson head of the organization after he had served for several months as acting-secretary.

Johnson brought to the NAACP abilities the association badly needed. He had developed considerable organizational and leadership skills during his careers as school principal, consular official, and editorial writer. His more than three years as field secretary had given him an understanding of the methods and goals of the NAACP; during that period he had also come to know thoroughly the strengths and weaknesses of his co-workers. When Johnson took over as secretary in 1920, he needed to exercise all his skills as a leader to make the NAACP the effective organization it deserved to be.

The initial, and in many ways the continuing, task Johnson faced was to develop further and make more effective the organization itself. In the early years of the NAACP unpaid volunteers had done much of the work, with a high turnover among the few paid staff members. Johnson increased the number of full-time professionals and reduced the turnover almost to nil.

Johnson brought Walter White onto the staff in 1918, and throughout the 1920s he served as Johnson's assistant. White was a native of Atlanta and a recent graduate of Atlanta University. He was twenty years junior to Johnson, and perhaps because of this there was something of a father-son relationship between the two. White participated actively in the planning of most of the NAACP activities, frequently carried out field investigations, coordinated legal activities, and often served as a publicist for the association. White was especially effective in the South, for his white skin belied his African ancestry. Thus he was able to move among both blacks and whites when he investigated the causes of a lynching or other violent manifestations of racial hostility. White was not popular with his co-workers, for he was strong-willed and self-centered, but few questioned his energy or skill.

Johnson relied on William Pickens and Robert Bagnall to carry on the organizing and maintaining of branches. Pickens, the son of a sharecropper, had graduated from Yale University and had taught at several black colleges. Bagnall had been the minister of an Episcopal church in Detroit before joining the New York staff in 1921. The task of organizing branches put a great deal of strain on them, for the health of the organization depended on the vitality of its branches. Pickens especially had a reputation of being an effective organizer; he was also known among his co-workers as argumentative and sarcastic, and one who did not take criticism easily.

Du Bois was a close co-worker of Johnson's during the 1920s. Du Bois had created the *Crisis* as the voice of the NAACP, but the force of his ideas and personality had identified it intimately with its creator more than with the organization. Du Bois brilliantly interpreted twentieth-century ideas and social movements in the *Crisis* and in other writings during his long and productive life. He was also well aware of his accomplishments and often acerbic toward those he felt were not his equals. Du Bois had his conflicts with almost everyone connected with the NAACP's staff and board of directors from the start of his editorship in 1911 until he was forced out of the position (by White) in 1934. Johnson, however, remained on excellent terms with Du Bois; in fact, Du Bois relied heavily on Johnson for advice and counsel. Their friendship enabled Johnson to keep Du Bois in a productive, if at times stormy, working relationship with other NAACP workers during the 1920s.

Johnson managed to create a smoothly functioning organization by placing himself as an equal among equals and then, by working through suggestions rather than orders, inducing others to do more or less what he wanted them to do. He suggested, for example, that Du Bois rewrite his annual report for 1926. The report, Johnson pointed out in a quiet but firm manner, "is too much of an apology or an argument" and "induces the wrong psychology." Du Bois, strong-willed though he was, listened to the carefully phrased words of advice from his friend and co-worker. Again working by indirection, Johnson suggested that the legal committee could best keep up with court actions if the central office prepared a monthly summary of cases. He urged Arthur Spingarn, head of the legal committee, to request such a summary. Spingarn did make the request; Johnson passed it on to White, who generally handled legal matters in the office, for action, noting that it was a "splendid idea." Board member Mary White Ovington, who had worked with the association since its beginning, certainly knew what she was talking about when in 1929, after watching Johnson's leadership in action for a decade, she praised him for "the marvelous way in which you get people to do things for you."

Johnson directed his efforts and the efforts of the NAACP staff in the use of certain basic tools, which enabled the association to develop its resources and to bargain more effectively for a significant improvement in the lives of black Americans. Johnson emphasized the use of publicity to expose both the physical and psychological cruelties of the Jim Crow system; he furthered the carefully planned legal attacks on the system in local, state, and federal courts; and he pressured government officials to treat blacks justly. Johnson did not introduce these tools—they had been used by the NAACP for a decade—but he did rapidly expand their use and make them considerably more effective.

Johnson coordinated the work of staff members, the board of directors, and the branches, so that each would use the principal tools most effectively in reaching the association's goals. Sometimes that meant sending White to investigate an incident; at other times he channeled advice and funds to a branch to fight a local case of discrimination. In other cases he brought pressure to bear to convince government officials or politicians to change or at least modify a discriminatory practice. Coordination was vital, for new cases constantly appeared while some old ones remained unresolved for years. By the mid-1920s Johnson could write with deep feeling to a friend, "I do not believe you can understand the pressure under which I work."

Johnson spent most of his time in a seemingly endless series of efforts to secure rights for blacks throughout the nation. By the early 1920s the NAACP was a clearinghouse for civil rights cases. Johnson reviewed hundreds of appeals for aid each year, most involving requests for financial aid to fight everything from attempts to segregate schools in the North to efforts to end or at least modify Jim Crow practices in the South. Johnson provided effective leadership to guide the small staff in the New York office as well as to inspire the local branches that had to do much of the work.

In many instances the NAACP turned to the courts in its search for a solution. Ralph Bunche, in his study memorandum for Gunnar Myrdal's *An American Dilemma* (1944), indicated that in this period the NAACP's legal work involved three areas. The first was the legal redress of individual cases of injustice due to race. The second area of activity lay in attacking the disfranchisement of black voters throughout the South. Finally, the NAACP brought a series of court cases against the Jim Crow system, that is, segregation by law, as it existed throughout the South and to some extent in other regions of the nation.

Only a few cases drew national publicity or raised major constitutional issues. A case of attempted racial discrimination that did generate national interest occurred in 1925 when Ossian Sweet, a black physician, and his family moved into a house he had purchased in a white neighborhood of Detroit. A mob besieged the house, and during one tense evening shots were fired from the house, killing a white man. The twelve people in the Sweet home were charged with murder. The NAACP retained Clarence Darrow and Arthur Garfield Hays, two of America's best-known civil liberties lawyers, and after two trials the Sweets were completely exonerated.

Perhaps the most significant of the cases the NAACP carried to the Supreme Court was *Nixon* v. *Herndon*. In 1924 Democratic party leaders in El Paso, Texas, began to enforce a state law, common in one form or another in most southern states, that limited primary elections to whites. The NAACP protested that, given the dominate power of white Democrats, the primary election was the only election that counted in the South. The local branch and then the national office fought the case up to the U.S. Supreme Court. In 1927 the Court ruled unconstitutional the "white primary" as constituted in Texas. Johnson did not expect anything "magical" to happen in the South because of the decision, but he wrote Moorfield Storey that "we have at least battered down one more wall between the Negro and his full citizenship rights." In fact, *Nixon* v. *Herndon* was the first in a series of NAACP-argued cases that would lead the Court in 1944 to declare unconstitutional all forms of the white-only primary election.

In the Sweet case, in *Nixon* v. *Herndon,* and in numerous other cases Johnson and White performed the essential behind-the-scenes role of managers. White took the lead in coordinating the efforts of local lawyers and the NAACP's legal experts working out of Boston, New York, and Washington, while Johnson directed fund-raising, an absolutely essential task given the cost of court action.

It was here that Johnson's network of connections paid off. For several years he had been on the board of directors of the American Fund for Public Service, a foundation devoted to liberal causes. In September 1925 he urged Storey to make an application to the fund for the NAACP's legal defense efforts. Johnson, in fact, wrote the application that Storey signed. The American Fund board shortly approved a grant of $15,000 if the NAACP raised an additional $30,000. Johnson led the fund-raising campaign over the next few months. The successful fund drive not only paid for the Sweet defense but also for the first time put the association's legal defense fund on a relatively firm financial footing.

Johnson firmly believed the NAACP had to change white public opinion as well as win court cases. He quickly made heavy use of publicity to put across the association's message. Herbert Seligmann, the only white member of the staff, had joined as director of publicity just before Johnson took over as secretary. All during the 1920s Johnson worked closely with Seligmann to develop a highly efficient distribution system for the association's press releases.

Johnson chose to emphasize the most brutal aspect of America's racial system in many press releases; he was not going to let America forget that lynchings were occurrences not of the past but of the present. Johnson, after all, could not forget it. With depressing regularity he had to report on deaths by lynching to the NAACP board of directors.

Woodville, Texas

A mob of forty masked men, on May 8, 1920, took Charles Arline, a Negro, from officers and flogged him to death. Arline was arrested on the charge of threatening to kill a white man.

Lakeland, Florida

On May 9, an unidentified Negro porter on an Atlantic Coast Line train, who was charged by a white woman passenger with having insulted her, was taken from the train by a mob . . . and shot to death.

Worth County, Georgia

The lynching of three Negroes recently . . . has been reported to the National Office by the Secretary of the Albany, Ga., Branch. The matter is being investigated by the Legal Committee.

Publicity exposing the brutality of lynching was an important weapon in the association's arsenal, and Johnson believed in using it fully to bring pressure to bear on local and national political leaders. He had no patience with a member of the NAACP's board of directors who in 1921 complained there was too much emphasis on the horrors of lynching and not enough on "the good things done to bring the races together." Johnson bluntly rejected such advice: "What we need to do is to root out the thing which makes possible these horrible details. I am of the opinion that this can be done only through the fullest publicity."

The combination of the NAACP's role as a pressure group and its attack on lynching clearly illustrate Johnson's skill as a leader. In 1921 and 1922 Johnson led the association's fight in Washington for federal anti-lynching legislation. In his role as lobbyist for the passage of the Dyer anti-lynching bill, Johnson introduced the association to the give and take of national politics, a fact that was as important as the outcome of the legislative fight itself.

The NAACP had vehemently opposed mob violence for years. One of its most widely distributed pamphlets, *30 Years of Lynching in the United States, 1889–1919*, provided grimly graphic details of this especially common American practice. Over 3,000 men and women, almost all black, had been lynched during this period. Lynching, of course, was murder; it was the taking of life *without* due process of law, but it was murder rarely punished by the forces of law and order.

But publicity alone did not seem to be enough. For a number of years the NAACP had sought the passage of laws specifically aimed at both the perpetrators of lynchings and at those law officers who failed to protect the victims. At first the association concentrated on state legislation designed to force local sheriffs and judges to protect citizens against mob violence. A number of states passed such laws, but they were rarely enforced. By 1920 it was evident that effective action against lynching would have to come at the national level.

The first clear opportunity came in 1918, when L. C. Dyer, a congressman representing a St. Louis, Missouri, district, introduced a bill making lynching a federal crime and the participants in a lynch mob guilty of murder. The bill also subjected state and local law enforcement officials to a fine or imprisonment for failing to protect the victim of a mob. Over the next several years the NAACP vigorously supported one form or another of the Dyer bill, seeing the struggle for passage both as a way to call America's attention to lynching and as a means of stopping the practice itself.

This was the NAACP's first significant attempt at shaping national legislation. Johnson took the lead in the fight for passage. In fact at the height of the struggle in 1921–22 he was the dominant force, far surpassing the efforts of the bill's author.

The major push to pass the anti-lynching bill began in the spring of 1921, shortly after Warren G. Harding's inauguration as president. Dyer again introduced his bill in the House, and it was referred to the Judiciary Committee. Johnson quickly began a campaign to influence members of the committee. He urged branches in states represented on the committee to convince as many black organizations as possible to write their congressmen to support the Dyer bill. He also urged branches to win the approval of leading newspapers and the support of prominent whites. Johnson made a special effort to distribute statements supporting the bill's constitutionality. This was a tough issue, for the attorney general of the United States as well as others believed that the Supreme Court had so narrowly interpreted the equal protection clause of the Fourteenth Amendment as to make it impossible for the federal government to involve itself in punishing those responsible for lynchings. Even Storey, renowned civil rights lawyer and president of the NAACP, acknowledged difficulties concerning the bill's constitutionality. But Storey argued forcefully, "We are face to face with a necessity which needs a law, and I do not like to admit that the United States is powerless to protect its own people."

Johnson spent much of his time over the next months in Washington. In the fall he worked to have the Dyer bill, now favorably reported out of the Judiciary Committee, placed on the House calendar. Johnson won the backing of Congressman Martin Madden, whose Chicago district contained a large number of black voters. Madden, in turn, influenced Republican members of both the Rules Committee and the Steering Committee. By November the anti-lynching bill was on the calendar, and Johnson began lobbying to have it brought to a vote.

Johnson hammered at two themes in his discussions with the Republican leadership. The GOP, Johnson emphasized to Speaker of the House Frederick Gillett, owed blacks a significant piece of legislation for their long-time political loyalty. In fact, Johnson told Ohio's influential Nicholas Longworth, blacks would regard a lack of enthusiastic support as a mark of "betrayal." He could not, however, gain any support for the Dyer bill from the new president. Harding condemned lynching, Johnson reported with some bitterness, but he would do nothing to pass legislation to prevent it.

The anti-lynching bill reached the floor of the House in December. Southern representatives immediately began delaying tactics. They also began to fire up the rhetoric with traditional "nigger-baiting," including a charge that a band of "hired Negro agitators and white Negroettes" made up the Dyer bill lobby.

In the midst of the often bitter floor debate Johnson kept up the pressure on House Republicans. While White minded the New York office, Johnson persuaded those in the House who in the least measure might support the bill. Dyer exercised little influence. "I saw Dyer," Johnson wrote White in January, and he "seemed to be as happy as a child and just about as innocent of what was going on in the inner circle." Given the realities of black political powerlessness in 1922, Johnson indicated he preferred to persuade congressmen in the "inner circle" rather than to try to intimidate them: *The method is still tact and diplomacy and firm but friendly pressure.* Threats will at this time do no particular good, and at no other times unless we are fully determined to carry them out."

Johnson's efforts were in large measure responsible for the House passage of the Dyer bill in late January. By combining a reaction to the horrors of lynching with the potential loss of black votes, he was able to win over initially indifferent Republicans to provide a 230–119 vote in favor of passage.

Winning Senate approval, however, would be much more difficult. Early on Johnson had hoped to have the strong support of William Borah of Idaho, one of the Senate's most influential members. Johnson plied the senator with information supporting the Dyer bill's constitutionality, knowing that Borah, a strict interpreter of the Constitution, had serious reservations on the matter. Johnson's efforts failed; Borah came out openly against the bill, claiming that the Constitution prevented the federal government's involvement in local law enforcement.

Johnson did win the support of a number of other Senators, including such conservatives as Henry Cabot Lodge of Massachusetts, William Calder of New York, and Charles Townsend of Michigan. After much hard work Johnson also convinced such Republican progressives as Arthur Capper of Kansas and Albert Cummins of Iowa to back the bill.

Republican leaders' fear that black voters would cut the party in the coming November congressional elections had carried the Dyer bill a considerable way in Congress. Johnson tried to use that fear to force the bill to the Senate floor before the election. He failed, but he intended to make the Dyer bill an issue in every election where black votes were a factor. Over the years the Republican party had made many promises to black Americans, Johnson declared in a September press release. "We must hold the Party and hold the President and hold the Republican majority in the Senate strictly to these promises, and if the enactment of anti-lynching legislation is not fulfilled . . . we should consider all of these promises as broken."

The NAACP worked hard in Michigan, New York, and Pennsylvania, where Johnson saw a significant number of black votes and a friendly senator up for reelection. In a close election a bloc of black voters might have made a difference, but 1922 did not provide a close election. The Republicans lost badly, their majorities in both houses reduced to a thin edge, largely because of voter dissatisfaction with the Harding administration.

A final opportunity to push the Senate on the Dyer bill came in late November when Harding called Congress into special session. Harding was not interested in the Dyer bill; he wanted the legislators to approve subsidies for America's overseas shipping industry. Johnson immediately began pressuring Republican conservatives to bring up the anti-lynching measure; at the same time he urged Senate progressives to take the same tack as a means of delaying consideration on the ship subsidy bill.

Johnson's tactics succeeded; on November 28 the Senate began debate on the anti-lynching bill. Southern senators immediately launched a filibuster to prevent the Senate from voting on the bill. Johnson hoped for one of two outcomes. Either the debate would go on until the date of adjournment, March 4, 1923, or public opinion would force enough northern Democratic senators to support the bill, thus enabling a two-thirds vote to invoke cloture and end the filibuster.

Neither alternative occurred. Storey, president of the NAACP, correctly diagnosed the situation: "The opponents of the Dyer Bill are in earnest, and its friends in Congress are not." After a few days the Republican leadership gave in to the demands of southern Democrats and dropped the anti-lynching bill from consideration.

Johnson felt betrayed by the "abject surrender" of such Republican leaders as Senators Lodge and James Watson, and for that matter, of Harding. "The Southern Democrats roar like lions," he noted caustically, "and the Republicans lay down like scared 'possums." Johnson went on to charge that both groups were responsible for the continuing "barbarism, anarchy and degenerate bestiality" symbolized by the four lynchings that had occurred in the week following the defeat of the Dyer bill. Johnson, however, did not let either his ire or his frustration diminish his efforts. Unlike his predecessor, Johnson saw that building an organization for a long and difficult struggle was as important as gaining a sought-after victory like the enactment of a federal anti-lynching law.

The struggle for passage of the Dyer bill clearly illustrates how Johnson increased the long-term effectiveness of the NAACP. For the first time a black-led interracial civil rights organization had engineered the push for legislation in Congress. Johnson certainly used ethical arguments in his appeals to the legislators, but he also manipulated their sense of political self-interest in his efforts to win support for the bill. The failure of his efforts can be linked to the problem of power. Johnson and the NAACP had ample motive to combat lynching; what he lacked in the Senate fight were the resources to bargain effectively with political leaders. Johnson's initial success and ultimate failure, however, only heightened the need for the NAACP to develop the resources to negotiate successfully within the political system.

Johnson summed up the lessons he learned in the Dyer bill fight in the October 1924 issue of the *Crisis*. In "The Gentlemen's Agreement and the Negro Vote," Johnson addressed the issue of the political power held by the two major parties. With the bitter experience of the Dyer bill fight still with him, he bluntly noted that "the Republican Party will hold the Negro and do as little for him as possible, and the Democratic Party will have none of him at all." Johnson went on to label the Republican party in the South as an "office holding oligarchy," uninterested in developing a viable vote-getting policy. Republican leaders, in fact, believed that a strong party was undesirable, for it would mean too many potential competitors for federal patronage jobs.

Johnson described the political situation for blacks in the North as "still in the Fourth of July stage." Blacks exercised too little judgment in evaluating what the two parties had to offer in the major cities of the North. Despite these problems it is to the North, Johnson emphasized, that blacks must look for their twentieth-century political emancipation. Democrats elected to Congress by black voters in the North would "go further to curb the anti-Negro activities of their Southern colleagues than weak-kneed, sycophantic Republican leaders." Johnson pointed out that black Democrats represented Harlem in the state legislature and on the city's board of aldermen. The rise of the Democrats in Harlem had so frightened the GOP, Johnson wrote with enthusiasm, that Republicans had now selected a Harlem black to run for Congress.

Johnson concluded by demanding a stronger bargaining position for blacks in both parties: "The Negro can serve notice that he is no longer a part of the agreement by voting in the coming elections in each State against Republicans who have betrayed him, who are in league with the Ku Klux Klan, who are found to be hypocrites and liars on the question of the Negro's essential rights, and by letting them know he has done it. I am in favor of doing the job at once."

Johnson's experiences in the 1920s convinced him that the political future of blacks lay in the North. The *Crisis* article put him among that small group of black leaders who believed that a slowly emerging northern urban coalition would provide the necessary power base from which blacks could substantially influence political decisions on a national level.

Johnson retired from the leadership of the NAACP at the end of 1930 to become professor of Creative Literature and Writing at Fisk University. At first glance this might seem an unusual move for him to make. Yet intense as it was, Johnson's leadership of the NAACP made up but one of the two interrelated careers he followed in the 1920s. As head of the NAACP, he led a campaign to end lynching; as a writer and poet, Johnson helped shape the cultural movement known as the Harlem Renaissance.

The Harlem Renaissance is most closely associated with a relatively small number of creative young blacks who in the 1920s brought black life to the center stage of American consciousness. Writers, novelists, and poets such as Alain Locke, Charles S. Johnson, Claude McKay, Countee Cullen, Langston Hughes, and Zora Neale Hurston explored what Hughes called the "racial mountain" and demonstrated a living, vibrant racial tradition. And Americans were paying attention. As Rudolph Fisher, an important writer of the Renaissance vividly put it in 1927, "Negro stock is going up, and everybody's buying."

Johnson's first significant literary efforts predated the Renaissance. He explored racial themes in half a dozen poems published between 1907 and 1915, as well as in his novel *The Autobiography of an Ex-Colored Man* (originally published, 1912; reissued, 1927). In "O Black and Unknown Bards" (1908) Johnson extolled the largely unknown creators of Afro-American folk music, while in "Fifty Years" (1913) he chronicled black history in the half century since the Emancipation Proclamation. The plot of *The Autobiography of an Ex-Colored Man* centered on a protagonist who is light enough to pass as white, but who initially chooses to identify with his black heritage. Johnson describes early twentieth-century race relations in both the North and South, finally having the central character traveling the South to research black folk music. It is in the South that the novel's hero witnesses a lynching, an experience he finds so frightening that he decides to give up his black identity for the safety of passing as white. The "ex-colored man" at novel's end laments: "I have sold my birthright for a mess of pottage."

These early writings made Johnson something of an elder statesman to the younger writers of the Harlem Renaissance. In addition, Johnson was a creative force in his own right during the 1920s. His *The Book of American Negro Poetry* (1922) became the standard anthology for the decade, as did *The Book of American Negro Spirituals* (1925), which he edited with his brother, Rosamond. In *God's Trombones* (1927) Johnson presented a set of original poems based on the sermon style of southern black preachers. Finally, at the end of the decade, he wrote *Black Manhattan* (1930), a history of black cultural life in New York City.

Johnson heavily emphasized the contribution of blacks to American cultural life. The Harlem Renaissance represented to him an "awakening" on the part of some whites and many blacks to the fact that blacks, both during the slave era and in the quasi-free decades since, had through their artistic efforts profoundly shaped American culture. Johnson rejected the idea that a writer should deal only with the respectable, middle-class side of black life. He defended Hughes and McKay, who drew much of their prose and poetry from the lives of the black poor, when they were described as "sewer dwellers" and members of the "debauched tenth." Spirituals, jazz, and black folk stories came out of the lives of the black masses, Johnson argued, and not from the unfortunately thin stratum of the black middle class.

Johnson spent much of his time, as he did in his work in the NAACP, reshaping American attitudes. He was recognized in the 1920s by both blacks and whites as a leading interpreter of black literature and culture. His own works were widely read, and he gave many talks around the country in which he called to his listeners' attention the works of the writers of the Renaissance and the wider contribution of blacks to American culture. Johnson, unlike Du Bois, did not see art as simply another propaganda tool. Great art worked subtly to shape the attitudes of its audience. Thus Johnson worked mightily to show all Americans that blacks of the past had produced great art and that the new generation of black writers and poets were building on firm foundations.

Johnson continued to be active during the 1930s. In his autobiography, *Along This Way* (1933), and in his final work, *Negro Americans, What Now?* (1934), he reiterated his commitment to the NAACP and its interracial strategy. Johnson had little sympathy for black-only movements, such as Marcus Garvey's. As much as he extolled black culture and achievements, he did not believe blacks could gain both their full rights and economic opportunity without the aid of whites. Du Bois thought Johnson both naive and old-fashioned in believing that whites would share power with blacks or that a capitalist economy based on greed and mired in a prolonged depression could offer a fair share of wealth to blacks. Johnson recognized the possibility that he was wrong. In his autobiography he warned whites that if they did not share both power and prosperity, "there will be only one way of salvation for the race that I can see, and that will be through the making of its isolation into a religion and the cultivation of a hard, keen, relentless hatred for everything white."

In the spring of 1931, a few months after he retired from the NAACP, Johnson's many friends from both his careers gave a testimonial dinner in his honor. Speaker after speaker praised his ability to convince both blacks and whites to work together efficiently and effectively. Johnson's qualities as a leader who could organize and inspire were best caught by Du Bois, who spoke with passion of how Johnson "easily created a role of interpretation and sympathetic contact, both with his fellow workers and with the outer world, while *at the same time* he pushed a furious anti-lynching campaign and besieged the courts with cases of color discrimination which could not easily be dismissed."

At the time of his tragic death in an automobile accident in 1938, Johnson was widely acknowledged both as a leader among black creative writers and as a leader in civil rights agitation. It was a dual role that has not been duplicated among black leaders since that time.

Note on Sources

Johnson's autobiography, *Along This Way* (New York: Viking Press, 1933), is a classic of the genre, both readable and enlightening. The standard scholarly biography is Eugene Levy, *James Weldon Johnson: Black Leader, Black Voice* (Chicago: University of Chicago Press, 1973). For the early years of the NAACP, see Charles Flint Kellogg, *NAACP: A History of the National Association for the Advancement of Colored People. Volume 1: 1909–1920* (Baltimore, Md.: Johns Hopkins University Press, 1967). For a biography of a white active in the NAACP, see William B. Hixson, *Moorfield Storey and the Abolitionist Tradition* (New York: Oxford University Press, 1972). The NAACP's anti-lynching efforts are fully explored in Robert Zangrando, *The NAACP Campaigns against Lynching, 1909–1950* (Philadelphia: Temple University Press, 1980). For the context of Johnson's literary efforts, see Robert Bone, *The Negro Novel in America* (New Haven, Conn.: Yale University Press, 1956); Nathan Huggins, *Harlem Renaissance* (New York: Oxford University Press, 1971); and David L. Lewis, *When Harlem Was in Vogue* (New York: Alfred A. Knopf, 1981).

Lawrence W. Levine   **6**

Marcus Garvey and the Politics
of Revitalization

The legal and legislative drive of the National Association for the Advancement of Colored People for fulfillment of the Negro's constitutional rights and the integration of blacks into American society did not go uncriticized in the Afro-American community. Among the leading critics of the association and its integrationist policy was the West Indian black nationalist, Marcus Garvey. Arriving in the United States at the height of the flood of black migration to northern cities during World War I, Garvey capitalized upon the disillusionment of the hundreds of thousands of new black city dwellers, who bore the brunt of economic discrimination and the wave of racial violence that followed the war. Garvey was a charismatic leader who offered his followers a sense of pride and self-esteem by celebrating the glories of the African past. He proposed a twofold nationalist solution for the problems of America's black citizens: one, the achievement of economic security by banding together to build their own enterprises if they stayed in the United States; and two, the creation of a glorious new empire on an African continent that was, at the time, controlled by the European imperialist powers.

> *The world has made being black a crime, . . . I hope
> to make it a virtue.*
>
> > —Marcus Garvey

In 1916, Marcus Garvey, a West Indian black without funds, influence, or substantial contacts, arrived in the United States for the first time. By the early 1920s he had built the largest and most influential Afro-American mass movement in American history. Before the decade ended, the movement he created and led, though it continued to exist both in the United States and abroad, was a weakened shadow of itself—internally divided and bereft of mass support. To understand the brief, dramatic, and profoundly significant career of Garvey and his Universal Negro Improvement Association (UNIA), one needs to understand the dynamic mix of personality and historical situation. Accordingly, this essay focuses upon the formative experiences of Garvey, the situation of American blacks when Garvey first arrived on

American soil, and the interaction between the leader and the people he wanted to lead.

Marcus Mosiah Garvey, the eleventh child of Marcus and Sarah Garvey, was born in 1887 in St. Ann's Bay, a rural town on the north coast of Jamaica in the British West Indies. In a 1923 magazine article, Garvey shared his memories of his parents:

> My parents were black negroes. My father was a man of brilliant intellect and dashing courage. He was unafraid of consequences. He took human chances in the course of life, as most bold men do, and he failed at the close of his career. He once had a fortune; he died poor. My mother was a sober and conscientious Christian, too soft and good for the time in which she lived. She was the direct opposite of my father. He was severe, firm, determined, bold and strong, refusing to yield even to superior forces if he believed he was right. My mother, on the other hand, was always willing to return a smile for a blow, and ever ready to bestow charity upon her enemy. Of this strange combination I was born.

Garvey's account was corroborated by a white neighbor who testified that the elder Garvey, a master stonemason who took jobs only sporadically, preferring to lock himself in his room and read, "always acted as if he did not belong among the villagers; he was well read, and gave advice as a local lawyer. He was silent, stern. . . . He was 'Mr. Garvey' to every one, even to Sarah—his wife and children." Mrs. Garvey "was just the opposite to him in every way. She was one of the most beautiful black women I have ever seen. . . . Her voice was gentle and caressing, her figure well shaped and erect. She was a regular Church-goer at the Wesleyan Methodist Church."

Because nine of his siblings died in childhood, Garvey seems to have grown up close only to his older sister, Indiana. Among his other daily playmates were the nine children of the two white families that lived on the adjoining land. "To me, at home in my early days," Garvey recalled, "there was no difference between white and black." His closest friend, a white girl, "knew no better than I did myself. We were two innocent fools who never dreamed of a race feeling and problem." Their innocence ended abruptly when Garvey's friend informed him that she was being sent away to school in Scotland and that she was instructed by her parents "never to write or try to get in touch with me, for I was a 'nigger.' " His friendship with white boys lasted a bit longer: "We played cricket and baseball, ran races and rode bicycles together, took each other to the river and to the sea beach to learn to swim." At maturity, these associations, too, ended. "I grew up then to see the difference between the races more and more. My schoolmates as young men did not know or remember me any more. Then I realized that I had to make a fight for a place in the world."

The young Garvey's fight was complicated by his father's growing stubbornness and reclusiveness, which damaged the family's financial position. At fourteen, Garvey left school to be apprenticed to his god-father, Mr. Burrowes, a printer. Though Garvey always felt insecure about his lack of formal education, this development was in many ways a happy one. At this small country printing establishment, Garvey was able to learn all facets of a trade that was to constitute one of his main means of communicating with those he wanted to influence. An added bonus was Burrowes's large library in which Garvey could continue to develop his interest in books. This experience only seems to have increased Garvey's resolve to succeed. As a schoolboy he had rebelled against those teachers who wanted to punish him physically: "I simply refused to be whipped. I was not made to be whipped. It annoys me to be defeated." In the printing trade he learned that he had sufficient intelligence and experience to manage men: "I was strong and manly, and I made them respect me. I developed a strong and forceful character."

At the age of sixteen Garvey made the first of a series of moves that were to take him from the periphery to the center of events: he left his rural apprenticeship to take a position as a printer with his uncle in the city of Kingston. Here Garvey furthered his knowledge of the newspaper business. It was in Kingston, too, that Garvey became impressed with the power of oratory. Struck by the skill of the speakers he heard at barbershop forums and debates in local parks, Garvey set about learning the art with his characteristic energy. He went from church to church, absorbing the oratorical and platform styles of a variety of preachers. He would spend long hours alone in his room reciting poetry and passages from school readers and experimenting with different gestures. As his confidence grew, Garvey took an increasingly active role in the Saturday night discussion groups at Victoria Pier, where speakers debated and explored subjects of every sort. His acquaintances during these years were impressed by Garvey's enormous zeal. "He carried a pocket dictionary with him," one of them recalled, "and said he studied three or four words daily, and in his room he would write a paragraph or two using these words." Such energy led this teenager to rise to the position of foreman at one of Jamaica's largest printing establishments. But his ambitions extended beyond his own career. He helped to train black youth in elocution and arranged concerts and

107

elocution contests for their edification. "He was always busy, planning and doing something for the underprivileged youth. Uplift work we called it," another early companion remembered. "I started to take an interest in the politics of my country," Garvey himself wrote of these years, "and then I saw the injustice done to my race because it was black, and I became dissatisfied on that account."

Garvey's dissatisfaction disrupted the orderly progress of his career. During the printers' strike of 1907, Garvey was the only foreman who took the side of the workers. Becoming a leading spokesman for their cause, Garvey found himself blacklisted once the strike failed. Though he was able to secure employment with the Government Printing Office, Garvey's mind was clearly on politics and the need for organization rather than on his vocation. In 1910 Garvey helped to found a political organization—the National Club—and created the *Watchman*, the first of his many newspapers. The failure of both ventures made evident the need for money to fund his political activities, and Garvey joined the stream of West Indian workers migrating to Central and South America in search of better opportunities. Thus, at the age of twenty-three, Garvey began a restless journey that was to keep him out of his native Jamaica for much of the remainder of his life.

In Costa Rica Garvey's uncle helped him secure a job as timekeeper on one of the United Fruit Company's banana plantations. Appalled at the conditions under which the West Indian migrants were forced to live and work, Garvey soon left the plantation and journeyed to Limón to protest to the British consul the treatment accorded those black British subjects. Met by an indifference that convinced him that black lives were simply of no consequence to white officials, Garvey tried more direct action by founding a paper, *La Nacionale*, which soon failed for lack of funds. Going next to Panama, Garvey was similarly disturbed by the condition of the West Indian workers on the Panama Canal. Again he protested, again he tried to establish a newspaper, *La Prensa*, and again he failed. In Ecuador, Nicaragua, Spanish Honduras, Colombia, and Venezuela the story was the same. Everywhere he traveled, Garvey was sickened by the exploitation of his people in the fields, mines, and cities. Returning to Jamaica in 1911, Garvey demanded that the governor take steps to protect overseas Jamaicans and was told—in a modern version of "Let them eat cake"—that if the Jamaicans disliked their treatment abroad they could always return home. If His Majesty's representatives proved indifferent, Garvey decided to see what might be done in England itself. Aided by his sister

Indiana, who was working in England as a child's nurse, Garvey set out for London in 1912.

Garvey's two-year sojourn in England proved to be of great importance in shaping his future. Arriving in England with his plans still fluid and uncertain, he departed with a much clearer notion of what he wanted to accomplish. His own version of how this happened is a model of simplicity: "I read 'Up From Slavery,' by Booker T. Washington, and then my doom—if I may so call it—of being a race leader dawned upon me in London. . . . I asked, 'Where is the black man's Government?' 'Where is his King and his kingdom?' 'Where is his President, his country, and his ambassador, his army, his navy, his men of big affairs?' I could not find them, and then I declared, 'I will help to make them.' " Garvey's poetic rendition of his conversion to race leadership should not be taken literally. His decision was neither so simple nor so sudden; it had been in the making for years. A man of Garvey's temperament and upbringing had long chafed under Jamaica's tripartite racial system, which placed the island's 630,000 blacks under the 168,000 coloreds or mixed-bloods, with the 15,000 whites at the top of the racial pyramid. His years in London were important not merely for his reading of Washington—as crucial as this proved to be—but even more so for the blacks from all over the world he met and with whom he exchanged ideas. A British Consul General Report notes that "when in London, Garvey met a number of his own race from Africa and the West Indies . . . he heard form the lips of his countrymen and other coloured people about the sufferings of the darker races, and of their desire to unite for mutual understanding and protection."

Garvey and his movement have become so closely identified with the United States, where indeed they enjoyed their greatest success, that it is sometimes forgotten that Garvey grew up as a colonial in the British Empire and thus had most in common with the Africans and other West Indians who like himself had been living as part of a colonized majority in their own lands. Though he does not mention them in his scant autobiographical writings, there can be no doubt that Garvey was privy to the ideas and dreams of that group of black colonial writers and intellectuals who coalesced in London around the *African Times and Orient Review* for which Garvey himself wrote. Within this circle, the young Garvey was exposed to ideas concerning race conservation, the preservation of group identity, anticolonialism, and African unity. It is not surprising, then, that when Garvey came to espouse the philosophy of Washington, it was with such significant additions as an emphasis on blackness and the glories of the black past and a determination to work for the redemption of Africa from foreign rule.

Before leaving England, Garvey articulated a new mission that coupled his sense of himself as a Jamaican with his growing identification with the entire black race. There would soon be a turning point in the history of the West Indies, he prophesied in the fall of 1913: "The people who inhabit that portion of the Western Hemisphere will be the instruments of uniting a scattered race who, before the close of many centuries, will found an Empire on which the sun shall shine as ceaselessly as it shines on the Empire of the North today." With this vision of himself and his fellow West Indians as the mechanism through which "the beloved and scattered millions" of the black diaspora would be united, Garvey found it impossible to remain any longer in London. "My brain was afire. There was a world of thought to conquer."

Garvey arrived home in Jamaica on July 15, 1914, and on the first of August—the anniversary of emancipation in the British West Indies— he established the Universal Negro Improvement and Conservation Association and African Communities' League, later shortened to the UNIA. The association's aims were stated in two parts. Those having to do with local conditions in Jamaica, which stressed the establishment of educational and industrial colleges, the elevation of the degraded to a "state of good citizenship," the promotion of commerce and industry, and the strengthening of "the bonds of brotherhood and unity among the races," could have been endorsed fully by Washington. The association's "General Objects" went a bit further and included such aims as the following: "To establish a Universal Confraternity among the race," "to promote the spirit of race pride and love," "to establish Commissionaries or Agencies in the principal countries of the world for the protection of all Negroes irrespective of nationality," "to conduct a world-wide commercial and industrial intercourse," and the vaguely worded "to strengthen the imperialism of independent African States."

If the goals of Garvey's new organization—with its bold motto: "ONE GOD! ONE AIM! ONE DESTINY!"—indicated the ways in which Garvey would supplement the goals of his mentor, Garvey's language in this period often remained pure Washingtonian. In his address to the first annual meeting of the UNIA in August 1915, Garvey stated that "the bulk of our people are in darkness and are really unfit for good society." Six months later he advised his fellow Jamaicans that

Europeans were "longing to see the Negro do something for himself." Once the Negro raised himself to a higher state of civilization, "all the other races would be glad to meet him on the plane of equality and comradeship. It is indeed unfair to demand equality when one of himself has done nothing to establish the right to equality."

Garvey found it easier to proclaim the existence and aims of the UNIA than to get others, especially Jamaica's powerful middle class of coloreds, to share his vision of the destiny of West Indians and of the black race. Indeed, he found white government officials and clergy frequently more willing to help than were the affluent members of his own race. "I was openly hated and persecuted by some of these colored men of the island who did not want to be classified as negroes, but as white. They hated me worse than poison. They opposed me at every step," Garvey recalled. It was not only his organization, but his very pretensions to leadership they opposed: "I was a black man and therefore had absolutely no right to lead; in the opinion of the 'colored' element, leadership should have been in the hands of a yellow or a very light man." It was while he was suffering these shattering blows to his dreams that Garvey began, perhaps unconsciously, to explore other alternatives. If the Negro population of Jamaica was too divided and myopic to provide the leadership necessary to unite the world's blacks, Garvey would have to search elsewhere. Whether he came to this determination before or only after arriving in the United States is not clear. Nevertheless, it was during this crisis that Garvey wrote to Washington of his desire to travel to the United States to acquaint himself with America's black people. Washington's death in November 1915 deprived Garvey of the chance to meet the man who had influenced him so profoundly, but it did not alter his determination, or his need, to visit the United States. Before leaving Jamaica, Garvey wrote a final appeal to his fellow "Afro-West Indians":

> For God's sake, you men and women who have been keeping yourselves away from the people of your own African race, cease the ignorance; unite your hands and hearts with the people Afric, . . . Sons and daughters of Africa, I say to you arise, take on the toga of race pride, and throw off the brand of ignominy which has kept you back for so many centuries. Dash asunder the petty prejudices within your own fold; set at defiance the scornful designation of "nigger" uttered even by yourselves, and be a Negro in the light of the Pharaohs of Egypt, Simons of Cyrene, Hannibals of Carthage, L'Ouvertures and Dessalines of Haiti, Blydens, Barclays and Johnsons of Liberia, Lewises of Sierra Leone, and

111

Douglasses and Du Boises of America, who have made, and are making history for the race.

In this mood, Garvey made his way to America.

Garvey had chosen precisely the right time for his American journey. The black population of the United States was in the midst of an experience that was to make it an ideal constituency for a man with Garvey's mission, energies, and oratorical abilities. To understand the ethos characterizing black America in the years following Garvey's arrival in March 1916, it is necessary to comprehend the impact of World War I on the dreams and expectations of many black Americans. Fifty years earlier blacks had emerged from the Civil War with hope in the American political process that, in the immediate aftermath of the war, produced three constitutional amendments and a host of Reconstruction reforms positively affecting the position of blacks within the system. "The Republican party is the deck," Frederick Douglass declared, "all else is the sea." The abandonment of the freedmen by the Republican party in the 1870s and 1880s abruptly ended the dream that Negro rights could be secured through conventional political behavior and gave rise to the view, advanced by some teachers and leaders, that no one had to be poor, that there was no need to fail, that the individual was the architect of his own fortune. Thus it is not surprising that with the blocking of political channels by federal indifference and southern disfranchisement, the new Negro leadership, epitomized by Washington, preached the possibilities of advancement through moral and economic development. Blacks must prove themselves worthy of freedom by developing their own capabilities. Tact, good manners, a resolute will, a tireless capacity for hard work ensured success for the individual and for the race, Washington insisted.

Although variations of this philosophy persisted long after 1918, World War I dealt it a blow from which it never fully recovered. With few exceptions, black Americans entered the armed forces with alacrity and served with enthusiasm and hope. Here was a perfect opportunity to prove their worth; a situation made to order for the Horatio Alger philosophy whose heroes had always proved themselves through inspired acts of heroism and devotion. The Texas Grand Master of the Negro Masons articulated the expectations of many when he announced: "We believe that our second emancipation will be the outcome of this war." This loyalty and hope were rewarded by segregating black troops; by subjecting them to untold indignities in training camps; by assigning them to labor battalions far out of proportion to their skills and intelligence; by warning the French not to fraternize with them lest they rape French women; by cautioning black troops at the end of the war not to expect in their homeland the kind of latitude they had enjoyed abroad.

Indeed, the America to which black troops returned was frighteningly familiar. Black soldiers were greeted not with gratitude but with fear. Ten returned soldiers were among the more than seventy blacks lynched in 1919; a far larger number were among those blacks assaulted in the year's twenty-five race riots. One veteran, returning from work during the Chicago race riot, was set upon by a white mob shouting, "There's a nigger! Let's get him!" "The injustice of the whole thing overwhelmed me," he later testified. "Had the ten months I spent in France been all in vain? Were those little white crosses over the dead bodies of those dark-skinned boys lying in Flanders field for naught? Was democracy merely a hollow sentiment?"

His question and his anger were reflected throughout black America. Blacks had played the game by the rules and discovered that the rules simply did not apply to them. "We have been fighting the wrong fellow," a Negro Masonic leader in California insisted. "The low American, and not the German, is the brute who has ravished our women, lynched, flayed, burned and massacred our men and women." Black people should practice the Christian virtues, Bishop John Hurst maintained. "If while exercising these virtues, however, his assailants . . . persist in molesting him, let him do what self respecting people should do—namely use his gun with effect and impose respect." "Let every Negro arm himself," the black New York *Commoner* advised, "and swear to die fighting in defense of his home, his rights and his person."

Implicit in all of these reactions was a heightened tendency to look inward, to reach within the community for protection, understanding, and sustenance. Not the least of the results of the great tension produced by the demonstrated failure of the American success ethos for black Americans was the impetus it gave to internal development and to searching within Afro-American culture and looking to the black people themselves for those things necessary to survival and the building of a meaningful dream. The anthropologist Anthony F. C. Wallace has argued that when a perceptible gap arises between the images and expectations a culture has created within its citizens and the realities of the culture, the resulting anxiety can often be relieved only through the agency of what he has called a *revitalization movement:* "a deliberate, organized conscious effort by members of a society to construct a more satisfying culture," one that comes closer to their longstanding dreams

113

and expectations. The forms such movements take vary from culture to culture. In the United States they have tended to stress the revival of central cultural beliefs and values and the elimination of alien influences. While the importance of such movements in the 1920s has been emphasized for some time now, there has been less recognition of the extent to which black America was characterized by them as well.

Garvey came to the United States prepared to preach the message of revitalization to a people ready, often eager, to hear it. The time had come, Garvey insisted, for blacks to stop emulating heroes of other races: "We must canonize our own saints, create our own martyrs, and elevate to positions of fame and honor black men and women who have made their distinct contributions to our racial history." When Europe was inhabited by savages, heathens, and pagans, he reminded his listeners, "Africa was peopled with a race of cultured black men, who were masters in art, science and literature; men who were cultured and refined; men, who, it was said, were like the gods. . . . Black men, you were once great; you shall be great again." He enjoined his audiences to "take down the pictures of white women from your walls. Elevate your own women to that place of honour. . . . Mothers! give your children dolls that look like them to play with and cuddle." God, he insisted, "made no mistake when he made us black with kinky hair. . . . We have outgrown slavery, but our minds are still enslaved to the thinking of the Master Race. Now take these kinks out of your mind, instead of out of your hair. You are capable of all that is common to men of other Races." "We have a beautiful history," he thundered, "and we shall create another one in the future." Over and over he insisted, "The faith we have is a faith that will ultimately take us back to that ancient place, that ancient position that we once occupied, when Ethiopia was in her glory."

In all of this Garvey articulated—more brilliantly than any other Afro-American spokesman of the time—the doctrine of revitalization. In 1933 one of his supporters wrote that "Garvey sold the Negro to himself." This theme has been picked up by a number of scholars so that one author writes that "Garvey tried to restore to the black man the masculinity stolen from him during the centuries of slavery," another that "Garvey put steel in the spine of many Negroes . . . [and] helped to destroy their inferiority complex," and still another that "he stirred some two million Negroes to a fierce race-consciousness which is still a compelling force in Negro life." While there is validity in such observations, their total effect is to obscure the substantial reservoir of pride, strength, and sense of history that existed in the black folk throughout slavery and the years that followed. Blacks certainly had hoped and worked to become part of the nation's economic and political fabric, but they continued to retain a vivid sense of who and what they were. Garvey did not create "race consciousness." How could black men and women living in the racial situation that prevailed in the United States in the early decades of the twentieth century not have been race conscious? Indeed, Garvey was able to rise so suddenly and attract a following so dramatically precisely because blacks retained a healthy consciousness of identity and community. What Garvey did was to provide a political channel and a global perspective for that consciousness.

Before exploring the movement Garvey built, it is important to remember that he was not the only force for black revitalization in the 1920s. The black writers of the Harlem Renaissance expressed revitalization in their search for their African past. "I was a black man," lamented Langston Hughes:

But the white men came.
And they drove me out of the forest.
They took me away from the jungles.
I lost my trees.
I lost my silver moons.
Now they've caged me
In the circus of civilization.

They expressed it in their search for themselves. "What she needed to do now," Wallace Thurman wrote of one of his characters whose complexion ostracized her within the middle class, "was to accept her black skin as being real and unchangeable, to realize that certain things were, and would be, and with this in mind begin life new, always fighting, not so much for acceptance by other people, but for acceptance of herself." And, finally, they expressed it in their rediscovery of the black folk and their culture. Only among "the working girls and boys of the country," one of Claude McKay's characters in *Banjo* concludes, could one find cultural integrity: "that raw unconscious and the-devil-with-them-pride in being Negro that was his own natural birthright. . . . Down there the ideal skin was brown skin. Boys and girls were proud of their brown, sealskin brown, teasing brown, tantalizing brown, high-brown, low-brown, velvet brown, chocolate brown."

Among the black folk themselves one can see revitalization in a number of ways: in the continued revival of traditional black religious practices and their spread from the Holiness churches to the larger de-

115

nominations; in the inclusion of traditional Afro-American musical forms in jazz and gospel music; and in the rise of the blues—an inward-looking music that insisted upon the meaningfulness of the daily yearnings, problems, and dreams of everyday black people. Garvey, then, for all of his uniqueness, was not an isolated force in the 1920s. His power and influence proceeded from his superb articulation of what many of his followers had long believed and acted upon in quiet dignity and strength: that blackness was nothing to apologize for; that black men and women shared a common proud heritage; and that the future was by no means hostage to white people. From the days of slavery, this had been the message of black Christianity in various forms, and it had been reiterated in myriad ways by the black folk in their songs, tales, proverbs, and anecdotes. The disillusioning difficult postwar years gave it added impetus. Like so many leaders, Garvey's influence was based upon not how far he was from, but how close he was to, the mass of the people to whom and for whom he tried to speak.

Garvey's initial activities in the United States were less those of organizing and politicking than of traveling and observing. He did deliver speeches in Harlem and elsewhere, but his main energies were devoted to learning about the conditions of American blacks. Washington was dead, but there was still much to be gained from trips to Tuskeegee Institute and other Afro-American institutions in the thirty-eight states Garvey visited. Everywhere he went Garvey endeavored to meet black leaders, and with few exceptions he perceived in them the same qualities that characterized their Jamaican counterparts. What passed for race leadership in the United States, Garvey asserted, was little more than "treachery and treason of the worst kind," since anyone who wanted to lead had to first find some wealthy white benefactor "who will dictate to him what he should do in the leadership of the Negro race." Worse yet, Garvey was certain that the identical pettiness and self-hatred that plagued his race in Jamaica existed in the United States as well. Visiting W. E. B. Du Bois in the offices of the National Association for the Advancement of Colored People Garvey was "dumbfounded" to find that it was impossible to tell whether one was in a white office or that of a black protest organization. "There was no representation of the race there that any one could recognize. . . . you had to be as near white as possible, otherwise there was no place for you as stenographer, clerk or attendant in the office of the National Association for the Advancement of 'Colored' People." In America as in Jamaica, Garvey concluded, the race's leaders "had no program, but were mere opportunists who were living off their so-called leadership while the poor people were groping in the dark."

Convinced that he had found a leadership vacuum, Garvey in 1917 established the New York Division of the UNIA. Garvey later claimed that he had had no intention of shifting his center of operations to the United States and that he remained only when it became necessary for him to defeat the aims of local politicians who threatened to take over and pervert the purposes of the new organization. It is doubtful that Garvey needed this kind of inducement to stay in the United States. A man so perceptive and ambitious must have realized at once that Jamaica simply could not match the potential of America's large, diverse black population. Indeed, Garvey himself made this point just eight months after he arrived in the United States, calling the American Negro "the most progressive and the foremost unit in the expansive chain of scattered Ethiopia." Industrially, financially, educationally, and socially "the Negroes of both hemispheres have to defer to the American brother." Most crucially, he concluded, American blacks were far ahead of West Indians in "the spirit of self-consciousness and reliance." Garvey could not have failed to arrive at the corollary conclusion that the ideal place to build a movement for the unification of the world's blacks was not his native island, where he had recently failed so badly, but the United States. His "brief" visit was to last eleven years.

Garvey's ultimate intentions may be revealed as well by the fact that almost from the moment of his arrival he spoke as an integral part of the American black community. During the 1917 race riot in East St. Louis, Illinois, he denounced America's "continuous round of oppression" of black people who for three hundred years had "given their life blood" to help build the republic. His refusal to act or to speak like an alien visitor continued with his repeated opposition to black participation in World War I. Shortly after the armistice, as disillusioned black troops returned to America, Garvey warned that his people would not allow themselves to be exploited in this way again. "The first dying that is to be done by the black man in the future will be done to make himself free. And then when we are finished, if we have any charity to bestow, we may die for the white man. But as for me, I think I have stopped dying for him."

Statements like these, of course, matched the mood of many American blacks in those difficult postwar years and were responsible for increasing Garvey's popularity and his audience. "I am the equal of any white man; I want you to feel the same way," Garvey told his listeners. "No more fear," he thundered, "no more cringing, no more sycophantic begging and pleading." Blacks were demanding "that freedom that Victoria of England never gave; that liberty that Lincoln never meant; that freedom, that liberty that will see us men among men, that will make us a great and powerful people." Garvey's appeal was based not only upon his militance but also upon his sense of destiny and hope. "There is much to live for," he declared. "I see before me a picture of a redeemed Africa, with her dotted cities, with her beautiful civilization, with her millions of happy children, going to and fro. Why should I lose hope? . . . Lift up yourselves, men, take yourselves out of the mire and hitch your hopes to the stars; yes, rise as high as the very stars themselves. Let no man pull you down, let no man destroy your ambition, because . . . man is your brother; he is not your lord."

Words like these make it evident that if Garvey's rhetoric was revolutionary as racial doctrine, it was also appealingly familiar, steeped as it was in traditional nineteenth-century American ideology. Many of Garvey's widely circulated aphorisms could have been inserted into any American primer for schoolchildren: "Whatsoever man has done, man can do." "A man's bread and butter is only insured when he works for it." "If you have no confidence in self, you are twice defeated in the race of life." "[Man is] master of his own destiny, and architect of his own fate." No prophet of the American success ethos could have put these things better. Thus Garvey won an immediate audience not only because he preached the doctrine of revitalization at precisely the right time, but because he preached it in the right syllables. He used a tone and an ideological context that were instantly recognizable to those to whom traditional American ideology was still familiar. He was able to show his followers that the ideas they were raised on could lead to their own liberation.

When Garvey shouted out to his audiences, "Up, you mighty race!" he was not reciting totally new doctrine. Blacks had been enjoined to rise since they were emancipated. Garvey was appealing to a set of dreams and ideals that had long existed among American blacks. He was able to take Washington's philosophy and transform it from a doctrine geared to help one up the ladder of American mobility into a mechanism designed to increase the worldwide consciousness, unity, power, and autonomy of the race. He took a philosophy suffused with overtones of individualism and bent it to serve the purposes of the group.

Much of Garvey's labors were geared to instill a sense of responsibility in blacks for their place in the world. "Blame not God," he told his listeners, "blame not the white man for physical conditions for which

118

we ourselves are responsible." The Creator intended humanity to be free. "That the Negro race became a race of slaves was not the fault of God Almighty . . . it was the fault of the race." "Sloth, neglect, indifference caused us to be slaves," he insisted. "Confidence, conviction, action will cause us to be free men to-day." He told the UNIA's Second International Convention in 1921: "If you want liberty you yourselves must strike the blow. If you must be free you must become so through your own effort, through your own initiative." Garvey was able to aim the Social Darwinist arguments that were so intertwined in his thought against the whites as well. If the latter really were convinced that the Negro was inferior, why did they find it necessary to hedge him in with laws enforcing his inferior state? The answer was obvious: whites feared black capabilities and talents, were afraid that blacks would outshine them. Give blacks a chance, Garvey taunted, and in fifty years "I will show you a nation of proud, refined and cultured black men and women, whose comeliness will outshine that of the age of Solomon." It was because Garvey did not expect whites to accept his challenge that he worked so hard to convince blacks they had to rise on their own.

The Negro, Garvey taught, was not at the bottom because he was held in contempt, he was held in contempt because he was at the bottom. Only when the race lifted itself up through its own initiative would it be in a position to demand respect. Many of his aphorisms were designed to illustrate that: "A race without authority and power, is a race without respect." "Don't be deceived; there is no justice but strength." "A race that is solely dependent upon another for its economic existence sooner or later dies." If power and autonomy were the goals, organization was the only viable means. One of the fundamental messages of Garvey's speeches, editorials, and articles was: organize as a race or perish as a race! He was convinced that "the greatest weapon used against the Negro is DISORGANIZATION." If Washington had lived, Garvey maintained, he would have had to change his program, for the New Negro needed a political voice as well as industrial opportunity. In the short run, political organization meant the creation of a strong and effective UNIA; ultimately, it entailed building an independent African nation powerful enough to protect black people everywhere.

Unlike most other black American political leaders of the period, Garvey understood the need to reach out with his message and his organization to the black people in general and not just the more educated classes. "The masses," he was convinced, "make the nation and

119

the race." Certainly no other black spokesman was better equipped to affect the masses. Not only the content of Garvey's message, but the eloquence with which he propounded it, the skillful use he made of his weekly newspaper, and the spectacular pageantry that soon became characteristic of UNIA events were all designed to reach a maximum audience. In 1919 Garvey purchased an auditorium on 138th Street in Harlem, renamed it Liberty Hall, and held nightly meetings to bring his message to as many as 6,000 listeners at a time. In the next few years liberty halls appeared in such UNIA centers as Philadelphia, Pittsburgh, Cleveland, Detroit, Cincinnati, Chicago, and Los Angeles. On the platforms of these meeting halls, Garvey, whose wife described him as "calm, almost phlegmatic in conversation," was transformed into a charismatic speaker whose rich voice and dramatic gestures converted many of his listeners into followers. For all of his criticisms, Du Bois conceded that Garvey's "singular eloquence" made him "an extraordinary leader of men."

Those not within the reach of Garvey's voice were exposed to his message through the *Negro World*, which Garvey began in 1918 and which by the early 1920s had a weekly circulation of from 50,000 to 200,000. In order to communicate with blacks throughout the world, it carried columns in Spanish and French. That its readership did go beyond the United States is attested to by those colonial administrators who held it partially responsible for anti-white riots in 1919 in Jamaica, Trinidad, and British Honduras, by other authorities who banned it from their jurisdictions in the New World and Africa, and by Jomo Kenyatta, the future president of Kenya, who testified that "in 1921 Kenya nationalists, unable to read, would gather round a reader of Garvey's newspaper, the *Negro World*, and listen to an article two or three times. Then they would run various ways through the forest, carefully to repeat the whole, which they had memorised, to Africans hungry for some doctrine which lifted them from the servile consciousness in which Africans lived."

Garvey did not base his appeal exclusively upon his impressive oratorical and journalistic skills. Organization depended upon more than an audience; it required participants. To ensure the maximum number of participants, Garvey created a host of groups: an African Legion clad in blue military garb, Black Cross Nurses, uniformed marching bands, choristers, and various auxiliaries. The pageantry implicit in all of this was revealed during the UNIA's First International Convention in 1920. Spectators lined the streets of Harlem for miles to watch Garvey in military uniform and plumed hat lead his impressively arrayed

120

followers marching under such banners as: "We Want a Black Civilization," "God and the Negro Shall Triumph," "Uncle Tom's Dead and Buried," "Africa Must be Free," and, at the head of the Woman's Auxiliary, "God Give Us Real Men!" The onlookers, according to Mrs. Garvey, "could not help but catch the spirit of the occasion; they clapped, waved flags and cheered themselves hoarse." Garvey, who was elected president general of the UNIA and provisional president of Africa, and who created numerous titles for his associates, seemed to have an insatiable appetite for ceremony. His wife described the court reception held during the convention of 1921:

> The Hall was transformed into a magnificent tropical setting, with lighting effects, appropriate music being played. Each Dignitary was timed to arrive according to his rank, and an anthem or appropriate music played until he was seated. . . . Young ladies were presented, and honours conferred on persons who had served the Race faithfully and well. Titles were: Kight Commander of the Nile, Distinguished Service Order of Ethiopia, and the Star of African Redemption. After the ceremonies, supper was served; guests were seated according to rank. Then followed the Grand Ball, with all the courtliness of training, natural gift for dancing and love of music.

Garvey's need to garb himself and his associates in the anachronistic trappings of aristocracy brought him enormous ridicule, especially from whites and the black middle class. He was "a clown strutting around in gaudy uniforms," a charlatan "who led big parades of ignorant people down the street selling pie in the sky." But there were other reactions as well, particularly from those groups Garvey was attempting to reach: "I remember as a lad in Cleveland, Ohio, during the hungry days of 1921, standing on Central Avenue, watching a parade one Sunday afternoon when thousands of Garvey Legionnaires, resplendent in their uniforms marched by. When Garvey rode by in his plumed hat, I got an emotional lift, which swept me up above the poverty and the prejudice by which my life was limited."

It seems to be indisputable that Garvey attracted millions of followers. It is more difficult to determine how many of them joined the UNIA. By the end of 1919, Garvey claimed two million members. Two years later he counted twice that number, and in June 1923 he announced that six million blacks were members of the UNIA. These figures reflected Garvey's hope and pride more than they did reality. Still, Garvey had much to be proud of. He had built not only the largest but the broadest mass movement in Afro-American history. The Communist party, surely no friend of Garvey's, was impressed by his success with the very elements the party itself had failed to enlist in substantial numbers: black workers and farmers. While it is not certain just how successful Garvey was outside the large northern cities, the organizational records of the UNIA indicate that the movement was not confined to these urban centers. By the mid-1920s the UNIA had established more than 700 branches in thirty-eight states in every section of the country including the Deep South. In addition, it had established more than 200 branches outside the United States, with the bulk of these clustering in the West Indies, Central America, and northern South America.

A clue to Garvey's unprecedented success in building a mass movement can be found in William L. Sherril's description of how he came to join the UNIA in Baltimore:

> One night on my way to a Show, I saw a huge crowd outside a Church, I went up and said, "what's going on in there?" A lady turned to me and said, "man alive, don't you know that Marcus Garvey is in there talking, yes, indeed, Garvey in person." "Shucks," I said, "I may as well see what he looks like." . . . I squeezed in, until I could get a good look at him; then suddenly he turned in my direction, and in a voice like thunder from Heaven he said, "men and women, what are you here for? To live unto yourself, until your body manures the earth, or to live God's Purpose to the fullest?" He continued to complete his thought in that compelling, yet pleading voice for nearly an hour. I stood there like one in a trance, every sentence ringing in my ears, and finding an echo in my heart. When I walked out of that Church, I was a different man—I knew my sacred obligations to my Creator, and my responsibilities to my fellow men, and so help me! I am still on the Garvey train.

Sherril, of course, was describing a conversion experience. For him, and presumably for many other members of the UNIA, Garvey's movement had deep religious overtones and significance.

Throughout the years of bondage American slaves had continued the African practice of drawing no clear line between the sacred and the secular, between the spiritual and the temporal world. This tendency remained strong in Afro-American culture in the years of freedom as well. Certainly it came to characterize the movement Garvey built and the style of leadership he created. One of Garvey's greatest assets was his comprehension of the importance of religion in black culture and his ability to incorporate so many of its elements in his movement.

It was not uncommon for Garvey's followers to refer to him as a Black Moses, a John the Baptist. Nor was it surprising, since Garvey himself invited such comparisons. He regularly employed a religious vocabulary, as in this speech he delivered in Liberty Hall in February 1921: "I wish I could convert the world of Negroes overnight to the tremendous possibilities of the Universal Negro Improvement Association. Let all the world know that this is the hour; this is the time for our salvation. Prayer alone will not save us; sentiment alone will not save us. We have to work and work and work if we are to be saved. . . . the time is now to preach the beatitude of bread and butter. I have contributed my bit to preaching this doctrine." More than this, Garvey dwelt endlessly on the suffering and betrayal of Jesus Christ, frequently casting himself in the role of Jesus. "If Garvey dies," he told his followers, "Garvey lives." "Christ died to make men free," he wrote in 1923; "I shall die to give courage and inspiration to my race." In his first message from Atlanta Prison in 1925, Garvey assumed the mantle of a full-fledged prophet assuring his fellow blacks: "Would I not die a million deaths for you? Then why be sad? . . . I tell you the world shall hear from my principles even two thousand years hence. . . . Look for me in the whirlwind or the storm, look for me all around you, for with God's grace, I shall come."

The religious quality of the UNIA was not confined to its leader's messianic style and rhetoric. Garvey utilized religion not merely to strengthen his own leadership, but to bolster the will and determination of those he wanted to lead. One of Garvey's favorite biblical texts was Psalms 68:31, which promised that "princes shall come forth from Egypt; Ethiopia shall soon stretch forth her hand to God." But before Africa could be redeemed, black men and women had to redeem themselves from the errors they had learned through the white people's religion. In his 1922 Easter Sunday sermon Garvey called for a new resurrection: "A resurrection from the lethargy of the past—the sleep of the past—from that feeling that made us accept the idea and opinion that God intended that we should occupy an inferior place in the world." No God, he insisted a year later, "would create me a black man, to be a hewer of wood and a drawer of water. It is a lie! It is a damned lie." The God that blacks worshiped and adored created them the equals of all humanity and expected them to take control of their own destiny. God, Garvey taught, gave humans the gift of life and sovereignty over the earth, but He did not run an employment bureau; He

123

did not dispense jobs to His children. He gave people the opportunities, the accomplishment was up to them.

Though Garvey taught of an impartial God who created all as equals, his anger at the way blacks had been treated led him at times to imply that suffering had rendered blacks more noble, more Christ-like than other races. "The Cross," he wrote, "is the property of the Negro in his religion because it was he who bore it." Although this dualism between universalism and particularism existed in Garvey's thought, he fell short of committing the error for which he condemned whites: advocating that God had a chosen race. In essence Garvey followed the spirit of the Old Testament itself and urged his fellow blacks to act not as a chosen but as a *choosing* people, a people with the same opportunities, the same possibilities, the same potential control over their destiny as every other people. Thus for Garvey religion was not an otherworldly affair; it taught ethical and practical principles that needed to be acted upon in this world: "I trust that you will so live to-day as to realize that you are masters of your own destiny, masters of your fate; if there is anything you want in this world it is for you to strike out with confidence and faith in self and reach for it, because God has created it for your happiness wheresover you may find it in nature."

Garvey was often ridiculed for picturing God as black. What he actually taught was more subtle and interesting. God, Garvey repeated over and over, had no color. However, since human beings were able to think of Him only in human terms, it was natural for them to conceive of God in their own physical shape. Whites, who had long done this themselves, had been successful in denying blacks the same privilege. It was now time "to see God through our own spectacles. . . . we shall worship Him through the spectacles of Ethiopia." "God is not white or black," he told a Cincinnati audience in 1921, "angels have no color, and they are not white peaches from Georgia. But if [whites] say that God is white, this organization says that God is black; if they are going to make the angels beautiful white peaches from Georgia, we are going to make them beautiful black peaches from Africa." Accordingly, the 1924 convention canonized Jesus Christ as a "Black Man of Sorrows," the Virgin Mary as a "Black Madonna," and resolved to idealize "God as a Holy Spirit, without physical form, but a Creature of imaginary semblance of the black race, being of like image and likeness."

James Weldon Johnson, who attended a number of UNIA meetings in New York's Liberty Hall, noted the elaborate liturgy and religious zeal he found there. Johnson's perceptions were quite accurate. The weekly meetings—generally held Sunday evenings—in liberty halls in New York and elsewhere closely resembled religious services. They were filled with the pomp and ceremony Garvey so loved and often featured processions of uniformed African Legionnaires or Black Cross Nurses. Hymns were sung, prayers recited, offerings received, just as in church. When Garvey was present, he delivered the major talk in his emotional, sermonizing style. When he was not, there would be a public reading of his front-page editorial in the week's *Negro World*. In addition, there would be talks by other UNIA leaders and sermons by clergy in attendance. And generally there were members of the clergy present, since a substantial number of black clergymen— Professor Randall Burkett has painstakingly identified more than 250— were active in the UNIA and helped to intensify the religious character already prominent in the movement.

Garvey worked hard to recruit clergy, hoping through them to reach their congregations. On occasion the strategy was more successful than Garvey could have hoped. At the 1924 convention, the Reverend R. H. Cosgrove of Natchez, Mississippi, reported that every one of the 500 members of his church was a member of the UNIA. Not surprisingly, those clergymen who became prominent in the UNIA tended to share Garvey's views and his militance. In 1923 the Reverend Thomas W. Anderson of the Second Baptist Church of Adrian, Michigan, told his Christmas Day audience that "the black man . . . must learn to fight; he must believe that God almighty. . . believes also in fighting." Blacks had to take charge of their own destiny. "If you don't have a bit of heaven here," he assured his audience, "don't worry, you won't have any hereafter.

The most important and influential of these ministers was the Episcopal priest George Alexander McGuire, who electrified the UNIA's first annual convention in 1920 by insisting that "the Uncle Tom nigger has got to go and his place must be taken . . . by a black man with a black heart." The element of revitalization was central to McGuire's appeal: "You must forget the white gods. Erase the white gods from your hearts. We must go back to the native church, to our own true God." The 1920 convention elected McGuire chaplain-general of the UNIA, and he quickly set about creating a *Universal Negro Ritual* and a *Universal Negro Catechism* intended to help reshape black religion. "O blessed Lord Jesus," read one of his suggested prayers, "Redeem Africa from the hands of those who exploit and ravish her. Renew her ancient glory, and grant that her oppressed and down-trodden children . . . may shortly be restored to their divine inheritance." In 1921

125

McGuire founded the African Orthodox Church and became its first bishop. Though there were many ties between the African Orthodox Church and the UNIA, Garvey neither endorsed nor joined McGuire's church for fear of alienating the many ministers and congregants of other denominations who were active in his movement, including such eclectic bands of non-Christian followers as black Jews and black Muslims. Whatever tensions existed between the two leaders, Garvey completely agreed with, and always acted upon, a principle McGuire enunciated at the 1924 convention: "Let it be understood, once and for all, that no constructive program for the Negro can be effective which underestimates the hold his religious institutions have upon him."

Garvey never made the mistake of underestimating the significance of religion. Nor did he commit the opposite error of focusing upon the spiritual to the neglect of the material needs of his people. From the beginning, fraternal sickness and death benefits were one of the features for which members were urged to pay their monthly 35-cent dues. Liberty halls served not only as scenes of inspirational public rituals but also as community centers sponsoring such social events as concerts, dances, and classes of various kinds. Notice boards held news of rooms or jobs. Liberty halls were sometimes converted into soup kitchens to feed the unemployed or into temporary dormitories for those without housing. "In the freezing winter days," Amy Jacques Garvey remembered, "stoves had to be kept going to accommodate the cold and homeless until they 'got on their feet' again."

Important as they were, Garvey considered such activities mere stopgaps. His organization was to function not as a welfare agency administering aid to the indigent, but as the center of a vast series of enterprises that would finally end black economic dependence. The Negro had for too long been a consumer, not a producer. "Let Edison turn off his electric light and we are in darkness in Liberty Hall in two minutes. The Negro is living on borrowed goods." In order to reverse this situation, Garvey established the Negro Factories Corporation in 1919 and offered "200,000 shares of common stock to the Negro race at par value of $5.00 per share." The ultimate object was to operate factories throughout the Western Hemisphere and Africa "to manufacture every marketable commodity." In New York City the corporation operated three grocery stores, two restaurants, a printing plant, a steam laundry, and a men's and women's manufacturing department that made the uniforms, hats, and shirts worn by members along with other items of clothing. In addition, the New York division owned several buildings, trucks, and the *Negro World.* Similar enterprises were operated or planned in other parts of the United States as well as in Central America and the West Indies. During the early 1920s, there were times when the UNIA and its allied corporations employed more than 1,000 blacks in the United States alone. The UNIA, Garvey pointed out to the white world, "employs thousands of black girls and black boys. Girls who could only be washer women in your homes, we made clerks and stenographers. . . . You will see from the start we tried to dignify our race." Here was a step toward Garvey's dream of a self-contained world of Negro producers, distributors, and consumers who could deal with or be independent of the rest of the world as necessity and circumstances dictated.

Garvey's attempts to lift the black world up economically were bedeviled by the very forces that Garvey decried: the difficulties of raising sufficient capital from an economically depressed and dependent group and the problems of dealing with white businessmen who were all too willing to exploit the economic disadvantages of blacks. Nothing demonstrated this more graphically than the failure of Garvey's most spectacular and significant economic activity: the Black Star Line that he created in June 1919 to operate a worldwide network of steamships. Within three months the Black Star Line had raised enough money through the sale of $5 stock certificates to purchase its first ship. Within a year the line had raised $610,000 and owned three ships. In spite of these initial successes, Garvey's dream of creating a great fleet of ships manned by black officers and men, so that "our race, too, would be respected in the mercantile and commercial world," was not to be. By the beginning of 1922, the Black Star Line was forced to suspend its operations, a victim of white businessmen who sold it decrepit vessels at inflated prices, of the inexperience and carelessness of Garvey and his chief associates, and of the dishonesty of some of its officers.

Economically, Garvey's venture into the maritime world left much to be desired. Its political capital, however, was considerable. Garvey pointed to the line as "the great attraction that brought to the Universal Negro Improvement Association millions of supporters." That attraction was manifest in the widespread sale of Black Star Line stock, which was limited to members of the Negro race. "I have sent twice to buy shares amounting to $125," one supporter wrote. "Now I am sending $35 for seven more shares. You might think I have money, but the truth, as I stated before, is that I have no money now. But if I'm to die of hunger it will be all right because I'm determined to do all that's in my power to better the conditions of my race." The child of another supporter recalled: "My mother was an intense Garveyite. She bought stock in it. . . . She lost money in its ventures and was disillusioned, but not in the principles involved. . . . The Back-to-Africa part was not important. Pride was. Negroes should have something of their own." The Black Star Line, the lawyer Henry Lincoln Johnson asserted, "was a loss in money but it was a gain in soul."

That gain was felt throughout the Western Hemisphere. Hugh Mulzac, a black ship's officer who sailed for Garvey on the *Yarmouth* in 1920, recorded the reception the ship received everywhere it docked. When it entered the harbor at Havana, "sympathizers flocked from all parts of the island toward the docks to greet the first ship they had ever seen entirely owned and operated by colored men. They came out in boats when we arrived, showering us with flowers and fruit . . . [we] were overrun with visitors from dawn until sunset." When the ship docked at Colon, "literally thousands of Panamanians swarmed the docks with baskets of fruit, vegetables and gifts. I was amazed that the *Yarmouth* had become a symbol for colored people of every land." In Costa Rica "we were accorded the welcome of conquering heroes. At Bocas del Toro thousands of peasants came down from the hills on horses, donkeys, and in makeshift carts . . . In the tumult that followed dancing broke out on the deck, great piles of fruit and flowers mounted on the hatch covers, and UNIA agents signed up hundreds of new members." In Philadelphia, Boston, and New York as well, there were spectacular receptions for the ship "with thousands joining the parades. Garvey made impassioned speeches, whipping the people into frenzied support of the association." The problem, Mulzac discovered, was that little or no distinction was being made between the commercial and symbolic functions of the voyage. There was no economic reason to be in many of these ports, and while the demonstrations were going on, hundreds of passengers aboard had to be fed and cared for, and hundreds of tons of coconuts were rotting in the hold. "It was," Mulzac concluded, "a helluva way to run a steamship."

The tension between the pragmatic and the symbolic was evident in other aspects of the Garvey movement as well. Garvey employed no symbol more frequently or more effectively than that of the African homeland. "Hail! United States of Africa!" he entitled a poem:

The treason of the centuries is dead,
All alien whites are forever gone;
The glad home of Sheba is once more free.

Garvey embroidered this portrait of a free, independent African continent endlessly and argued for its necessity incessantly. "Show me the race or the nation without a flag, and I will show you a race of people without any pride," he proclaimed. Consequently, the convention of 1920 added to the "objects" of the UNIA the establishment of "a central nation for the race," created a red, black, and green flag for the African republic, and adopted a national anthem that began: "Ethiopia, thou land of our fathers, / Thou land where the gods loved to be."

The "brilliant, noble and grand" African past was a constant theme for Garvey in speech after speech, but he reminded his followers in 1923, "WE CANNOT LIVE BY THE PAST." The only "salvation for the Negro" was "through a free and independent Africa." Without that, blacks would be forever the exploited wards of other races, eternally incapable of demonstrating what they could accomplish. If the race remained a scattered, drifting remnant, "it will be only a question of time when the Negro will be as completely and complacently dead as the North American Indian, or the Australian Bushman." The question of independence was too crucial for Garvey to contemplate failure. African redemption, he prophesied, "is in the wind. It is coming. One day, like a storm, it will be here." He warned the white world: "We are coming 400,000,000 strong and we mean to retake every square inch of the 12,000,000 square miles of African territory belonging to us by right Divine."

Garvey utilized the idea of Africa to touch deeply many of the yearnings and needs of his people. He was preaching more than the redemption of Africa; he was preaching the redemption of the entire Negro people, the revitalization of the entire black race. Nevertheless, when Garvey cried out, "Wake up Ethiopia! Wake up Africa! Let us work towards the one glorious end of a free, redeemed and mighty nation," he was not being merely allegorical. He really did want to end white hegemony and substitute a black republic stretching, as he put it in one of his poems, "From Liberia's peaceful western coast / To the foaming Cape at the southern end." He did believe that so long as blacks lacked an autonomous, powerful nation of their own they would never be accorded their rights anywhere in the world. The diplomatic pressure an independent Africa could exert, for example, would be far more effective in protecting American Negroes than any anti-lynching bill.

Consequently, Garvey worked in every way he could for African independence, insisting that his goal was the exact counterpart of the Jewish yearning for a homeland in Palestine or the Irish desire for an independent Eire. He supported Senator Joseph France's plan to have the United States liquidate its allies' war debts in return for enough of their African territory to establish an independent nation for American Negroes. He petitioned the League of Nations to deliver the ex-German colonies in Africa to the custody of the UNIA. He negotiated with Liberia for a UNIA immigrant settlement on the Cavalla River in southern Liberia. This latter arrangement, scheduled to begin with 500 American families in 1924, failed on the eve of its birth due to a combination of British and French pressure to keep the deeply anticolonial Garveyites out of Africa and the growing fear of the elite Liberian governing class that an influx of American immigrants would ultimately threaten the Liberian status quo.

Garvey was deeply disappointed at his failure to win a settlement in Liberia, which he had envisioned as a beachhead from which Western Negroes could spread modern technical, scientific, and humanistic knowledge throughout the continent. There is no indication that Garvey ever worried about what effects the accelerated imposition of the body of Western knowledge would have upon indigenous African cultures. It is important to remember that Garvey's opposition to the West was political; he did not disdain Western culture, which he was, after all, part of. "Those of us who lead are well versed in Western civilization and are determined that the black man shall not be a creature of the past, but a full-fledged man of the present." In this respect, Garvey was never a cultural nationalist. He looked back to the glories of the African past, but even there he was proudest of those attributes that had contributed directly to the store of Western culture. He had little, if anything, to say about the glories of African religion or expressive art or social mores and patterns. These were not concerns of his, and he seems to have been willing to see them replaced as expeditiously as possible with their Western counterparts. It is not surprising, then, that one of the consistent "objects" of the UNIA was "to assist in civilizing the backward tribes of Africa."

In spite of Garvey's many activities concerning Africa, his widow insisted that "the term, back-to-Africa, was used and promoted by newspapers, Negro newspapers mostly, to ridicule Garvey. There was no back-to-Africa movement except in a spiritual sense." Mrs. Garvey was essentially correct. Garvey envisioned African independence as a gradual, long-term process and never seems to have advocated the massive return of blacks from the diaspora. Nevertheless, Garvey's vagueness and perhaps confusion about his plans, coupled with his tendency toward rhetorical excess, often gave a different impression. Thus, in 1921 he insisted that "we are not preaching any doctrine to ask all the negroes of Harlem and of the United States to leave for Africa. The majority of us may remain here." But he also declared that when the pioneer mechanics and artisans had built the necessary railroads and institutions, "The time will come for the command to be given, 'Come home!' " The vision of the biblical exodus often informed his speeches: "We shall gather together our children, our treasures and our loved ones, and, as the children of Israel, by the command of God, faced the promised land, so in time we shall also."

Above all, it was his pessimism about the possibility of whites and blacks living in harmony that made him appear a champion of total repatriation. One of the salient messages emerging from his speeches and writings was his conviction that American blacks would never be accorded true equality. As the white population grew, blacks would be pushed out of the marketplace and become increasingly redundant economically. Nor could they look for protection to a government controlled by a white majority. He reminded those who believed that the black minority would win a share of the white majority's economic and political power that "nothing of the kind has happened in all human history." So long as whites feared black competition, so long would there be "not only prejudice, but riots, lynchings, burnings." The only solution was to provide an outlet for black energy and ambition where it would not threaten whites. The conclusion was obvious: "The future of the Negro therefore, outside of Africa, spells ruin and disaster."

If Garvey's distrust of whites and his desire to build a sense of black solidarity produced ambiguities in his attitudes regarding emigration to Africa, they created a consistent set of racial policies—too consistent, perhaps, for Garvey's own good. Garvey wanted to unite his people not only politically and economically but racially. "I believe in a pure black race," he announced and argued that it was time to end "the curse of many colors within the Negro race" that slavery had produced; it was time to stop this "wholesale bastardy" and to create "a race type and standard of our own." The UNIA, Garvey announced, "is against miscegenation and race suicide. . . . It believes in the social and political physical separation of all peoples to the extent that they promote their own ideals and civilization." He assured the whites that blacks did not want racial amalgamation, and he pleaded with his people to be true to themselves: "The Anglo-Saxon doesn't want to be a Japanese; the Japanese doesn't want to be a Negro. Then, in the name of God and all that is holy, why should we want to be somebody else?" Garvey insisted that he was not attempting to exclude anyone. "For once we will agree with the American white man, that one drop of Negro blood makes a man a Negro." In the UNIA "100 per cent Negroes and even 1 per cent Negroes will stand together as one mighty whole."

Garvey's zeal on the race issue led him to promote blackness wherever he could. He banned ads for skin lighteners and hair straighteners from his papers; he urged that children be given black dolls to play with and black role models to admire; he wrote odes to the beauty of black women: "Black Queen of beauty, thou has given colour to the world, / Among other women thou art royal and the fairest." His zeal led him also into more dangerous waters. In the postwar years the black urge to revitalization clashed with such white revitalization movements as the Ku Klux Klan. These separate movements looked back with nostalgia on different heritages and forward with longing to distinct futures. Garvey, however, saw race policy as a means of bridging the gap. In 1922 Garvey met with leaders of the Klan in Atlanta to explain how close the UNIA and the KKK were on such matters as miscegenation and social equality. No other act of Garvey's brought him more criticism or cost him more support. Yet he refused to apologize for it. Compared with the "farce, hypocrisy and lie" typical of most whites, he welcomed the "honesty of purpose" of the Klan. "They are better friends to my race, for telling us what they are, and what they mean, thereby giving us a chance to stir for ourselves." Potentially, he warned, "every whiteman is a Klansman . . . and there is no use lying about it."

It would be a mistake to see Garvey's attitudes toward the Klan as an aberration. They were deeply representative of Garvey's racial views and his abiding pessimism concerning the future of blacks in the United States. When President Warren G. Harding spoke out in 1921 "against every suggestion of social equality," Garvey sent him a telegram of congratulations. Speaking in North Carolina in 1922, Garvey thanked southern whites for having "lynched race pride into the Negro." In 1925 he forged an alliance with the Anglo-Saxon Clubs, invited their leader, John Powell, to speak in Liberty Hall, and announced: "I unhesitatingly endorse the race purity idea of Mr. Powell and his organization." A year and a half before he died, Garvey endorsed the bill of the racist Mississippi Senator Theodore Bilbo for the repatriation of American Negroes to Africa and instructed all divisions of the UNIA to give it their "undivided and wholehearted support."

Garvey's racial ideology helped to determine his response to politics in general. In 1924 he answered a friendly overture from the Workers' party by stating: "We belong to the Negro party, first, last and all the time." His fear of the racism of the white working class, combined with his lingering affection for Washingtonian self-help, gave his domestic politics a conservative cast. He was a consistent foe of the Communists, whom he branded "a group of lazy men and women who desire to level all initiative and intelligence and set a premium on stagnation." Communists and trade unionists, he warned, were "more dangerous to the Negro's welfare than any other group at present." He attributed the failure of modern government to individual selfishness and greed, which could be remedied by paying government officials enough to remove them from temptation and punishing them by death should they succumb anyway. He proposed to reform capitalism by limiting individual fortunes to one million dollars and preventing any corporation from controlling more than five million dollars. While reforms were necessary, Garvey hailed capitalism as "necessary to the progress of the world" and branded its opponents "enemies to human advancement." "The only convenient friend the Negro worker or laborer has, in America, at the present time, is the white capitalist," Garvey announced, since the capitalist's desire to maximize profits made him willing to use the cheapest available labor. Garvey urged the black worker to "keep his scale of wage a little lower than the whites until he is able to become, through proper leadership, his own employer."

One of Garvey's most remarkable achievements was the ease with which he bridged the cultural and political gulf between Jamaica and the United States and learned to comprehend and speak to the needs and aspirations of millions of American blacks. The areas in which he failed to make this transition sufficiently were ones in which he committed his most serious errors. Among these were those aspects of his racial ideology that led him to attempt to form a common front with white racists and that affected his relations with his fellow black leaders. Given the nature of many of his programs, it was inevitable that Garvey would make a number of potent enemies within the ranks of black intellectuals, editors, civil rights leaders, and political activists. His very attempt to articulate the feelings of the masses was bound to create some animus among a significant number of the educated and affluent. However inevitable some of this might have been, it cannot be attributed—as Garvey liked to do—wholly to his opponents. Not only Garvey's programs but his style and temperament helped to create the impossibly poor relations with other black leaders that constituted one of Garvey's greatest weaknesses and hampered his cause significantly.

Certainly Garvey was provoked. To give but two examples, Du Bois described him as "a little, fat black man, ugly, but with intelligent eyes and big head," who was "the most dangerous enemy of the Negro race in America and the world . . . either a lunatic or a traitor," and A. Philip Randolph's *Messenger* referred to him as "the supreme Negro Jamaican Jackass," a "monumental monkey," and an "unquestioned fool and ignoramus." Garvey bore more than a little responsibility for determining the tone of this debate and surely for setting its racial dimensions. He brought with him from Jamaica an abiding distrust of the light-skinned, middle-class Negroes who constituted so many of the leaders in America. The basis of his distrust was not only, or even primarily, their program but their class and color. He attacked Cyril Briggs, the light-complexioned leader of the militant African Blood Brotherhood, with which Garvey certainly might have forged an alliance, as a "white man." He criticized the "near-white" leaders of the NAACP, which Garvey delighted in calling the "National Association for the Advancement of Certain People." His favorite target was Du Bois, whom he branded a "lazy dependent mulatto" whose mixed Dutch, French, and Negro ancestry made him "a monstrosity" who "bewails every day the drop of Negro blood in his veins." The Negro press, "controlled by crafty and unscrupulous persons who have no love of race," was "the most venal, ignorant and corrupt of our time." Du Bois and his allies were planning the extinction of the black race through miscegenation and were thus "the greatest enemies the black people have in the world."

This unhappy, unproductive debate not only drained the energies of all involved and rendered impossible the kind of unified black community Garvey claimed he wanted, but also it ultimately undermined Garvey's leadership and the effectiveness of his organization. A number of black leaders and journalists with whom Garvey had been feuding mounted a campaign against Garvey's operation of the Black Star Line, alerting government officials to alleged illegalities. In January 1922 Garvey and three of his associates were arrested and in February indicted on twelve counts of fraudulent use of the mails to sell Black Star stocks. A prolonged delay in beginning the trial, during which Garvey was released on bail, annoyed his opponents and on January 15, 1923, eight prominent black men and women, including three editors, two NAACP officials, and three business people, wrote to the attorney general of the United States, denouncing Garvey as a demagogue who preached "distrust and hatred of all white people," and demanded that the attorney general "disband and extirpate" Garvey's "vicious movement" and speedily push the government's case against him. The trial began within four months. Though there was no evidence that Garvey was guilty of anything more than poor management, inexperience, and bad judgment in choosing some of his associates, he alone of the four defendants was found guilty and sentenced to five years in prison.

From New York City's Tombs Prison, which Garvey entered in the middle of June 1923, he asserted, "I am not here because I committed any crime against society or defrauded anyone, but because I have led the way to Africa's redemption." In September he was released on bail pending his appeal and enjoyed his last seventeen months of freedom in America. On February 2, 1925, Garvey's appeal was denied, and six days later he entered Atlanta Penitentiary. In his many prison messages and editorials, Garvey was at his most prophetic and messianic: "If I die in Atlanta my work shall then only begin." Garvey was not destined to die in Atlanta. On November 18, 1927, President Calvin Coolidge commuted Garvey's sentence, which still had slightly more than two years to run. Early the next month, Garvey was deported as an undesirable alien. Hundreds of Garvey's followers gathered at the New Orleans pier to bid him farewell. "Be not dismayed," he told them. "Africa's sun is steadily and surely rising, and soon shall shed its rays around the world. I live and shall die for Africa redeemed. Steady yourselves and go forward!"

Despite Garvey's optimistic rhetoric and the considerable personal courage he exhibited during his prosecution and imprisonment, his incarceration and deportation separated him from the most powerful constituency he had and effectively destroyed his movement in the United States. Certainly it is true, as Amy Jacques Garvey has pointed out, that though Garvey was forced to leave America, "Garveyism remained." But it remained in severely diminished circumstances. In Garvey's absence its following declined drastically, and its leadership became hopelessly divided. At the time of Garvey's deportation, the UNIA was bankrupt with liabilities of over $200,000. The final ship in its fleet had been auctioned off for payment of debts; it had lost its liberty halls in New York and Pittsburgh as well as its New York office buildings and publishing plant. The UNIA continued to function, but its days of power and glory were behind it.

Garvey was to live more than twelve years in forced exile from the United States. They were years of characteristic energy and activity and of uncharacteristic isolation and futility. Making Jamaica his base of operations, Garvey edited several newspapers, hosted international conventions of the UNIA in 1929 and 1934, served three months in prison for contempt of court, was elected to the governing body of

Kingston and its parish but was defeated in his bid for the Jamaican legislature, made an abortive attempt to organize a Jamaican People's party, and spent much time and energy feuding with his former UNIA colleagues in America and seeking financial support for his movement. Once again, Garvey was to find his native island too confining. On his way down, no less than on his way up, Garvey needed to be near the center of events.

In March 1935 Garvey took his magazine, the *Black Man*, which he had begun the year before, and moved permanently to London. When the colonial secretary in Jamaica warned British Military Intelligence that Garvey might relocate in London, the reply was: "he can do very little harm over here." That judgment proved to be correct. Garvey continued the patterns of the past: he edited his impressive magazine, he spoke in Hyde Park whenever the weather was fair and indoors wherever he could find a hall and an audience, but he seems not to have had meaningful interaction with London's black population, which had grown somewhat larger and more diverse since Garvey had lived there before World War I. Throughout these final years the major outlines of his philosophy remained familiar. He continued to be a proponent of racial separation, of success through individual and group initiative, and of African redemption. Nevertheless, he was no more predictable at the end of his life than he had been in the beginning. Even as he denounced Benito Mussolini for his rape of Ethiopia, he openly admired aspects of his regime and complained: "Mussolini copied fascism from me. . . . Mussolini and Hitler copied the program of the UNIA." Even as he championed the principles of liberty and the rights of oppressed peoples, he proved strangely indifferent to the plight of the Jews in Germany, charging that their troubles had "been brought on by themselves," because—of all reasons—"their particular method of living is inconsistent with the broader human principles that go to make all people homogeneous."

Garvey longed to return to the United States, if only for a visit, but was denied permission. He came as close as he could, spending three summers, from 1936 to 1938, in Toronto, where he held two regional UNIA conferences and his last international convention. Though the days of his own leadership were behind him, one of his final gestures was to establish a School of African Philosophy in Toronto to recruit and train prospective new leaders for the UNIA. In June 1939 his precarious financial situation forced him to suspend publication of the *Black Man*. For almost the first time since his youth, Garvey was without a journalistic voice. The last year of his life in London was lived in

136

silent penury. In January 1940 he suffered a stroke that left him partially paralyzed, and on June 10, nine weeks short of his fifty-third birthday, he died.

Though he died in isolation, Garvey was not to be forgotten. Decades after his death, his name was still invoked, his ideas still discussed, his influence still felt. Garvey would not have been surprised; it was always his conviction that this would be so. Throughout his stormy, difficult life, Garvey had nurtured his vision of a proud, united black race and an independent Africa. He may not have always worked for it wisely or effectively, but he never ceased working for it and believing in it. In his "Appeal to Racial Pride," printed in the penultimate issue of the *Black Man,* Garvey closed with words that might well serve as his epitaph: "The end is not in our day but in our time we can make certain contribution toward it. . . . Let us not turn back, let us hold on, so that when the final history of man is to be written, there will not only be glory for others but there will be glory for us."

Note on Sources

Those interested in Garvey should begin with his own writings, especially *Philosophy and Opinions of Marcus Garvey*, ed. Amy Jacques Garvey (New York: Atheneum, 1969), and *More Philosophy and Opinions of Marcus Garvey*, ed. E. U. Essien-Udom and Amy Jacques Garvey (London: Frank Cass, 1977). Garvey's final magazine, *The Black Man*, has been reprinted in full in an edition edited by Robert A. Hill (Millwood, N.Y.: Kraus-Thomson, 1975). Garvey's revealing autobiographical article, "The Negro's Greatest Enemy," *Current History*, 18 (Sept. 1923), has been reprinted in John Henrik Clarke, ed., *Marcus Garvey and the Vision of Africa* (New York: Random House, 1974), which also contains other important pieces by Garvey. Garvey's long narrative poem, *The Tragedy of White Injustice* (1927), has also been reprinted (New York: Haskell House, 1972).

The most useful biographical overview is Edmund David Cronon, *Black Moses: The Story of Marcus Garvey and the Universal Negro Improvement Association* (Madison: University of Wisconsin Press, 1955). It should be supplemented by Theodore G. Vincent, *Black Power and the Garvey Movement* (Berkeley, Calif.: Ramparts Press [1971]), and Tony Martin, *Race First: The Ideological and Organizational Struggles of Marcus Garvey and the Universal Negro Improvement Association* (Westport, Conn.: Greenwood Press, 1976). Amy Jacques Garvey's biography of her husband, *Garvey and Garveyism* (Kingston: A. Jacques Garvey, 1963), is especially interesting on Garvey's final years in the West Indies and London. For her article, "The Early Years of Marcus Garvey," and Robert A. Hill's important article, "The First England Years and After, 1912–1916," see the Clarke volume cited above. Robert A. Hill's introduction to *The Black Man*, also cited above, contains an excellent detailed discussion of Garvey's years in exile. Hugh Mulzac's autobiography,

A Star to Steer By (New York: International Publishers, 1963), provides a fascinating inside picture of the Black Star Line. Finally, the most indispensable recent study of Garvey and his followers is Randall K. Burkett, *Garveyism as a Religious Movement: The Institutionalization of a Black Civil Religion* (Metuchen, N.J.: Scarecrow Press, 1978).

Benjamin Quarles

7

A. Philip Randolph:
Labor Leader at Large

In addition to the nationalist critique of the legal struggle for constitutional rights that was advocated by most northern race spokesmen during and after World War I, a radical Socialist critique also appeared. The most important representative of this school of thought was the militant black orator and editor, A. Philip Randolph, who saw the solution to the race's problems in an alliance with the white working class. His magazine, the Messenger, *not only demonstrated Randolph's radicalism, but beginning in the mid-1920s, it became the organ through which Randolph promoted his work in forming and winning recognition for the Brotherhood of Sleeping Car Porters. From his base in this union Randolph moved into larger arenas, attacking discrimination in white-dominated trade unions. At critical junctures he emerged as a magnetic, electrifying leader of national importance who temporarily welded the diverse protest organizations into grand coalitions that battled successfully for greater federal action against economic and other forms of discrimination.*

AT THE TIME of his death in 1979, at the age of ninety, A. Philip Randolph had a reputation as the first national labor leader to emerge among black Americans and as a figure of major force in the mid-twentieth century civil rights movement. Randolph had become a dominant figure in black circles in 1937, when the Pullman Company grudgingly gave official recognition to the union that he organized and led, the Brotherhood of Sleeping Car Porters. Randolph's leadership image had been foreshadowed the preceding year, when he had prodded the American Federation of Labor (AFL) to grant an international charter to the Brotherhood, thereby making it equal to the other unions in the federation. From this double-barreled labor base Randolph had not only pressed insistently for further racial reforms in labor and industry but had joined in the battle against color discrimination on a broad-based front, whether in the armed services and the public schools or in government and politics.

Randolph's leadership was characterized by its receptive attitude toward new strategies in combating racial discrimination. In black circles he was a pioneer in the use of mass protest, a trail-blazing technique that he brought into play in the summer of 1941 on the eve of America's entry into World War II. Deeply concerned because black workers were denied an equal share in the newly created jobs in the production of defense and military equipment and supplies, Randolph called for a "March on Washington." Not caring to run the risk of a mass of protesters converging on the nation's capital, President Franklin D. Roosevelt issued an executive order establishing a committee to ensure fair employment practices. A breakthrough in enlisting the support of the federal government in striking at job discrimination, Roosevelt's decree was "the most significant executive action in the field of race relations since President Lincoln issued the Emancipation Proclamation."

Randolph's role as a black leader resulted from the pattern of race relations that prevailed during his formative years and, in equal measure, from his own qualities of mind and spirit. Born in 1889 in Crescent City, Florida, his father a struggling African Methodist minister, his mother a hard-working helpmate, Asa Philip Randolph grew up in a family marked by its respect for learning. Working at a variety of unskilled or semiskilled jobs during his teens, Randolph was graduated from the high school at Cookman Institute in Jacksonville.

In 1911, at age twenty-two, he left Florida, coming to New York City, his first and last migration. Taking odd jobs during the day, he attended City College during the evenings, his wide-ranging choice of courses embracing political science, philosophy, economics, and history. During the summer of 1914, Randolph married beautician Lucille Campbell Green, a most compatible union that lasted until her death in 1963.

The wedding of the Randolphs took place a few months after the outbreak of World War I, a development that brought a flood of southern blacks to northern cities like New York. Totaling nearly one-third of a million blacks during the decade 1910 to 1920, these migrations tended to raise the aspirations of urban northern blacks, old inhabitants as well as newcomers, leading them to press for equal rights in general and better job opportunities in particular. It was in the wake of this "northern fever" that swept the South that Randolph would seek his way, in the social and economic ferment of the war years and their aftermath that he would launch his career.

It was inevitable that Randolph would view the black working class as offering the greatest potential for an aspiring leader. Neither of the two existing major black betterment organizations, the National Association for the Advancement of Colored People nor the Urban League, had worked directly with laborers, nor had the black leadership in these organizations come from the working class. Considering the marked influx of blacks in the industrial labor market during World War I, there was much to be done in stimulating a labor consciousness among them, particularly in promoting labor unionism. To Randolph the trade union movement was the major remedy for the ills that beset blacks. In the labor movement lay the power to challenge the oppressors of the people.

Young Randolph's formulations of programs and strategies for blacks was typical of the analytical approach that would characterize his career. Unlike some black leaders, Randolph was not antitheoretical. A wide reader with a meditative turn of mind, he was at home in the world of ideas. Reflecting this somewhat scholarly temperament, his speeches and writings bore a steady note of high seriousness with few light or humorous touches. His rich vocabulary sometimes took on scriptural accents; a word like "verily" would not come unnaturally to one who had been a Bible reader since boyhood.

Randolph's readiness in diagnosis was matched by an equal penchant for prescription. To him theory and application were inseparable; vision must be linked to reality. As he pointed out in 1926, a reformer must go further than calling attention to social evils—he must also "indicate the cause and prescribe a remedy." A born organizer, Randolph would perpetually be trying to form unions of working people and coalitions of reformers to carry out the strategies he had conceived and publicized.

To the tasks he set for himself Randolph brought an array of leadership qualities. To begin with, he was never daunted by the thought of failure, never dismayed by the enormity of the odds against him. His struggle against the Pullman Company pitted him, as a contemporary put it, against "Pullman's millions of dollars when half the time he didn't have a dime in his pocket." According to George S. Schuyler, a staff worker on a monthly edited by Randolph in the 1920s, his employer was a man of unshakable aplomb "whether the rent was due and he did not have it, whether an unexpected donation failed to materialize, or whether the long-suffering printer in Brooklyn was demanding money." Of a silver-lining temperament, Randolph maintained an air of confidence however adverse the circumstances.

Another facet of Randolph's leadership was his integrity, a trait that endowed him with an air of moral authority. He could not be bought or

141

bribed, easy money having no allure for him. His private life was likewise unassailable; a private, nonbusiness letter coming to his office from a woman trying to make his acquaintance would be routinely filed away and forgotten. Scandal-lovers and gossip columnists knew better than to waste their time on him.

Randolph's leadership qualities owed something to his bearing and manner, even though he conveyed more of an air of aloofness than any other twentieth-century black leader, including W. E. B. Du Bois. Never folksy or "down home," Randolph kept his distance. In a tête-à-tête he tended to speak as if addressing a public meeting. A visitor to his office would find, as in the case of Edwin R. Embree, president of the Julius Rosenwald Fund, that although Randolph kept his eyes on his caller's face, they "seem focussed on far-distant places."

Randolph's formality, however, was mitigated by his innate graciousness and by a courtesy bordering on politeness. After forty years as his close friend and associate, Bayard Rustin said that he had never "once seen Mr. Randolph treat any human being with anything less than complete dignity and respect." Hence if Randolph seemed preoccupied, even remote, in his contacts with others, he certainly did not give them the impression that he looked down on them.

Randolph's leadership, however, did not rest in person-to-person negotiations behind closed doors. His strength rested more in addressing himself to the public. Bent on becoming a leader, he had schooled himself in the forms of public address. His deep bass voice had been trained by his courses in oratory at the College of the City of New York, by his study with a private tutor, and by his membership in "Ye Friends of Shakespeare," an amateur group of thespians—when he first came to New York he had thought of becoming a stage actor. During these early years of leadership preparation Randolph acquired the so-called "Harvard accent," which his followers regarded not as an affection but as another manifestation of his inherent dignity. And finally as to his image as a public figure, Randolph made an appeal to the eye as well as to the ear. His good looks and well-built physique were put to their best advantage by a carefully selected wardrobe.

Endowed with a combination of leadership qualities and confident he could acquire those he initially lacked, Randolph was ready by 1915 to take his first steps toward the making of a career that, he hoped, would give new meanings to the whole concept of black leadership in action. As it turned out, he did not underestimate himself. His impressive record as a mover and shaker for half a century might be illustrated by reviewing his activities as a Socialist, a labor organizer, a proponent of mass action along a united front, a disciple of nonviolent protest, a shaper of black thought, and, however paradoxical it might appear, a consciously black leader whose outlook was not circumscribed by the color line.

Accepting an award at Carnegie Hall in 1944 from the Workers' Defense League, a Socialist-oriented group that raised money for the legal defense of union workers, Randolph said that one of the fundamental forces that shaped his life was his study and reading in Socialist philosophy and literature and his participation in the Socialist movement. To this movement, he added, he owed his understanding of social forces, his awareness of the mission of the working class, and his world perspective.

Randolph's introduction to the tenets of Socialism came from his courses at City College in 1912 and 1914 and from his contacts with campus activist groups. By 1917 when the United States entered World War I, Randolph had become a Socialist, and his attitude toward this conflict and America's participation in it reflected the standard Socialist theory that wars were brought about by the machinations of contending groups of capitalists and hence were of little concern to the workers of the world. After the United States entered the war, Randolph advised blacks to resist the draft and confine their fighting to the home front.

Fortunately for Randolph, his views about the war and on other issues could be expressed not only in personal appearances on tours to northern cities but also through the pages of the *Messenger*, a monthly magazine he edited in partnership with Chandler Owen, another black Socialist. The duo worked well together, although Randolph was much the more influential of the two, his the more dominant voice. Moreover, Owen's participation would come to an end in 1923, when he left amicably to begin a new career in Chicago.

The *Messenger* drew much of its financial support from the predominantly white Socialist-oriented needle trades and clothing unions, and it, in turn, favorably reported their activities and carried their advertisements. Asserting that blacks had been lulled into a false sense of security by the Booker T. Washington type of leader and by the gradualist approaches of the National Association for the Advancement of Colored People and the National Urban League, the *Messenger* called for a bold, black Socialist leadership. Proudly announcing the magazine's radical orientation, its editors defined radicals as those who had the courage of their convictions, who sought "to get at the root of our social problems," in essence, seekers after truth.

Radicalism as interpreted by Randolph and Owen embraced the use of the strongest language and the open advocacy of the most controversial of causes. The *Messenger* did not hesitate to denounce those in the highest places, President Woodrow Wilson among them. In an article summarizing his two terms in the White House up to September 1919 the *Messenger* stated that "the chief beneficiaries of his public career are the combined manufacturers and capitalists and himself." Others, such as liberals, radicals, and Negroes, "would willingly witness the setting of his sun in public without grief. Unhonored, he will go down to the narrow, bigoted grave of private life from whence he sprang."

The *Messenger*'s boldness reached its peak in its support of the new regime in Russia. Coming at a time when the country was in the grip of a "red scare," the *Messenger*'s support of a government run by Communists inevitably drew fire. In a speech in the House of Representatives on August 15, 1919, James F. Byrnes charged that Randolph and Owen were "Bolsheviks." In a lengthy "Reply to Congressman James F. Byrnes of South Carolina," the accused editors stated that "they would be glad to see a Bolshevik government substituted in the South in place of your Bourbon, reactionary, vote-stolen, misrepresentative Democratic regime." Not to be silenced in the matter, the *Messenger*'s December 1919 issue, a so-called "Thanksgiving" issue, reported that among the things for which it was thankful was "the Russian Revolution, the greatest achievement of the twentieth century."

The pro-revolutionary stance of the magazine had not escaped the attention of the Department of Justice, Randolph and Owen falling under its surveillance. While addressing a mass meeting in Cleveland on August 4, 1919, the two black Socialists were arrested by an agent of the Department of Justice and spent two days in jail. Three months later the department submitted to the Senate Judiciary Committee a lengthy report dealing with radicalism in general and with due attention to its incidence among blacks. J. Edgar Hoover drafted this report, which characterized the *Messenger* as "the exponent of open defiance and sedition" and as "by long odds the most able and most dangerous of all the Negro publications." Almost half of the section of the report that concentrated on blacks was devoted to a reprinting of articles, editorials, and poems that had appeared in the *Messenger*. Additional censure and condemnation were visited upon the magazine by the New York state legislature through its Joint Committee Investigating Seditious Activities.

Although hailing the violent overthrow of the czarist regime in Russia, Randolph and Owen had in mind a more orderly Socialist revolution for the United States. Their method was to unionize the workers and then get them to support the Socialist party. To this end Randolph and Owen formed a short-lived union of blacks who worked in hotels and apartments, the United Brotherhood of Elevator and Switchboard Operators. For a few months in 1917 the duo edited a trade journal published by the Headwaiters and Sidewaiters Society of New York, a monthly that went out of existence a few weeks before the birth of the *Messenger.* In 1919 Randolph and Owen served on the board of directors of the National Brotherhood Workers of America, an umbrella organization that tried to establish a national federation of labor but without success.

Undaunted by this succession of initial failures, Randolph and Owen in 1920 launched the Friends of Negro Freedom, an interracial but black-controlled organization whose overly ambitious program included the organizing of black laborers on an international scale. Almost simultaneously, however, the Randolph-Owen duo diluted the strength of the Friends by creating an overlapping organization, the National Association for the Promotion of Labor Unionism among Negroes. In 1923, after these two groups had become moribund, Randolph and Owen announced the formation of a United Negro Trades. Its objectives—to unionize and upgrade the black workers—were similar to those of its predecessors, and so was its fate.

Supplementing their efforts to unionize blacks, Randolph and Chandler, particularly the former, were active in Socialist party activities. Noting the Republican party's hold on Negroes, the *Messenger* asserted that inasmuch as blacks were workers they had nothing in common with a party dominated by capitalists and employers. "The Negro was a Republican and had been a Republican for fifty years because his father was a Republican and Abraham Lincoln was a Republican. But awake, old black brother Republican." As far as Negroes were concerned there was, said Randolph, no difference between the Republicans and the Democrats because "whichever wins, the people lose."

In 1917 Randolph and Chandler campaigned for the Socialist party candidate for mayor of New York, Morris Hillquit. In 1920, having served his apprenticeship, Randolph was nominated by the Socialists as their candidate for the state comptroller of New York, and two years later the party nominated him for the office of secretary of state of New

York. (He would never run for public office again, graciously declining—"because of union duties"—an invitation in 1944 to become the Socialist party candidate for vice-president of the United States.)

For all his dedication to the Socialist cause Randolph could hardly have been surprised that he was able to make few converts among his fellow blacks. He may not have given sufficient weight to the class lines within the black community, but he was well aware of the strength of the Republican party therein. He knew, too, that most blacks and their leaders saw little point in voting for Socialist and other third-party candidates not likely to be elected.

In seeking to win blacks to Socialism, however, Randolph tended to give insufficient consideration to certain race-related conditions. Holding that the black people needed allies, Randolph advocated working class solidarity across the line. Randolph himself worked smoothly with white Socialists, never seeking to establish a black wing of the group.

Interracial cooperation and harmony among Socialists, however, were not as simple as they might sound. Most white Socialists regarded race and color as incidental to the larger problem of race conflict. They did not sense that the black American was the victim not only of class oppression but also of race oppression. Hence, they did not think of the Negro question as one that required special approaches and remedies. It did not escape the notice of blacks that some white Socialists were prejudiced against them, and that in deference to its southern wing the party tended to gloss over the disfranchisement and lynching of Negroes in southern states. Hence, although the Socialists began a campaign to woo blacks during the years that Randolph was an active party member, the obstacles against them were formidable, the fruits were few.

Despite the Socialist party's lack of success in recruiting blacks, Randolph found much to be pleased with as a result of their work. The Socialists had, he claimed, succeeded in forcing black organizations to examine anew their programs and their leadership and in forcing the two major political parties to become more liberal in matters of race and color. The *Messenger* had broken new ground in organizing "the Radical Movement among Negroes in America" and in presenting "the Negro workers' question to the European workers, radicals and liberals." In an article published in *Opportunity* in January 1926 touching on Negro Radicals, Randolph credited them with having shaped "a working class economic perspective in Negro thought." If any of his readers were ignorant of Randolph's own role in shaping this perspective, they certainly must have surmised it.

But by the time he wrote this article Randolph himself had become much less doctrinaire, having learned that blacks, even among the working masses, would not easily be converted to Socialism. By the mid-1920s the *Messenger* had dropped its tone of ridicule as to black business and the black bourgeoisie and had begun to pay more attention to predominantly black issues and programs. During this period Randolph began to channel his energies into the practical and time-consuming work of trade-union organizing, with fewer precious moments to spare in holding forth on Socialist theory and reformist doctrine.

The event that signaled Randolph's newer orientation and gave a whole new thrust was a mass meeting held in the Elks auditorium in Harlem on August 25, 1925, at which time Randolph accepted an offer to become the "general organizer" of the Brotherhood of Sleeping Car Porters. A newly formed organization, the Brotherhood sought to induce other porters to join them and to induce the Pullman Company to recognize it as the bargaining agent for the porters.

If the Brotherhood viewed the appointment of Randolph as advantageous, so did he. Its leaders had selected him because he had made a reputation as a forceful and well-informed public speaker; because he was not inexperienced as a labor organizer (although admittedly with little success thus far); and because he was not a porter and thus he was not subject to reprisals by the Pullman Company. Randolph, moreover, was editor of the *Messenger*, which, as he pointed out, "could be used to spread the propaganda of the organization," and which indeed became the Brotherhood's official organ, exchanging its more revolutionary accents for the less exciting tones of a trade journal.

Randolph, in turn, was pleased with the appointment, viewing it as an opportunity to test himself as a leader. Having schooled himself well in the theory of labor reform, he was now ready to tackle a job that would require more than a skill in dialectics. He must now face a more practical challenge, demonstrating the ability to cope with a formidable array of concrete problems, including the task of working cooperatively with a variety of other leaders and organizations. And nobody was more aware than he that blacks who attempted to form labor unions encountered peculiar difficulties, their color and marginal status making reprisals easier, not to mention their inequality before the law and their relative lack of personal security.

The most obvious and immediate problem confronting the new union and its general organizer was the economic plight of the Pullman porters. Their wages were low, making it necessary for them to depend upon tips, and out of their earnings they had to pay for their uniforms for the first ten years of service, for shoe polish, and for meals during runs. Porters averaged 400 hours a month on the job as contrasted with 240 hours for other train-service employees. Porters also wanted pay for preparatory time—the time from which a porter reported for work rather than from the time the train pulled out of the station.

The Pullman Company's attitude toward the new union was predictably hostile. In 1920, in order to forestall an earlier effort at union organization by the porters and maids, Pullman had formed a company union, the Employees Representation Plan. To combat the Brotherhood the Pullman Company hired detectives to identify porters who were union members, and it threatened to replace Negro porters with Asians, particularly Filipinos. In its opposition to the union the company sought to enlist the support of blacks in all walks of life.

Such anti-Brotherhood blacks were not hard to find. Reflecting their middle-class orientation, most black professionals and intellectuals were cool toward organized labor. Some Pullman porters, too, according to Sterling D. Spero and Abraham Harris, contemporary authorities on black labor, "had all of the familiar middle-class prejudices of the white-collar worker and the upper servant," thus tending to identify with the rich and influential passengers who rode their cars.

With some notable exceptions, a majority of the black newspapers were against the Brotherhood. At its meeting in Atlanta in 1924 the National Negro Press Association went on record as "condemning all forms of Unionism and economic radicalism." Perry Howard, Republican national committeeman from Mississippi, charged that the Brotherhood was Communist-supported, but his criticism lost some of its force when it became known that he was a paid consultant to the Pullman Company. Opposition also came from the black clergy, particularly from those black congregations that depended upon white financial support. Reflecting their religious traditionalism, the more evangelical denominations were either anti-union or indifferent ("the greater the religiosity, the less the militancy," writes Preston Valien).

Randolph was quick to strike back at the Brotherhood's black critics. In January 1926 he charged two Chicago weeklies, the *Whip* and the *Defender*, with having surrendered to "gold and power." A month later, in a more sweeping indictment, he accused "hypocritical and corrupt Negro leaders" with having been "bought and paid with

Pullman money. Like the dog before the gramaphone, they are listening to their master's voice, the Pullman Company.''

Not able to count on the black church, Randolph sought assistance in other black quarters, soon enlisting the support of the NAACP and the Urban League. In early 1926 James Weldon Johnson, executive secretary of the NAACP, wrote public letters endorsing the Brotherhood, and in its April 1926 issue the *Crisis*, organ of the NAACP, carried an editorial by Du Bois condemning the Pullman Company for its machinations in trying "to block the belated effort of the Pullman porters to form a real and effective labor union." Randolph successfully wooed the influential black fraternal organization, the Improved and Benevolent Order of Elks of the World, winning its endorsement in 1928, not an inconsiderable feat inasmuch as the fraternity at its convention in 1925 had unanimously condemned organized labor. To no one's surprise, at its first national convention in 1929 in Chicago, the Brotherhood elected Randolph as president.

Whether coming in contact with him through the Brotherhood releases or from listening to him in public address, the porters were favorably impressed by their leader, viewing him as one who was wholeheartedly and single-mindedly devoted to their welfare. Warming to their high appraisal, Randolph exerted his spell, stirring them with words of hope and exhortation interspersed with snatches of fatherly advice. "A new Pullman porter is born," he informed them in the April 1926 issue of the *Messenger*. "He has caught a new vision. His creed is independence without insolence; courtesy without fawning; service without servility."

Randolph urged the porters to do their best on the job despite their multiple grievances. "The Brotherhood will not injure the Pullman Company," he wrote. "It does not counsel insubordination, but efficient discipline." Sounding like a latter-day Washington, Randolph preached the gospel of work and habits of industry. (In 1940, in the *Black Worker*, a Brotherhood periodical, Randolph would present to the porters a list of ten "Don'ts," beginning with "Don't drink on the job," and ending with "Don't annoy women.")

Viewing Randolph in terms of his external relationships to them and in the light of the public image he cast, the Brotherhood rank and file could hardly be aware of any leadership flaws with which his closer associates, the second echelon administrators, had to cope. On them fell the real task of organizing and operating the Brotherhood, Randolph showing little interest in administrative work or grasp of its content and perhaps not fully sensing its importance. At home in reading a treatise

on theoretical economics on a global scale, Randolph found less satis-
faction in scanning a Brotherhood balance sheet placed on his desk.

Fortunately for Randolph, throughout his long leadership of the
Brotherhood he was able to develop a cordial relationship with one or
another able subordinate who was willing to assume the major responsibilities for administrative operations. In the early years this role was
admirably filled by Milton P. Webster, a former Pullman porter himself, who had come from Chicago, where he had been influential in
black political and labor circles. Holding the rank of first vice-
president of the Brotherhood, Webster was second only to Randolph
in command. No "yes-man," Webster never hesitated to differ with
"the Chief," vigorously defending his viewpoints but winning or losing
with equal grace. Early in their relationships the two leaders had
learned to respect and trust each other.

During the early years of the Brotherhood Randolph was equally
successful in winning the strong personal loyalty of a countrywide network of dedicated lieutenants, whether in Oakland, Detroit, Pittsburgh, or St. Louis. Their dual devotion to Randolph and the Brotherhood was one of the major causes of the union's ultimate success.

After a twelve-year fight the persistence of Randolph and the patience of his followers was rewarded. The Railway Labor Act of 1934
outlawed company unions and granted railroad employees the right to
organize without interference by the employer. Such legislative sanction of collective bargaining, a long-sought Randolph goal, was a
significant victory for organized labor as a whole. The following year
the Brotherhood, in an election contest with a union loyal to the Pullman Company (the Pullman Porters and Maids Protective Association), decisively won the right to represent the porters in collective bargaining. The Pullman Company held out for two more years, finally
capitulating in August 1937 when it recognized the Brotherhood as the
bargaining agent for the porters and maids, negotiating a contract covering wages, hours, and working rules.

The Randolph-led union had won an important victory. In a letter to
Du Bois two years earlier (May 24, 1935) Randolph asserted that
"when the Brotherhood wins this fight, it will probably be the most
significant economic victory and stride of substantial and constructive
progress the Negro has made in history." Randolph's evaluation was
not without substance, if we grant that leaders as a class are entitled to
a touch of hyperbole.

For indeed, the victory over the Pullman Company was a demonstration of the ability of blacks to organize and run a union despite a

"sea of troubles." It made blacks more union-aware, decreasing their anti-labor sentiment; it provided an organized group whose resources and leadership could be enlisted for service in other black causes, and it marked the beginning of black influence on national labor policy and in national labor circles.

The capitulation of the Pullman Company came at a propitious juncture in Randolph's fortunes, coming just when AFL, growing weary of his continuous strictures, had considered ejecting the Brotherhood from the federation. In 1929 the Brotherhood had joined the AFL, although it had not received the kind of charter it sought. Randolph and his followers wanted an international charter that would make the Brotherhood equal with the other member unions, thereby wielding more influence in national labor circles and enabling it to operate independently in negotiating its own working conditions. Instead of receiving such autonomy the Brotherhood was placed under the direct jurisdiction of the president of the AFL, William Green, and its Executive Council. Randolph accepted this more limited "federal" charter because he deemed such a step as a temporary expedient, "establishing a beach-head," as he phrased it.

Randolph proceeded to use the annual conventions of the AFL as a forum, pressing for an international charter for the Brotherhood and sharply condemning the racial practices and policies of the member unions. He called for the elimination of the color clauses in their constitutions and the color pledges in their rituals, demanding the expulsion of "any union maintaining the color bar." In light of the deeply rooted patterns of racial exclusion and job discrimination so typical of its craft-union membership, the AFL could hardly deny Randolph's charges. At the annual meetings, however, Randolph's resolutions were generally referred to a committee which either pigeonholed them, recommended nonconcurrence, counseled patience, or expressed hopes for a more friendly spirit in the house of labor.

In 1936, however, upon the heels of the Brotherhood's decisive victory over the union sponsored by the Pullman Company, the AFL decided to grant Randolph's application for an international charter. The first predominantly black union to receive such a charter, the Brotherhood now became an autonomous unit, equal to other international units.

The organized labor movement would continue to discriminate against Negroes, and for more than one-third of a century Randolph would be a leader in the fight against such practices. But this recalcitrance on the part of white labor did not diminish the importance of the

Brotherhood's feat in obtaining an international charter. However slow the organized labor movement might be in erasing the color line, its membership from top to bottom now became much more conscious of the Negro workers, their problems and possibilities.

Strengthened by its international union status and by its victory over the Pullman Company, the Brotherhood had become a dominant force in Negro circles by the late 1930s. Its cohesiveness and power enabled it to exert a major influence both in coming to the aid of other black unions and in assisting other black betterment movements and efforts. And, as a concomitant factor, Randolph himself now became a figure of consequence in black life. Girded by the power and prestige of the Brotherhood, and by the accolades his leadership of the Brotherhood had brought him, he bore a new confidence and authority as he moved onto a wider stage.

Grounded in theory, Randolph knew something of black leadership as a type. In black life so little power was available that the competitive struggle for its exercise was bound to be intense, often ruthless. Randolph knew, too, that there was a multiplicity of black leaders and organizations, varying in strategy and tactics, and that no one of them spoke for all blacks. But if there were no universal leader, Randolph, by the late 1930s, was prepared to speak to and for an ever widening constituency, having already indicated his own broad social concerns and having already demonstrated his ability to work with other black leaders and other black protest and improvement organizations. In black leadership he aspired to exemplify the principle of collective action.

However inclusive his leadership outreach, Randolph spurned the overtures of one group, the Communists. Randolph had hailed the Russian revolution of World War I years, but when the American Socialists divided into right and left shortly after the war Randolph remained with the former. Hence, when the American Communist party was organized in 1921, he did not become a member.

To Randolph, the Communists imperiled all efforts toward joint action and interorganizational unity. From the year of its founding in 1925 Randolph denounced the American Negro Labor Congress, charging in September of that year that it was "not representative of the American Negro worker because its seat of control is Moscow." During the long struggle between the Pullman porters and the Pullman Company Randolph reiterated the point that the Brotherhood of Sleeping Car Porters was "not backed by Moscow, nor has it any Communistic connections." In a letter written in June 1928 he referred to the Communists as a "sinister and destructive crowd."

Randolph's highly critical appraisal of the Communists was heightened in the late 1930s as a result of his experience as president of the National Negro Congress. Organized in 1930, this was an umbrella-like combination of about twenty organizations, white and black, whose goal was racial advancement in general with emphasis on the problems of the black worker. To Randolph this seemed to be the kind of a "united front of all Negro organizations," which had become the dominant goal in his life. In his presidential address of 1936 (read in his absence) he opened by invoking "the spirit of Frederick Douglass and Nat Turner, of Gabriel and Denmark Vesey, of Harriet Tubman and Sojourner Truth—those noble rebels who struck out in the dark days of slavery that Negro men and women might be free." Randolph closed this initial presidential address by reminding the delegates that the ambitious program envisioned by the Congress would require the cooperation of various Negro organizations—"church, fraternal, civil, trade-union, farmer, professional, college and what not—into a framework of a united front, together with white groups of workers, lovers of liberty and those whose liberties are similarly menaced."

During its first four years, nearly half of its brief existence, the National Negro Congress did much to improve the lot of blacks, locally and nationally. But its significant accomplishments were obscured by the rising role and influence of the Communists within the organization. They had stayed in the background at first, but within two years it had become obvious that theirs was the dominant voice, theirs the source of funding. During these first years Randolph took little time in the operation of the Congress, his energies devoted to the Brotherhood's culminating struggles with the Pullman Company on one hand and the AFL on the other. Moreover, as in his leadership of the porters, Randolph showed little interest in administrative work. In the Brotherhood this shortcoming had been covered up by able and loyal subordinates, but in the Congress it emerged for all to see, thus diminishing his effectiveness.

The Congress did not convene in 1938 and 1939, and hence it was not until 1940 that the issue of Communist control reached its denouement. At that meeting Randolph resigned, charging the the Congress was Communist-dominated. "I quit the Congress because it was not truly a Negro Congress," he wrote in an article in the *Black Worker*, "Why I Would Not Stand for Re-election for President of the National

Negro Congress." During his speech of resignation the Communists staged a demonstration, followed by a walk-out.

The Communist party would not enroll many blacks. Not ideology-oriented, Negro Americans sought to improve the capitalist system rather than to liquidate it. Nonetheless the Communists had some success, in America and abroad, in dramatizing the grievances of black Americans, particularly of the black workers. Moreover, Randolph's own exposure to Marxist theory and practice had contributed to the tone and militance of his vocabulary and to his convictions as to the use of mass direct action techniques. But whatever their contribution to black advancement or to his own outlook or approaches, the Communists could only count Randolph as one of their most bitter black critics. In 1944 in proposing a "non-partisan political bloc," he called for their exclusion, asserting that "the Communist Party seeks only to rule or ruin a movement." In 1946, at the twenty-first anniversary celebration of the Brotherhood of Sleeping Car Porters, he characterized the Communists as "one of the greatest menaces to labor, the Negro, and other minorities."

Randolph's mindset about Communists was a factor in his decision to exclude all whites from participation in the "March on Washington" he scheduled for the summer of 1941. The possibility of Communist infiltration into this projected demonstration was, however, but one reason, and not the major reason, for Randolph's announced policy of racial exclusion. To white liberal groups and associates, such as the Fellowship of Reconciliation and its leader, A. J. Muste, who questioned this policy, Randolph had a ready answer. The proposed march, he explained, was "pro-Negro, not anti-white." Such an all-black movement would "create faith by Negroes in Negroes," developing "a sense of self-reliance with Negroes depending upon Negroes in vital matters."

Destined to be of major importance for its accomplishments and for its trail-blazing techniques in direct mass black pressure and action, the March on Washington Movement was a cooperative venture, with Randolph as its operating head. The movement grew out of the plight of the urban Negro worker on the eve of America's entry into World War II, black unemployment having reached 25 percent in 1940. The long-existent discriminatory practices in hiring, in on-the-job training, and in upgrading were more aggravating than ever to the Negro workers as they noted their country's eagerness to contrast the American creed of liberty and equality with the suppressions that characterized the Fascist nations, Hitler's Germany in particular. And although

American industry was increasing its production to meet the needs of the national defense program, blacks were being turned away at the defense-plant gates.

On September 27, 1940, Randolph and two other black spokesmen, Walter White of the NAACP and T. Arnold Hill of the National Urban League, conferred with Roosevelt, but this White House meeting accomplished little, thus convincing Randolph that nothing short of mass action by blacks would suffice. Hence through the Negro newspapers (see, for example, the *Pittsburgh Courier,* January 25, 1941) he issued a call. Negro Americans, ran his summons, must bring their "power and pressure to bear upon the agencies and representatives of the Federal Government to exact their rights in National Defense employment and the armed forces of the country." He suggested that 10,000 Negroes march on Washington, their slogan, "We Loyal Negro American Citizens Demand the Right to Work and Fight for our Country."

Randolph's appeal exceeded even his characteristically optimistic expectations, drawing enthusiastic support throughout the black community, including the clergy, the press, and the rank and file. The leaders of other black organizations, including the Urban League and the NAACP, found themselves swept into the fold. However much Randolph's growing popularity might threaten their own leadership standing in black uplift, these spokesmen and spokeswomen could hardly stay on the sidelines, even though direct mass action of a marching kind took on a somewhat more confrontational style than some of them preferred. Their choice was predictable. "No Negro leader could risk the Uncle Tom label," explains Herbert Garfinkel in analyzing their uniformly affirmative response.

It would not be the last time that Randolph would put other black leaders in a position in which they felt themselves to be somewhat coerced into supporting a strategy he espoused. But it is to be noted that if Randolph made constant use of other organizations and their leaders, he in turn reciprocated in full measure. He was, for example, a longtime supporter of the NAACP's crusade against lynching.

Their groundwork laid, Randolph and seven other black leaders formed a March on Washington Committee, scheduling the march for July 1, 1941, and multiplying their projections as to the number of marchers. "Dear fellow Negro Americans," exhorted Randolph, with growing confidence, "be not dismayed in these terrible times. You possess power, great power. Our problem is to harness and hitch it up for action on the broadest, daring and most gigantic scale."

In early June the mushrooming march movement forced itself upon Roosevelt. Exercising his political skills, he tried to have the march called off, enlisting the services of his wife Eleanor, whose popularity among blacks was already legendary, and of New York's mayor, Fiorello H. La Guardia, also a favorite in black circles. The failure of such emissaries made it necessary to arrange a White House conference on June 18 with four black leaders, including Randolph. Calling the idea of a march "bad and unintelligent," Roosevelt strongly urged the leaders to cancel it. When it became evident that his plea was unacceptable without a quid pro quo, Roosevelt brought the thirty-minute conference to a close by appointing a committee of five high-ranking whites to meet with the black leaders in order to reach an agreement.

Following a quickly arranged series of meetings and telephone conversations, the two groups resolved their differences, and on June 25, one week after the White House conference, Roosevelt issued Executive Order 8802, decreeing that "there shall be no discrimination in the employment of workers in defense industries or government because of race, creed, color or national origin" and establishing a Committee on Fair Employment Practices (FEPC). Appointed on July 19, 1941, this six-member committee included Webster, vice-president of the Brotherhood, Randolph having declined an invitation to serve. In the meantime, in exchange for Roosevelt's order, Randolph called off the scheduled march, proceeding instead to form a new organization, the March on Washington Movement, to act as a watchdog over the FEPC, among other activities.

Randolph's success in persuading Roosevelt to issue Executive Order 8802 illustrated a technique familiar in black leadership circles for over a hundred years. This was the practice of operating from a relatively weak power base, but of making demands nonetheless, hoping to achieve the group's goal by the use of strong rhetoric along with the threat of a disruptive physical confrontation that would certainly reach the public eye, even if it failed to touch the public conscience. Bearing some semblance to the game of bluff, this technique sometimes failed, as in the Brotherhood's threat to strike against the Pullman Company in 1928. Keenly aware of the riskiness of this technique, Randolph also knew full well that a black leader does not enjoy a wide range of weapons.

A group, or coalition of groups, whose power was problematic faced another disheartening possibility, i.e., the victory they won might turn out to be less fruitful than they had expected. The aftermath of Randolph's march was a case in point. Despite its leader's vigorous efforts, the campaign for a permanent FEPC was unsuccessful, the wartime committee quietly expiring in the spring of 1946. Inadequately financed by the Congress and with little power to enforce its findings, the committee encountered bitter and unrelenting attacks. Malcolm Ross, its chairman beginning in October 1943, described it as the most hated agency in Washington, southern Congressmen and their constituents regarding it as an attempt to impose social equality upon their states.

The National Council for a Permanent FEPC, established in 1943, had been unable to halt its demise, running completely out of funds in 1946 and facing internal dissension with a rift between co-chairman Randolph and executive secretary Anna Arnold Hedgeman. Nonetheless, the FEPC was important for its pioneering role—for "making the issue part of the national consciousness," as Hedgeman said later. In the some 10,000 cases it handled during its five-year existence it met with some success in changing the discriminatory policies of employers and trade unions. Rather than face charges by the commission, some employers erased their color line, and others broadened their hiring policies.

Moreover, the existence of the FEPC meant that the federal government had now assumed a role in the elimination of Jim Crow practices in employment, that a precedent had been established for considering job discrimination a denial of one's civil rights. In addition the FEPC had its influence on the issuing of court decrees against job discrimination and on the establishment of state FEPC laws and of federal government contract compliance committees, the last-named capped by a committee on equal employment opportunity. And to Randolph, as to other black opinion-makers, no movement could be counted a failure that had succeeded in establishing among Negroes a greater sense of collective self-reliance.

Along with mass action and public demonstrations, Randolph made use of another technique that would foreshadow the civil rights revolution of the 1950s and 1960s, i.e., the Gandhian approach of nonviolent civil disobedience. During his *Messenger* days Randolph had been an exponent of retaliatory violence, but an older Randolph, under the influence of such pacifists as Rustin, then on the threshold of a long career in reformist causes, modified his views. At its founding in 1942 the Congress of Racial Equality named Randolph to its National Advisory Committee, well aware that he shared its philosophy of nonviolent direct action. At the annual meeting of the March on Washington Movement in 1943 in Detroit, Randolph challenged the 1,200 delegates "to adopt nonviolent, goodwill, direct action as organizational policy." Such an approach, as Randolph pointed out later that year, would require persons "who had undergone a rigid training and discipline to develop self-control and the requisite moral and spiritual resources to meet the most trying ordeal."

Randolph himself put this technique to the test in his campaign against segregation in the armed forces during the 1940s. During World War I Randolph had spoken out against discrimination in the armed forces, and he sounded a similar note on the eve of World War II. The White House meeting on September 14, 1940, between Roosevelt and the three black leaders, Randolph included, discussed the participation of Negroes not only in defense industries but in the military. The call to the March on Washington, issued in the spring of 1941, included a petition "for the integration of Negroes in the armed forces, such as the Air Corps, Navy, Army and Marine Corps of the Nation." To Randolph's disappointment, however, Roosevelt's Executive Order 8802 was confined to defense industries. Hence the abolition of Jim Crow policies in the armed services, including the Women's Auxiliary Army Corps and the Waves, became one of the major objectives of the March on Washington Movement.

The war ended but not the issue, the latter taking a new momentum in 1947 when a Universal Military Training bill came before the Congress. A peacetime draft, it contained no antidiscrimination proviso. Responding to this omission, Randolph and Grant Reynolds, the black New York State Commissioner of Correction, established in November 1947 a Committee Against Jim Crow in Military Service and Training, a step that was hailed by blacks throughout the country.

The effort of this committee to persuade Congress to enact an antisegregation law for the armed services, or to persuade President Harry Truman to establish such a policy by executive decree, met with opposition from southern Congressmen and from high army officials. Reflecting the mood of their constituents, a group of black leaders met with Truman late in March 1948, urging him to insist that the proposed draft law include an antisegregation amendment. Not mincing his words, Randolph reported that in his travels around the country he "found Negroes not wanting to shoulder a gun to fight for democracy abroad unless they get democracy at home." Following a further exchange of views between Truman and the black delegation, the meeting came to an inconclusive end.

In his testimony before the Senate Armed Services Committee nine days later, Randolph was just as frank as he had been at the White

House. If Congress passed a "jimcrow draft," he warned, he would advise blacks to resort to "mass civil disobedience" along the line of Gandhi's struggles against the British in India. Randolph openly pledged himself to counsel and assist young people, white and black, to "quarantine" a segregated "conscript system." When one senator raised the question of treason, Randolph replied that "we are serving a higher law than the law which applies to the act of treason."

When Congress, on June 22, 1948, passed a draft law that did not ban Jim Crow practices, Randolph announced the formation of a League for Non-Violent Civil Disobedience Against Military Segregation, which proposed to concentrate its efforts on persuading the president to alter the situation by executive order. The league called upon Truman to issue such an antidiscrimination order, stating that if such a step were not taken by August 16 (when the new draft law became operative), the league would conduct a campaign of noncompliance. Again making use of a technique that bore the earmarks of bluff, Randolph operated from no substantial base of power, and his willingness to go to jail in such a cause is open to question.

Truman, however, needed little further convincing. During his presidency he had grown more liberal on race issues, more concerned about civil rights. Moreover, in the presidential election to be held later that year, he needed the black vote, which had become increasingly important as the black population shifted from the South, where blacks could not vote, to the North, where they could. On July 26 Truman issued Executive Order 9981 declaring, as presidential policy, "that there shall be equality of treatment and opportunity for all persons in the armed services." A month later Randolph and Reynolds announced the termination of the league, the latter pointing out that the league had accomplished its mission "not in familiar legal or Constitutional terms" but in a program of noncompliance that had gone outside the traditionally accepted boundaries.

Randolph's crowning experience as an advocate of direct mass action by a coalition of reform-minded groups and agencies came in the summer of 1963 with the "march on Washington for Jobs and Freedom." Publicly announced from Randolph's office in Harlem in February of that year, the idea for such a demonstration grew out of a conversation between Randolph and Rustin, his assistant, a few weeks earlier. Originally concentrating on black unemployment, the march soon broadened its scope to include the whole range of civil rights in response to the cry "Freedom Now!"—the slogan of blacks during the hundredth anniversary of the Emancipation Proclamation. Sponsors of the march sought to bring pressure on Congress to enact a civil rights bill, then dormant in the House Rules Committee. "Politicians," said Randolph, "don't move unless you move them."

A labor leader himself, it was natural for Randolph to have originally thought of the proposed march as primarily a demonstration for jobs. But he had no quarrel with the slogan, "March on Washington for Jobs and Freedom," inasmuch as he held that economic freedom was the base of other freedoms, for, as he said, "Freedom requires a material foundation." But Randolph also knew that freedom had a protean quality, taking on a myriad of guises and fulfilling itself in many ways. Indeed, it was in quest of such an indivisible freedom that Randolph, now in his mid-seventies at the time of the march in 1963, had devoted his long career, as a moment of reflection would tend to indicate.

As to his sensitivity in the matter of jobs for blacks, Randolph stood above all other black leaders. During the twenty-five years between the granting of an international charter to the Brotherhood of Sleeping Car Porters and the proposed march on Washington in 1963, Randolph's devotion to the cause of the black workers had been unflagging and these workers needed such dedication. From his position as international president of the Brotherhood, Randolph raised an insistent voice for racial justice in the councils of the AFL. At its annual meetings in the 1940s and 1950s he proposed a series of resolutions, including those calling for the appointment of committees to investigate discriminatory practices among the member unions. As a rule the AFL reaffirmed its policy of opposition to Jim Crow practices but confessed itself without sufficient power to influence the autonomous individual unions. Randolph's own union, he noted, did not practice racial discrimination; of its 12,000 members in 1947 approximately 20 percent were whites, including Filipinos and Mexicans.

Randolph was hardly popular at the annual meetings of the AFL. Boos were not uncommon when he arose to speak, some delegates walking out and milling around in the halls until he took his seat. But Randolph was not to be silenced, winning the title, "the conscience of the AFL," and forcing the leaders to address themselves to the touchy questions of race and color.

In 1955 when the AFL merged with the Congress of Industrial Organizations (CIO) to form the AFL-CIO, the new federation named two blacks as vice-presidents, Randolph and Willard S. Townsend of the United Transport Service Employees. Founded in 1935, the CIO had made a strong effort to win the support of blacks. Organized along industrywide lines rather than the more restrictive craft lines, and forming new unions unburdened by a history of racial discrimination, the CIO's racial and social policies were broader than those of the AFL, even though Randolph had preferred to keep the Brotherhood in the latter. By the time of the merger, however, the CIO had become less vigorous in pressing for racial equality.

To Randolph's gratification the constitution of the new federation provided for a Civil Rights Committee, one pledged to "the effective implementation of the principle of non-discrimination." Randolph became disenchanted, however, at the union's failure to expel locals that were guilty of discriminatory racial practices. Randolph's insistent charges that the AFL-CIO's attack on color barriers was halfhearted became increasingly galling to George Meany, its president. Meany had grown impatient with Randolph, charging that his indictments were overdrawn and that he failed to give the federation any credit for its successes against segregation. The Meany-Randolph imbroglio came to a head in 1959 at the annual convention of the union. In a sharp exchange between the two, Meany gave way to his ire, saying to Randolph, "Who in hell appointed you as guardian of the Negro members in America?"

Bent on exerting pressure on the AFL-CIO, Randolph in 1960 founded the Negro American Labor Council, made up of black officials of existing unions. Representing the council as its president, Randolph presented to the AFL-CIO a list of grievances accompanied by suggested remedies. The federation leadership responded by denying the charges and sharply criticizing Randolph himself for causing "the gap that has been developed between organized labor and the Negro community." This rift in the Negro-labor alliance, however, was relatively short-lived, with Meany a featured speaker at the annual meeting of the Negro American Labor Council in 1962.

If the black worker and the organized labor movement were indebted to Randolph, the same was true, if to a lesser extent, of the civil rights movement as a whole. Randolph's social vision was broad. As president of the Brotherhood of Sleeping Car Porters, he reminded its membership of the necessity of supporting "progressive forces for the securing and maintaining of democratic institutions for the Negro." In 1957, at the request of Martin Luther King, Jr., Randolph became one of the sponsors of the Prayer Pilgrimage to Washington, an effort to prod the federal government to take further action on "the unresolved civil-rights issue." Randolph delivered a moving address to the some 20,000 gathered at the Lincoln Memorial on May 17, the third anniversary of the Supreme Court decree against segregation in the public schools.

To the seventy-four-year-old Randolph, therefore, a march was nothing new; "Mr. Randolph is a march man," observed Whitney M. Young, Jr., in 1963. "He's been marching since 1941." A march focusing on jobs and freedom was a fitting climax to a career such as his. It was Randolph, wrote King, who "proposed a March on Washington to unite in one luminous action all the forces along the far-flung front." It was Randolph who headed the march's organizing committee of six blacks and four whites, and it was Randolph's deputy director, Rustin, who planned and coordinated the operations, handled the complex details, and recruited the volunteers. Joining forces with Randolph in 1950, Rustin had soon become a trusted and efficient lieutenant, skilled as a troubleshooter.

To Randolph the 1963 march was the high point of his public life. Over 200,000 marchers took the mile-long walk from the Washington Monument to the Lincoln Memorial. At the more formal proceedings, held at the foot of the memorial, Randolph presided and also delivered the keynote address. The march "is not the climax of our struggle but a new beginning, not only for the Negro but for all Americans, for personal freedoms and a better life," he said. "The civil rights revolution is not confined to Negroes; nor is it confined to civil rights."

Randolph introduced the other nine speakers in turn, ending with King, whose address, "I Have a Dream Today," marked the high water mark in twentieth-century civil rights oratory. Orderly and inspiring, the march was characterized by a note of high seriousness from beginning to end. "The imposing dignity and patience of A. Philip Randolph toned the whole affair," observed *Newsweek* columnist Kenneth Crawford.

Randolph counted the 1963 march as the most memorable day of his life, the crowning event associated with his leadership. And indeed the march was notable both as a symbol of past struggles and aspirations and, as Randolph had said, the herald of a new beginning.

There were, however, two aspects of the emergent black protest and activism of the 1960s that the aging Randolph found questionable, i.e., the cry of "black power" and the call for black separatism. Randolph held that although "black power" could be construed as "a valid and poetic 'cry for deliverance,' " its advocates had not succeeded in formulating a concrete program that was "applicable to the needs of practical political action." To Randolph, "black power was a slogan and slogans solve no problems."

Randolph did not believe that blacks should "go it alone," and thus he was out of tune with the position paper adopted in August 1966 by the Student Nonviolent Coordinating Committee: "If we are to proceed toward true liberation, we must cut ourselves off from whites." Forty years earlier Randolph had condemned the racially separatist tenets of the Marcus Garvey movement. Holding that anti-white doctrines are dangerous and false, Randolph charged that Garveyism broadened the chasm between white workers and black workers and "engenders and fosters a virulent race prejudice." As for Garvey's cry that Negro Americans must establish an independent nation in Africa, Randolph replied that the liberation of Africa could come only "by allying the Negro liberation movement with the movements for the liberation of all the world's enslaved of all races, creeds and colors."

Randolph's attitude toward the black power militants of the 1960s was thus a reaffirmation of his essential ecumenism. Except for a brief spell while launching the 1941 March on Washington, Randolph's long leadership had consistently reflected a coalitionist bent. Randolph's concerns were global; for example, while most black leaders viewed World War II as an opportunity to win victory on the home front as well as victory over the Axis powers, Randolph viewed the conflict as an opportunity for a "Peoples' Revolution" that would "possess the fighting faith and crusading confidence of the masses of all colors and race," as he wrote in 1944. "The people can cause this war to usher in the Century of the Common Man."

Randolph's outlook embraced the generality of mankind. He strove to "win a decent place in America" for blacks, but he sought to win it without "destroying the possibilities for mutual goodwill." Within black circles he stressed the commonalities that transcended the lines of class and occupation, among other dividers. Beyond the color line he sought the universals in the human experience.

It might be noted that Randolph's faith in the power of reason and his belief in people's common destiny led him at times to underestimate the tenacity of race and color prejudice in his native land. Devoid of such feelings himself, he did not gauge fully the status advantages to be derived from racial discrimination—that whites in labor unions, for example, were fearful not only of losing their economic benefits but also of jeopardizing their social standing if blacks were accorded job equality. Randolph does not seem to have fully weighed the social uses of racism, its role as a form of cultural taboo, its service as an ego-prop.

To the end Randolph believed that self-interest balanced by a concern for the common good would ultimately prevail, and that the enlightened, particularly those who were the victims of oppression, would make common cause. Working toward this goal was Randolph's essential contribution, and it received its most cogent expression from Rustin, his close friend and associate. Shortly after Randolph's death in 1979, Rustin listed what he had learned from his mentor, including nonviolent protest and the economic roots of racism. "But, above all," wrote Rustin, "I learned that the struggle for the freedom of black people is intertwined with the struggle to free all mankind."

Rustin was fortunate in having had the opportunity to learn such things firsthand. Others, however, would not go unendowed, the Randolph legacy having an outreaching quality, embracing in particular the seekers of social insight.

Note on Sources

The important manuscript source on Randolph is the papers of the Brotherhood of Sleeping Car Porters in the Manuscript Division of the Library of Congress and in the Manuscript Division of the Chicago Historical Society.

In the periodical literature, the most valuable single source is the *Messenger,* which was published in New York City from 1917 until its cessation in 1928. It is indispensable for Randolph's early career as a labor organizer and a Socialist, and it describes his activities in laying the foundations for the Brotherhood and setting its course.

The secondary sources include one full-length study, Jervis B. Anderson's *A. Philip Randolph: A Biographical Portrait* (New York: Harcourt Brace, and Jovanovich, 1973), in style, content, and insight an admirable introduction to the man. This work may be supplemented by a body of specialized studies of high caliber in which Randolph is the central figure. Listed according to their chronological coverage, the first is Theodore Kornweibel, Jr.'s *No Crystal Stair: Black Life and the Messenger, 1919–1928* (Westport, Conn.: Greenwood Press, 1975), a scholarly exposition and analysis of that journal's viewpoints. A similarly thorough volume, William H. Harris's *Keeping the Faith: A. Philip Randolph, Milton P. Webster, and the Brotherhood of Sleeping Car Porters, 1925–1937* (Urbana: University of Illinois Press, 1977), traces in detail the long battle between the Brotherhood and the Pullman Company, pointedly analyzing Randolph's leadership characteristics throughout. Harris holds that even though Randolph and his Brotherhood associates viewed themselves as path-breakers and innovators, "they functioned much in the tradition of other black leaders." The pioneer study of the Randolph-led union is Brailsford R. Brazeal's *The Brotherhood of Sleeping Car Porters: Its Origin and Development* (New York: Harper and Brothers, 1946), a solid work with an interpretive touch.

Works that deal with issues about which Randolph was concerned and his role therein including the following. Herbert Garfinkel's *When Negroes March: The March on Washington Movement in the Organizational Politics for*

FEPC (Glencoe Ill.: The Free Press, 1959) is skillfully organized and copiously documented, its conclusions soundly reasoned. Garfinkel may be supplemented by two additional studies that add to our understanding of that agency: Louis C. Kesselman's *The Social Politics of FEPC: A Study in Reform Pressure Movements* (Chapel Hill: University of North Carolina Press, 1948) and Louis Ruchames's *Race, Jobs and Politics: The Story of FEPC* (New York: Columbia University Press, 1953). The fight against Jim Crow practices in the services, with due attention to Randolph's role, is recounted in Richard M. Dalfiume's *Fighting on Two Fronts: Desegregation of the U.S. Armed Forces, 1939–1953* (Columbia: University of Missouri Press, 1969). Histories of black labor union movement of the twentieth century include Sterling D. Spero and Abram L. Harris's *The Black Worker: The Negro and the Labor Movement* (New York: Columbia University Press, 1931), which is somewhat critical of Randolph's leadership during the early years of the Brotherhood. One of the best of the studies that broadly and comprehensively covers the black worker is Philip S. Foner's *Organized Labor and the Black Worker, 1619–1973* (New York: Praeger Publishers, 1974), its index listing over forty references to Randolph.

Walter Weare **8**

Charles Clinton Spaulding:
Middle-Class Leadership
in the Age of Segregation

The career of this North Carolina businessman illuminates the transition in the role of southern black leadership during the first half of the twentieth century—the transition between Booker T. Washington and Martin Luther King, Jr. Infused with Washington's self-help philosophy, Spaulding was the chief architect of the North Carolina Mutual Life Insurance Company, one of the most successful black business enterprises in this century. From his position as head of the company, he operated as the most influential black civic leader in Durham, serving as a symbolic model for the black middle class and as a functional link between the black community and the city's white establishment. Although always careful by temperament, as times changed he became more militant, quietly working with the National Association for the Advancement of Colored People and helping orchestrate the mobilization of Durham blacks into a cohesive and influential voting bloc.

I F Charles Clinton Spaulding—the leading black businessman of the first half of the twentieth century—had not existed, America would have invented him. The whole cloth of America's value system created him no less than if he were Poor Richard or the fabrication of a Horatio Alger novel. But Spaulding's story was better, a more functional variation of the theme, not just because it was true, but because he was black—a satisfying cultural surprise. If he, a barefoot, Negro farm boy from the piney woods of North Carolina, could make it in America, anybody could make it.

From 1900 until his death in 1952, Spaulding administered the nation's largest black business, the North Carolina Mutual Life Insurance Company. In doing so he garnered fame for himself as "Mr. Negro Business," and for his community, Durham, North Carolina, as "the Black Wall Street of America," or as E. Franklin Frazier styled it, "the Capital of the Black Middle Class." The white middle class of Durham, mostly boosters of banking and industry, adopted the Spaulding saga as its own, a prophetic fulfillment of the New South creed promising economic progress in the context of racial segregation as revealed by the prophet himself, Booker T. Washington.

But as one of Washington's "captains of industry," Spaulding was more than just a useful symbol for whites and more than just a business leader for blacks. In the judgment of his black contemporaries, he was a "race man"—a leader who believed in the combined doctrine of self-help and racial solidarity, who believed that the race stood to rise or fall on individual effort, and who believed that every personal action should meet the test of racial uplift. To be a race man was to be a public man in a special sense that private white citizens could scarcely understand; yet it was often with them in mind that the private black citizen molded his image, hoping that in the process of being a model before his own people he would destroy the racial prejudice of others. During the first half of his career, Spaulding believed that if his generation literally tended to business, the race problem would give way to the structural weight of a society that worshiped business enterprise, especially the underdogs who won success. By the 1930s Spaulding would find it possible to move from business leadership to civic leadership, a change marking not only a major transition in his personal leadership, but a change illustrating a larger transition in twentieth-century black political leadership. In any case, the race man was always a political man, and never more so than in the wake of disfranchisement when he embraced the politics of no politics. Such, of course, was the style of Washington, possibly the greatest politician in Afro-American history. Spaulding inherited the style, and even when buried in the depths of political intrigue he invariably protested, "I am a businessman, not a politician."

Spaulding also inherited a full-flowing stream of Afro-American thought that had run throughout the course of the nineteenth century, well before the emergence of Washington. The call for a positive withdrawal from the crush of white society into an organized black world, complete with a full range of separate institutions, extends back at least to the 1780s, when free Negroes in northern cities established mutual benefit societies, fraternal organizations, schools, and churches. Negro business institutions, especially insurance companies like the North Carolina Mutual, evolved out of such a tradition. Modernization transformed secret orders and fraternal lodges into secular enterprises managed by "scientific" businessmen like Spaulding—"New Negroes for a New Century," as Washington proclaimed them.

The new century also witnessed the nadir of race relations, and under such pressure the strategic withdrawal became more urgent. Black capitalism became a social movement arousing support across the spectrum of black leadership. W. E. B. Du Bois sponsored the idea behind the National Negro Business League before Washington launched it in 1900. John Hope, president of Atlanta Baptist College, champion of liberal education, and archenemy of the Tuskegee Machine, acknowledged that "we are now under the immediate sway of business, living among the so-called Anglo-Saxons who turn their conquests into their pockets. Business seems almost to be the civilization itself. Living among such a people it is not obvious that we cannot escape its most powerful motive and survive." The rhetoric of Washington's mouthpiece, the New York *Age*, was more typical: "There is commercial opportunity everywhere. Let us hammer away. The almighty dollar is the magic wand that knocks the bottom out of race prejudice and all the humbugs that fatten on it."

If there was a common denominator in Afro-American thought during the age of Washington, it was this gospel of progress. Its overweening zeal suggests a surrogate for politics and a platform to counter the racist doomsayers who predicted the extinction of the Negro race within fifty years. The black ministers of the secular gospel, Spaulding among them, turned the crude Darwinism on its head and announced that theirs was a rising race whose leaders would harness the natural law of material progress. In the Washingtonian dialectic, business was the great equalizer, with Negro entrepreneurs representing the advance guard of an ascendant bourgeoisie breaking out ahead of an oppressed peasantry in the process of apprehending industrialism, capitalism, and racism. To understand Spaulding is to understand this mission, this tangled requirement of his race and class, his elemental dual identity—an American businessman, an American Negro.

It is also necessary to understand time and place. Spaulding's lifetime (1874–1952) covered almost precisely the period between the first and second Reconstructions, a medieval epoch in modern Afro-American history, full of silent struggle. And he spent almost the whole of his adult years in a New South industrial city in an upper South state, suspended in political place and time somewhere between the rural Alabama of Booker T. Washington and the New York City of Adam Clayton Powell, Jr.

As the prototype of the self-made man, he entered this setting fresh from the countryside, his values and ethics a product of the family farm. Unlike Washington, whose Protestant ethic came at the hands of Yankee missionaries, Spaulding learned from the example of his parents. His birthplace, west of Wilmington in Columbus County, North

Carolina, was also the home of a traditional community of free Negro yeoman farmers who, like Spaulding's grandfather, had settled there in the early nineteenth century. Young Spaulding grew up on his father's farm in a puritanical environment of early risers who took immense pride in the crops and land, their homes and families, and who looked to work as the mainstay of life. His father, Benjamin McIver Spaulding, was not only a successful farmer but also a blacksmith and an artisan who forged plows and implements, built his own furniture, and contracted work from his neighbors, both black and white. He was a community patriarch who served as county sheriff during Reconstruction and ruled his immediate family of ten with a firm hand. Spaulding remembered that when he was not working with his father in the field, he was mending harness, and that all of the children helped their mother preserve food and scrub the board floors of the cabin with "soap and sand."

In 1894 Spaulding left Columbus County for Durham. There, under the tutelage of his uncle, Dr. Aaron McDuffie Moore, he worked at a succession of menial jobs and completed the equivalent of high school. In 1898 he took over the management of a cooperative Negro grocery, and it was in this capacity that his entrepreneurial talent captured the attention of Dr. Moore and John Merrick, both of whom had founded the North Carolina Mutual Life Insurance Company that same year. Neither Dr. Moore, Durham's only black physician, nor Merrick, the town's leading barber and black businessman, had time to manage the fledgling firm, which in 1900 appeared on the brink of failure.

What followed would fit the formula of America's most exuberant success literature, and often has been presented in such style. Merrick and Moore summoned Spaulding, who not only saved the flagging enterprise but built it into the unparalleled pride of black capitalism, "The World's Largest Negro Business." This was no one-man show, however, and it is more correct to portray Spaulding as a catalyst in a mixture of forces both personal and structural. As long as Merrick and Moore remained alive (Merrick died in 1919, Moore in 1923), he was never more than one-third of a famous "Triumvirate" that endured as a legend in older circles of the black bourgeoisie.

The three leaders possessed complementary qualities that proved highly functional in their New South setting, forming a matrix out of which Spaulding's leadership could develop. Merrick, the only ex-slave of the three, stood as a transition between the Old South and the New South, part aristocrat and part bourgeois. As a black barber he represented an antebellum tradition—a colored gentry serving a white elite. Like a manservant of old, he was the picture of propriety, more dignified than those he served, full of tact and nobility. But according to an oral tradition he was also full of calculation and purpose. He knew perfectly how to wear the mask; "with great poise he could tip his hat to the white man and at the same time call him a son-of-a-bitch under his breath." His "astuteness" in handling whites lent a necessary approval to the actions of the Triumvirate, especially to those of the brash, young Spaulding. And, as in the case of Spaulding, the robber barons of Durham also smiled on Merrick's astuteness as a New South businessman, with his six segregated barber shops (three for whites, three for blacks), his shrewdness in real estate speculation, and his prosperous construction of cheap housing for the waves of black workers who came to labor for the American Tobacco Company and to buy industrial insurance from the North Carolina Mutual.

Dr. Moore, on the other hand, is remembered as a man who transcended categories. He "spoke straight from the shoulder," played no roles, and approached white leaders from a posture of equality, assisted perhaps by his reputation as a physician and because he could nearly pass for white. Quietly he gave himself to his practice, to the Negro hospital he founded in 1901, to philanthropy, religion, and philosophy. Generalizations detract from his uniqueness, but he was more missionary than businessman. Like Du Bois he worried that New South materialism would corrupt the souls of black folk. His steady character brought ballast to his nephew's impetuous tendencies. Above all, Dr. Moore deepened Spaulding's commitment to his people and insured his legitimacy in the black community, a life-long legitimacy that enabled Spaulding to build an intricate political leadership precariously balanced between white power and black support.

Spaulding's intrinsic gifts were the least complicated of the Triumvirate. Biology blessed him with a quick mind and boundless energy, and he added to that an irrepressible optimism. For all black American leaders there must exist some explanation for their ability to sustain injustice and humiliation, frustration and contradiction, and yet keep themselves whole. For some, perhaps for Du Bois, James Weldon Johnson, and Martin Luther King, Jr., ideology, art, or religion explained this inner strength. For Spaulding, it was work. But for the race man, work provided more than personal salvation; it provided a social philosophy with cultural reinforcement from all sides. What was good for Spaulding was good for black America; work would uplift the race, counter stereotypes, solve the race problem. Spaulding personified the bourgeois motif of the New South. Work, thrift, enterprise, and planning could turn a benighted, spiritual people into modern, economic men—into equal Americans. Frazier, the black sociologist writing in the midst of the Harlem Renaissance, caught this theme as well as anyone: "Durham offers none of the color and creative life we find among Negroes in New York City. It is not a place where men write and dream; but a place where black men calculate and work." The head of a prominent white law firm in Durham agreed that Spaulding represented a "New Negro." Emphasizing the difference between Merrick and Spaulding, and appropriately missing the artistry of Merrick's mask, the white attorney contrasted the two as "the difference between the old-fashioned, contented Southern darkey and the new, restless, ambitious Negro. John Merrick would say 'Thank you, sir' for every fifty-cent tip that came his way." But not Spaulding. "Lean, Cassius-like, he seldom smiled. He sought no tips. All he asked of life was an open field and a fair chance. He was strictly business."

That white Durham could celebrate this new Negro as well as the old is a striking symbolic indication of what C. Vann Woodward characterized as the "divided mind of the New South," but more relevant here, it is an indication of structural forces, as well as personal forces, contributing to the rise of Spaulding and an urban black middle class. Recent studies citing the persistence of a static, plantation economy with little change in caste or class after the Civil War may fairly capture the essence of much of the New South, especially the cotton states, but the case of Durham introduces at least tension into the model. Perhaps more than any other city, Durham represented the raw, unabashed materialism of the industrial New South. Without surrounding plantations or antebellum traditions, it resembled in many ways a frontier community promising quick fortunes in the textile mills and tobacco factories rising up out of the red piedmont hills. Here a man was judged less by his past than by his ability to survive in a Darwinian struggle for success. In this struggle, Spaulding and his business partners witnessed the accumulation of one of the great American fortunes. Washington Duke, a dirt farmer, and his nouveau riche sons made no idle boast when they pledged to do for tobacco what the Rockefellers had done for oil. Not only did the industrial setting produce a white bourgeoisie, but a peripheral black bourgeoisie. Frazier observed that the city's celebrated Negro entrepreneurs "grew up with the exploitation of the New South." These black and white men on the make were, in Frazier's words, "brothers under the skin."

Such an assertion doubtless oversimplifies the subtle, functional complexity of the Triumvirate and overlooks a capacity for paternalism among the New South industrialists that would rival, indeed emulate, that of Old South planters. But Frazier did not exaggerate the mood, or what black and white leaders heralded as the "spirit" of Durham. Like Atlanta's subsequent claim that it was the city "too busy to hate," part of the Durham spirit can be written off as civic boosterism. But there was substance, too. The "whitecapping"—violent harassment—of black businessmen, which sometimes plagued parts of the deep South, would have been entirely alien to the political economy of Durham. Washington, during a visit in 1910, found Durham to have "the sanest attitude of the white people toward the black." Perhaps Washington said this about all the cities he visited, but Du Bois, two years later, wrote a piece full of lavish praise, entitled "The Upbuilding of Black Durham." Du Bois congratulated the black business community, but he also applauded the "disposition of the white citizens to say: 'Hands off—give them a chance—don't interfere.' " With the horrors of the 1906 Atlanta race riot and the fate of black shopkeepers still fresh in his memory, Du Bois wondered what "made white Durham willing to see black Durham rise without organizing mobs or secret societies to 'keep the niggers down.' " Du Bois speculated that "the high ideals of Trinity College" (Duke University) explained the difference, but more likely the explanation lay in the ideals of Tuskegee Institute and the reality of a labor-starved industrial economy.

In the pressing search for the place of ex-slaves in southern society, the white leadership of Durham was certain that Washington had found the answer. Removing Negroes from politics and employing them in segregated industries seemed a practical and humanitarian reform that would put the South at ease and at the same time arouse her economy. Blacks, for the most part, would be put to work in the tobacco factories, whites in the cotton mills. But in the early days of Durham's industrialization, the demand for workers of any color often went unrelieved, so much so that the racial division of labor yielded to a Jim Crow cotton mill that operated for over twenty years. It was this large pool of black industrial labor that explains Durham's demographic base for black business, and hence its duplicate black society and shadow bourgeoisie. The New South relationship between bourgeois elites departed from an Old South relationship between planters and servants—a relationship Durham never knew. Thus without a lingering antebellum social order, Durham experienced no institutional drag on its burgeoning economy. No aristocracy challenged Duke, and without sociological strain, Merrick could be both Duke's personal barber in the white world and Spaulding's role model in the black world. The kind of ideological conflict that found Charleston's cream of colored society resisting upstart advocates of racial solidarity had little meaning in Durham, where lineage stopped in 1870, and money bought status.

Sitting astride this social structure, white leaders looked down to see self-satisfying images of themselves managing a tractable labor force and a noncompeting black economy. It was from within this structure, this accord between capitalism and caste, that Spaulding would have to express his leadership. For whites the New South vision of an industrial economy and a biracial society represented an end, a utopian apartheid. For Spaulding it represented a means, a chance to calculate and work.

But he also dreamed. By 1912 the reality of Spaulding's business success made it tempting to interpret the dream as self-fulfilling. One black institution seemed to spring almost involuntarily from another. With the North Carolina Mutual acting as the mother institution, and Spaulding as midwife, a nascent Negro economy arrived in black Durham. Among the offspring appeared two newspapers, a drugstore, a bank, a real estate company, and a cotton mill. The Mechanics and Farmers Bank, founded in 1908, endures today as part of the legacy, but the two ephemeral newspapers, full of allegory, and co-edited by Spaulding, best summarized the race man's dream of a rising people. "Our every departure into business is a sign that we are eager to go from infancy to manhood. With such a wise determination we may safely say we are gliding out among the shoals and our view opens to a clearer, deeper sea." The vision went beyond Durham and the New South, perhaps beyond America. Such "substantial growth," testified the editor, "affords an interesting study in the history of the darker races."

By 1913 Spaulding had guided his company to achieve "old line legal reserve" status, a major milestone in the evolution of all industrial life insurance enterprises. In 1916 he decided to follow the Great Migration, and he extended the company's territory north, from the Carolinas and Georgia, to Virginia, Maryland, and the District of Columbia. By 1920 the firm had not only survived the influenza epidemic of 1918, but had expanded into virtually every southern state. And by 1924 Spaulding had inspired still another round of subordinate institutions, including a fire insurance company, a branch in Raleigh of the Mechanics and Farmers Bank, a savings and loan association, the Mortgage Company of Durham, and the National Negro Finance Corporation (NNFC). Again, he dreamed.

174

The NNFC, a visionary, all-black national clearinghouse for Negro business, symbolized a stage in the development of Spaulding's leadership, and perhaps a turning point in Afro-American thought. For a generation or more the idea of progress through Negro business had been building as a powerful myth among the black middle class who, as products of both Western civilization and racial oppression, had little choice except to believe passionately that the color blind forces of modernization would prevail. At least as early as the Chicago World's Fair in 1893, running through the Atlanta Cotton States Exposition, made famous by Booker T. Washington in 1895, to the St. Louis Exposition in 1904, the Jamestown Tercentennial in 1907, and climaxing with semicentennial "Fifty Years of Negro Progress" jubilees commemorating the Emancipation Proclamation in 1913, black leaders from all quarters had invested much of their faith and energy in the dual process of defending the integrity of the race and uplifting its condition. They celebrated all signs of racial progress, but to prove their people equal to the demands of a modern, industrial society they put a premium on technology and economics, with Negro inventors and entrepreneurs always on prominent display. Durham, the "magic city," with the completion in 1921 of the Mutual's marble-trimmed, ultramodern home office building, became the "hub in a wheel of Negro progress." More than that it became a shrine, the Mecca in the mythology, requiring a pilgrimage of its believers. In 1928 the editor of the *St. Luke Herald,* a Negro weekly in Richmond, Virginia, exhorted his bourgeois readers to go to Durham: "Go to Durham . . . you need the inspiration. Go to Durham and see Negro business with an aggregate capital of millions. Go to Durham and see twenty-two Negro men making modern history. Among your New Year's resolves, resolve to go to Durham!" Even Atlanta, the "Jewel of the New South," deferred to Durham, as did Chicago, the rising "Black Metropolis." Accordingly, nobody doubted that Durham should be the home of the NNFC. Robert Russa Moton, Washington's successor at Tuskegee, was appointed honorary president, but the management came from the Durham establishment. Everyone from Marcus Garvey to Herbert Hoover (especially Hoover, with his philosophy of cooperative capitalism) admired the idea, but the corporation scarcely got off the ground.

Ironically, a black confidence man from Kentucky had much to do with its immediate failure, but the seeds of destruction lay in the romance of black capitalism, propagated by powerful abstractions in Western culture and the singular example of Spaulding. The NNFC

175

stands as the little event in the larger event of Negro progress as mid-dle-class millenarianism. It is significant that this quixotic episode oc-curred in the 1920s, when the buoyancy of business expansion and bit-terness of postwar race relations placed an added strain on the tenuous balance between optimism and forbearance—the essence of the old black middle class. In a decade so full of material promise and racial hatred, perhaps the more likely responses were euphoria and frustra-tion. The Harlem Renaissance expressed some of this, as did the Gar-vey movement; in those cases, however, the euphoria was an expres-sion of repudiation, born out of alienation and disbelief. But at a time when "the business of America was business," Spaulding and his disci-ples tried to believe as never before. The overexpansion of the North Carolina Mutual and the grandiose plans of the NNFC testified to this belief, but after 1929 it would be more difficult to keep up the faith. Spaulding, however, did not resign his role as race man; indeed, the decanonizing of business carried him to a new level of leadership. He became less a one-dimensional symbol and more a multi-dimensional leader. The heavenly city of Negro business widened its gates, making room for civic affairs and partisan politics.

When Spaulding supported Franklin D. Roosevelt in 1932 and be-came a spokesman for the New Deal in 1933, his actions had less to do with a shift in his loyalties than a transformation in his leadership. His politics of sublimation gave way to a politics of participation. Hereto-fore, just by being a "credit to his race," Spaulding could be a race man; but in the 1930s he emerged as a racial statesman. He became what sociologist Guy Benton Johnson would later call a "neo-Washingtonian."

This evolution toward direct politics cannot be seen apart from larger changes taking place around Spaulding, nor apart from the unique institutional base that served him. Unlike many settings in New South Negro politics, Durham did not depend on churches and preachers to provide leadership. To be sure, they participated; but they did not dominate. Both the sense of moral authority and the sub-stance of community organization came more from the North Carolina Mutual and North Carolina College (North Carolina Central Univer-sity) than from the church.

By the end of the 1930s the Mutual had taken on a cultural legiti-macy that transcended Negro business. For nearly two generations the company had served as a landmark in the minds of visitors and towns-people, blacks and whites, and in the collective psyche of the commu-nity. Its mere presence evoked a compulsory response from everyone who knew its identity. As long as it stood six stories tall as a black institution in a southern town of squat warehouses and dimestores, and in the white rather than in the black business district, it commanded attention. Standing apart from the black community, uptown on Parrish Street, next door to the U.S. Post Office, so prominent, so proud, the Mutual violated what ought to be; yet it was so skillfully presented, so in tune with the white ethos, that it came to represent in the white mind a self-delusory promise of what the black community might be. The black success was made over into a white success, even a sectional success. Durham offered three glittering examples of southern achievement: Duke University, American Tobacco, and the North Carolina Mutual—three satisfying symbols of the New South.

For black Durham the company loomed from Parrish Street as a salient example of black success in the white world. Black people expected their communities to have big preachers and educators, but the "World's Largest Negro Business" and an internationally known Negro executive were beyond expectation. The Mutual gave the black population a certain psychic, if not economic, sustenance—a sense of identity, which despite class feelings, trickled down undiluted to the masses across the tracks. Doubtless, the uptown location strengthened the company's psychological impact. When Spaulding, impeccably dressed, rolled up to the white community in his Buick six mornings a week, he may have stirred resentment among his race brothers, but he stirred pride, too, and his dramatic exit upstaged the larger and more somber scene of black domestics going up to work in the white kitchens. Spaulding and his lieutenants, in contradiction to the general rule, did not set out each morning to serve the white man; instead, it appeared that they were intruding a small distance into the impenetrable mainstream. eroding the power structure, playing the white man's game in the white man's territory and winning. This, too, amounted to delusion—but an essential compensatory delusion in a world where economic success came hard, if at all, and where the need for vicarious achievement was compulsory.

Surviving the Depression added to the mystique of the Mutual, which in turn enlarged the responsibility of the race man. Since the days of Moore the rule had been that a company man must also be a community man. Historically, such a policy was implicit in the origins of the company and later explicit in its relationship with the black community's first newspaper, its hospital, library, churches, schools, recreation programs, and voluntary associations. Responsibility devolved upon Spaulding because of this heritage, and also because of the Mutual's great visibility as a plural institution with multiple functions cutting across the whole of Afro-American society. Through his leadership in this central institution of black Durham, Spaulding came to occupy a pivotal place in a mutually reinforcing power relationship between the black and white communities. To be sure, most of the power was on the white side, but Spaulding's ability to deliver favors from the white community reinforced his political power in the black community. He used this power, in turn, to bargain successfully for more patronage from the white community, thus enhancing his political power and perpetuating the cycle.

Whether he wanted to or not, Spaulding frequently found himself in a position to determine who in the black community found employment, who qualified for credit, who received welfare, who paid fines, and who escaped a sentence to the road gang or maybe even the gas chamber. He exercised authority over the press, the sermons, the morals, the arts, relations between the races, the curriculum of schools, the appropriation and allocation of public funds, political appointments, and the vote in the black community. From Howard to Tuskegee the internal affairs of black colleges often reflected his influence. A letter from him, like one from Washington a generation earlier, could win a scholarship or secure an honorary degree, a place on a board of trustees, a position on a faculty, a promotion, even a deanship or a presidency.

Because racial discrimination circumscribed the development of Afro-American institutions and leaders, those who did attain power necessarily took on plural functions and overlapping responsibilities often far removed from their nominal roles in society. In what might be described as a dialectic between the scarce and the conspicuous, individual leaders frequently assumed a vast array of responsibilities that would have been distributed more evenly throughout the black community had power and institutions not been such scarce commodities. But given this scarcity of power, any sign of influence loomed as an oasis of strength in a wilderness of black weakness, thus attracting clients and patrons, thus appearing all the more conspicuous, and so on. To the extent that this was ascribed power it could become a self-fulfilling prophecy—if the leader could achieve legitimacy in both the black and white communities. This Spaulding did; and although his power was necessarily incomplete, it was real enough. Unlike Negro principals or college presidents who depended on white legislatures, Spaulding, with his all-black constituency and autonomous institutional base, was relatively invulnerable to white economic sanctions. Moreover, much of his leadership had a life of its own within the black community, purposely invisible to whites. Pragmatically, he established himself in a strategic position that enabled him to act as a broker of patronage and philanthropy, as a racial ombudsman, and something of a community patriarch.

Nowhere was his broad jurisdiction more evident than in his relationship with the church. He took his Baptist religion seriously, to say the least. The sacred and the secular became an indistinguishable whole in which God's purpose was his purpose, and the proof of the unity was the success of the company. Anthropologists might argue that the spiritual and the secular have traditionally commingled in Afro-American culture, but Spaulding simply brought a renewed vitality to the Protestant ethic, with business and racial uplift as his combined calling. He was unconscious of any conflict in admonishing his insurance agents to use the church as their "most powerful contact" or in his regular five-dollar offerings to ministers in exchange for sermons on "Business Cooperation."

Black Baptists in Durham took it for granted that he would dominate their leading institution, the White Rock Baptist Church. White Rock, one of the most prestigious black churches in the South, bore a relationship to Spaulding not so different from that of the North Carolina Mutual. Under his direction, the Mutual financed the church; it also did the hiring and firing. With his contacts and the congregation's wealth, White Rock attracted the nation's finest black clergymen, many of whom chafed under company control and soon departed. One minister who probably would not have stayed long, had he gotten the call, was young Adam Clayton Powell, who in 1932 preached a trial sermon as a candidate for the empty pulpit. Spaulding left it to the older women of the church to declare, "That boy is too sporty for White Rock." Instead of Powell, Spaulding and the deacons chose Miles Mark Fisher, the son of another famous Baptist minister, Elijah Fisher, pastor of Mt. Olivet Church in Chicago. Fisher, a remarkable combination of higher education and old-time religion, held a divinity degree as well as a Ph.D. degree in history from the University of Chicago, where he wrote his prize-winning publication, *Negro Slave Songs in the United States.* Fisher had grown up under the spell of Chicago's black progressives—the elder Fisher, R. R. Wright, and Ida Wells-Barnett among them—and with Spaulding's blessing he carried their social gospel to Durham. In fact, Fisher's compassion for the poor and respect for folk culture brought out Spaulding's best instincts, encouraging his natural common touch and reinforcing his legitimacy among the masses.

With the Mutual often paying the piper in supporting other black institutions, Spaulding just as often called the tune. Lincoln Hospital, as much as White Rock Church, fell under his influence. If he was chairman of the board of deacons of the one, he was chairman of the board of trustees of the other. At times he must have appeared sovereign to those looking up through the institutional pyramid. For example, from his office at the Mutual he could write a letter as president of the Mechanics and Farmers Bank to Lincoln Hospital, where in his capacity as trustee he could unilaterally attach the salary of a resident physician who neglected his note at the bank. Or when evidence surfaced that a Lincoln Hospital official had accepted kickbacks for every corpse delivered to a certain undertaker, the hospital looked to Spaulding for discipline, not so much as trustee, but as the respected community leader, the moral chieftain entrusted to rule over an extended family within an informal system of subcommunity justice designed to seclude black errors from public view and to avoid the uncertainties of the larger system.

The Negro press in Durham met Spaulding on something closer to equal terms than did the hospital. Like Lincoln Hospital, the *Carolina Times* was often indebted to the Mutual, but the singular character of its editor, Louis Austin, made it a relatively independent institution. Austin proudly wore the label of town radical, earning him recognition in the white community as "that nigger communist from Massachusetts." Despite the difference in their political styles, or perhaps because of it, Spaulding and Austin had great respect for one another. Indeed, they functioned well as a team, one rocking the boat, the other stabilizing it, their reciprocal actions maintaining movement without upheaval. Together they pressured the city government to hire black policemen; registered black voters; battled against vice and the numbers racket; campaigned for sanitation, parks, and paved streets; petitioned the school board to adopt Carter G. Woodson's textbook in Negro history; and generally cooperated, sometimes in secret, to work for the welfare of the community. Spaulding occasionally asked Austin to tone down his editorials, and in justifying loans to Austin he told his board of directors that such assistance was necessary "to have a paper we can control." But outright control of the press never fit Spaulding's style. Instead, he needed a radical front to afford him greater mobility and safety in exploring a moderate position behind the lines; like

Washington, he needed a forum to his left, where he could anonymously present information for the purpose of protest. Austin understood this as well as Spaulding; moreover, they saw eye to eye on racial solidarity in support of black institutions. Austin, more than Fisher, lent Spaulding invaluable legitimacy with the black working class.

If the relationship between Spaulding and the *Carolina Times* was complementary, the relationship between Spaulding and North Carolina College was a close collaboration in the politics of Negro education that is little known or appreciated. James E. Shepard, founder and president of the college, shared with Spaulding the poignant consciousness of race men building their black institutions from the ground up against great odds on the dangerous frontiers of the New South. In retrospect Shepard's achievement was probably more difficult. He established his school in 1910 and by 1914 had lobbied to make it the first publicly supported black liberal arts college in the South, a nearly impossible task, considering the white resistance to liberal education for blacks. That the college survived and later opened graduate and law schools is a further tribute to Shepard's adroitness, but another part of the credit belongs to Spaulding.

In Shepard's view he and Spaulding working as a team, "standing each for the other," could be well nigh "invincible," especially at appropriations time. Ostensibly detached from the college and independent of white money, Spaulding operated as the front man of the team, Shepard's star witness at the legislative hearings. In white circles Spaulding's name added respect to any black cause, and he never failed to make a commanding appearance. Trim and poised, flawless in his banker's clothing, his rich brown skin set off with gold-rimmed spectacles and a crown of snow-white hair, always businesslike, and well armed with facts and figures, he knew precisely how far to point up injustice without appearing to be on the attack. Yet he never retreated to sycophancy. In dealing with powerful whites Spaulding probably could have taken lessons from the dexterous Shepard, but his position as businessman gave him advantages that may have made him the senior partner in the relationship—even to the extent of selecting Shepard's successor. The New South, after all, was full of Negro college presidents, but not world-famous black business executives. Thus Spaulding could command a larger hearing, especially in a section of the South, where business enterprise had displaced cotton as king.

By the 1940s Spaulding's "conspicuous" leadership had fed on itself until it had outgrown any proportionate relationship with "scarcity." He had become a public figure, even a media figure, and eventually he was spread too thin. He found his way into J. A. Rogers's *Great Men of Color* and Langston Hughes's *Famous Negroes*. Through black newspapers, he could issue press releases at will; white leaders gave him access to the radio waves, including a broadcast in 1939 from the New York World's Fair. He spent much of his time answering fan mail, especially in the 1940s after *Ebony, Reader's Digest,* and the *Saturday Evening Post* spread his story throughout America. The need for heroes sometimes blurred the distinction between him and Frederick Douglass. Schoolchildren wrote poems about him; black townspeople named their schools and streets after him.

Spaulding did not retreat before the limelight; after all, had not Washington predicted that universal recognition would follow economic achievement? He had no idea, however, that the publicity would make him a veritable caretaker for the race. He became all things to all black people: wealthy philanthropist, moral philosopher, financial and legal adviser, social worker, employment agent, labor mediator, child psychologist, and father confessor. "You are what keeps our heads up when we don't do enough to help ourselves," a black women acknowledged. Whites, too, assumed that he was responsible for the race. A lady on Long Island wanted to know why she couldn't get "reputable colored help" anymore. The white department stores of Durham used him as the supreme credit reference for the black community. A new Easter outfit might depend on his approval. And from West Africa, dozens of young men asked that he send for them, pay their way through Howard University (where they knew he was trustee), and then provide employment for them at the Mutual.

Many persons never understood that as a salaried officer of a mutual insurance company, Spaulding owned no stock and acquired little wealth. Indeed, his own philanthropy was much less important than the promise of what he might stimulate from others. The legendary relationship between the Duke family and the Mutual led some to believe that Spaulding held a blank check from the Duke Endowment. Beyond this vital connection, in 1931 he became the first Negro ever elected to the board of the Slater Fund, and he also acted as a regional broker for the Rosenwald Fund. With this in mind, virtually every black college at one time or another offered him a position on its board. He served on only three: Howard University, North Carolina College, and Shaw University, but he spread his influence around, helping Mary McLeod Bethune, for example, "set in motion a rescue campaign" for Bethune Cookman College in 1937. In black Durham, the politics of philanthropy had run through the good offices of the

North Carolina Mutual since the turn of the century when Merrick, Moore, and the Duke family joined forces to build Lincoln Hospital. Spaulding, a generation later, knew exactly how to keep the money flowing. He appealed to tradition, to the "memory of fathers and grandfathers" for "yet another monument in the name of the Dukes." That he understood symbol and psychology was perhaps best revealed by his celebrated fund-raising drive in the black community for the great Gothic chapel at segregated Duke University. He knew he would collect only a pittance among the black citizens, but they and he knew that this was a necessary symbolic gesture out of which he could skillfully bargain in turn for a new library, a college auditorium, a nursing home, and a new heating plant for Lincoln Hospital. Moreover, he could then use the Duke philanthropy as a stalking horse from which he could spur contributions from Liggett and Myers.

If Spaulding provided entrée into the private sector of white money and influence with its attendant politics, he did the same in the public sector. At the onset of the Depression, the governor of North Carolina appointed him to the state Council on Unemployment and Relief. He held a similar post on President Hoover's Federal Relief Committee; thus his informal private role in Negro welfare took on official public sanction, and his image as community patriarch grew to greater proportions in the minds of destitute black citizens who carried little notes bearing his signature to the relief office.

Beyond the local level, it was the National Urban League and the New Deal, however, that captured Spaulding's energy and gave him larger political standing. The Urban League, in coordination with the federal government, appointed Spaulding national chairman of its Emergency Advisory Council, a body organized to enlist black support for the National Recovery Administration and other New Deal agencies. Although Spaulding was primarily a public relations man for the New Deal, without commensurate power to oversee or to influence its policies, he did have access to influential persons in the government through members of Roosevelt's "black cabinet," most notably Robert C. Weaver, who had once worked for Spaulding at the Mutual, and Bethune, who had a long-standing friendship with Spaulding. Through them and other contacts, including Harold Ickes and Eleanor Roosevelt, he helped southern blacks secure a token number of federal jobs, and he assisted black property owners in acquiring federal farm loans. But in dealing with discrimination in the Civilian Conservation Corps, Tennessee Valley Authority, and Works Progress Administration, he found himself thoroughly frustrated by unwieldy layers of racist bureaucracy that would not bend before his style of personal politics. His efforts earned him recognition as the leading black Democrat in North Carolina, and he turned down offers to serve on the Fair Employment Practices Commission and as minister to Liberia, but he had worked with great zeal, as was his style, for very meager results, a sobering experience for him.

In the meantime, he was also moving toward political realism and maturity in Durham, where he put on display, for later scholars at least, a political style that pragmatically coupled accommodation with protest and represented in microcosm the fitful efforts that built the bridge between the age of Booker T. Washington and the "civil rights revolution." Nowhere was this style more in evidence than in his attempt to play off the threat of integration against the recalcitrance of the state to correct the gross inequities of the Jim Crow school system. His first venture, however, proved to be a painful learning experience.

Early in 1933, two black Durham attorneys, in collaboration with the national office of the National Association for the Advancement of Colored People, launched a case to integrate the University of North Carolina. *Hocutt v. North Carolina* began with Spaulding's blessing; in fact, it was none other than Spaulding who in a letter to NAACP Executive Secretary Walter White apprised the national office of the dramatic plans for the suit and vouched for the local lawyers as "two of our active and progressive young attorneys who are approaching you with a matter that I feel is of vital importance to Negroes." However, when Thomas Hocutt actually tried to enroll at Chapel Hill, the overpowering white reaction brought such pressure on Spaulding that, in the words of Charles Houston, he "promptly ran to cover." It is tempting to suggest that Spaulding worked both sides of the street, encouraging the case behind the scenes and disavowing it in public in order to stimulated greater white support for existing black institutions. Unfortunately for the sake of intrigue, it appears that he simply got caught in the middle and then tried to extricate himself.

But he learned quickly. He readopted the case as his hostage in trying to ransom a bill from the state legislature providing out-of-state tuition grants for black students seeking graduate and professional education not available in the black colleges. Disingenuously, he advised the state superintendent of education that he was trying to "work quietly on the Hocutt situation, but now the NAACP has charge, and I am afraid our good state is going to be embarrassed." Hoping that white leaders might rush to negotiate the integration suit for the tuition bill, he sought to convince the state official that he could arrest the Hocutt case "if some arrangements are made to take care of the tuition."

Spaulding emerged from the Hocutt case considerably chastened (the case failed, as did the tuition bill), but he took on a new sophistication. The Scottsboro case and a physical assault he had suffered in a Raleigh drugstore for drinking a Coca Cola across the color line toughened his idealism. Widespread accounts of his self-defense in the drugstore also strengthened his image. And during the Hocutt proceedings, his contacts with the NAACP, especially its distinguished attorney William H. Hastie, who had Durham "agog," heightened his respect for "radicalism."

With a clearer sense of the *realpolitik,* then, he set to work with White to organize the NAACP throughout the state in the fight for equal salaries for black teachers. He sent White funds and asked him to use the money to dispatch NAACP organizers to North Carolina. Simultaneously, he went into his "frightening act" and alerted the state superintendent that "serious threats are being made to organize an active branch of the NAACP in this state, and nobody wants that!" Spaulding knew what he was doing this time. He lay in the background, stroking the big whites, while his lieutenants marshaled the resources of the North Carolina Mutual on behalf of the NAACP. The vast agency network of the Mutual proved to be the perfect instrument for organizing the NAACP, but for the moment this was to be the only achievement. The state legislature, with the masses of blacks still disfranchised, could not be moved by a lobby of the black elite.

Spaulding had no choice but to recognize the limitations of his political style, especially at the state and federal levels, and he joined his more aggressive colleagues in Durham in the judgment that "a voteless people is a hopeless people." The political ground shifted beneath him during the 1930s, and he merely shifted with it, shielded by a growing body of white liberals and black "radicals." He ran to catch his people, realizing the need for direct politics, and not to be outdistanced he took his place at the head of the most significant political movement in the history of black Durham: the Durham Committee on Negro Affairs (DCNA).

The DCNA, organized in 1935, openly asserted that it planned to put political power in the hands of black people. The committee remains today the most important political force in the Durham black community, and as an Afro-American institution it anticipated by as much as twenty-five years the pattern of Negro politics and community organization in the New South. According to political scientist Everett Carll Ladd, Jr., the DCNA became the South's most effective "peak organization," that is, a single organization that embraced what often stood as three separate movements: economic welfare, civil rights, and electoral politics—a kind of Urban League, NAACP, and non-partisan political machine in one.

Parrish Street easily dominated the DCNA, commanding a majority on an executive committee that had Spaulding as its chairman. The intent, however, was to build a coalition; thus Austin served on the executive committee, as did Shepard. Austin, typically ahead of his times, had tried to organize a similar movement in the 1920s, but perhaps the most important precondition for the DCNA was a growing tendency of the state Democratic party to acquiesce in reenfranchisement. So close was the 1928 Senate race between Furnifold Simmons and Josiah W. Bailey that North Carolina Democrats, who had never rigidly enforced the white primary and had outlawed the poll tax in 1920, began openly to buy black votes, particularly in piedmont cities like Durham, where white majorities offset the fear of "Negro rule." For a righteous Spaulding and a radical Austin, a corrupt, white-owned black vote was worse than no vote at all, and on this common ground they could build a coalition to salvage and extend the gains in registration.

Endorsement of candidates as well as voter registration became the principal activities of the DCNA in its effort to educate the community and to build an independent political force. Endorsement often amounted to an edict of the executive committee distributed to the black community on election eve or printed in the *Carolina Times*. White candidates took the endorsement seriously, appearing in person before the committee, because they knew the DCNA could deliver the Negro vote with "extraordinary efficiency." Doubtless the key function of Spaulding's leadership was to lend such broad respectability to the DCNA so as neither to plant the kiss of death on white candidates nor to lose the trust and discipline of black voters. Obviously white Democrats would never bargain with the DCNA if its endorsement cost them white votes, and blacks would never support the DCNA if its leadership appeared too conservative.

The success of the DCNA in voter registration, turnout, and cohesion has been well reported by social scientists, but the larger historical significance would seem to lie in this early passage from one era of southern politics to another. And there is little doubt that Spaulding and his institutional resources made that passage possible. Behind this assumption one acknowledges the important hypothesis that if whites make up two-thirds of a local population, they will not rise up in terror and crush the fetal signs of black political development; nonetheless, among the dozens of communities in the upper South demographically similar to Durham, none gave birth to anything like the DCNA. Working within this golden mean of permissible black power, Spaulding functioned as the catalyst in the conversion from the old politics of abstinence to the new politics of reenfranchisment. He also worked within an institutional base that gave him enormous support and unique advantages. For the first fifty years of its history, the North Carolina Mutual and its offspring drew their executives from the ranks of the underemployed Talented Tenth. Among the administrators one could find ex-politicians, writers, orators, lawyers, college presidents, professors, physicians, and preachers—creative talent for community organization. One of Spaulding's skills was to surround himself with able colleagues who often stood to his left and could bring moderate change under his aegis. And they had at their disposal the indispensable sinews of modern politics: money, offices, staff, printing machines, telephones, plus Spaulding's pervasive good will. Such a strong, independent, indigenous black base having local legitimacy (even sanctity) was quite unlike the northern labor unions, NAACP chapters, or Communist party movements that attempted to organize other southern Negro communities during Spaulding's lifetime.

Spaulding provided the personal transition in this process of political modernization. He moved amphibian-like between two environments—advancing with dexterity in the new land of direct politics and black protest, then retreating with grace to the ancestral home of personal politics and white patrons. Implicit in the acceptance of the new was the inevitable rejection of the old; thus in the transitional short run, Spaulding's function was to exploit the advantages of both, that is, to preserve the benefits of patron-client relationships while at the same time to represent a suffrage movement designed to replace these whimsical relationships. Under his influence the two systems comfortably overlapped, constituting perhaps a southern version of what Martin Kilson has identified as "neoclientage." Being chairman of the DCNA, for example, did not mean that Spaulding gave up his personal pleading with the governor to commute sentences or to hire more token blacks in the state government. Nor did it mean that he stopped flattering the city manager and police chief whenever a new street light appeared in the black community or whenever a white policeman showed discretion in dealing with black citizens; or that he felt it no longer necessary to send turkey, hams, and other personal gifts to city and state officials at Christmas time. On the contrary, Spaulding expanded his personal politics, much of it simply smooth public relations, and neatly complemented the operations of the DCNA. In this special New South setting he was no machine politician promising to deliver the black vote indiscriminately to the Democratic party. Rather in a long-standing institutionalized relationship with the white community, he promised, symbolically in the minds of whites, to deliver something far more important: social control.

In this connection, Spaulding described himself as a "shock absorber between the races," with the ultimate test being his ability to prevent violent contact. Apparently he could. On a summer night in 1937 when Joe Louis became the first black heavyweight boxing champion since Jack Johnson, the black citizens of Durham, like others across the nation, poured spontaneously onto the streets, expressing a mixed mood of jubilation and hostility. Symbolically black America had whipped white America, and white citizens driving through black Durham at that historic instant were stunned beyond belief to see erstwhile "well-behaved" black men racing alongside their automobiles, hurling rocks, and shouting insults. Within minutes Spaulding had mounted a running board and moved through the community, calling the celebrants by their first names and commanding them to return to their homes, lest they invite the holocaust. Realism returned as quickly as it had departed, the patriarch prevailed, and the "race riot" dissolved. This dramatic, symbolic act earned Spaulding a political fortune that he could spend for years to come.

On a formal basis, Spaulding tried to improve race relations through his leadership in the Commission on the Interracial Cooperation, an Atlanta-based human relations group founded during the violence of 1919 by a white Methodist minister, Will W. Alexander. Spaulding was easily the most important black figure in the North Carolina commission, and he played a conspicuous role in the larger commission as a member of its executive committee. Charles S. Johnson, black sociologist and later president of Fisk University, remembered that he and Spaulding were on one occasion the only *"gens d' couleur"* sitting on the high council in Atlanta. Indeed, most of Spaulding's contacts in the commission were with white southern liberals, men like Howard Odum and Guy Johnson, both distinguished sociologists at the University of North Carolina. Critics of the commission characterized its work as "sanctimonious talk," but the hundreds of interracial meetings that Spaulding attended taught him to speak more directly and to

188

challenge the subtleties of racism that he had previously taken for granted. He discovered, for example, that he could influence the language and selection of stories on blacks as reported in white newspapers. The larger significance of his interracial efforts, however, lay in the relationship between southern liberalism and the evolutionary development of his leadership. Surely he could move as fast as respectable southern white men. Under the protection of their particular liberalism he could embrace what Washington had renounced—overt politics—and still stand as an honored heir-apparent to the Tuskegean. His steady absorption of the politics to his immediate left is perhaps a test case for what Washington himself might have done. It is intriguing to imagine what Spaulding might have done had he lived after 1954.

The chances are that by 1952 he had lived out his assignment, a difficult one in Afro-American history demanding uncommon faith and endurance. Obviously he was no longer a new Negro for a new century. The black New South creed, with its belief in a bourgeoisie leading a rising people in a developing country, belonged to an earlier faith, as did the race man and the gospel of progress. Indeed, whites were beginning to preach Negro progress, while blacks voiced suspicion. Others would have to find a new passage to a newer South. In Spaulding's final years there was less and less to separate "Mr. Negro Business" from the business world at large. For whites his symbolism assumed renewed prominence during the Cold War as counterpropaganda to Communism. For blacks he would continue to symbolize "achievement against the odds." For Afro-American history he symbolized an era.

His leadership illustrates one of the inner stories of those often invisible years suspended between the two reconstructions. He represented a middle range of leadership—bishops, editors, college presidents, government functionaries, and fellow businessmen—who quietly dominated the interregnum between Booker T. Washington and Martin Luther King, Jr. Between the A. Philip Randolphs and the Paul Robesons on the one hand, and the small-time puppets on the other hand, stood the Mary McLeod Bethunes and the C. C. Spauldings, men and women practicing the "art of the possible," believing that faith and work along with patience and protest could carry the victory, and believing fundamentally that their moderation staved off genocide. They protested within the status quo, believing that America, despite the gravity of its sins, was still capable of redemption.

Note on Sources

Apart from Abram L. Harris's old standard *The Negro as Capitalist* (Philadelphia: American Academy of Political and Social Sciences, 1936) and my more recent *Black Business in the New South: A Social History of the North Carolina Mutual Life Insurance Company* (Urbana: University of Illinois Press, 1973), there is little scholarly literature on Spaulding. This can be explained in part by the inaccessibility of Spaulding's private papers; these voluminous papers are in the possession of the North Carolina Mutual Life Insurance Company and are not generally open to scholars. As a businessman, generally viewed as being outside the all-important tradition of Afro-American protest, Spaulding has attracted little interest from modern scholars. Much of what has been written about him belongs to an earlier tradition of laudatory writing about "builders and heroes"—notable black figures in all walks of life who were celebrated as evidence of racial progress and as role models for black children; two such examples on Spaulding are in Langston Hughes, *Famous Negro Heroes of America* (New York: Dodd Mead and Co., 1958), and Joel A. Rogers, *World's Great Men of Color* (New York: J. A. Rogers, 1947). Both sociologists and political scientists have been interested in the special character of black leadership in Durham; E. Franklin Frazier first called this to scholarly attention in his essay, "Durham: Capital of the Black Middle Class," in Alain Locke, ed., *The New Negro* (New York: Albert and Charles Boni, 1925). More recently, largely out of interest in the civil rights movement and the legacy of the DCNA, scholars have studied black leadership and political organization in Durham; the best examples are Margaret Elaine Burgess, *Negro Leadership in a Southern City* (Chapel Hill: University of North Carolina Press, 1960); Everett Carll Ladd, Jr., *Negro Political Leadership in the South* (Ithaca, N.Y.: Cornell University Press, 1966); and William R. Keech, *The Impact of Negro Voting* (Chicago: University of Chicago Press, 1968). Also for special emphasis on Durham and Spaulding's role in the politics of education, see Augustus M. Burns III, "Graduate Education for Blacks in North Carolina, 1930-1951," *Journal of Southern History,* 46 (May 1980).

Mary McLeod Bethune and the National
Youth Administration:
A Case Study of Power Relationships
in the Black Cabinet of Franklin D. Roosevelt

*Mary McLeod Bethune, who rose from poverty to become one of the
nation's most distinguished Afro-American leaders, had three different
careers: as an educator, she was the architect of Florida's Bethune-
Cookman College; as founder and president of the National Council of
Negro Women, she was a central figure in the development of the black
women's club movement; and, as a worker in politics, she was one of the
few blacks who held influential posts in the federal bureaucracy during
the administration of Franklin D. Roosevelt.*

B. Joyce Ross's essay, reprinted from the Journal of Negro History,
*deals with Bethune's career in a New Deal agency, the National Youth
Administration, and is a case study in how the members of what was
popularly dubbed the "black cabinet" functioned. While occupying the
highest posts in the federal service that blacks had had since the early
part of the century, these officeholders all served as special advisors on
Negro affairs. Among the most important of them, in addition to Bethune, were Frank Horne, a specialist in housing; William H. Hastie,
who served in various capacities, including civilian aide to the secretary
of war during the first part of World War II; and Robert C. Weaver, who
advised on housing and labor policies, and who would subsequently be
the first Negro elevated to a cabinet post when Lyndon B. Johnson made
him secretary of the Department of Housing and Urban Development.*

*While supposedly representing black interests, the members of the
"black cabinet" all found themselves working under serious constraints
imposed by membership in the federal bureaucracy. Each individual
handled this problem in his own way. Weaver, operating with great care,
proved to be the most durable of this group of officeholders; Hastie, on
the other hand, militantly resigned his post in the War Department because of the intransigent policy of discrimination and segregation that
pervaded the Army's operations. In dealing with the only woman member of this "black cabinet," Ross illuminates the problems faced by these
officials, and the limited progress they had to settle for, as they worked to
advance Negro interests in the New Deal agencies.*

Reprinted from the *Journal of Negro History* (60 [Jan. 1975]: 1–28), with permission
of the Association of Afro-American Life and History.

IN TERMS of black people's history, the New Deal primarily is important because it marked for the first time since the Reconstruction era
the revival of the principle of federal auspices of racial equality. Second, it is important because not since the Reconstruction era did Negroes enjoy such a large number of significant governmental posts on
the national, state, and local levels. Such New Deal provisions as the
Fair Employment Practices Act, ostensibly equitable consideration of
blacks under the federal housing program, and the authority and the
avowed policy of federal agencies such as the National Youth Administration to force equitable representation and participation of blacks
in even deep southern states marked the first occasion since the passage of the Thirteenth, Fourteenth, and Fifteenth amendments and
the Civil Rights Acts of the 1860s and 1870s that the federal government assumed a major portion of the responsibility for insuring the
equality of Negroes within the larger society. Indeed, the passage of
the Voting Rights Act and other federally sponsored legislation during
the 1960s has led some historians to describe the administration of
Lyndon Johnson as the "Second Reconstruction." Yet, because it was
the principle of federal auspices of racial equality which constituted the
most important facet of the civil rights movement of the Reconstruction era, the initial revival of this principle during the 1930s rather than
in the 1960s suggests that it was the New Deal which technically deserves the sobriquet "Second Reconstruction."

Nevertheless, the New Deal's application of the principle of federal
auspices of racial equality was unique among the three eras, for unlike
the Reconstruction era and the 1960s, federal auspices of racial equality during the Roosevelt administrations often enhanced the trend toward separate but equal accommodations for Negroes. On the other
hand, the bulk of the federal civil rights legislation of the 1860s and
1960s decidedly favored an integrated society; Negroes were federally
supported in their right to sit where they chose on interstate public car-
riers and to be served and seated without racial considerations in res-
taurants, theaters, and other public establishments. President Roosevelt often needed the support of the powerful southern bloc in
Congress; therefore, he did not lend the full weight of his office to
overturning southern laws and customs which had long governed the
region's race relations. Despite the lobbying of the National Association for the Advancement of Colored People and other groups, he
would not lend his personal support to anti-lynching legislation. Historians such as Charles Abrams convincingly have argued that, in the

final analysis, New Deal housing legislation actually enhanced residential segregation.[1] In the case of agencies like the National Youth Administration (NYA), the administration's policy was tacit acceptance of separate, albeit ostensibly equal, consideration of blacks in the programs of the southern and border states. Thus, the greatest shortcoming of the New Deal was its failure to link inextricably the principle of federal auspices of racial equality with the concept of a desegregated society.

Though New Deal racial stances are vital to this study, its concerns are the power and interpersonal relationships surrounding Mary McLeod Bethune,[2] one of the members of the so-called black cabinet of Franklin D. Roosevelt—that coterie of blacks including Bethune, Robert Weaver, H. A. Hunt, William Hastie, Lawrence Oxley, Frank Horne, and others who served as "advisors," "assistants," and "directors" of Negro affairs in both the myriad of New Deal relief and recovery agencies, as well as in the majority of cabinet divisions of government. Though a projected full-length study of the black cabinet is not yet completed, the basic methodological questions that will be asked of the study are instructive of the role of Bethune and other appointees of the group.

More than a dozen black New Deal appointees are loosely classified as members of the black cabinet; an in-depth study of each is neither entirely feasible nor necessary. The study will seek to focus upon eight to ten carefully selected appointees whose tenure, when viewed collectively, will reflect a wide spectrum of variables. Not all of the cabinet members served contemporaneously; indeed, it might well be argued that there were several black cabinets during Roosevelt's extensive tenure. Hence, while Bethune is an excellent representative of those individuals whose service primarily spanned the depths of the Depression and the pre–World War II period, it is also imperative to select an appointee such as Hastie, the assistant to the secretary of war for Negro Affairs, who attained prominence near the end of the Roosevelt administration and after the outbreak of hostilities. Such a comparison in time aids in determining how cabinet members' influence was affected. Such factors as the importance of Negroes to the war effort as a determinant in the comparative authority accorded black advisors in peace and war time, their relative strength during the two time periods of the major civil rights organizations, their role, if any, in enhancing the cabinet members' authority, and nuances of change over time in the social and political thought of the larger black community are significant. Meanwhile, the extent to which the respective cabinet members' personal and public philosophies reflected currents of black thought is also important.

Needless to say, it is even more important to focus upon Bethune and Weaver who did serve contemporaneously. Since all of the black cabinet members occupied top-level administrative posts, the primary perspective from which they must be studied is that of power relationships—the degree to which the individual cabinet member was able to influence the policies of his respective agency toward Negroes. It is not premature to project the conclusion that in addition to the pressure which black community groups were able to exert upon the administration, there were other major determinants. Two of these determinants were the influence that any given cabinet member could exercise over the relative authority officially and technically accorded his office within the total administrative structure of the agency, and the extra-official means available to white superiors and subordinates for circumventing or enhancing the cabinet member's official authority. A study of the latter two variables in regard to several cabinet members who served simultaneously illuminates such factors as the varying policies of the several agencies toward black affairs and the public and personal attitudes of white superiors and subordinates within each agency. Taken as a whole, such comparisons should do much toward explaining the fundamental question of why some of the black cabinet members apparently were more influential than others.

These cabinet members were appointed by federal officials rather than selected by the black community per se; the study does not accept as a foregone conclusion that they necessarily were spokesmen of the mainstream of contemporary black thought. Indeed, the forthcoming full-length study of the black cabinet will reveal that there were instances in which highly placed blacks in agencies other than the NYA were virtually publicly taken to task by the NAACP for pronouncements which the organization deemed racially conservative. Thus, a study of the interpersonal relationships among black cabinet members and their black subordinates within the respective agencies is imperative. It provides one of the most important yardsticks for measuring the extent to which the respective cabinet members were entitled to be designated as spokesmen of the mainstream of black thought during the 1930s and early 1940s. In other words, a comparison of Bethune's racial philosophy with that of black contemporaries who served as her assistants and subordinates within the NYA provides a major approach to determining whether her racial philosophy can be termed conservative, moderate, or radical.

However, this study assumes that an even more valid means of placing personal racial philosophies within a broad spectrum is the use of the official public racial stances during the period under consideration of two of the nation's black advancement organizations—the NAACP and the National Urban League. These organizations were chosen because they claimed the largest contingents of black followers during the period under consideration. Hence, to utilize a hypothetical case, if at a given time the NAACP held a position on segregation that differed significantly from the public position on this issue taken by Bethune, then this study assumes that there are reasonable grounds for suspecting that her approach to that particular issue was not representative of an appreciable, and perhaps not the major, segment of the contemporary black community.

Some of these fundamental questions are applied to Bethune's tenure as director of the NYA's Division of Negro Affairs from the division's inception in 1935 until its termination in 1943. The most important result was the failure of Bethune's division in many instances to challenge the Roosevelt administration's reluctance to demand a desegregated society.

The pertinent files show Bethune to have been a Janus-faced figure who presented a public position to biracial and white groups that often differed appreciably from her privately expressed attitudes. When addressing biracial groups, her appeals for racial equality often were couched in terms which could only be flattering to white people, while her demeanor was usually that of a supplicant whose primary approach lay in appeals to white people's consciences and sense of fair play. Her remarks in 1939, to the predominantly white NYA National Advisory Committee, a group of thirty-five civic and professional leaders appointed by President Roosevelt to formulate NYA policy, typify her public approach to biracial groups. In appealing for more blacks to be appointed to NYA state and local posts, she was quoted by the stenographer as stating that she would "like to see more of those darkies dotting around here."[3] When asked to make a few remarks at the close of the same meeting, Bethune noted: "After being down in Harlem, I'm glad to have the opportunity of being up here in the Waldorf-Astoria with you white folks. I wish more of my people could share this opportunity."[4] Extemporaneous remarks and speeches were usually profusely laced with religious homilies and southern-style analogies, of which one of her best was that of the chicken: "You white folks have long been eating the white meat of the chicken. We Negroes are now ready for some of the white meat instead of the dark meat."[5]

Nor can the general tenor of these remarks be dismissed as growing out of any initial timorousness which Bethune may have experienced as a result of occupying an important national office, for her pronouncements before the National Advisory Committee were made as late as 1939, more than four years after she had assumed office. Moreover, in light of the fact that the late 1920s and early 1930s had witnessed a protracted struggle by the NAACP, the Association for the Study of Negro Life and History,[6] and other groups to have the term Negro recognized as a proper noun, it seems fair to view Bethune's public reference to darkies as being decidedly passé in 1939.

However, the demeanor within which Bethune's public remarks were couched should not be confused with the content of her pronouncements. When her statements to the National Advisory Committee and her other public pronouncements are viewed collectively, it is apparent that despite her homespun homilies and subdued approach, she explicitly advocated a program centered in equitable representation of blacks in every level of the NYA's administration. Black youth were included in activities that prepared them for skilled, high-salaried positions in the labor market and for total equality for Negroes in every facet of the American society. Thus, the same NYA National Advisory Committee members who heard Bethune unabashedly utilize the term darkies also listened to the following mettlesome comments: "May I advise the committee that it does not matter how equipped your white supervision might be, or your white leadership, it is impossible for you to enter as sympathetically and understandingly, into the program of the Negro, as the Negro can do."[7] In the final analysis Bethune presented the public image of a woman who was so affable that even southern whites could hardly be offended by her approach, but who, at the same time, clearly expressed a vision of racial equality.

More important, the forcefulness of Bethune in her private behind-the-scenes official and interpersonal relationships with white and black administrators more than atones for her public shortcomings. As will be discussed shortly, she pragmatically accepted segregated consideration of Negroes under the NYA program and, therefore, only rarely utilized her personal and official power in demanding desegregation. The value of her tenure as NYA director of Negro Affairs was her unyielding demand, especially in her private contacts with colleagues, upon absolutely co-equal, albeit often separate, consideration of blacks.[8] A discussion of Bethune's officially designated power relationship within the NYA administrative hierarchy more appropriately belongs to a later section of this study. Suffice it to say at this point that in the wake of southern white state NYA officials' attempts to circumscribe the number of black state appointees, she stood firm, with the backing of black leaders, in demanding that white NYA national officials overrule southern administrators.[9] Indeed, it is not an exaggeration to state that her constant pressure in regard to the appointment of increasing numbers of black NYA officials on the state and local levels was perhaps her most outstanding administrative accomplishment and, in itself, justified the existence of her office and the Division of Negro Affairs. Similarly, for example, her behind-the-scenes correspondence with NYA white administrators regarding the inclusion of black youth in NYA work projects that afforded training aimed at the skilled and semiskilled positions in the job market yields the portrait of an aggressive and often outspoken woman. "It is about time," she told the NYA national director in 1937, "that white folks recognize that Negroes are human too, and will not much longer stand to be the dregs of the work force."[10] In the final analysis it would, therefore, appear that Bethune's subdued public approach probably was not an engrained part of her personality, but, rather, was a deliberate act, consciously and adeptly performed.

Perhaps historians will be left to speculate as to whether Bethune's public approach was the most advantageous for her race at that particular point in history. It is instructive that the demeanor and approach of the only other black member of the National Advisory Committee, Dr. Mordecai Johnson, the president of Howard University, was antithetical to hers. Described by one contemporary as being "extremely fair complexioned but in reality very black," Johnson presented to the advisory committee the image of an articulate, candid black representative who spoke in terms of the "right" of Negroes to equality, the "consequences" to the nation of segregating itself into two distinct races, and the validity of the "demands" which blacks advanced. Indeed, one can only imagine what thoughts must have gone through his mind when his colleague spoke at the 1939 meeting and employed the term darkies. Nevertheless, though Johnson presented a forceful public image, unlike Bethune, he was rarely obliged to test his pronouncements within the context of official or semi-official NYA power relationships. During virtually the entire existence of the NYA, one of the shortcomings of the National Advisory Committee was rooted in the fact that the preoccupation of its highly prestigious members with personal professional concerns precluded the service which they were able to render as NYA advisors. Within a year after being appointed to the committee, Johnson admitted that his duties as a university president severely circumscribed his attendance at meetings and greatly diminished even his awareness of the committee's policies and activities. In fact, it was not uncommon for him to call upon Bethune during meetings to apprise him of developments in NYA Negro activities.[11] Thus, in comparison to the director of the Division of Negro Affairs, the more publicly forceful Johnson was not a major figure within the power relationships surrounding Negro activities of the NYA. It was largely the Janus-faced Bethune who stood in the midst of the proverbial lion's den.

Bethune's racial philosophy can be closely defined through a comparison of her philosophy with that of her black subordinates within the NYA. The official administrative structure of the national NYA Division of Negro Affairs designated the major officers as Bethune in the top ranking position of director, followed by an "administrative assistant" to the director, then several stenographers and clerks. In 1937 T. Arnold Hill, an executive of the National Urban League, became an advisor to Bethune on industrial relations. This post was necessitated by the division's desire, in the wake of the resolutions of an NYA conference on the problems of the Negro, to incorporate more black youth into skilled manpower training programs and private industrial employment. Though Bethune served as the division's director during its existence, the turnover rate of her administrative assistants was high, which Bethune basically and correctly attributed to better job and salary opportunities elsewhere. The more well-known assistants included Juanita J. Saddler, a young national executive of the student division, YWCA; Horne, assistant superintendent of education in Fort Valley, Georgia; and Charles P. Browning, who was elevated to the post following his service as state director of Negro NYA affairs in Illinois (the counterpart of Bethune's position on the state level). The administrative assistants were charged with the responsibility of devising techniques for implementing the director's program, serving as liaisons between the national Division of Negro Affairs and the NYA Negro agencies on the state and local levels, and providing firsthand information to the director regarding state and local Negro activities through field trips to black projects in the several states. Thus, in terms of sheer numbers, Bethune commanded a relatively modest work force.[12]

A discussion of the philosophies of all of Bethune's assistants is not practical in a study of this length. However, Saddler[13] deserves special mention, although she served for less than two years. Saddler, aside from Bethune, probably was the most impressive administrator in the national Division of Negro Affairs during the organization's formative period. There is a possibility that she might have been a better choice than Bethune for the position of director. Bethune's official reports and her correspondence with white and black co-workers lacked depth of analysis on the programmatical problems that confronted the Division of Negro Affairs. She visited black NYA programs in every state of the union as director; her written reports were largely detailed. These reports were analytically superficial accounts of what she had seen, together with her speaking itinerary and notations regarding the group that had been her host. Her annual reports and official reports to such groups as the National Advisory Committee largely consisted of statistical and factual data, which were more descriptive than analytical. Furthermore, some of these reports, and especially those prepared during the formative period of the division, obviously were presented verbatim by Bethune from original drafts bearing Saddler's signature. Similarly, the content of her official and personal correspondence to co-workers suggests that while she clearly possessed a vision of equal participation of blacks in the NYA program, she rarely advanced commentaries on the underlying racial, economic, and social problems that governed the attainment of her goal. Nor does this preclude recognition of the fact that much of Bethune's correspondence was deliberately guarded—especially that which pertained to delicate racial matters. For example, when Ralph W. Bullock, a black southern NYA official, complained to her regarding southern white people's inequitable treatment of Negroes, she indicated that she would rather discuss the matter privately during her next visit to the South. There were also other memorable occasions on which Bethune, in the avowed interest of privacy, invited black state or local officials to visit her in Washington rather than convey her opinions in written communications.[14] In the final analysis, the files simply do not yield a clear conception of her intellectual prowess.

Among national NYA black administrators, one who wishes an astute, in-depth analysis of the formative phase of the program of Negro activities should turn to Saddler's field reports and correspondence rather than to the files of Bethune. After visiting a given area, Saddler usually proved adept at concisely and candidly analyzing the total economic, social, and political milieus of the community. Her observations regarding the impact of intergroup relations among blacks upon NYA Negro activities are perhaps the most illuminating in the NYA files. For example, she pointed out to one NYA state director that friction had developed in the conduct of Negro activities because he had afforded representation to one black religious domination on the local advisory committee but had omitted its major rival. In the case of another state she warned that the Urban League official who had been appointed to the local advisory committee was not the best representative of blacks in that area. In reports which were designed for white NYA administrators as well as for Bethune, she did not hesitate in denouncing ostensibly liberal whites in agencies such as the YWCA for deliberately seeking to control local NYA Negro activities. In a number of instances she made field trips to southern states that were openly hostile to black participation in the NYA program, and, for example, in Texas she was largely responsible for inducing the then racially conservative state director, Lyndon B. Johnson, to afford blacks representation in the administration of the program in the form of a segregated all-black Texas state advisory committee. Moreover, Saddler often advanced her ideas and conclusions directly to white national officials over her own signature.[15]

More important, Saddler questioned more candidly than any other national black NYA administrator the propriety of both the NYA's and the Roosevelt administration's position on desegregation. She expressed her ideal of integration openly and forcefully, though she often was obliged to accept much less in reality. Not only was she opposed to enforced segregation of blacks by the larger society, but she also maintained that the only grounds (particularly in reference to the NYA program) which justified Negroes voluntarily segregating themselves was when they might "have a chance for initiative and self-expression and the development of latent abilities within the group itself." Even when she discovered that whites in parts of upstate New York were attempting to control local NYA Negro activities, she agreed only reluctantly to the establishment of all-black local policy-making bodies, maintaining that "I, myself, question whether [segregation] is ever a wise step to take." Saddler perceived that federal funding of programs like NYA afforded an opening wedge for altering the South's historic racial attitudes. For example, when Johnson proved reluctant to place blacks in policy-making and supervisory positions, she suggested to him that "the fact that the Government is aiding and supporting various projects in the State [of Texas], seems to me to allow leeway for liberal and tolerant groups and individuals in the community to try to make the social patterns more just and equitable for all the people in the community." Though Saddler candidly spoke her ideal, the refusal of white

200

national NYA administrators to "press" Johnson led her to accept the "half-loaf" of a segregated Texas committee.[16]

In contrast, Bethune adopted the pragmatic position that segregation was an unfortunate reality and that while it remained a reality, Negroes must seek to insure equal, though separate, consideration. She told the National Advisory Committee in 1936: "In places where there is no need for a separate program, for Negro and white groups, we most heartily recommend the one program. And in fields where it is necessary for us to have a separate program, we most heartily recommend a separate program, taking, of course, under advisement, the necessity of the proper leadership and guidance."[17] In 1936 she advanced her philosophy even more succinctly to a conference of southern whites: "You white folks have your swimming pool if you think that best. Just give us one to enjoy too."[18] In regards to the NYA program, Bethune, in keeping with resolutions passed by several conferences of black leaders, interpreted separate but equal as meaning black supervisors for black projects; black participation in the policy-making phase of the program; and NYA activities for black youth which enhanced their training beyond traditional Negro jobs such as maids and janitors. She never waivered in her insistence upon these three principles in her private and public contacts with white and black administrators.[19]

Yet Bethune should not be harshly judged for her pragmatism, for scores of blacks who could hardly be termed conservative practiced, though without fanfare, the philosophy she openly preached. Throughout the tenure of the NYA, black leaders like the fiery Roscoe Dunjee, editor of the Oklahoma *Black Dispatch*, Dr. William Stuart Nelson, president of Dillard University in Louisiana, and Dr. Richard Grant, the president of a local Illinois branch of the NAACP, served on segregated NYA local advisory committees.[20] It should also be kept in mind that during the 1930s the NAACP, despite its idealistic integrationist position, tacitly bowed to southern segregation patterns. For example, after repeated, unsuccessful attempts to force integration of the southern school system, the organization adopted the tactic of demanding that black school facilities and teachers' salaries should be so nearly equal to those of whites that southern segregation would die from the weight of the financial expense. Thus, on what was perhaps the most important issue governing the conduct of NYA affairs, Bethune can safely be placed well within the mainstream of contemporary black thought and action.

In my opinion, the greatest shortcoming of Bethune's tenure as NYA director of Negro Affairs was that in so many instances she was forced to accept not only separate but also less than equal consideration for her people. The root of the problem was the failure of national NYA administrators, even in the wake of demands of the director of the Division of Negro Affairs and the resolutions of black conferences, to apply fully the principle of federal auspices of racial equality at the state and local levels. A discussion of the role and activities of black NYA appointees on the state and local levels cannot be taken up at length in a study of this brevity. Suffice it to say that each state director was assisted in formulating NYA activities by a state advisory committee, which the national office dictated should be composed of representatives of predesignated occupational and minority groups—labor leaders, educators, welfare workers, Negroes, and civil leaders. In addition, each city or county within each state utilized a so-called local advisory committee, originally projected by the national office to be composed of the same occupational and racial categories as the state committees. The concept of integrated committees at both levels was implicit in this structure.[21]

The first major retreat of national executives from the policy of integrated committees came in 1935, when they failed to "press" Johnson about his insistence that whites in Texas would object to an integrated state committee. Aside from the Roosevelt administration's general reluctance to breach southern law and custom, national NYA administrators deliberately sought to foster local community participation and control out of consideration of the fact that the success of the NYA program largely depended upon the financial co-sponsorship of programs by community civic groups. The perennially destitute black race harbored little power in the realm of funding on a statewide basis, especially since Negroes were concentrated in only certain sections of the cities. The result was the paralleling of the white Texas state committee by an all-black Texas state advisory committee chaired by Dr. Joseph J. Rhoads, president of Bishop College.[22]

However, by the end of 1936, a series of factors had enhanced the existence of integrated NYA state advisory committees even in the states of the Confederacy. The actual functioning of the black Texas committee demonstrated that segregated committees created a duplication of expenses. A few months after the committee had been operating, Saddler complained that the white Texas committee was supplied stenographic and other assistance but that black committee members, despite their full-time personal professions, were expected to perform even routine chores personally. Richard R. Brown, the NYA deputy administrator, concluded that duplicate financing was one of the major drawbacks of segregated committees. Second, it should be noted that as a general trend, southern states looked first toward totally white administration of even the Negro phases of the NYA program, then preferred integrated administration, and only lastly agreed to totally segregated administration. Almost all of the southern states initially delayed in appointing Negroes to state committees, and a handful, the most notable of which was Tennessee, insisted that blacks had no objections to whites representing them. Even after constant, though subtle, pressure from the national office, Mississippi attempted to avoid the issue by permitting white state government officials, rather than black civic groups, to nominate the Negro candidate. Furthermore, it was a constant complaint of Bethune and participants at black NYA conferences that even when NYA work projects were comprised entirely of black youth, most southern states insisted upon white project supervisors. Nor would any southern state permit Negroes to supervise integrated work projects.[23]

On the other hand, the majority of southern states appear to have considered affording Negroes separate and distinct administration of Negro activities an even greater evil. This contention is supported by the reluctance of all but a handful of southern states as well as some northern states to appoint black state directors of Negro activities. It was only after constant insistence by Bethune and black conference participants that national executives began, around the end of 1936, to pressure states to appoint Negro state directors because "Mrs. Bethune expects the office and Negro pressure demands it." In some states such as Alabama resistance seems to have been rooted in the intention not to provide any NYA activities whatsoever for Negroes. The fact that even after Negro state directors had been appointed the overwhelming majority enjoyed no official power and received extremely low salaries further suggests that whites did not wish to give the administration of NYA Negro activities to blacks.[24] It was undoubtedly for this reason that when national executives insisted upon Negro representation on NYA state committees, no southern state except Texas seriously pushed the idea of a parallel, all-black state advisory committee. The result was, ironically, that even die-hard southern states like Alabama, Arkansas, Mississippi, and Georgia had integrated state advisory committees, although segregated NYA activities. In the final analysis, less than a half dozen states utilized all-black state advisory committees. In the majority of these cases, such as

Oklahoma and California, the heavy geographical concentration of Negroes in certain areas, for example, Los Angeles, Oakland, and Oklahoma City, together with strong black community organization and aggressive leadership—Dunjee in Oklahoma and Augustus Hawkins and Vivian Osborne-Marsh in California—led blacks to seek voluntary control of Negro NYA activities as a reflex action to actual and potential white discrimination. The only states that were permitted by the national office not to appoint Negro state advisory committee members and Negro state directors were Wyoming, New Mexico, Vermont, and Montana, where the black percentage of the total population was infinitesimal. Some of these states appointed Indians to the state advisory committees since this racial group, rather than blacks, constituted the largest racial minority. But even in these states Negroes served on city and county local advisory committees wherever small residential pockets of blacks so warranted.[25] Consequently, though all states did not have Negro representatives on their state advisory committees, blacks were represented on at least some of the city and county local advisory committees of every state.

On the city and county levels the preferential order of segregation-integration was reversed. As has just been noted, all-black local advisory committees were common in both northern and southern states. Because the local advisory committees were expected to reflect and be knowledgeable of the problems of their particular community, the segregated residential patterns of both northern and southern cities favored all-black committees, which could relate the needs of the ghetto. There were also cases like those reported by Saddler in Buffalo, Poughkeepsie, and other sections of up-state New York in which Negroes gave up their positions on integrated local advisory committees to form segregated committees because whites deliberately sought to dominate the administration of Negro activities. Thus, both integrated and all-black local advisory committees existed simultaneously in New York, Delaware, Pennsylvania, and other northern states. Furthermore, that black community agencies—YMCAs, colleges, high schools, local branches of the Urban League, and others—financially co-sponsored many NYA projects gave blacks a major springboard for demanding administrative control of segregated neighborhood programs. Indeed, it was not at all unusual for Florida A. & M. College and Tuskegee Institute in Alabama to be given virtually complete supervision of projects that they sponsored on their campuses. NYA financial statistics demonstrate that blacks contributed more than 35 percent of the costs of NYA Negro activities on a nationwide average.

204

This is not incompatible with our earlier contention that blacks did not harbor much financial clout in demanding representation on state advisory committees, for statistics also show that their financial contributions, though commendable, constituted less than 25 percent of total community-donated funds during the existence of the NYA.[26]

Hence, the shortcoming of Bethune's insistence upon equal, albeit separate, consideration of Negroes lay not in Negroes' failure to be represented on virtually all state and local advisory committees, but rather in the overwhelming majority of states in which blacks constituted an appreciable proportion of the total population but were not accorded representation on state advisory committees in proportion to their population percentage. Though the bulk of the black population was concentrated in southern states, Negroes usually were accorded no greater representation on southern state advisory committees than in states like Iowa, Ohio, and New Hampshire, where their percentage of the state population was relatively small. Though by 1938, some states, including North Carolina, Alabama, and Florida, had at least two Negro representatives on their state committees (North Carolina had six), other states with heavy concentrations of blacks, including Tennessee, Virginia, and South Carolina, each had only one black state representative. The degree of activism of the black community appears to have been the decisive factor in each case where Negroes approached equitable representation. North Carolina Negroes skirted the state director by nominating state advisory committee members during a personal visit by Bethune. She urged their selection of national executives. In Alabama the first Negro NYA project was initiated by Negroes alone in the wake of white apathy, and Tuskegee's president, F. D. Patterson (who served as one of Alabama's state committee members) became a trusted unofficial advisor on NYA Negro Affairs to the Alabama state director. In Miami, Tampa, and Pensacola, Negroes were organized into strong local advisory committees and chose even lower echelon black NYA personnel. In Omaha and Lincoln, Nebraska, the local branches of the Urban League sustained such agitation that they were virtually solely responsible for the appointment of a black to Nebraska's state advisory committee, despite the state's relatively small black population.[27] Nevertheless, despite Bethune's warnings that "token" Negro representation was not acceptable, only in rare instances did national officials, in the absence of black community pressure, voluntarily press states to appoint more than a minimum number of Negro representatives.

It should be remembered, however, that more blacks held important governmental posts on all levels during the New Deal than during any previous period since the Reconstruction era. But whereas historians are increasingly demonstrating that black officeholding during Reconstruction largely grew out of white initiative and white expediency, an in-depth study of the NYA suggests that black officeholding during the New Deal "Second Reconstruction" essentially was rooted in the growing political, economic, and numerical strength of Negroes.

The second most important failure of Bethune's avowed aim of totally equal consideration of Negroes lay in the realm of inequitable salaries for black NYA state officials. Positions on state and local advisory committees were totally without remuneration, but the office of state director of Negro Affairs, or the assistant to the state director in charge of Negro Affairs, was a full-time salaried position. The constant insistence of Bethune and NYA conferences of blacks that this office be instituted in the states already has been noted. In North Carolina, Alabama, and a handful of other states Negro members of the state advisory committees additionally pressured state directors to establish the office. By 1940 national NYA executives had devised a number of subtle ways to force state directors to appoint a Negro director: Indiana was told that Bethune and the black community demanded the office; Mississippi was told that if it did not wish to nominate a candidate, the national office would do so; Tennessee was informed that the national office had provided special funds in the state's budget for the office and that it was expected that an appointment would soon be made. Under this pressure all but those states with very small black populations had appointed Negro directors by 1940.

However, in no northern or southern state were the Negro directors afforded salaries commensurate with white assistants or assistant directors. Indeed, a comparison of state officials' salaries on a nationwide basis reveals that on the average the pay scale for Negro assistants was more nearly commensurate with that of low-ranking district supervisors and, in some states, common project foremen. As early as 1936 Bethune warned national executives that the major technical problem in the NYA program of Negro activities was the inability to secure competent black employees because of inadequate salaries. That this situation was never remedied is borne out by the complaint as late as 1942, by Bullock, one of the nation's most outstanding southern black NYA officials, that Negroes might withdraw from the NYA program completely if southern states did not accord them more equitable pay.

The pertinent files simply do not explicitly disclose why national executives responded so decisively to demands for the institution of the office of Negro state assistant, yet displayed no similar inclination to force more equitable pay scales. Their official authority to have made such demands upon the states was not in question, for all state budgets had to be approved by the national office and were subject to revisions. One of the most plausible explanations is that national officials were not fully convinced of the importance or necessity of the office of Negro state director. Shortly after the first of these positions was instituted, Gerald Barnes, the white NYA regional director of the northeast, complained to Brown, the NYA deputy executive director, that on several occasions Bethune had referred to the new officials as directors and questioned whether Brown wished "to take it up with her." Brown skirted the issue by noting that designation of titles was "no serious matter." It is also likely that Aubrey Williams, the NYA director, harbored reservations about the Negro directors, for he questioned the existence of even the national Division of Negro Affairs on the grounds that Negroes defeated their own purposes when they drew sharp racial distinctions in programs and activities. Whatever the case, the net result was that Bethune, time after time during her tenure as director, personally approved discriminatory salaries for black state directors.[28]

Finally, the study of Bethune would not be complete without mention of her conception of her role as juxtaposed against the actual power relationship which accrued to her office and the Division of Negro Affairs. It is my conclusion that the Division of Negro Affairs, as a subunit of a larger agency, never attained the authority projected by Bethune because of (1) the NYA's failure to clarify and define the division's power relationship with other subunits of the agency or with the top echelon of the agency's administration, and (2) the extra-official means available to Bethune's subordinates and co-equals for potentially circumventing her division's authority. The net result was that the national Division of Negro Affairs never developed co-equal authority in the control of NYA Negro activities on the state and local levels, and Bethune, the division's director, never attained a power relationship with the agency's top administrative echelon beyond that of an advisor whose opinions were not officially binding.

It should be kept in mind that the NYA was a compound organization, having not only a central office in Washington, but also subordinate units in the form of state and local administration. Technically, the agency was predicated upon highly centralized authority, for although local officials were responsible to the state offices, and the state directors nominated members of the state advisory committees, the national office selected the state directors, approved or rejected nominees to the state advisory committees, formulated the budgets for the state offices, and laid down the broad parameters of the NYA activities that the state and local divisions could sponsor. It has already been suggested that the national office's desire to foster community financing and its reluctance to breach southern racial laws and customs significantly softened the national office's exercise of its full authority.

More important to the study of the Division of Negro Affairs is the fact that the national office sought to delegate authority and responsibility along geographical rather than functional lines. Geographical lines imply that the state offices handled all aspects of NYA activities and problems for a particular state, as opposed to functional delegation of authority whereby a given field office would handle, for example, only financial matters or other specific aspects of the total program of an area. Under a centralized arrangement, geographical delegation of authority almost always entails progressions of power relationships in which the lowest echelon of officials reports first to unit chiefs (in the case of NYA, the state directors) who, in turn, are responsible to the national top echelon or their designated intermediary representatives. [29]

One of the initial problems was that Bethune conceived of the national Division of Negro Affairs as exercising authority over Negro activities on all levels within a context of functional authority, although the NYA was predicated upon a geographical authority arrangement. According to Bethune's account, her division began operation in December 1935 with no clearly designated functions or procedures. After remaining in her office for two weeks without having any contacts with national executives, she unilaterally formulated a tentative outline of the division's potential work, which included the establishment of a national Negro NYA advisory committee (a projected parallel to the National Advisory Committee that was never inaugurated), the maintenance of satisfactory press relations, the compilation of files on the programs and philosophies of black organizations, and cooperation with black NYA appointees on the state and local levels. Obviously, this initial job description depicted the Division of Negro Affairs as largely a fact-finding and public relations agency and implied that it was to enjoy no significant power relationship vis à vis national executives or state directors. Bethune submitted the outline to Brown "in an endeavor to having him think with me in defining the job," but she later observed that "our interview did not net much that was definite however, in the way of establishing standards of procedures and working out relationships here and in the field." Six months later Bethune reported that still no provisions had been made with national executives regarding the role and function of the Division of Negro Affairs.[30]

Undoubtedly the limbo in which the division began operation was partially because of its establishment after the structure and program of the NYA had been formalized. President Roosevelt invited Bethune and Mordecai Johnson to represent Negroes at the White House planning conference for launching the NYA; shortly afterward, the president, in recognition of their reputations as foremost educators of black youth, appointed both of them as the two black representatives on the National Advisory Committee. However, Roosevelt initially demurred in approving a distinct Negro unit largely because of the expressed fears of southern Congressmen that such a division would usurp authority over NYA Negro Affairs on the state level. Williams initially was hesitant because of the NYA's limited budget and his personal conviction that a separate Negro division would enhance, rather than diminish, the trend toward segregation. It was only in the wake of the demands of a 1935 conference of blacks, convened to discuss the participation of Negroes in the NYA, together with the sustained contention by the NAACP that the interests of blacks in the New Deal programs could not be adequately safeguarded by even the most well-intentioned white administrators, that Roosevelt approved the establishment of a distinct NYA Division of Negro Affairs. Nevertheless, Williams candidly informed the first NYA conference of blacks to be convened after the inauguration of the division that he still was not certain that a Division of Negro Affairs was not self-defeating for the best interests of blacks.[31]

The most important consequence of the belated establishment of the Division of Negro Affairs was Bethune's concession, shortly after taking office, that because the broad parameters of the NYA program already had been formulated, the policy-making role of her division largely would be limited to "the adaptation of the [already established NYA] program to the needs of Negro people and the interpreting of the program to them." Yet she never wholly lived up to this initial statement. During her tenure as director she strongly urged national executives to approve a program of consumer education for blacks and a foundation for black crippled children similar to that at Warm Springs, Georgia, and she planned for the Division of Negro Affairs to compile studies of black workers' education councils, which were being newly debated and inaugurated by the NAACP and the Urban

League. Each of these proposed programs was outside of the realm of the NYA's project offerings; each was rejected by national officials on the grounds of inadequate funds and the fear of duplicating the work of other private and governmental agencies. A discussion of actual NYA Negro projects cannot be taken up in this study.[32] Suffice it to say that Bethune largely was confined during her tenure as director to efforts to insure equitable consideration of Negroes under the NYA program which existed at the time of her division's establishment.

It was not until 1936, after Bethune had conferred with black national leaders and NYA black state appointees, that she presented to national executives a forceful, three-point statement of the proposed power relationship between the Division of Negro Affairs and the NYA. The document, entitled "Relation of the Division of Negro Affairs to the General Program of the National Youth Association," partially was occasioned by the virtual ignoring of Bethune's division by white state officials and, to a certain extent, by national executives as well. Even where strictly Negro problems were concerned, northern and southern state directors almost always wrote directly to Williams and Brown or to the regional directors. Conversely, regional directors usually dealt with Negro problems and matters in direct consultation with national executives or state directors. Though national executives often requested Bethune's advice, there were numerous occasions on which they unilaterally dealt with Negro problems. Again, no guidelines had been established regarding the division's and the director's power relationship with national and state officials. Bethune also was informed by black state officials that because black state assistants were the subordinates of the state directors, the latter retained the authority to administer Negro programs as they saw fit, which portended discrimination, especially in the South.[33]

The document regarding the relationship of Bethune's division of the NYA was of major importance, because it called for the division to exercise authority over national Negro affairs along functional, rather than geographical, lines of administration. It requested (1) representation of the division at any meetings of the NYA national executives which concerned the division; (2) the handling of all correspondence pertaining to the Negro program "directly" by this office in cooperation with and with the approval of the deputy executive director; and (3) the referral of all complaints from Negroes (presumably on the state and local levels) "directly" to the Division of Negro Affairs, with the understanding that Bethune was to investigate and adjudicate them in consultation with national executives. In the same document Bethune set forth her main duties as interpreting the needs of blacks to NYA officials; reviewing and seeking to adjudicate Negroes' complaints; advising black state and local NYA officials; representing the NYA at all Negro conferences; and formulating new ideas and programs for black NYA activities, an aim she never realized fully.

In light of recognized principles of organization and administration this document contained both sound and unsound tenets. Bethune was correct in recognizing that no organization's divisions could be completely autonomous, because there must be at least one office—in the case of NYA, that of the executive director—which could unify command by taking ultimate responsibility. The insufficiency of her proposal is best illustrated through a comparison of the power relationship between other divisions of the NYA national office and the state offices. The predominant hierarchical line of authority seems to have favored the state director's right to channel initially all problems and complaints directly to the state office, followed by his option of referring these matters for final adjudication either directly to the executive director or directly to the division concerned. In the case of the former, the executive director's office usually either adjudicated the matter or referred it to the division immediately concerned. In other words, it was not standard procedure for employees or groups on the state level—for example, Negro officials or NYA participants in Mississippi—to bypass the state director, as Bethune was requesting, in lieu of communicating directly with a national division or the national executives of the agency.

Neither national nor state NYA officials sustained the powers that Bethune requested for her division. When the state director of Mississippi found that the Negro state assistant was communicating directly with Bethune's office, he became the first of nearly a half dozen southern state directors to complain to national executives that the state directors' authority was being circumvented. He requested reaffirmation of their immediate jurisdiction over affairs within their respective states. Nor was the controversy confined to the South. For example, the state director of Connecticut complained to national executives that confusion had resulted form Bethune's informing Connecticut's black state assistant while he was visiting her in Washington that he was entitled to a higher salary when, according to the state director, no funds for a salary increase were available. In all of these cases, national executives overruled Bethune in recognition of the fact that the NYA was structured along geographical lines of administration, and that state directors had prior authority first to review matters within their jurisdictions.[34]

Officially, therefore, Bethune had no direct relationship with Negro assistants or other black NYA officials on the state and local levels. National executives did request state directors to send her division copies of all correspondence pertaining to Negro affairs, but generally the overall absence of such correspondence in the official files of the division indicates that this request was not generally honored. Indeed, one of the most strikingly obvious features of the official files of the NYA is the relative paucity of material that comprises the files of the Division of Negro Affairs; the total of collected material for its nearly decade of existence consumes less than fifteen small boxes of correspondence and reports (out of a total of more than 1,200 file boxes for the entire NYA). Even when correspondence of the division, which is scattered throughout the general files of the agency, is taken into consideration, the division and its director appear to have amassed a total of less than thirty file boxes of material.

This dearth of material offers an important, though indirect, commentary on the extent of the division's involvement, both officially and unofficially, in Negro affairs on the state and local levels. In addition to a paucity of correspondence from white state directors to the division, there is a lack of any sustained flow of correspondence between the division and black officials on the state and local levels. For example, there is nothing in the files to suggest that most Negro state assistants regularly corresponded, either officially or unofficially, with Bethune or her division. However, Bethune repeatedly urged Negro state assistants to send her division copies of their official reports to the state directors. These fairly complete reports comprise much of the division's files. The volume of the division's correspondence with black local advisory committee members and superintendents of projects was very small; in fact, she admitted that her office did not possess a complete roster of Negro state and local advisory committee members on a nationwide basis.[35] Finally, the files indirectly indicate that Bethune bowed to state directors' prior jurisdiction over Negro affairs. Official correspondence and documents from her division in reference to Negro affairs usually were sent first to state directors for their subsequent distribution to Negro state assistants and other black state officials.

The official and extra-official functions of the NYA regional directors, together with the appointment of so-called regional Negro affairs representatives after 1940, enhanced the tendency toward geographical rather than functional lines of administration, resulting in a further bifurcation of the autonomy which the Division of Negro Affairs hoped to exercise over Negro activities on the state and local levels. In addition to state and local organizations, the NYA initially divided the country into four regions, each consisting of approximately a dozen contiguous states, which corresponded to the regions of the Works Progress Administration. The regional directors were appointed by the national NYA director to serve as liaisons with state administrators and as field representatives who could provide the national office first-hand information regarding the actual operation of state programs. Officially the regional directors had virtually no administrative powers. They were observers and coordinators with no authority over state directors or the national NYA divisions. However, from the inception of the NYA, the regional directors functioned as unofficial, semi-autonomous administrative agents of the national executives, semi-independently approving and disallowing state budgets and programs, in general consultation with their superiors.[36]

With the shift of the NYA to manpower training on the eve of World War II, the necessity of precise coordination of manpower led to the increase of the number of NYA regions and regional directors to twelve, together with the enhancement and formalization of the previous extra-official supervisory authority of the regional directors. Simultaneously, general recognition of Negroes' importance to the war effort, coupled with the pressure exerted by the NAACP, the Urban League, and other black groups, led to the appointment for the first time of black regional Negro affairs representatives. Nominated by the regional directors and approved by Bethune in consultation with national executives, the regional Negro affairs representatives usually were former state assistants of Negro activities whose experience and meritorious service as state officials easily warranted their promotions. They were subordinates of the regional directors and were charged with the responsibility of coordinating state Negro activities and advising the regional directors of the best utilization of black manpower resources. As coordinators and advisors, their opinions, like those of the Negro state assistants, were not binding upon either state directors or regional directors.[37]

The central point regarding the regional arrangement, both before and after 1940, was that this particular feature of the NYA's administrative structure afforded additional officials outside of Bethune and national executives a direct voice in Negro affairs. Sometimes, as in the case of Barnes's observations about Bethune's reference to Negro state assistants as "directors," the regional directors questioned policies of the Division of Negro Affairs. At other times, they pointed out factual errors in the information disseminated by Bethune's division. For example, Garth Akridge, director of the southern region, called to the attention of national executives in 1936 the fact that Bethune had requested additional NYA student aid funds for several black colleges, but that upon personally investigating he had found that the schools had not utilized already allocated funds. After the powers of the regional directors were increased after 1940, it became necessary for Bethune to lobby with them on behalf of blacks as much as with national executives. When Bullock, one of the most aggressive southern regional affairs representatives, complained to Bethune that the regional director could approve available funds for salary increases of blacks, but that he simply refused to do so, she proved powerless. National executives took the position that regional directors had general decision-making powers over budgetary allocations. Similarly, one of the northeastern regional directors, John N. Patterson, squashed the protests of Bethune and Philadelphia Negroes regarding NYA employment discrimination by informing her that his thorough personal investigation disclosed that there were no grounds for such charges.[38]

In the final analysis, Bethune can best be termed a coordinator and advisor on Negro affairs in the NYA throughout her tenure as director. Mordecai Johnson perhaps best summarized the meaning of her tenure during a telephone interview with the writer in July 1974. "I believe with all my heart that she sincerely worked on behalf of her people," said Johnson, "and had their best interests at heart. . . . She was not primarily an administrator; she was more a symbol of Negroes' aspirations, and she knew how to wield influence."

Notes

1. See, for example, Burke Marshall, *Federalism and Civil Rights* (New York: Columbia University Press, 1964); James C. Harvey, *Black Civil Rights during the Johnson Administration* (Jackson, Miss.: University and College Press, 1973); B. Joyce Ross, *J. E. Spingarn and the Rise of the NAACP* (New York: Atheneum, 1972); Charles Abrams, *Forbidden Neighbors: A Study of Prejudice in Housing* (New York: Harper, 1955).

2. For discussions of Bethune's rise from a poverty-stricken childhood in South Carolina to a role as advisor to presidents, see Catherine Owens Peare, *Mary McLeod Bethune* (New York: Vanguard Press, 1951), and Rackham Hold, *Mary McLeod Bethune* (Garden City, N.Y.: Doubleday, 1964).

3. Quoted in "Minutes of the Meeting of the National Advisory Committee," Aug. 1939, typescript, Files of the National Advisory Committee, Na-

tional Youth Administration Archives, National Archives, Washington, D.C., hereafter cited as the NYA Archives.

4. Ibid.

5. Bethune, "Report of Field Trip to Nebraska, Kansas, Missouri," n.d. [1937], Files of the Division of Negro Affairs, NYA Archives.

6. Carter G. Woodson (head of Association for the Study of Negro Life and History) to W. E. B. Du Bois, Aug. 4, 1927, Papers of Carter G. Woodson, Library of Congress, Washington, D.C., and James Weldon Johnson to Walter White, Apr. 13, 1933, NAACP Administrative Files, Personal Correspondence, Library of Congress.

7. Quoted in Lucy Ficklin (admin. sec., National Advisory Comm.) to Richard R. Brown, May 25, 1937, NYA Administrative Files, NYA Archives.

8. See, for example, Bethune to Aubrey Williams, June 10, 1938, copy in Files of the Division of Negro Affairs, July 12, 1938, copy in NYA Administrative Files, to Juanita J. Saddler, Feb. 3, 1936, Apr. 12, 1936, Files of the Division of Negro Affairs, NYA Archives.

9. Bethune to Brown, Jan. 12, 1936, Apr. 7, 1936, Sept. 5, 1936, NYA Administrative Files, NYA Archives; to Jesse O. Thomas (exec. sec., National Urban League), Dec. 4, 1937, Dec. 20, 1938, Files of the National Urban League, Library of Congress; Daisy Lampkin (field sec., NAACP) to Bethune, Nov. 29, 1938, NAACP Administrative Files.

10. [Bethune], "Report for the Meeting of the [National] Advisory Committee," Mar. 17, 1937; Bethune to Williams, June 10, 1937, Jan. 15, 1938, to Brown, May 12, 1936, July 3, 1937, Files of the Division of Negro Affairs, NYA Archives.

11. For a summary of the function and composition of the National Advisory Committee, see NYA, *Information Exchange*, Bulletin no. 5, Apr. 1940, File of H. Dreiser, 1941–42, NYA Archives. Membership lists, minutes of meetings of the committee, and plans of reorganization are grouped in the Administrative Files, National Advisory Committee, NYA Archives.

12. Personal background material, correspondence, and personnel data regarding the administrative assistants to Bethune are scattered throughout the Files of the Division of Negro Affairs. However, for reasons that are not clear, very little information is extant in the files on Saddler. A small amount of personal data is also found in the Administrative, Budget, and Personnel Files, all in the NYA Archives. For statements of the assistants' duties, see "Relation of the Division of Negro Affairs to the General Program of the National Youth Administration" [1936], and "Need for an Assistant for Negro Press and Public in the Division of Negro Affairs National Youth Administration" [1935], Files of the Division of Negro Affairs, NYA Archives.

13. Saddler was born in Guthrie, Okla., in 1892. In 1915 she graduated from Fisk University, Nashville, Tenn., and received a master's degree in education from Teachers College of Columbia University in 1935. Between 1920 and 1933 her principal work was with the national student department of the YWCA. Widely recognized as an integrationist, she prepared a statement on the role of student YWCAs in integration that became the basis for the national organization's interracial charter adopted in 1946. In 1933 she interrupted her work with the YWCA to become dean of women at Fisk University and was called from the post to serve as Bethune's first assistant in the Division

of Negro Affairs in 1935. In July 1936 Saddler resigned her post in the NYA, partially because of dissatisfaction with the pace of the organization's integration efforts, and returned largely to her YWCA work. Prior to her death in 1970, she organized and became executive director of the Cambridge (Mass.) Community Relations Committee, which integrated Boston nursing schools and offered other opportunities to young black women. Her last notable achievement was the operation of a pilot project for Church Women United during the 1960s in the Morningside area of New York to promote interracial and ecumenical activities among the churches of that area. New York *Times*, Jan. 13, 1970; Saddler to Bethune, June 14, 1936, to Brown, June 17, 1936, Files of the Division of Negro Affairs, NYA Archives.

14. For examples of Bethune's public statements on the NYA program, see her speech at the dedication of the center for Negro youth, Baltimore, Md., Sept. 1936; [Bethune], Statement [1937], Files of the Division of Negro Affairs; Bethune to Bullock, Dec. 3, 1941, Jan. 7, 1942, Files of the Regional Directors, NYA Archives. Cf. Saddler, Statement [Mar. 1936], with [Bethune], Statement on Need for Negro Assistants in the Division of Negro Affairs, n.d. [Apr. 1936]., Files of the Division of Negro Affairs, NYA Archives.

15. Saddler to Brown, Apr. 27, 1936 (copy), Dec. 16, 1935, Mar. 31, 1936, June 23, 1936, Mar. 28, 1936, to Bethune, July 13, 1936 (copy), Files of the Division of Negro Affairs; Saddler, "Report of Visits to Ithaca, Albany, Dutchess Junction and Buffalo, January 2–9, 1936," Administrative Correspondence Files, NYA Archives.

16. Saddler, "Report of Visits to Ithaca, Albany, Dutchess Junction and Buffalo, January 2–9, 1936"; Saddler to Johnson, Apr. 9, 1936 (copy), Administrative Correspondence Files; John J. Corson (NYA admin. asst.) to Williams, Sept. 25, 1935, Files of NYA Memorandums, 1935–38, NYA Archives.

17. "Minutes of the Meeting of the NYA National Advisory Committee," Apr. 1936, Administrative Files, NYA Archives.

18. Bethune, draft of speech in her handwriting, n.d. [1936], Files of the Division of Negro Affairs, NYA Archives.

19. See especially Bethune's remarks at the several conferences of black leaders and black NYA officials in the Files of the Division of Negro Affairs, NYA Archives. See also Bethune to Williams, May 5, 1936, July 14, 1938, to Brown, Feb. 12, 1938, Mar. 7, 1938, Administrative Correspondence Files, NYA Archives.

20. NYA of La., "Monthly Narrative Report," Mar. 1938, File of Administrative Reports; "Recommendations for NYA Advisory Committee: Winnebago County, Illinois, County District 1" [Dec. 1936], Administrative Correspondence Files; NYA of Okla., "Monthly Narrative Reports of Activities," 1937–39, File of Administrative Reports, NYA Archives.

21. Almost every aspect of state and local advisory committee composition and functions is grouped in data in the files of the National Advisory Committee, NYA Archives. Random material is scattered throughout the Administrative Correspondence Files, NYA Archives.

22. Corson to Williams, memo, Sept. 25, 1935, Files of Administrative Memorandums, NYA Archives. On the importance of community co-

sponsorship of programs, see, for example, John E. Bryan (state dir., Ala. NYA) to John Pritchard, Oct. 20, 1941, Files of the Regional Directors; "Preliminary Draft of Recommendations of the President of the United States Submitted by the National Advisory Committee," n.d. [1936], Files of the National Advisory Committee, NYA Archives.

23. See the narrative monthly reports of activities of the several states in the Administrative Reports Files. For data on Negro superintendents, see the Reports of State Directors of Negro Affairs (two boxes) in the Files of the Division of Negro Affairs, NYA Archives. See especially "Annual Report of the Division of Negro Affairs," 1938–39, ibid.; NYA of Ala., "Narrative Report of Negro Activities," Jan. 1939, State Director of Negro Affairs Reports in Files of the Division of Negro Affairs; D. B. Lasseter (state dir., Ga. NYA) to Garth Akridge (NYA regional field rep.), Feb. 28, 1938, Miscellaneous File; Bryan to Brown, July 5, 1938, Administrative, Budget, and Personnel Correspondence Files, NYA Archives.

24. For examples of pressure upon states to appoint Negro state assistants, see Gerald Barnes (northeast regional field rep.) to Thomas J. Dodd (state dir., Conn. NYA), Mar. 15, 1937; Dodd to Barnes, Mar. 19, 1937, Field Reports of Barnes in Files of Regional Directors; Brown to Robert Richey (state dir., Ind. NYA), Jan. 11, 1938, Apr. 16, 1938, Administrative, Budget, and Personnel Correspondence Files, NYA Archives. On functions and appointments of Negro state assistants, see the Reports of State Directors of Negro Affairs in Files of the Division of Negro Affairs, NYA Archives. Additional data on these officials are scattered throughout the Administrative Files, NYA Archives. See also "Negro State Reports on NYA" [Sept. 1938], Files of the Division of Negro Affairs; Corson to Gladys J. Shamp (state dir., Nebr. NYA), Sept. 19, 1935, Files of the National Advisory Committee; Bethune to Brown [Oct. 1936]; Brown to J. C. Flowers (state dir., Miss. NYA), Oct. 15, 1936, Administrative, Budget, and Personnel Correspondence Files, NYA Archives.

25. Each state's summary of Negroes on state and local advisory committees as of 1941 is found in the File of H. Dreiser (NYA admin. asst.). See also Lucy Ficklin (as field rep. of the National Advisory Committee) to Pritchard, June 30, 1941, Files of the Regional Directors, NYA Archives. It should be noted that the majority of state advisory committees in the nation rarely met as a group because state directors experienced various problems in convening them. Negro members thus rendered the greatest service (as did white members) through individual contacts with state directors and the black community. By the time the national NYA office began urging regular convening of the committees around 1940, the NYA was on the verge of termination. Circular letter signed by Williams, Dec. 1940, Files of the National Advisory Committee; Margaret M. Griffin (state dir., Nev. NYA) to Brown, Oct. 15, 1937, File of Administrative Reports; telephone conversation between Bethune and Richey, Sept. 29, 1938, Files of the Division of Negro Affairs, NYA Archives. For an example of a state with virtually no Negro activities and personnel, see Nev. NYA, "Outline for State Youth Director's Monthly Reports," Dec. 28, 1935, Administrative Reports Files, NYA Archives. The number of Negroes on state advisory committees showed a sight decrease after 1940. The national

office could not provide an adequate explanation. "Summary of National, State, and Local Advisory Committees," Oct. 1940, Files of the National Advisory Committee, NYA Archives.

26. For examples of the participation of Negroes in local programs, see NYA of Ga., "Narrative Report on NYA Work Projects," Oct. 1938; "Report of the National Youth Administration of South Carolina for September 1936," File of Administrative Reports; "Suggestions for the Activities of the Coordinator of the National Youth Administration in the Southern Area," n.d.; "Minutes of the North Carolina State Advisory Committee on Negro Affairs," Mar. 31, 1939, Files of the Division of Negro Affairs, NYA Archives.

27. For examples of black pressure for more Negro officials on the state and local levels, see Saddler to Brown, Mar. 28, 1936, Files of the Division of Negro Affairs; Statement, n.n., n.d. [1938], Files of the National Advisory Committee; NYA Conn., "Report" [1937], File of Administrative Reports; Paul G. Prayer (exec. sec., Asbury Park, N.J., Urban League) to Williams, Sept. 5, 1936, Charles W. Washington (exec. sec., Minneapolis Urban League) to C. B. Lund (NYA adm. asst.), Apr. 28, 1941, S. Vincent Owens (exec. sec., St. Paul Urban League) to Lund, Feb. 11, 1942, Raymond R. Brown (exec. sec., Omaha, Nebr., Urban League) to Williams, Sept. 25, 1942, Files of the Regional Directors, NYA Archives. For Patterson's role, see, for example, Bryan (state dir., Ala. NYA) to Richard Brown, Aug. 5, 1936; Brown to Bryan, Aug. 11, 1936, Administrative, Budget, and Personnel Correspondence Files, NYA Archives.

28. See, for example, Richey to Brown, May 9, 1938, Brown to Richey, May 12, 1938, May 16, 1938, O. H. Lull (dep. exec. dir., NYA) to Richey, Sept. 30, 1938, Brown to John Bryan, Sept. 11, 1937, Brown to Flowers, Dec. 5, 1936, Administrative, Budget, and Personnel Correspondence Files, NYA Archives.

29. See Paul C. Bartholomew, *Public Administration*, 3rd ed. (Totowa, N.J.: Littlefield, Adams and Co., 1972); Catheryn Seckler-Hudson, *Organization and Management: Theory and Practice* (Washington, D.C.: American University Press, 1955).

30. "Report Covering First Six Months of the Work of the Office of the Negro Affairs National Youth Administration" [1935–36], Files of the Division of Negro Affairs, NYA Archives.

31. Ibid.; "Minutes of Meeting of Conference of Advisory Group on Negro Questions," Aug. 8, 1935, R. R. Brown File, NYA Archives. Participants at the conference included White, NAACP; Channing Tobias, National YMCA; Johnson, president of Howard University; Robert Weaver and William Hastie, advisors in Dept. of Interior. Roosevelt to Williams, Feb. 11, 1935, Administrative Files, NYA Archives.

32. "Report Covering First Six Months of the Work of the Office of the Negro Affairs National Youth Administration" [1935–36], Files of the Division of Negro Affairs; [Bethune], "Cooperatives," Sept. 1939, Administrative Files; Bethune to Brown, memo, Oct. 8, 1936, Files of the Division of Negro Affairs, NYA Archives.

33. "Relation of the Division of Negro Affairs to the National Youth Administration" [1936], Files of the Division of Negro Affairs, NYA Archives. For examples of the flow of correspondence between white officials regarding

Negro affairs, see Barnes to Bankson T. Holcomb (state dir., Dela. NYA), Jan. 25, 1937 (copy), Barnes Field Reports in Files of the Regional Directors; William J. Campbell (state dir., Ill. NYA) to Brown, Nov. 5, 1936; Bryan to Brown, Sept. 9, 1937, Administrative, Budget, and Personnel Correspondence Files, NYA Archives. At times national executives overruled state directors on Bethune's advice. See, for example, Bethune to Brown, Nov. 11, 1936, Brown to Campbell, Nov. 17, 1936 (copy), Administrative, Budget, and Personnel Correspondence Files; record of telephone conversation between Dr. John M. Gandy and Bethune, Sept. 25, 1939, Files of the Regional Directors, NYA Archives.

34. Flowers to Brown, Feb. 9, 1937, Mar. 2, 1937, Brown to Williams, May 5, 1937, Dodd to Brown, Dec. 30, 1937, Brown to Dodd, Jan. 6, 1938, Administrative Correspondence Files, NYA Archives.

35. Bethune to Robert Brown, May 17, 1943, Files of the Regional Directors; Bethune to Brown, Sept. 3, 1936, Files of the Division of Negro Affairs, NYA Archives.

36. For the role and functions of the regional directors, see Brown to Edward L. Casey (state dir., Mass. NYA), Sept. 8, 1937, Williams to Robert K. Salyers (dep. state dir., Ky. NYA), Oct. 22, 1938, Administrative Correspondence Files, NYA Archives.

37. See especially Bullock, "A Brief Resume of the Regional Office of Negro Affairs of the National Youth Administration . . .," 1941, Files of the Regional Directors, NYA Archives. For examples of the duties and activities of regional Negro affairs representatives, see Bullock to Bethune, Apr. 29, 1942, July 2, 1941, to Pritchard, June 8, 1942, May 14, 1942, to Charles G. Lavin (state dir., Fla. NYA), Apr. 30, 1942, Robert Brown to Bethune, Jan. 13, 1943, to Wilford Frerschknecht (regional dir., Pacific states), May 31, 1943, June 25, 1943, Rufus Watson (regional Negro affairs rep., region III) to Bethune, June 8, 1943, Files of the Regional Directors, NYA Archives. For Negroes' importance to the war effort in relationship to the NYA, see, for example, "Summary of Conference on the Negro in New Jersey Defense Program," Trenton, Sept. 14, 1940; Bethune to Johnson, June 10, 1940, Harriett West (Johnson's sec.) to Bethune, June 26, 1940; "A Statement on the Negro's Participation in National Defense" [1940], Files of the Division of Negro Affairs, NYA Archives.

38. Bethune to Bullock, May 3, 1942, July 3, 1942, to Pritchard, May 1, 1941, Aug. 7, 1941, to John N. Patterson, Aug. 12, 1942, Files of the Regional Directors, NYA Archives.

Genna Rae McNeil   **10**

Charles Hamilton Houston:
Social Engineer for Civil Rights

The legal attack of the National Association for the Advancement of Colored People on disfranchisement, segregation, and mob violence had from its early years been conducted largely by distinguished white constitutional lawyers, the most important of whom argued the organization's cases before the U.S. Supreme Court. By the 1930s the maturation of a group of brilliant young black lawyers well versed in constitutional law, the growing strength of the NAACP, and the increasing respect for Negro attorneys on the part of the white-dominated courts led to a new policy, whereby the NAACP relied on a staff of black lawyers. In the forefront of this change was Harvard University–trained Charles H. Houston, the first full-time NAACP counsel. He handled a variety of cases and advised Executive Secretary Walter F. White on many other matters. Yet Houston is most noted as the chief strategist of the long-range NAACP campaign against educational discrimination that culminated, two decades later, in the celebrated Brown decision of 1954, declaring segregation in public schools unconstitutional. Though Houston had long since left the NAACP—in fact, he died before the case was heard—the decision was not only a major victory for the NAACP, but a fulfillment of Houston's vision of using the law as a tool of social engineering that could dramatically improve the legal status of Negroes in America.

O<small>N</small> M<small>AY</small> 17, 1954, the U.S. Supreme Court announced a series of decisions in which the justices declared segregation in public schools unconstitutional. These landmark cases set the stage for massive legal and extralegal attacks on segregation in every phase of the nation's life. Addressing an audience at Amherst College in April 1978, Justice Thurgood Marshall recalled that "Charlie Houston" was the "engineer of it all." Marshall spoke at length in paying homage to his former law professor, mentor, and colleague, Charles Hamilton Houston. Because few knew of Houston's contribution to civil rights but most most were well-acquainted with Marshall's important role in the 1954 cases, his assessment was telling. He explained that when *Brown* v. *Board of Education* (1954) and *Bolling* v. *Sharpe* (1954) were argued before the

Supreme Court, "there were some two dozen lawyers on the side of the Negroes fighting for their schools. . . . Of those . . . there were only two who hadn't been touched by Charlie Houston."

For over two decades, Houston taught and practiced laws, championed civil rights for black Americans, defended black workers facing unfair, racist labor policies or practices, and expounded the use of the law as an instrument of fundamental social change—"social engineering"—that would promote justice and liberty in the United States for blacks as well as whites. Houston's intellect, skill, and ingenuity during an era of racist state policies, laws, and practices, severe economic depression, and heightened class and racial conflicts all served to place him in a high position among Afro-American leaders. Among Howard University Law School students, faculty, and alumni he was the respected and inspiring "Dean Houston." Among civil rights veterans, there is a consensus that he was the first "Mr. Civil Rights"—an expert in constitutional law and a strategist and litigator in education, labor, and housing rights cases. This examination of Houston focuses on his activities as an educator, lawyer, and civil rights leader from 1929 to 1950.

Houston was born in Washington, D.C., in 1895, the grandson of former slaves and son of a lawyer and a hairdresser. He attended the District of Columbia's segregated public schools and was graduated from the excellent M Street college-preparatory high school. After earning a Bachelor of Arts degree at Amherst, he served as an officer in the American Expeditionary Forces from 1917 to 1919. These were genuinely formative years. Observing the court martial of a black officer for following orders, being adjudged unfit to command white field artillery soldiers, and having his life capriciously threatened by a lynch mob of enlisted men etched the meaning of racism on his mind. Houston left the "war to save democracy" and America's army with fiery determination. "I made up my mind that I would never get caught . . . without knowing . . . my rights, that I would study law and use my time fighting for men who could not strike back."

Houston attended Harvard Law School from September 1919 to June 1923, specializing in the study of constitutional law under the noted future Supreme Court Justice Felix Frankfurter. He absorbed much of the philosophy of "sociological jurisprudence" then in its ascendancy at Harvard under the influence of the celebrated Dean Roscoe Pound and attained the distinction of being the first black to serve on the editorial board of the *Harvard Law Review*. After winning a

222

fellowship for a year of foreign study, Houston returned to Washington in the summer of 1924, where he joined his father, William L. Houston, in private practice and accepted a professorship at Howard University's Law School.

When Houston began teaching at Howard's Law School, its curriculum was typical of most successful evening law schools, which students could attend part-time, and its alumni had distinguished themselves in various areas of law and politics. Many of them, especially in the border states, had provided the backbone of the legal work of local branches for the National Association for the Advancement of Colored People. Nonetheless, Howard's standing in the field of legal education was in jeopardy. Like all schools for part-time students, it was suspect due to a confluence of factors. Legal authorities insisted that part-time law schools were not comparable in quality to full-time institutions and ought to be improved. The American Bar Association (ABA), which excluded black lawyers from membership, had set standards that Howard University Law School could hardly meet. Howard was ineligible for membership in the Association of American Law Schools (AALS), the key agency for establishing or maintaining credibility in legal education, because it could not meet the AALS's standards for law libraries, faculty, or admissions policies.

Houston replaced the last white dean of Howard's Law School in 1929. Already, cautious steps had been taken to insure its upgrading. In 1927–28, supported by a grant from the Laura Spelman Rockefeller Memorial, Houston had undertaken a study of black lawyers. His findings revealed a striking shortage of black lawyers and, in particular, only a negligible number, in the North or South, with training and experience in constitutional law and thus equipped to handle effectively civil rights cases in the federal courts. Houston believed—and he convinced Howard University President Mordecai Johnson—that Howard should offer a fully accredited program of legal education to students attending classes on a full-time basis and that Howard's formal legal training should include preparation for civil rights litigation. Johnson, the university's first black president, was intrigued with the possibility of producing outstanding lawyers whose work could benefit the entire race. Consequently, he authorized Houston to take charge of a new program for full-time day students and a law school accreditation drive.

Under Houston the school became fully accredited by the ABA and the AALS. It was no small accomplishment, nor was it easily achieved. The requisite approvals were obtained between 1929 and 1931, in part, because Houston relished the challenge and knew how to stay on top of a variety of projects.

The law school's reorganization during Houston's leadership transformed the institution into one committed to excellence in both the study of law and in the defense of Afro-Americans' civil rights. Houston repeatedly pointed out that the future required what he was attempting to do. Already, "Howard University School of Law is performing an indispensable social function," he stressed, but the black lawyer must be especially "trained . . . [and] prepared to anticipate, guide and interpret his group's advancement." He expressed his views with an intensity that could frequently move to passion: "I believe that the race problem is one of the most fundamental problems in American life today. . . . The orderly process of the solution of this problem depends largely upon the prompt, just and efficient administration of the law." Under Houston, self-conscious racial advancement and the pursuit of full freedom and justice became central to the work of the school. In the university setting Houston developed and expounded his philosophy of "social engineering." This view that law could be used to effect social change imbued the law students and faculty as well as the civil libertarians who would participate in the decades of civil rights struggles after 1935.

Houston's philosophy was grounded in two beliefs about law: that law could be used to promote and secure fundamental social change for the betterment of society and that law was an instrument available to minority groups who were unable to achieve their rightful places in the nation through direct action. More specifically, Houston maintained that Afro-American lawyers were obliged to understand the Constitution and explore its uses, both in the solution of problems of local communities and in the improvement of conditions under which black and poor citizens lived. In 1932 he wrote that social engineering should ensure that "the course of change is . . . orderly, with a minimum of human loss and suffering." At the same time, it should also articulate the demands and expectations of the weak and oppressed.

As Houston directed the work of the law school and taught his courses, he challenged the law students to become "sentinels guarding against wrong." For the black lawyer–social engineer, Houston underscored commitment and skilled advocacy. Two of his high-ranking students readily admitted that Houston was "absolutely fair," but they recalled even more vividly that he was not one to equivocate—"a lawyer's either a social engineer or he's a parasite on society." Moreover, as the head of the law school, Houston seized every opportunity

224

to dispel myths about the inferiority of black lawyers and to use black lawyers from Howard in the cause of civil rights. He recognized the important contribution that prominent white constitutional lawyers like Moorfield Storey and Louis Marshall had made in arguing important NAACP cases before the Supreme Court until they both died in 1929, but he felt strongly that the time had come for black lawyers to play the commanding role in defending and advancing the rights of the race. Securing the accreditation for Howard University's Law School and making it a major source of black attorneys highly competent in civil rights litigation were directed toward this end. He told an NAACP national convention that, "for its greatest effectiveness," it ought to be "of the Negroes, by the Negroes . . . for all the Negroes," committing itself to a program of "intelligent leadership plus intelligent mass action." He also expressed the belief that black Americans should attempt to "unite with the 'poor white' . . . [although] the minds of both . . . have been poisoned against each other" by the ruling class that exploited both groups. Houston's view that blacks and poor whites needed to work out common objectives brought a new perspective to the work of the NAACP.

Houston's close friend and fellow Harvard Law School alumnus, William H. Hastie, underscored the magnitude of Houston's achievement at Howard when he noted, after Houston's death, that "a transformation which ordinarily requires a generation in the history of an educational institution" Houston accomplished in less than six years. All subsequent objective assessments of Howard Law School's modern growth and development reveal that the years of Houston's administration were the era during which the law school moved into a sphere of larger usefulness and national prominence. Supreme Court Justice Marshall is the most famous illustration of the lawyer that Houston's reorganization of the Howard University Law School produced.

Houston's work at the law school and his philosophy of social engineering brought him to the attention of civil rights/civil libertarian groups. In the early 1930s, on matters of due process, equal protection of the laws, lynching, voting rights, and employment security, he became a leading activist. He marched for the freedom of the "Scottsboro Boys," who were accused of raping two white women in Alabama, and he filed a brief on their behalf in the U.S. Supreme Court. On another occasion, he enlisted a Howard colleague and an alumnus to prepare a special legal memorandum arguing against lynching and for prosecution of derelict or conspiring officials under federal law.

Recognizing Houston's potential contribution beyond Washington, leaders of both the NAACP and the Communist-oriented International Labor Defense (ILD), which was at the time very active in civil rights litigation, approached Houston about greater participation in nationwide civil rights advocacy. This was also the time when many groups, including the NAACP and the ILD, were seeking ways to help the vast numbers of blacks hit by the Great Depression. It was an appeal that Houston could not resist. Houston himself, deeply concerned with the economic problems of the black working class, did not flinch from cooperating with the Communists on occasion, but he opted to work within the framework of the black-controlled, reformist NAACP, even though that organization was being widely criticized for clinging too closely to its civil rights litigation program and not concerning itself enough with the economic problems of the masses. The first case he took for the NAACP involved an indigent Virginia black, accused of murder. Although Houston lost this case in 1933, it was a landmark for the NAACP, which used it to demonstrate that a black lawyer could handle a delicate, highly emotional case in a small southern town, with the respect and even admiration of local lawyers and judges. Two years later in the case of *Hollins* v. *State of Oklahoma*, Houston established an even more important precedent. Successfully defending a black man sentenced to death for criminal assault on a white girl, Houston—in the first case in which the NAACP employed exclusively black counsel before the Supreme Court—convinced the high tribunal to overturn the conviction because blacks had been illegally excluded from the jury panel.

Soon afterward Houston obtained a leave of absence from Howard University to serve as full-time special counsel for the NAACP. This position and title he retained from July 1935 until 1940, although beginning in 1938 he handled special legal projects from his Washington firm, leaving Marshall to work from the New York headquarters. For the rest of his life Houston remained deeply involved in a wide range of litigation affecting the rights and welfare of American blacks. The most notable civil rights cases resulting from this work were in the areas of education, labor, and housing. He argued civil rights cases before the Supreme Court, and he aided in the preparation of lower court suits. Between 1939 and 1950 he was the general counsel for the Association of Colored Railway Trainmen and for the International Association of Railway Employees. For nearly a decade he represented clients seeking relief from restrictive covenants (discriminatory agreements entered into by white homeowners to prevent movement of blacks into their neighborhoods).

The man who became head of the NAACP's first permanent salaried legal department in July 1935 was imposing—over six feet tall,
roughly two hundred pounds, with features and bronze coloring that
left no doubt about his Afro-American descent. An intense gaze, a
steady baritone voice, and a confident demeanor worked together to
create an aura of authority and immense competence. Both Walter
White, the executive secretary, and Roy Wilkins, the assistant secretary, were optimistic about the man who was selected to take charge of
the NAACP's legal program and develop a legal department that
could effectively work for social change through law.

Among Houston's dozen or more legal defense inquiries in his first
year with the NAACP were critical life and death matters. A telephone call or some papers left on his desk could place him in the middle
of hearings for clients whom he had never met, but who required his
help for successful appeals. Then there were request for speeches
about the new NAACP legal program. Sometimes traveling with
White, other times with Eddie Lovett or Oliver Hill, both Howard
graduates, and occasionally alone, Houston spoke at meetings and rallies of civic bodies, teachers' associations, interracial councils, church
congregations, parents' groups, sororities, fraternities, and student organizations throughout black communities in the cities and rural areas
of the South. He logged nearly 25,000 miles for the campaign against
discrimination in education during his first year as special counsel.

Houston's reputation is undoubtedly most indelibly linked with his
role in initiating the NAACP's long-range and ultimately successful
campaign against segregation in southern public schools. Even before
Houston joined its staff, the NAACP had decided to make its attack on
this form of discrimination the central focus of its legal work. Houston
was well aware that even under the more liberal climate of the New
Deal, the conservative policies and cautious procedures of the American judicial system militated against judges entertaining an immediate
direct attack on segregation that would force them to overrule an earlier court's decision on the constitutionality of segregation. Moreover,
Houston knew that nothing in the history of the United States or the
history of the Supreme Court justified the assumption that either
would suddenly decide to promote racial equality. To secure both
equal protection under the laws and justice for Afro-Americans required a protracted struggle, which would include successive legal battles (handled by lawyers working with black communities) that would
be designed to undercut the legality of discrimination and segregation.
Rather than waiting for cases to be referred to the NAACP's national

227

office, Houston established not only a long range goal for the legal campaign—the elimination of segregation—but also limited objectives, priorities for blacks' civil rights, and criteria for suitable cases. Thereafter, Houston sought cases and test litigants that would effectively advance the NAACP's cause. Houston based the NAACP's legal strategy on his understanding of the United States, the American legal system, history, and racism. As a result the NAACP won a series of court battles that paved the way for successful attacks on the constitutionality of segregation itself.

Accordingly, Houston was careful not to move immediately against the separate-but-equal dictum, enunciated in 1896 in the case of *Plessy* v. *Ferguson*, which declared constitutional laws providing for segregation in public transportation. A carefully drawn, long-term assault on the citadel of southern school segregation was required. Houston developed a two-pronged strategy to topple the edifice of school segregation. On the one hand, the NAACP attacked the inequities, especially in teachers' salaries, that characterized the southern elementary and high school systems; on the other hand, Houston and his associates conducted litigation against the exclusion of blacks from the graduate and professional courses offered in state-owned white universities but not in the black colleges. In addition to the purely legal aspects of this work, Houston believed that the development of "a sustaining mass interest behind the program . . . along with or before litigation" was essential. Houston's message was clearly and simply expressed. If ignorance prevails among the masses of any race, they are bound to become "the tools of a small exploiting class," he explained to one gathering. And on the matter of racially segregated schools and inequities, Houston repeatedly told black Americans: "The mass of Negroes . . . are a part of the public which owns and controls the schools. . . . Both schools belong to one and the same system and the system belongs to the public."

Parents, teachers, and black community leaders in Maryland, Virginia, Tennessee, and Missouri took action to achieve equality of educational opportunities and to equalize the salaries of teachers. In Virginia and Maryland Houston consulted with local leaders and by 1936 launched a successful attack on racial discrimination in the appropriation of funds affecting black students and teachers in elementary and secondary schools. In Tennessee and Missouri the focus was on exclusion from graduate-professional public education. Interested adults and students with good academic records came forward to volunteer for court battles. As part of his overall strategy, Houston planned for

228

every situation and consequence he could anticipate, including when to accept or reject volunteers. Each case had to be measured against exacting standards, so that funds would not be expended unless there were some reasonable expectation of success on the appellate level.

As special counsel and chief legal officer of the NAACP, Houston developed test case requirements. Plaintiffs had to be "proper parties," representing "the discrimination which we desire to attack," and the situation had to represent "a sharply defined issue . . . support[able] . . . by auxiliary legal proceedings," and it should "present key discriminations," thereby furnishing "a focus or springboard for extending the attacks on a larger front."

With his eye on the Supreme Court, Houston took the situation of one Lloyd Lionel Gaines of Missouri under advisement. Gaines, a young college graduate, wanted to be a lawyer and did not want to wait until the state black institution, Lincoln University, had been voted sufficient appropriations to offer a legal education equal to that offered to white students. He therefore asked the St. Louis local chapter and the national office of the NAACP to handle his case against the white university. Using a complaint similar to a Maryland law school admissions case (in which Marshall and Houston had earlier prevailed on the state appellate level), the NAACP filed suit in 1936 on behalf of Gaines against the University of Missouri.

Houston's decision to handle the Gaines case was a tactical maneuver in the long-range plan to secure a favorable U.S. Supreme Court ruling against racial discrimination. Test cases that would systematically eviscerate the separate-but-equal principle of *Plessy* v. *Ferguson* were to be planned deliberately and prosecuted. Each case would progressively establish both a precedent for equality where segregation existed and the prerogative of the Supreme Court to determine what constituted equality consistent with the Constitution. (Concurrently, the NAACP through its magazine *Crisis* and in press releases provided interpretation of the significance of each case.) Houston targeted state-supported legal education because he reasoned that judges were qualified to compare legal education at various institutions and certainly, when they were asked to rule on the equality of law school offerings, they could not demur on the basis of lack of expertise or experience.

Everywhere Houston involved local black lawyers and community institutions in the law suits. In St. Louis Sidney Redmond and Henry Espy of the Mound City Bar Association worked on the case. The black press reported regularly on each step of the litigation, and black

229

residents attended the hearings. One of the highlights of the case was the reaction of the dean of the Missouri Law School, William Edward Masterson, who not only had a "complete lapse of memory" when Houston asked him telling question, but who also "wiggled like an earthworm" on the stand.

As Houston had anticipated, the case was lost in Missouri's Supreme Court. (An understanding of jurisdiction necessitated that lawyers present in state courts claims regarding a state's obligation to its black citizens, but rarely had southern or border states ruled in favor of blacks.) Houston, with the assistance of his former students and colleagues at Howard University—Leon Ransom, NAACP Assistant Special Counsel Marshall, and Lovett, as well as Redmond and Epsy—prepared to appeal. Houston appeared before the Supreme Court in 1938 for the oral arguments in the Gaines case. On trial was more than Gaines's individual claim. Houston challenged white supremacy as illegal, immoral, and inequitable when he made assertions about myths and biased interpretations of *Plessy* v. *Ferguson*. Was it not true that equal protection of the laws meant that if white Missourians were entitled to legal education by the state, then black citizens were entitled to legal education of the same quality? The contention was unambiguous: Missouri had denied Gaines equal protection by excluding him from the law school of the tax-supported University of Missouri for no reason other than his race; further, the university had failed to prove its out-of-state scholarships for blacks provided an equal opportunity for legal training.

Hardly had one month elapsed before the Supreme Court held that Missouri's Supreme Court had erred in denying the petitioner, Gaines, his federal rights. Chief Justice Charles Evans Hughes delivered the opinion that vindicated the NAACP's position, and he enunciated the new controlling precedent: the "obligation of the State to give the protection of equal laws" is imposed upon the state by the Constitution and must be "performed . . . within its own jurisdiction. . . . Here the petitioner's right was a personal one . . . and the State was bound to furnish him within its borders facilities for legal education substantially equal to those which the State . . . afforded for persons of the white race."

The implications of the decision were far-reaching, as the precedent inevitably extended beyond tax-supported law schools. It outlawed out-of-state scholarships and regional university programs for blacks as a means by which states might maintain segregation and shirk constitutional duties within their borders. Houston's success in the case of

Gaines ushered in a period of widespread influence among NAACP-affiliated lawyers. The results of the Gaines case also provided a basis for changes in his personal life.

Ideally Houston should have been directing legal affairs for the NAACP from its Manhattan headquarters, but in mid-1938 he had responded to other responsibilities. In order to keep the firm, Houston, Houston & Hastie, out of jeopardy while his father served as special assistant to the U.S. attorney general and his colleague Hastie served as U.S. district court judge in the Virgin Islands, Houston had moved back to Washington, D.C. From here he supervised the education cases; his protégé Marshall—elevated to co-special counsel—worked in New York City. Whatever doubts might have existed about the arrangement were quieted by the impact of the Gaines's victory and the momentum it provided. No one presented a formidable challenge to Houston's NAACP strategy, which aimed at laying a social and legal foundation for direct attacks on racial discrimination and segregation.

Though he relinquished the title "special counsel" in 1940, Houston continued to cooperate with the NAACP Legal Department and its tax-exempt arm (which was established by the NAACP in 1939), the NAACP Legal Defense and Educational Fund, Incorporated (Inc. Fund) until his death in 1950. The Inc. Fund concentrated on racial discrimination in public education, while the NAACP's own legal work was concerned with a wide variety of litigation on other civil rights matters. Under Houston's leadership as member and later chairman of the NAACP's National Legal Committee, the NAACP's policy and practice were to support and promote the activities of the Inc. Fund. Due to Houston's unusual interpersonal skills, the NAACP board and staff, its legal committee, and the Inc. Fund all worked together and in effect spoke with one voice.

Houston remained the greatly admired and heavily leaned-upon philosopher-teacher, legal strategist, and tactician. His propensity for entertaining a broad range of views regarding the civil rights struggle and for arriving at sound approaches through careful analysis and discussion was striking. Marshall himself was accustomed to writing Houston for "suggestions as to [a NAACP lawyers'] meeting . . . [and] working together between the National Legal Committee, the legal staff of the national office [Inc. Fund] and . . . branch lawyers." In the years between Houston's death and the 1954 school segregation decision, Marshall and others at the Inc. Fund continued to ask, "What would Charlie say?"

For both Houston and the NAACP the goal of complete elimination of segregation remained compelling. As Houston had expressed it initially, "Equality of education is not enough. . . . No segregation operates fairly on a minority group unless it is a dominant minority." By the late 1940s the impressive series of successful NAACP cases had turned the attack from an indirect one into a direct one. In 1947 Houston wrote in a major black newspaper that "one of the most interesting developments in the entire campaign is the change in the way the issue of segregation has been handled. . . . The NAACP lawyers in order to get the campaign underway accepted the doctrine that the state could segregate . . . provided equal accommodations were afforded. . . . Now the NAACP is making a direct, open, all-out fight against segregation. . . . There is no such thing as 'separate but equal.' . . . Segregation itself imports inequality." Gradually, however, as his health failed, he withdrew from direct participation. As he wrote one of the NAACP's chief new leaders in the campaign in 1949: "These education cases are now tight sufficiently so that anyone familiar with the course of the decisions should be able to guide the cases through. You and Thurgood can proceed without any fear of crossing any plans I might have."

Houston had been interested in the problems of the black workers, and after returning to private practice in 1938 much of his attention was given to pioneering litigation on their behalf. No philanthropist or national civil rights organization offered funds with which to fight racial discrimination and injustice in employment when Houston decided to turn his attention to labor law and inequities affecting black workers. Samuel Clark and J. A. Reynolds, members of the Association of Colored Railway Trainmen and Locomotive Firemen (ACR) of Virginia, an all-black union, had come to Houston, Houston & Hastie because of Houston's reputation with the NAACP. Clark recalled, "I wanted to go to Washington to go before Congress or anybody that I could to find out what we should do to protect our rights." The workers felt virtually helpless in the face of large racist unions, unsympathetic employers, and the new collective-bargaining procedures of the amended National Railway Labor Act of 1934. Under the law only bargaining agents chosen by the majority of members in a union could be statutory representatives in collective-bargaining negotiations. Invariably this seemed to work to the detriment of the minority black workers, since all of the railroad brotherhood excluded blacks from membership. In 1940 Houston became the general counsel for both the ACR and a sister organization, the International Association of Railway Employees

(IARE). The pace for pursuing the rights of these black railroad workers was less cautious than that of the NAACP's education campaign. Nonetheless, it was a carefully designed assault on bastions of white supremacy in the world of labor. Houston, with a young Howard law graduate, Joseph Waddy, assisting him, expressed the militancy and urgency of the workers in legal papers fashioned for judges.

In another important respect this fight differed from the campaign against discrimination in education. Minor skirmishes and battles to invalidate a particularly unfavorable precedent gradually would not be acceptable "positionary tactics." In the case of black workers' rights, a direct attack was imperative. There was virtual silence from both Congress and the Supreme Court on the issue at hand, and in the one significant precedent (*Hodges* v. *United States*, 1906) the Supreme Court had held that even though they were covered by union contract, black workers dismissed from their jobs had no federally protected rights under which they could sue. Houston summarized the situation for Clark: "You don't have any laws to protect you, but I'm going to make some laws that will."

Two primary concerns dictated how forcefully and how uncompromisingly the attack was to be launched. First, the well-being of Houston's clients and their unions had to be considered. Acts of hostility toward blacks by national unions dated back to 1863 and included the removal of blacks from upwardly mobile or steady jobs by exclusion from craft unions, secret union-management agreements, and even murder. Second, the lawyers needed to establish as soon as possible, through a test case, that there was a constitutional principle of fair representation regardless of race. Houston and Waddy sued on behalf of the ACR and IARE, articulating grievances that ranged from loss of wages, destruction of seniority rights, breach of contract, and fraud to the federal question of breach of duty under the Railway Labor Act.

Recognizing that the success and the credibility of his leadership in any battle for workers' employment rights hinged on more than legal expertise, Houston came to know the black union people and to move in their circles. The ACR and IARE were independent unions of men who operated trains—i.e., operating workers—therefore, he went to where they were meeting in their locals and on their jobs, climbing piers and examining tracks to "find out how the work was, what they had to do."

In *Steele* v. *Louisville & Nashville* and *Tunstall* v. *Brotherhood of Locomotive Firemen* (1944), Houston first clarified for the courts the relation of fairness and freedom under the Constitution to the racially discriminatory activities of railway labor unions acting under federal law. Houston planned and with the aid of Waddy and an Alabama attorney, Arthur Shores, promptly prosecuted Bester William Steele's case through the Alabama state court system while petitioning the federal court system for relief on behalf of Tom Tunstall. Carefully constructed arguments and strong records in both cases won the workers a hearing before the U.S. Supreme Court after the Alabama Supreme Court and the U.S. Court of Appeals ruled against Steele and Tunstall, respectively.

Arguing both cases before the U.S. Supreme Court, Houston declared that an agent designated under federal law as the exclusive bargaining agent had a good faith duty to the minority workers. That duty minimally included representing the minority equally with the majority, which had selected the agent, and seeking no profit for union members in the majority over the non-union or minority union members. "An opposite interpretation," Houston insisted, "would legitimize a federal law permitting the denial of equal protection and due process."

The Court's decision in December 1944 vindicating Houston's position was a signal constitutional achievement. It established a precedent for fair representation of all workers regardless of race or union affiliation. Nevertheless, Houston perceived it as no final victory. The Supreme Court extended to the men the opportunity to sue for their rights in accordance with the principle established in the cases, but the principle would have to be developed further to "make sure that [the cases] give our people real protection," Houston reported to the ACR and IARE. Moreover, consistent with his view of judges and other public officers—whom he labelled generally "servants of the class which places them in office and maintains them there"—Houston quickly reminded a friend the mass "agitation . . . over the plight of the Negro [locomotive] firemen" and "the work of the President's Committee on Fair Employment Practices . . . served as the background" for the high court's action. Subsequently Houston and Waddy handled a series of cases for railroad workers. The practical benefits of their legal victories proved limited, given the context of the times, but they were of utmost importance in establishing the precedents on which A. Philip Randolph's Brotherhood of Sleeping Car Porters and others succeeded in fashioning a body of labor law that eventually proved highly effective in breaking down barriers of discrimination by both industry and unions.

Convinced that all the questions about workers' rights and fairness "cannot be fought out in . . . courts because the courts are too slow and litigation . . . too expensive," Houston had supported the wartime Fair Employment Practices Committee (FEPC) since its inception in 1941. The FEPC had been created under pressure by Franklin D. Roosevelt's executive order in response to Randolph's threatened March on Washington during 1941. Houston's vocal and persistent advocacy of black workers' rights had led to his appointment to the FEPC by Roosevelt in February 1944. The Norfolk *Journal & Guide* reporter remarked then, "Mr. Houston's appointment, because of his militancy and ability will undoubtedly meet with . . . hearty approval from the Negro and other liberal organizations."

Hard-working, outspoken, and unyielding in his demand for fairness regardless of race, Houston personally investigated workers' complaints against corporations across the country, but especially on the West Coast. In late 1945 he became a spokesman for the committee, focusing on the problem of employment discrimination in the urban transit industry. This problem had a low priority in the view of the executive branch of the federal government, and Houston voiced his discontent. Subsequently he made public his criticism of President Harry Truman's alleged commitment to racially fair employment practices when the president's office blocked, on the basis of specious logic, the FEPC's directive to Capital Transit of the District of Columbia that it cease discriminatory hiring and promotion practices. At first evasive and finally unresponsive, White House aides flaunted their lack of respect for the FEPC and Houston during the entire transit controversy.

The refusal of Truman to meet with the FEPC, despite the committee's urgent request, compelled Houston to conclude that the president was both repudiating the committee and nullifying the executive orders that created the administrative body. In a letter to Truman, in December 1945, which received wide press coverage, Houston resigned from FEPC. Telling Truman that "the effect of your intervention in the Capital Transit case is not to eliminate the discrimination but to condone it," Houston could not see himself remaining a part of an administration marked by its "failure to enforce democratic practices and to protect minorities."

Houston had not sought greater recognition and acclaim from civil libertarian lawyers and Afro-Americans in connection with his challenges to racially discriminatory employment practices and policies, but he had gained it anyway. Although he fell out of favor with the Truman administration, Houston managed to move in and out of a presidential appointment with his militancy and integrity in tact. According to Houston, it was the duty of the lawyers to "find a way to

235

make the United State Supreme Court change" rulings that permitted denials of liberty.

It would have sounded self-serving if Houston had hinted to anyone except Henrietta, his wife of eight years, how responsible for blacks and America he felt. Sometimes he felt driven. He really believed what he so often told his Howard students and colleagues—"no tea for the feeble, no crepe for the dead." Although Houston wanted to be with his family and he was quite attached to his son, he could not be satisfied with less than superior effort in any professional undertaking, so he was often absent from his family. Getting the job done right was one of the important attributes that all of his students, colleagues, family, and friends remembered about Houston. So when Henrietta Houston heard him explain, before he left for an NAACP conference on restrictive covenants, that "the test of character is the amount of strain it can bear," she was not surprised.

The NAACP had decided upon a full-fledged attack on racially restrictive covenants, and at this planning conference Houston was undoubtedly the most respected lawyer present. Contracts that contained restrictions on the buying and selling of houses to a particular race or ethnic group were major impediments to equal housing opportunities. Since 1940 Houston had been handling restrictive covenant cases in the District of Columbia through his firm. He had spent years on strategy and tactics because he was unalterably opposed to infringements on the rights to convey property and to live in a house of one's choice in the land of one's birth.

As in the education and the employee-rights cases, there existed a negative precedent from the Supreme Court. The Court, in an NAACP-supported case, *Corrigan* v. *Buckley* (1926), had refused to rule against the practice. Now in the fall of 1947 a new NAACP-supported case, the Missouri case of *Shelley* v. *Kraemer*, had been certified for review by the Supreme Court. Houston, with his acute sense of timing, was anxious that a District of Columbia case, *Hurd* v. *Hodge*, for which he was attorney, should be considered by the Court at the same time. In the litigation concerning Houston's clients, lower court judgments had restricted the Hurds' purchase and occupancy of a covenanted house. The U.S. District Court and the U.S. Court of Appeals ruled against them. Even a motion for rehearing at the Court of Appeals level had been denied. Their attorney's last resort was to petition the U.S. Supreme Court. Timing was critical to Houston, because he was certain that the attack on this restrictive covenant would be most effective if heard in conjunction with the NAACP cases.

Working with Howard law alumnus and future judge of the U.S. Court of Appeals, Spottswood Robinson III, and a white civil libertarian attorney, Phineas Indritz, who volunteered his services without fee, Houston worked on the case in his usual intensive way. Robinson recalled that "long hours, incessant toil and meticulous attention to each element of the problem were the keys. . . . And at no time when I worked with him did I see any 'tea for the feeble.' " As they worked on the request for a hearing in the U.S. Supreme Court, Houston returned drafts to Robinson for refinement with regularity and, as Robinson remembered, Houston's "wide advice, accompanied by explanation of the analysis and synthesis forerunning it, was a revelation in itself." The three men researched and wrote painstakingly in order to show the applicability of the Fifth Amendement and the federal Civil Rights Act of 1866 to their clients' claim. Conrad Harper writes that "*Hurd*, in which Houston's richly comprehensive presentation drew on constitutional, statutory, common law, public policy and social science materials, was one of his most extensively prepared cases." The central question of the brief was also a challenge to the justices and the system of which they were a part: "Shall we in the United States have ghettoes for racial, religious and other minorities, or even exclude such minorities entirely from whole areas of our country, by a system of judicially enforced restrictions based on private prejudices and made effective through the use of government authority and power?"

As in all of his civil rights cases, Houston considered public support a necessity. He and the NAACP lawyers invited organizations interested in the battle to file briefs as friends of the court. He was most gratified, for obvious reasons, by such a brief filed by the office of the U.S. attorney general. And Houston created his own propaganda. In the *Afro-American,* he publicized the housing rights cases during 1947 and January 1948.

In oral argument before the Supreme Court, Houston called the attention of the Court to the meaninglessness of the right to own property without the right to be protected from judicially enforced discrimination. Houston stressed the racism inherent in the right his opponents claimed, discussed the legal propositions that clarified federal duty, and pointed out the record of facts pertaining to race relations. After his opponents confidently reminded the Court of its precedent in *Corrigan* v. *Buckley,* Houston forced the issue out of its private-agreement vacuum. In rebuttal he asked how such privacy could be reconciled with participation in World War II and with national security concerns. Robinson allowed that "just to watch him in action was to witness a demonstration of the way it ought to be done," as others in attendance remembered Houston exhibiting an intrepidity not frequently witnessed in the U.S. Supreme Court. To be certain that the justices understood the fundamental matter before them, Houston concluded with startling clarity, "Racism must go!"

Hurd v. *Hodge* and *Shelley* v. *Kraemer* settled the issues of judicial enforcement of restrictive covenants. Delivering opinions on both of these cases in May 1948, the justices declared such contracts unenforceable in the courts of the land. The equal protection clause of the Fourteenth Amendment prohibited such state action and the U.S. Code invalidated federal court enforcement of such agreements.

By the last years of the 1940s, Houston had enormous influence among civil rights and civil liberties proponents, but his court arguments did not reach the masses of black people as he had hoped. He was litigating education, labor, and housing cases. He was in demand throughout the United States to speak in defense of the rights of black Americans in every area of life. His legal advice was often coveted. Supporting the National Negro Congress's appeal to the United Nations, Houston told the readers of his weekly newspaper column that "discrimination and denial of human and civil rights [had] reach[ed] a national level" and the national government was not protecting black Americans against "local aggression." Houston encouraged Afro-Americans to see themselves a part of the non-white majority in a world that included Africans and Asians intent upon freeing themselves from the bonds of Western imperialism and colonialism. Regarding white America, he added, we have a "spiritual responsibility to lead . . . white United States brethren into the real fellowship of nations."

In Houston's last years, black people saw him as part of black leadership delegations in the White House protesting segregation or as a keynote speaker for rallies on the rights of blacks and he was. In 1950, when both the black and white press prominently reported his death from a heart attack, blacks of all classes knew that they had lost a champion in Houston. Mourners at his funeral included five U.S. Supreme Court justices, federal judges, the secretary of the Department of the Interior, journalists who had covered Houston's many activities, colleagues such as Marshall, Wilkins, and White of the NAACP, Waddy, and Robinson as well as a score of other lawyers who identified themselves as "social engineers" and civil rights lawyers. As Hastie reminded those present, Houston engaged in struggle with full knowledge of its risks, yet he believed that "every battle must be fought until it is won . . . without pause to take account of those stricken in the fray."

Charles Hamilton Houston, as an educator and civil rights lawyer/ activist, played a principal role in defining and pacing the legal phase of the Afro-American struggle for freedom from 1935 until his death. He always tried to take into account not only racial and class violence and exploitation, but also the *modus operandi* of the judicial system, limited minority access to law-making branches of government, and an historically racist, undemocratic, non-egalitarian society. In the context of this legal struggle he operated primarily in the judicial arena. Nevertheless, Houston also worked through other arms of the legal system because he recognized that "courts [were] too slow." He believed, however, that disfranchisement and racial repression militated against the immediately successful use of Congress, state legislatures, or executive agencies with no enforcement power as weapons in the struggle. Convinced that mass agitation and protest were essential, Houston supported direct action and participated in demonstrations, although his own major contribution lay in working through the courts.

Houston consistently held a position of leadership among Afro-Americans between 1935 and 1950. His legal accomplishments were the consequence of carefully considered, well-developed legal strategies and skillful arguments. Justice William O. Douglas of the U.S. Supreme Court, who was appointed in 1939 and had occasion to assess Houston as a litigator, noted: "I knew Charles H. Houston; and I sincerely believe he was one of the top ten advocates to appear before this court in my 35 years." His philosophy of social engineering—using the law to secure fundamental social change for the improvement of society and to establish and protect minority rights—had wide acceptance among civil rights lawyers. Moreover Houston maintained a strong leadership position among black people because of his skill at interpersonal relationships. His successes in the Supreme Court were shared accomplishments. They resulted from the cooperation of many legal associates throughout the nation and even the active efforts of communities, individuals, and protest organizations. He was a respected leader because people could sense that he was neither arrogant nor manipulative. He regarded himself as a "technician probing in the

239

courts . . . how far the existing system will permit the exercise of freedom," and therefore he openly entertained a wide range of views pertaining to the struggle for freedom and justice. Finally, his legal strategy for promoting judicial recognition of the Afro-Americans' rights was successful. Not only did his work have some immediate impact on the opportunities for blacks to explore or exercise rights in some areas of American life, but his Supreme Court victories had far-reaching significance for the future progress of blacks in American society.

Note on Sources

MANUSCRIPT SOURCES

The most important manuscript sources are:
The NAACP Papers at the Library of Congress, Washington, D.C.
The Charles H. Houston Papers. Howard University, Washington, D.C.

SELECTED PUBLICATIONS BY HOUSTON

"A Challenge to Negro College Youth," *Crisis*, 45 (Jan. 1938): 14–15.
"Foul Employment Practices on the Rails," *Crisis,* 56 (Oct. 1949): 269–71, 284–85.
"Future Policies and Practices Which Should Govern the Relationship of the Federal Government to Negro Separate Schools," *Journal of Negro Education,* 7 (July 1938): 460–62.
"How to Fight for Better Schools," *Crisis*, 43 (Feb. 1936): 52, 59.
"The Need for Negro Lawyers," *Journal of Negro Education*, 4 (Jan. 1935): 49–52.

SELECTED SECONDARY WORKS

Jerold Auerbach, *Unequal Justice*. New York: Oxford University Press, 1976.
Conrad Harper. "Charles Hamilton Houston" in R. Logan and M. Winston, eds., *Dictionary of American Negro Biography*, forthcoming.
William Hastie. "Charles Hamilton Houston," *Negro History Bulletin*, 13 (June 1950): 207–8.
Richard Kluger. *Simple Justice: The History of Brown v. Board of Education and Black America's Struggle for Equality*. New York: Alfred A. Knopf, 1976.
Genna Rae McNeil. "Charles Hamilton Houston (1895–1950) and the Struggle for Civil Rights" (Ph.D. diss., University of Chicago, 1975).
August Meier and Elliott Rudwick. "Attorneys Black and White: A Case Study of Race Relations within the NAACP," *Journal of American History,* 62 (Mar. 1976): 913–46.
Spottswood Robinson. "No Tea for the Feeble," *Howard Law Journal,* 20 (1977): 1–9.
Geraldine Segal. *In Any Fight Some Fall*. Rockville, Md.: Mercury Press, 1975.

Darlene Clark Hine   **11**

Mabel K. Staupers
and the Integration of Black Nurses
into the Armed Forces

*The social and economic changes associated with the New Deal and the
fairer hearing that race advancement organizations were receiving in the
courts and federal executive offices brought a rising black militance that
escalated with the coming of World War II. Two of the best examples of
the achievements of this wartime militance were A. Philip Randolph's
March on Washington and the creation of the Fair Employment Practices Committee discussed earlier and Mabel Keaton Staupers's crusade
for the employment and integration of Negro nurses in the armed services. Staupers's career provides an illuminating case study of the way in
which many Negro leaders have made skillful use of pressure by both
blacks and well-placed white sympathizers to advance the cause of equal
opportunity.*

WORLD WAR II was a watershed in black history. Many blacks, both
men and women, resolved to take advantage of the war emergency and
to push for the full realization of their rights as American citizens and
as human beings. Scholars have justifiably dubbed this period as "the
forgotten years of the Negro Revolution." Black leaders such as A.
Philip Randolph of the Brotherhood of Sleeping Car Porters and organizer of the March on Washington Movement; Walter White of the
National Association for the Advancement of Colored People; Lester
Granger of the National Urban League; Claude Barnett of the Associated Negro Press; James Farmer and Bayard Rustin of the Committee
(later Congress) of Racial Equality employed a variety of tactics and
struggled to dismantle the entire edifice of white supremacy and racial
proscription.

To the dismay of black Americans, the federal government proved

I thank Professors Leonora Woodman and Harold D. Woodman of Purdue University and William C. Hine of South Carolina State College for their thoughtful comments
and thorough reading of earlier drafts of this essay. I also thank the Rockefeller Foundation, the Eleanor Roosevelt Institute, and the Rockefeller Foundation Archive Center
for research grants.

slow in responding to their attacks and charges of discrimination. Blacks already situated on the bottom rung of the socioeconomic ladder had suffered to a remarkable degree during the Great Depression. Much of the New Deal relief legislation designed to ameliorate the deprivation and suffering of impoverished Americans actually preserved Jim Crow practices. To be sure, blacks received significant amounts of work, housing, and federal relief, but this was certainly not sufficient to solve the basic problems arising from white prejudice and discrimination.

The resurgence of economic activity at the outset of World War II registered only imperceptible changes in the black condition. Private industries with and without government defense contracts continued to discriminate against blacks in hiring, wages, and promotion. While many white unions excluded blacks, the U.S. Employment Service, a federal agency, continued to fill "white only" requests from employers of defense labor. The Fair Employment Practices Committee (FEPC) appointed by President Franklin Delano Roosevelt to implement Executive Order 8802 banning employment discrimination in government defense industries lacked enforcement powers and proved to be of only limited effectiveness. Yet, stimulated by the limited reforms of the New Deal and the democratic ideology stressed by U.S. anti-Nazi propaganda, blacks became much more militant in attacks on the racial status quo. Thus the vigilance with which black editors observed and reported accounts of racial segregation, discrimination, and civil inequalities surpassed all previous coverage.

One black leader, Mabel Keaton Staupers, heretofore unheralded and virtually ignored as executive secretary of the National Association of Colored Graduate Nurses (NACGN), successfully challenged the highly racist top echelons of the U.S. Army and Navy and forced them to accept black women nurses into the military nurses corps during World War II. This essay focuses on her leadership in the campaign to win long-denied rights for black women nurses.

Within the federal government, the Army and Navy displayed the strongest adherence to and defense of the ideology and practice of racial discrimination and segregation. Military leaders saw nothing amiss in sending a segregated Army and Navy to obliterate the forces of Fascism and Nazism to make the world safe for democracy. These contradictions were not lost upon black Americans. Walter White wrote at the time, "World War II has immeasurably magnified the Negro's awareness of the disparity between the American profession and practice of democracy."

242

As the country mobilized for the impending conflict, government authorities informed the major nursing organizations of the increased need for nurses. Staupers and the members of the NACGN heeded the alert. The NACGN had been founded in 1908 to champion the interests and promote the professional development of black women nurses. The leading nurses organizations, the American Nurses Association (ANA) and the National League of Nursing Education (NLNE), refused to accept individual membership from black nurses residing in seventeen, primarily southern, states. Every southern state association barred black women, thereby making the majority of black women nurses professional outcasts.

Handicapped by lack of a permanent headquarters, low membership, and insufficient funds with which to pay a salaried executive, the NACGN accomplished little during its first two decades. Thus, as late as 1930 black nurses had not obtained membership in the ANA, were excluded from the vast majority of nurse training schools, and suffered employment discrimination. One black nurse succinctly described the NACGN's plight, "There was a great need for a program which would bring into clear focus the fact that Negro nurses not only needed better educational and employment opportunities, but that these needs were aggravated by racial bias."

In 1934 the NACGN secured grants from the Julius Rosenwald Fund and the General Education Board of the Rockefeller Foundation. The money enabled the organization to move into permanent headquarters at Rockefeller Center, where all of the major national nursing organizations resided. More significantly, the grant enabled the NACGN to employ an executive secretary. The time was never more propitious. The reorganization brought together Staupers and Estelle Massey Riddle, two exceptionally talented black nurses who immediately contacted the white nursing leaders of the ANA and the NLNE and who lobbied for the removal of discriminatory policies that denied black nurses membership in state professional organizations. Staupers served as the first executive secretary from 1934 to 1946, and Riddle reigned as president of the NACGN from 1934 to 1938. Riddle, a native of Palestine, Texas, had attended the Homer G. Phillips Hospital and Nurses Training School in St. Louis, Missouri. She moved to New York in 1927 and entered Teachers College, Columbia University, becoming the first black recipient of a Rosenwald Fund Fellowship for nurses and the first black woman nurse to earn an M.A. degree.

Staupers, born in Barbados, West Indies, in 1890, had migrated with her parents to New York in 1903. After graduating from Freedmen's Hospital School of Nursing in Washington, D.C., in 1917, Staupers began her professional career as a private duty nurse in New York City. She was instrumental in organizing the Booker T. Washington Sanatorium, the first facility in the Harlem area where black doctors could treat their patients. Later Staupers served for twelve years as the executive secretary of the Harlem Committee of the New York Tuberculosis and Health Association. When the opportunity came, she unhesitatingly embraced the challenge of rebuilding and leading the NACGN. An ardent integrationist and feminist, Staupers set as her prime objective the full integration of black women nurses into the mainstream of American nursing. It would take years before her dream became a reality.

The long and arduous struggle for the professional recognition and integration of black nurses into American nursing acquired new momentum and a heightened sense of urgency with the outbreak of World War II. Between 1934 and 1940 Staupers's efforts to win for black women nurses unfettered membership in the major professional associations, particularly on the state level, had been unsuccessful. Staupers resolved therefore to seize the opportunity created by the war emergency and the increased demand for nurses to project the plight of the black nurse into the national limelight. Fully cognizant of the discrimination and exclusion black nurses suffered in World War I, Staupers vowed that history would not be repeated. In a long letter to William H. Hastie, the black civilian aide to the secretary of war, Staupers laid bare the strategy of mobilizing both blacks and whites that she would pursue in the campaign to force the complete integration of black nurses into the total war effort. Staupers viewed the acceptance of black nurses into the Army and Navy Nurse Corps as critical to the achievement of her major objective, that is, the full integration of black women into American nursing. Fortunately, the NACGN was in a much stronger position to coordinate the struggle for inclusion than it had been during the previous world conflict. She confided to Hastie: "Although we know that pressure from Negro groups will mean something, nevertheless I am spending all of my time contacting white groups, especially nursing groups. I have a feeling that if enough white nursing organizations can register a protest and enough white organizations of influence other than nurses do the same, it will create in the minds of the people in the War Department the feeling that white people do not need protection in order to save themselves from being cared for by Negro personnel."

Staupers adopted this particular strategy in order to address simultaneously two interrelated concerns. She was fully cognizant that the white American public's appreciation for nurses and the status of the nursing profession as a whole increased sharply whenever the country was involved in a war. This had been especially true during World War I. Therefore, to improve the economic, social, and educational opportunties of black nurses and their relationship with the professional nursing establishment, Staupers had to make sure that the larger white society recognized and valued the contributions of black women nurses in the Army and Navy Nurse Corps because these agencies possessed high public visibility. If the white public, especially the armed forces nurse corps, approved of and accepted black women as competent and desirable nurses, then surely the white professional nursing groups would follow suit. Her strategy was further complicated by the fact that any struggle to win public support mandated that she also attract the allegiance of sympathetic white nurses within the nursing profession.

By the time of the Japanese attack on Pearl Harbor in December 1941, Staupers had already developed a sharp sense of political timing and possessed a finely tuned facility for strategic maneuvering. She had skillfully cultivated close interaction with white nursing leaders, and as a consequence the NACGN's interests were well represented by its former president, Riddle, on the National Defense Council, which was renamed in 1942 the National Nursing Council for War Service. Staupers would continue to nurture her earlier long-term friendship with Congresswoman Frances Payne Bolton of Ohio, and before long she would make contact with First Lady Eleanor Roosevelt to solicit her assistance in the integration campaign. Also, as of 1940 Staupers had purposefully arranged for officers of the major civil rights organizations to be placed on the NACGN National Advisory Committee. Finally, Staupers appreciated the value of the black press and remained in constant communication with several black editors, sending them a constant stream of NACGN press releases.

Grants from various philanthropic foundations provided the money used for her continuous travel and feminist networking activities. Staupers logged thousands of miles, spoke with hundreds of black nurses, and wielded the NACGN into a powerful instrument for social change. She urged black nurses in major urban areas to form cells of local citizens, so that they could more effectively implement the programs and strategies designed at NACGN headquarters. The NACGN organized and sponsored regional institutes to which it invited key nursing figures, white and black, to discuss openly plans for further action. They particularly emphasized the need to arouse public support against the discrimination and segregation of black women nurses.

Plans to effect the complete integration of black women into the U.S. armed forces unfolded gradually as the war progressed. During the first year of peace time mobilization, 1940–41, Staupers concentrated on preventing the exclusion of black women from the Army and Navy Nurse Corps; once the war began she fought to have abolished the quotas that had been established by the Army. Throughout 1943 and 1944 she challenged the Army's practice of assigning black nurses only to care for German prisoners of war and not to white American soldiers. In addition Staupers cooperated with other groups to ensure that legislative measures proposed in Congress concerning nurses and hospitals contained anti-discrimination clauses. In spite of the continuous NACGN pressure, the U.S. Navy proved to be unalterably opposed to the induction of black women into the Navy Nurse Corps.

The American Red Cross Nursing Service under the leadership of Mary Beard in 1939 was, as in World War I, designated the official agency for the procurement of nursing personnel for the armed services. In the summer of that year Virginia Dunbar, Beard's assistant director, contacted Staupers to formulate the requirements for black nurses who desired to serve in the armed forces nurse corps. As most black nurses residing in southern states were barred from membership in state nurses associations, Staupers and Dunbar agreed to consider membership in the NACGN an acceptable substitute. Dunbar expressed concern that large numbers of black women would decide not to enroll, the likelihood of which was great, considering the continued hostility many blacks harbored towards the American Red Cross. For example, Hastie and Granger both questioned the desirability of designating the Red Cross as the chief procurement agency for nursing personnel in the armed forces. They cited the Red Cross's policy of separating blood donated by blacks from that given by whites as an indication of the organization's racial bias. In spite of these reservations Staupers nevertheless urged Dunbar to send letters and application forms to all black nurses training schools, nurse superintendents, and hospitals. She appealed to Barnett to publicize the fact that black nurses should enroll in the Red Cross in order to enter Army service. She asserted with determination that "we will not be left out" this time.

In addition to membership in a professional nurses association, armed forces nurses were required to be between the ages of eighteen and thirty-five. Nurses were expected to be single, divorced, or widowed. Another set of stipulations required that the potential nurse corps recruit provide references of her good moral character. Nurses in the Army and Navy Corps received a lower initial salary than any other nurse in government employ.

In spite of these deterrents, and the fact that there was so much reluctance about recruiting them, black women responded well to the call. Approximately 350 black women enrolled in the Red Cross Nursing Service, anticipating appointment in the Army Nursing Corps. As it turned out, only 117 were judged eligible for the First Reserve. Many were eliminated because of marriage and age. Several other black enrollees saw their hopes of being inducted dashed against the wall of racial exclusion. In mid-1940 they received letters informing them that the Army did not have a program that would permit the utilization of the services of black nurses. A few of the black nurses angrily forwarded copies of the rejection letters to Staupers at NACGN headquarters. An incensed Staupers wrote Beard and railed against the hypocrisy of urging black women to join up and serve their country and then callously rejecting their applications. She exploded, "We fail to understand how America can say to the World that in this country we are ready to defend democracy when its Army and Navy is committed to a policy of discrimination." The die was cast. Clearly then, the next move was up to the Army.

On October 25, 1940, on the same day Secretary of War Henry Stimson appointed Hastie, then dean of the Howard University Law School, as his civilian aide on Negro Affairs, James C. Magee, surgeon general of the U.S. Army, had announced the War Department's "plan for the use of colored personnel." According to the policy statement separate black wards were to be designated in station hospitals where the number of black troops was sufficient to warrant separate facilities. In the South and Southwest, where the overwhelming percentage of black troops was located, several exclusively black hospitals were to be established: Camp Livingston in Louisiana, Ft. Bragg in North Carolina, and Fort Huachuca in Arizona. The black wards and hospitals were to be manned entirely by black doctors, dentists, nurses, and attendants. In a later official clarification, Magee stated, "Where only a few of that race are to be hospitalized in any given hospital . . it would . . . be poor economy to set aside separate wards for the segregation of such cases."

The black press, nursing organizations, and black physicians immediately rallied to protest the War Department's segregation policy. In defense of his position, Magee asserted that he "would not place white soldiers in the position where they would have to accept service from Negro professionals." The War Department from the very beginning disclaimed to be an "appropriate medium for effecting social adjustments." One War Department officer would later explain to Staupers that the racial segregation supported and practiced by the U.S. Army derived from the conviction that "men who are fulfilling the same obligations, suffering the same dislocation of their private lives, and wearing the identical uniform should, within the confines of the military establishment, have the same privileges for rest and relaxation" that they enjoyed at home.

Staupers and a group of black nurses requested a meeting with Julia O. Flikke, head of the Army Nurse Corps. A few weeks following the October announcement black nurses met with Flikke, Major General George F. Lull, the deputy surgeon general for the War Department, and Colonel Love. Both Love and Lull simply reiterated the official policy: black nurses in limited numbers would be called upon to serve black troops in segregated wards and in separate military hospitals. Staupers and the NACGN committee found themselves in a dilemma. They had envisioned a broader use of black women and what had been offered fell far short of their desires. Yet it was better than total rejection. Consequently, the NACGN decided to accept, for the time being, the half-opened door. They reasoned that once a hand full of black nurses penetrated, then they could intensify agitation for more complete integration. The group refused, however, to compromise on the second proposal. Love had asked if the NACGN would be willing to assume responsibility for the recruitment of black nurses for the Army Nurse Corps as the need arose. Staupers adamantly rejected the suggestion, reminding the colonel that such tasks were the responsibility of the American Red Cross Nursing Service of which black nurses were members.

Although the meeting resulted in very little change in official Army and War Department policy, nevertheless the NACGN's militant stance initiated later changes. Magee announced in January 1941 the Army's decision to recruit fifty-six black nurses who would be assigned to the black installations at Camp Livingston and Fort Bragg. Staupers, desiring to strengthen the NACGN and to present a semblance of advancement to her followers, quickly sought to capitalize upon the announced quota. She confided to Marion B. Seymour, the chairman of the NACGN's National Defense Committee, "I hope this

story will get to the newspapers as coming from this organization before [Walter White] gets a chance to claim credit for it after all the work
we have done." She quickly sent press releases to the editors of the
leading black newspapers: Chicago *Defender,* Amsterdam *News,* New
York *Age,* Pittsburgh *Courier,* and the Norfolk *Journal and Guide.*

Although she desired to obtain credit for the NACGN for the announcement of the induction of black women nurses into the Army
Nurse Corps, Staupers realized that the quota of fifty-six was a slap in
the face. As she pointed out, the quota implied that black nurses were
inferior to the other nurses. Quotas were both floors and ceilings. The
important question, simply put, now became how could she secure the
foundation yet raise the roof. Like many other black leaders, Staupers
found herself in a double bind, being pulled in two directions: the first
toward the elimination of segregation and discrimination, while in the
second attempting to exploit to the fullest the possibilities for the use of
black nurses within a segregated system. For the time being, however,
she turned her attention to another matter and informed a nurse colleague, "Our next job is to see that our nurses are not segregated in
those states where segregation is not approved by law."

Opportunity to fight for this objective came a few months later. In
March 1941 members of the subcommittee on Negro Health of the
Health and Medical Committee of the National Defense Council met
with Magee, all of the assistant surgeons general, Brigadier General
Fairbanks, Colonel Love, and civilian aide Hastie. The subcommittee
on Negro Health was comprised of the black Chicago physician, M. O.
Bousfield, chair and director of Negro Health of the Julius Rosenwald
Fund; Russel Dixon, dean of the Howard University School of Dentis-
try; A. N. Vaughn, president of the black National Medical Association; Albert W. Dent, Dillard University president and superintendent of the black Flint-Goodridge Hospital in New Orleans, and
Staupers. The subcommittee at Staupers's insistence strongly urged
that the plan for segregated wards for black troops not be extended to
areas outside the South. Staupers pointed out that blacks had made
very substantial progress in civilian life in the integration of black patients and professionals into general hospitals. The subcommittee argued that "the extension of the segregated ward plan to many areas of
the country would represent an unfortunate reversal of current
trends."

The members spent much discussing the quotas which called for, in
addition to the fifty-six nurses, only 120 doctors and forty-four dentists. They unanimously objected to the quotas as being disproportion-

ately small even for the service of black troops stationed in the South. They implored Magee to use his influence in favor of an increase. Magee adamantly supported the official policy of "segregation without discrimination." The black press castigated the obdurate Magee. The Philadelphia *Tribune* editor observed, "It has become apparent to on-lookers in Washington, that at least some of the difficulties which have been experienced by black professionals in the medical branches of the armed forces have their origin in the office of one man. He is Major General James C. Magee." Most members of the military bureaucracy staunchly adhered to the quota system. Magee was, of course, reflecting the views of his superiors in the War Department, who proved unyielding in its position. Robert P. Patterson, the undersecretary of war, declared that in establishing separate units the War Department could not be judged guilty of any discrimination against black nurses or physicians. He maintained that "the Medical Department has not discriminated in any sense against the Negro medical professions, nurses, or enlisted men. It has assigned Negro personnel in keeping with War Department policy and provided field and service units in support of Negro troops with Negro Personnel." Patterson continued, smugly noting that for the first time in the history of the Army opportunity had been furnished the black medical profession and ancillary services "to exercise full professional talent through the establishment of separate departments at two of our large cantonment hospitals for the care of Negro soldiers."

Thus, as far as War Department officials were concerned, segregation, implying only separation, was nondiscriminatory if equal facilities were provided. Blacks, on the other hand, considered the concept of enforced segregation discriminatory. From their perspective separation prevented freedom of movement and produced inequalities of facilities and opportunities. Traditionally minority groups possessed few means of enforcing equality guarantees. Staupers, arguing from a black perspective, contended, "My position is that, as long as either one of the Services reject Negro nurses they are discriminated against and as long as either Services continue to assign them to duty as separate Units they are segregated."

Hastie in his function as civilian aide to the secretary of war tried valiantly to convince the War Department of the unfairness of quotas and segregation. He urged that these flaws be rectified or abolished before they became too entrenched. His carefully drafted recommendations for the desegregation of the Army were summarily rejected.

According to one student of the era, the general staff took the point of view that Hastie wished the Army "to carry out a complete social revolution against the will of the nation." Days before the Japanese bombed Pearl Harbor Hastie and the Army's high command had reached an impasse. General George C. Marshall wrote in response to Hastie's desegregation memorandum, "The War Department cannot ignore the social relationships between negroes and whites which have been established by the American people through custom and habit." Marshall added that "either through lack of opportunity or other causes the level of intelligence and occupational skill of the negro population is considerably below that of the white." He predicted that were the Army to engage in social experiments only "danger to efficiency, discipline, and morale" would result. Finally, he observed that the Army had attained maximum strength by properly placing its personnel in accordance with individual capabilities. This racist response coupled with several other examples of blatant disregard for him and his recommendations left Hastie no alternative than to resign as civilian aide to the secretary of war. This he did on January 31, 1943.

However, compared to the position adopted by the U.S. Navy, the Army was a model of racial enlightenment. The Navy found unnecessary the establishment of quotas, for it held black women simply ineligible and undesirable for service in the Navy Nurse Corps. According to Lt. Commander Sue S. Dauser, superintendent of the Navy Nurse Corps, Navy nurses were special nurses. They combined the responsibilities and roles of teacher, counselor, dietist, laboratory technician, X-ray operator, bookkeeper, and confidante of the sick. The Navy nurse was required to instruct hospital corpsmen in modern nursing methods. In turn the men so taught would be responsible for the welfare of the patients in the sickbays of battleships, cruisers, destroyers, and other combat vessels to which members of the Nurse Corps were not assigned. While the Army nurse engaged in some teaching activity, this was considered incidental when compared to ward or bedside duties. In sum, a Navy nurse had to be a "tactful, clearminded administrator and teacher." Presumably black women were devoid of such qualities. Furthermore, there were very few black sailors in the Navy.

Yet midway through the war both the Army and Navy moved hesitatingly towards greater integration. Staupers received notice in 1943 that the Navy had decided, at last, to place the matter of inducting black nurses "under consideration." The Army, on the other hand, had raised its quota of black nurses to 160: thirty of them were assigned to foreign duty and another thirty-one were deployed to form a new separate unit at Ft. Clark, Texas. These actions did not appease Staupers.

Frustrated by her inability to persuade the Navy and War Department to abolish quotas completely and to institute plans for the immediate and full integration of black nurses, Staupers resolved to present the case of the black nurses to America's First Lady. Shortly after she made contact with Eleanor Roosevelt, the First Lady sent discreet inquiries to Secretary of War Stimson and to Beard. She wrote, "I have several protests lately that due to the shortage of nurses, the colored nurses be allowed to serve where there is not serious objection to it." While Stimson's response was essentially defensive and noncommittal, Beard confessed that the American Red Cross Nursing Service had been "greatly concerned with the unequal treatment of qualified Negro nurses as compared with the white nurses" servicing in the armed forces. She reassured the First Lady that the National Nursing Council for War Service was attempting quietly to influence the assignment policy of the Army and Navy Nurse Corps. Elmira B. Wickenden, executive secretary of the National Council, offered similar reassurances. Indeed, the National Nursing Council in late 1943 had sent the following resolution to the surgeon generals of the Army and Navy Medical Corps: "Be it resolved that Negro graduate registered nurses be appointed to the Army (or Navy) Nurse Corps on the same basis as any other American nurses who meet the professional requirements, as was done in the last war."

Staupers's patience had grown thin; she wanted results, not promises or resolutions. Propitiously, 1944 was a presidential election year. Staupers let it be known in the appropriate political circles that she was an avowed Roosevelt supporter and did not wish to make a fuss or "give any publicity to the present situation during this pre-election period." A friend, Anna Arnold Hedgeman, the executive secretary of A. Philip Randolph's National Council for a Permanent Fair Employment Practice Committee, interceded and suggested to Eleanor Roosevelt that she invite Staupers to meet with her.

Staupers and Roosevelt met in November 1944, whereupon the NACGN executive secretary described in detail the black nurses' relationship with the armed forces. She informed the First Lady that eighty-two black nurses were serving 150 patients at the Station Hospital at Ft. Huachuca at a time when the Army was complaining of a dire nursing shortage. Staupers expounded at length on the practice of using black women to take care of German prisoners of war. She asked, rhetorically, if this was to be the special role of the black nurse in the war. Staupers elaborated, "When our women hear of the great need for nurses in the Army and when they enter the Service it is with the high hopes that they will be used to nurse sick and wounded soldiers who are fighting our country's enemies and not primarily to care for these enemies." Roosevelt, apparently moved by the discussion, applied her own subtle pressure to Norman T. Kirk, surgeon general of the U.S. Army, Secretary Stimson, and the Navy's Rear Admiral W. J. C. Agnew.

As 1944 faded into 1945, events on the black nursing front took a sudden upswing. In early January 1945, Kirk announced to a crowd of 300 nurses, politicians, and private citizens assembled at the Hotel Pierre in New York City that in order for the Army to be adequately supplied with nurses it might be advisable to institute a draft. Staupers immediately rose to her feet and pointedly asked the surgeon general, "If nurses are needed so desperately, why isn't the Army using colored nurses?" She continued, "Of 9,000 registered Negro nurses the Army has taken 247, the Navy takes none." Kirk, visibly uncomfortable according to press reports, replied, "There are 7,000 Negro nurses in comparison to a 200,000 total in the United States. I believe that the average share of colored nurses in the army is equal to the total number of Negro troops." News of the exchange received nationwide coverage and made the headlines of virtually every black newspaper in the country. The Boston *Guardian* declared, "It is difficult to find calm words to describe the folly which color prejudice assumes in the desperate shortage of nurses." The editor anticipated the kind of future action that occurred when he predicted that "the Commander-in-chief will be backed up in this instance by the great majority of the people if he orders a cessation of the outrageous ban on nurses because of skin color and thus helps to modernize the armed forces by ridding them of the foggyism which is the greatest barrier to national growth."

Compounding the tension surrounding the Kirk-Staupers incident, on January 6, 1945, in a radio transmitted address to the U.S. Congress, President Roosevelt announced his strong desire for the enactment of legislation amending the Selective Service Act of 1940 to provide for the induction of nurses into the Army. He justified the need for such legislation on the grounds that volunteering had not produced the number of nurses required. Roosevelt adopted this position over the objections of Chief of Staff Marshall and Major General Stephen G. Henry, both of whom advised that the proposed legislation would be "most discriminatory in that it singles out a small group of especially trained women for induction under the Selective Service Act." As if on cue, however, Representative Andrew J. May (Democrat, Kentucky) introduced the Draft Nurse Bill, H. R. 1284 79th Congress, on January 9, 1945, and it was immediately referred to the Committee on Military Affairs.

An ensuing public outcry quickly forthcoming and totally unexpected jarred the military brass. Roosevelt apparently had not the slightest appreciation for the depth of public dissatisfaction with the restrictive quotas for black nurses. Staupers with alacrity sought to harness, direct, and channel the wave of public anger and sympathy. She urged black nurses, women's groups, and sympathetic white allies across the country to send telegrams directly to Roosevelt and May, protesting the exclusion, discrimination, and segregation of black nurses. Staupers in numerous press releases pleaded, "We stress again for the Negro nurses all over the country that they rally now as never before to the support of the NACGN." And rally they did. The sheer hypocrisy of calling for a draft of nurses while excluding large numbers of black nurses willing to serve was too much for many Americans to swallow. Telegrams poured into the White House from the NAACP, the Catholic Interracial Council, National Nursing Council for War Services, Congress of Industrial Organizations, American Federation of Labor, National YWCA Board, the Alpha Kappa Alpha Sorority, the Philadelphia Fellowship Commission, the New York Citizens' Committee of the Upper West Side, the National Negro Congress, National Council of Negro Women, the United Council of Church Women, and the American Civil Liberties Union. From Cleveland, Jane Edna Hunter, president of the Ohio State Federation of Colored Women's Club and former nurse, in a telegram to the president declared: "If the proposal to draft nurses must be resorted to, then we urge that all inductees be given consideration on bases of training and fitness and allowed to serve in all branches of the Army and Navy and not restricted to Negro soldiers alone."

Buried beneath the avalanche of telegrams and seared by the heat of an inflamed public, Kirk, Agnew, and the War Department declared an end to quotas and exclusion. On January 20, 1945, Kirk stated that nurses would be accepted into the Army Nurse Corps without regard to race. On January 25, 1945, Admiral Agnew announced that the Navy Nurse Corps was now open to black women, and a few weeks later Phyllis Dailey became the first black women to break the color barrier and receive induction into the Navy Nurse Corps. There was no outcry against the accepting of black nurses into the armed forces nurse corps.

Eventually the War Department decided to stop the entire scheme to enact a draft of nurses. Staupers's carefully orchestrated telegram campaign and tedious years of continuous effort had culminated in the breaking of at least this one link in the chain that oppressed, excluded, and prohibited black women from the full realization of their civil rights. This was by no means the end of their war. It was, however, a welcome victory in what had been a long struggle overwhelmingly characterized by defeat, setbacks, humiliation, and frustration. The proposed nurse draft legislation and ensuing congressional debate had been the catalytic component to which Staupers and black nurses had joined their struggle for full integration into the armed forces and had gained support and sympathy from both white and black Americans. Presidential and congressional speeches bemoaning the shortage of nurses had only fed the fire that Staupers's public protests had generated. While Staupers and black nurses may have supported in principle the nurse draft legislation, they nevertheless used it to draw attention to the fact that they had been excluded, segregated, and discriminated against. She displayed a flawless sense of timing and political maneuvering.

The battle to integrate black women nurses into the Army and Navy Nurse Corps had been an exhaustive and draining one. In 1946 Staupers relinquished her position as executive secretary to take a much needed and well-earned rest. This was to be of short duration, however, for Staupers considered her work incomplete. She had not accomplished her major objective, the integration of black women into the ANA. Beginning in 1934, Staupers and Riddle had appeared before the House of Delegates at the biennial meeting of the ANA. After ten years of fruitless persistence, Staupers wrote Congresswoman Bolton, "Each year although we have not gained our ultimate objective we have gained friends and are in a stronger position than ever before." After the 1944 meeting Staupers confided to Bolton her hope that "integration may be an accomplished fact before 1945."

General integration into the ANA did not come in 1945. It came three years later. In 1948 the ANA House of Delegates opened the gates to black membership, appointed a black women nurse as assistant executive secretary in its national headquarters, and witnessed the election of Riddle to the board of directors.

For Staupers, the breakdown of the exclusion barriers was a triumphant vindication of her leadership role. In 1950 Staupers, now president of the NACGN, convinced black nurses that the purpose for which the organization had been established had now been achieved and that it was time to dissolve the NACGN. Staupers wrote in a press release dated January 26, 1951, that as far as it was known the NACGN was the first major black national organization to terminate its work "because it feels that its program of activities is no longer necessary." She continued, "The doors have been opened," and the black nurse "has been given a seat in the top councils." Staupers later exulted, "We are now a part of the great organization of nurses, the American Nurses' Association."

Staupers received many accolades for her leadership in the integration fight and in the dissolution of the NACGN. By far, the crowning acknowledgement and recognition of Staupers's role and contribution in the quest of black nurses for civil rights and human dignity came from a rather unexpected source. The Spingarn Award Committee of the NACGN chose Staupers to be the recipient of the Spingarn Medal for 1951. Channing H. Tobias, director of the Phelps-Stokes Fund, confided to Staupers, "I know the committee was especially appreciative of the fact that you were willing to sacrifice organization to ideals when you advocated and succeeded in realizing the full integration of Negro nurses into the organized ranks of the nursing profession of this country."

Mabel Keaton Staupers was one of the truly outstanding black women leaders in this century. The key identifying characteristic of her leadership style was the establishment of close working relationships with leading white women, black male heads of organizations, and fellow black women nurses. She secured her base first, that is, the NACGN, by maintaining continuous communication and contact with the membership. Staupers furthermore manipulated the press extremely well by releasing statements at the most strategic moment. Her public remarks unfailingly emphasized the cause for which she was fighting. In so doing she constantly reminded the country of the plight of black women nurses, of the racism and sexism that robbed them of the opportunities to develop their full human potential. Small of frame, energetic, and fast-talking, Staupers knew when to accept a half-loaf of advancement and when to press on for total victory. It is unlikely that the successful integration of black women into American nursing on all levels could have been accomplished during the 1940s without Staupers at the helm of the NACGN.

Note on Sources

UNPUBLISHED SOURCES

American Red Cross Manuscript Collection. National Archives, Washington, D.C.

Claude Barnett Papers. Chicago Historical Society, Chicago, Ill.

Frances Payne Bolton Papers. Western Reserve Historical Society, Cleveland, Ohio.

National Association of Colored Graduate Nurses Collection. New York City Public Library, Schomburg Afro-American History Collection, New York, N.Y.

Eleanor Roosevelt Papers. Franklin Delano Roosevelt Library, Hyde Park, N.Y.

Rosenwald Fund Papers. Fisk University Library, Nashville, Tenn.

Mabel Keaton Staupers Papers. Amistad Research Center, New Orleans, La.

Mabel Keaton Staupers Papers. Moorland-Spingarn Research Center, Howard University, Washington, D.C.

Records of the Surgeon General's Office of the U.S. Army. National Archives Research Center, Suitland, Md.

Records of the War Department, General and Special Staff. National Archives Research Center, Suitland, Md.

PUBLISHED SOURCES

Staupers, Mabel Keaton. *No Time for Prejudice: A Story of the Integration of Negroes in Nursing in the United States.* New York: Macmillan Co., 1961.

Thoms, Adah B. *Pathfinders: A History of Progress of Colored Graduate Nurses.* New York: McKay, 1929.

Martin Kilson

12

Adam Clayton Powell, Jr.:
The Militant as Politician

Chicago's Southside "Black Metropolis" in 1928 was the first congressional district in the North—and the first since the turn of the century—to send a black man (Oscar DePriest) to Washington. Made feasible by the growth of the large urban ghettoes that accompanied the northward migration, the rise in the number of black congressmen was thwarted by skillful gerrymandering, and not until 1944 did Harlem become the second northern district to send a Negro to Congress.

Adam Clayton Powell, Jr., New York's first black congressman, combined a flair for militant oratory and social protest with his own political ambition; throughout his career he was a symbol of black protest as well as of black power and achievement. In this respect he was unlike his Chicago predecessors, who served as faithful lieutenants in white-dominated city machines; instead, Powell was akin to the growing ranks of the more outspoken black congressmen who achieved their high office in the wake of the civil rights revolution of the 1960s.

THE FAILURE of the federal government's policy of Reconstruction in the late 1870s was the prelude to the virtual political subjugation of emancipated blacks during the 1880s and 1890s. A combination of legal, illegal, and violent methods was used to reduce the majority of Afro-Americans to a status tantamount to political slavery—the late nineteenth and early twentieth century's counterpart to the socioeconomic slavery of the pre–Civil War era. Political rights for Afro-Americans were now available only through migration out of the South, a development that began in earnest during the early 1900s. Such migration was, however, a protracted process: in 1910 about 10 percent of black Americans lived outside the South, 23 percent by 1930, and in 1950, 33 percent of Afro-Americans were living in the North and West.

Overwhelmingly blacks outside the South resided in large industrial cities. The significance of urbanization to the political development of Afro-Americans cannot be overemphasized: it afforded them that quality of social organization and institutional specialization without which effective political influence is impossible. Yet black urbanization outside the South was not free of obstacles to effective social and political development. Northern blacks were stifled by that cluster of norms and behavior characterized by the term white racism. No other major American ethnic community—Irish, Jews, Italians, Poles, e.g.—faced a comparable range of restrictions upon its urban adaptation. Lloyd Warner, the sociologist of mainstream America, discovered this in Yankee City: "The caste barrier or color line, *rigid and unrelenting,* has cut off this small group [blacks—one-half percent of Yankee City's population] from the general life of the community." Such isolation of blacks "from the general life of the community" is central to understanding the dynamics of blacks' political status in cities in the first half of the twentieth century.

Whatever the general life of a modern community consists of, surely politics is a salient feature, for politics is the process through which a significant share of modern services and benefits is allocated among competing sectors of society. From World War I, the party and bureaucratic structures in northern cities functioned to preclude an effective political role for Afro-Americans. Not that the black city dwellers were ignored by white-controlled city politics, for their numbers alone argued against total indifference. Rather, white city machines—with the sole exception of Chicago's—simply dealt half-heartedly with the problem of the political inclusion of Afro-Americans on terms comparable to that of white ethnic groups. In order to ensure a truncated political status for blacks, the typical city machine gerrymandered ghetto neighborhoods. Such practices distorted black political development in northern cities for a half-century.

Above all, the stance toward blacks by city machines during the first several decades of the 1900s weakened Afro-Americans' quest for that primary mode of political organization and influence that had been available to white ethnic groups—namely, the politicization of ethnicity, that is, the use of ethnic patterns and solidarity features as the primary basis for political formations. It means building upon these to integrate a given ethnic community into the wider politics of the city and the nation. To the extent that a given ethnic group was successful in so organizing itself in the early decades of this century, it could claim an effective share of city-based rewards and, through congressional and presidential politics, of federal government benefits. On the other hand, to fall outside or to be only partially integrated into ethnic-based machine politics was necessarily to be without an effective basis for acquiring the benefits of American society.

260

In most cities, during the first three decades of the twentieth century, city machines related to blacks in such a manner as to neutralize or minimize the potential political clout of the black community. How was this achieved? Typically a powerful white boss or a clique of white politicians would select an influential black as a client of the city machine, casting this client in the role of the machine's political agent within the black community. Thus, in East St. Louis, Illinois, from around 1910 Dr. LeRoy Bundy, a black dentist, functioned as the agent between blacks and the East St. Louis Republican organization. A similar relationship, a patron-client axis as it were, was forged between New York City's black Harlem community and the Republican and Democratic organizations from the early 1900s. On the Republican side, Charles W. Anderson emerged from the lower ranks of Republican ward organizations in early twentieth-century Harlem, via a federal appointment as collector of Internal Revenue, to become the major black politician in the black community. As a member of the Republican organization in Harlem's 19th state assembly district, which was overwhelmingly black, Anderson helped to nominate and elect a black member of the city council, and in 1916 he directed the national Republican campaign among blacks. From his post as collector of Internal Revenue for New York, Anderson ruled Republican politics among blacks until his retirement in 1934.

The Democratic party, controlled through Tammany Hall, had its own political clients in the black community of New York City, most notably Ferdinand Q. Morton, a Harvard-educated lawyer who headed the United Colored Democracy (UCD), a black division of Tammany Hall. The UCD was formed as a split-off from the Republican organization in 1898. Morton gained leadership of it in 1915 and skillfully built a formal party organization in Harlem, putting down independent or wildcat candidacies and slowly overcoming the Republican dominance over black voters—a dominance that had helped to elect a black lawyer, Edward A. Johnson, to the state assembly from Harlem (the 19th district) in 1917 and four other black assemblymen over the next ten years. Morton influenced a 27 percent black vote for John Hylan, the Democratic mayoral candidate in 1917; in his reelection in 1921, Hylan gained 75 percent of Harlem's vote. With that, Morton emerged as New York City's most powerful black politician at that time. He was rewarded with appointment as civil service commissioner for New York City—there were three commissioners—and proceeded to gain Tammany's support for several black candidates for seats in the state assembly.

261

During the turbulent years of the 1930s, however, Morton displayed an increasingly dictatorial disposition, rejecting initiatives from a younger group of black politicians who sought to broaden the range of issues and appeals associated with Harlem politics. The Depression had hit black Harlem extremely hard, dislocating the lives of thousands upon thousands of hapless blacks, often recent migrants from the South or the West Indies. Also, a new black middle class was rising, seeking unprecedented opportunities in business and the professions and new modes of black ethnic expression and celebration. Even earlier, during the 1920s, the Harlem Renaissance and the Garvey Movement had been popular features of the new modes of such black ethnic expression. In face of these new dimensions of life in the Harlem of the 1930s, the politics of Morton and Tammany Hall proved both unresponsive and ill suited. There was, in short, a political vacuum; new forms and new personalities were increasingly required to fulfill the new needs of Harlem's black community. One personality who endeavored to fill this political and leadership vacuum was Adam Clayton Powell, Jr.

The political style of America's black leaders varies as much as that of its white leaders. It ranges from the soft-spoken, businesslike pragmatist, through the ethnic militant, to the exhibitionistic back-slapping demagogue, with infinite variation on each of these types. White leadership in this century has had numerous examples of the exhibitionistic demagogue, especially among the urban ethnic politicians (Irish, Jewish, Italian, Polish) and among the white-racist Protestant leaders in the South. This type has also existed among Afro-American politicians, often in combination with the ethnic-militant style—a style characterized by an uncompromising articulation of the bitter frustrations experienced by all sectors of black Americans in their quest for social and political equality with whites.

For the black politician, the ethnic-militant or black-racialist style afforded him the means for his own political base outside of the established political arrangement associated with city machine politics. Through the manipulation of black racialism or black solidarity, the Afro-American politician induced the emergence of latent energy and resources within black institutions, such as churches and fraternal bodies, within mutual-aid groups in the working class, and within professional associations, like the National Negro Bar Association and the National Negro Medical Association. In this way, then, some of the first black-controlled political structures in American cities were built, including the successful black political organization in Chicago that sent the first black to Congress in 1928 and kept William L. Dawson in Congress for nearly thirty years—from 1942 to 1970.

The political career of Powell was a model of the successful use of black solidarity in American politics. Unlike Dawson, who eventually discarded the use of black racialism for the pragmatic style, Powell clung to it throughout his career, shrewdly reinforcing black racialism with the demagogic style and forging it into a formidable national political force, centered on a twenty-six-year career in the U.S. Congress (1944–70). While Powell did not generate as many federal benefits for his black New York City constituents as Dawson did for Chicago's blacks, he nonetheless provided through his leadership style a national focal point around which many black Americans rallied in their opposition to white racism.

Born in 1908, within several years of the commencement of sizable black migration from the South to northern cities, Powell was the son of an upper middle-class Baptist clergyman. The Reverend Adam Clayton Powell, Sr., a fair-skinned Afro-American of white, Cherokee, and black ancestry, achieved enormous prominence in Harlem as pastor of the Abyssinian Baptist Church, a religious edifice with over 10,000 dues-paying congregants. He also speculated successfully in Harlem real estate, amassing a fair amount of wealth. In addition to his affluent upper middle-class household, Powell was reared in an era when the recent black migrants to the North faced enormous problems of adjustment to city life. They were maliciously harassed and impeded at every turn by white indifference to their needs, by corrupt city machines and brutal police practices, and not infrequently by mob violence. The younger Powell observed the perpetual failure of every stratum within the Harlem ghetto to sustain leadership long enough and effectively enough to make a dent in the ghetto's massive frustrations, problems, and social pathologies. But his contact with the plight of blacks was not particularly immediate during his school days and college years, for he attended public schools for high-achieving students and an elite white college—Colgate University.

Powell's political orientation was influenced by two political patterns that shaped Harlem's power structure during the years between the two world wars—the pressure group politics of middle-class Afro-Americans, exemplified best by the National Association for the Advancement of Colored People, and the black separatist politics of petty-bourgeois blacks (e.g., grocers, small businessmen, hairdressers, and poolroom operators), exemplified best by the Universal Negro Improvement Association, led by West Indian Marcus Garvey and often called the Garvey Movement. From the NAACP and similar organizations Powell learned the skills and tactics for linking middle-class and elite blacks to the political process. From the Garvey Movement Powell learned the skills and mannerisms of mass political appeal, including those rooted in demagogic populism. This mode, ironically enough, was frequently used by white politicians in the South during these years to oppress and disenfranchise Afro-Americans; but like all political styles it was equally serviceable to black politicians seeking to surmount political apathy, fear, and weakness among blacks in northern cities.

Powell synthesized these two strands of Afro-American political action during the interwar era, producing his own unique political instrument. Central to Powell's synthesis was the idea of aggregating a variety of black voluntary associations. In this situation a skillful and charismatic leader first maximizes the politicization of his own voluntary agency and then, having secured this initial base, branches out to penetrate other voluntary associations, employing militant ideological appeal. The new mechanism and influence from this process are put to the task of challenging the established political institutions, including the electoral process. Powell was the first major Afro-American politician to harness the resources associated with ethnic and ideological militancy in this way, transforming them ultimately into enormous political influence, both at the city and national level.

Thus in the 1930s Powell, now an assistant minister in his father's church—a 10,000-member organization—formed precisely this type of political instrument in the Greater New York Coordinating Committee. Through the resources of the Abyssinian Baptist Church in Harlem, Powell elaborated the coordinating committee to include a broad spectrum of Harlem's middle-class and lower-strata population, aligning these social groups into sharp opposition to the white-controlled political machine. Powell's committee made explicit use of black racialism or ethnic solidarity, attacking whites in general, white politicians in particular, and also black elites and politicians in alliance with the city machine. The result was the creation of a political machine of his own.

Powell helped pioneer the politics of boycotts and picketing in behalf of occupational mobility for Afro-Americans. His first attempt at this approach occurred when he responded to requests from five black doctors in Harlem, who charged racial discrimination in their dismissal from Harlem Hospital, a city institution. Dr. Ira McCown, the leading figure among Harlem's doctors during the 1930s and later the physician of the New York State Boxing Commission, invited Powell in 1930 to organize whatever political pressure he could muster in behalf of Harlem's beleaguered black doctors.

Run exclusively by white doctors and administrators (largely Irish-Americans), the Harlem Hospital served a largely black clientele. By the 1930s this clientele, especially the working and lower classes, had their usual frustrations compounded by the massive unemployment caused by the Great Depression. It was to this sector of black Harlem that Powell turned for the leverage necessary to influence change in the white supremacist practices of the Irish-American doctors and administrators in the hospital. Gifted at oratory and populist arousal, Powell fashioned tactics of mass direct action against white institutions, and by his reckoning he enticed some 6,000 of "the people of the streets, the failures, the misfits, the despised, the maimed, the beaten, the sightless, and the voiceless" to march on the hospital and city hall. In this action Powell discovered the style and the mode of organization and appeal that were to characterize his future political career. The concessions that the twenty-two-year-old Powell extracted from negotiations with the New York City Board of Estimates, while a mass of radicalized blacks stood at his back, are described by Powell:

> The Board of Estimates launched an investigation and finally all five doctors were reinstated, and Harlem Hospital was given an interracial staff, with a Negro as the Medical Director. The surgical and medical facilities, which had been so filthy that the hospital for years had been referred to as "The Butcher Shop," were cleaned up. The Nurses' Training School at the hospital was investigated and overhauled. And later I had the privilege of standing by Mayor LaGuardia [elected in 1933] and helping him lay the cornerstone of the hospital's new women's pavilion. The victory was very heady wine for a youngster of twenty-two.

With his political appetite whetted, Powell moved to expand both the range and depth of his politics of militant ethnic solidarity. This expansion was variegated and included boycotts of white businesses, alliances with white radicals (including Communists), a successful campaign for the city council, and an equally successful campaign for the U.S. House of Representatives. At the root of Powell's political metamorphosis from ad hoc activist to broad-gauged politician was, of course, the Depression-devastated plight of black Harlem. By 1936 rents were 20 percent higher than similar accommodations elsewhere in the city, foodstuffs were 17 percent higher than city norm, credit for blacks was usurious, and insurance rates were not much below the usury level. Over 20 percent of black Harlem was unemployed, about 63 percent of schoolchildren in the neighborhood of Powell's church suffered malnutrition, and over half of the black population was on relief or welfare.

Thus Powell's actions en route to becoming a politician had focus and purpose and were shaped by a combination of his genuine concern for the plight of black Harlem and his driving ambition—an ambition that preferred black prominence in black neighborhoods to deference to whites. Perhaps the most important event that wedded Powell's empathy for the poor and his self-serving quest was the Harlem riot on March 19, 1935—the first riot started by blacks in New York City's history, sparked by rumors of whites' rough-handling a Puerto Rican child for shoplifting—spreading fire, looting, and property damage worth millions of dollars from one end of 125th Street to the other. In 1937 Powell formed a new action organization—the Greater New York Coordinating Committee for Employment (comprising 207 groups with 170,000 members)—and by 1941 this agency was redesigned to embrace a variety of white radical organizations, including Communists, and became the People's party. Between 1937 and 1941 Powell used the Coordinating Committee for Employment and the People's party to boycott white businesses on 125th Street (businesses that in 1933 hired some 5,000 persons but only ninety-three blacks), to force the Omnibus Corporation that ran New York City's buses to upgrade black workers, and to negotiate hundreds of jobs for blacks in bottling and bread companies and in large firms like Consolidated Edison and the New York Telephone and Telegraph Company.

Powell capped these steps toward becoming a black politician with an appeal to a large number of diverse people by mounting a campaign for the city council in the fall of 1941. Powell faced competition from the Republicans, who nominated a black official of the national YMCA—Dr. Channing Tobias; from the Democrats, who nominated a trusted black district captain—Herman Stoute; and even from the radicals, who nominated a black boys club organizer and political activitist—Dr. Max Yergan. But no black politician in the years before World War II had acquired a wide-ranging presence in black Harlem comparable to Powell's, nor had any black politician a private infrastructure of linkages with Harlem comparable to Powell's Abyssinia Baptist Church—an infrastructure that during the Depression had taken on the additional burden of dispensing relief to about a thousand people a day. The campaign allowed Powell to test the effectiveness of the protracted politicization of the Abyssinian Baptist Church, which had commenced eleven years before. In the end, Powell received 65,000 votes, placed third out of twenty-nine candidates, and gained a seat on the New York city council—the first black to do so. Powell was now poised for the last stage of his political career—membership in the U.S. Congress.

Powell's ambition for national political status was overridden by only one factor: his endemic need to confront white authority, especially in its racist forms. This need translated into a compulsion to insist on parity for blacks in all matters of social and political equality and in his disregard for the opinions of whites over his poor attendance record in the House of Representatives, his galavanting, or other behavior. In this disregard, Powell was acting out of deep-rooted personality traits.

Powell's autobiography, *Adam by Adam,* offers some insight into his character. He portrays himself as a man of more than usual vanity, appearing to consider himself a savior of the weak and poor among Harlem's blacks. Though this posture was often a political technique that exploited the tendency of the black American lower classes to elevate political leaders, who represent secular authority, to messiahs, who represent sacred authority (a tendency I consider an Africanism), Powell also seems to have genuinely internalized a messiah complex.

Powell relates how he experienced in boyhood a gnawing urge to find an area of legitimate activity in which he could match the success and authority of his father. Politics is not an uncommon outlet for men with this father-competitive propensity, for, as Talcott Parsons has taught us, politics is often "functionally diffuse," requires few specialized resources, and attracts persons driven to achieve but who possess structurally inchoate attributes (e.g., a charismatic personality). Moreover, throughout the autobiography Powell reveals a deepseated, often manic, need to deviate from expected behavior, and again politics often affords more opportunity for fulfillment of this impulse than do other avocations. But politics also has pitfalls and booby traps for those who crave its rewards (authority, power, wealth) but reject its obligations (discipline and compromise). Thus Powell's career in Congress, which lasted twenty-six years, found him dangling precariously and perpetually between the pitfalls and obligations of politics; eventually he succumbed to the former.

He would, alas, have it no other way. Powell considered himself "the first bad nigger in Congress"—an appellation he gave himself. The deviant in Powell, apparent in all spheres of his behavior, surfaced at the start and persisted to the end of his congressional career. His campaign for Congress was born in the midst of the political chaos of Tammany Hall. Charles Francis Murphy, founder of the modernized Tammany Hall who had wedded the power-questing and reform-questing wings of Tammany, had died in 1925, leaving minions of limited talent and character—men like Mayor Jimmy Walker—to tear Tammany apart, spawning unprecedented levels of corruption. The rise of successful reform candidates like Mayor Fiorello LaGuardia—elected in 1933 as a Fusion party candidate—aided the spread of independent or wildcat candidacies among blacks in Harlem. Powell's successful candidacy for the city council in 1941 was in this vein. Even the political demography of New York City eluded Tammany Hall, for reapportionment created four new state assembly districts (numbers 11, 12, 13, and 14) out of Harlem, where about 90 percent of Manhattan's blacks resided; these four districts had a population in 1943 of 445,800, of which 67 percent or 289,000 were blacks. In turn, these four districts were restructured to form the 22nd congressional district, which replaced Harlem's 21st district and created only the second congressional district in the country in which a majority of the population was black.

The capacity for independence among black voters had been demonstrated during Powell's successful election to the city council in 1941. Harlem's blacks repeated this behavior in the 1942 gubernatorial election, supporting Republican Thomas E. Dewey over Democratic John J. Bennett. In a congressional by-election in February 1944 the unsuccessful Republican candidate, William S. Bennet, gained more black votes than his Democratic victor, James Torrens. Thus the stage was set for Powell's debut in a congressional election.

Powell's candidacy began on a discordant note. Herbert Bruce, the black district leader in the new 12th assembly district, had faced a bid by Powell in 1941 to unseat him, so when Powell announced his congressional candidacy as a Democrat in the summer of 1944 he was challenging the authority of Bruce, Harlem's first black district leader. But this mattered little to Powell, who had demonstrated for a decade his charismatic appeal in Harlem, as well as his skill at using both the sacred-cultural medium of the black church and the secular-cultural medium of a weekly newspaper, *The People's Voice,* which Powell founded in 1942. Powell's campaign immediately sparked a massive bandwagon in his favor and carried all of Harlem's political forces in its wake. Powell was overwhelmingly victorious in the primary election in August 1944, gaining not only the Democratic and Republican nomi-

268

nations but also that of the left-wing American Labor party. (In reality, Powell needed only the Democratic nomination, for Harlem blacks had voted 67 percent Democratic in the presidential election of 1932 and were voting 77 percent Democratic by 1940.) Powell's rout of the primary election launched him on his congressional career without the need for a general election.

In the twentieth century Powell was preceded in Congress by three other northern Afro-Americans, all elected from Chicago's Southside black community—Oscar DePriest (1929–34), Arthur Mitchell (1934–42), and Dawson (1942–71). Whereas these black predecessors gained office largely through use of pragmatic style and deference to a city machine, Powell launched his congressional career in the same way that he commenced his Harlem leadership—relying on ethnic militancy and black populist arousal. In Congress Powell encountered situations that reinforced his attachment to this political style—situations that made him proud to be "the first bad nigger in Congress." Thus while Dawson ignored the white supremacist life style of the Congress, Powell suffered these insults poorly. As he remarked in his autobiography:

> In that capital, along the banks of the quiet and muddy Potomac, witness and testimony were given by night and by day to the emasculation of the Bill of Rights and Constitution that I had sworn to uphold, even when there was no upholding done by those in high places. . . . Arriving from Chicago in 1943 [Dawson] found not a single hotel that would give him a room. Nor was there a restaurant where he could eat or a lunch counter where he could buy a cup of coffee. . . . This man who had come from Chicago, a member of the United States Congress, was even discouraged from eating in his own dining room although the sign said "Reserved for Members of Congress only." Even the black men and women who toiled for the government could not eat in the government employees' dining room, but stood abjectly in the corridor, waiting for their handout from a window.

Powell lashed out against Washington's white supremacist ways, within and without Congress, seldom following Dawson's strategy of restraining himself for the sake of political compromise and prudence. His first occasion was forced upon him. On January 8, 1945, Congressman John E. Rankin (Democrat, Mississippi) issued a statement that Powell's election to the House was a "disgrace" and that he would not "let Adam C. Powell sit by me." Seating in the House (unlike the Senate) is open, and when Powell heard of Rankin's racial slur, he replied

269

that Rankin's presence in Congress was "distasteful" and that the only people "fit for him to sit by are Hitler and Mussolini." But Powell, fond of confrontations, especially with white racists, did not leave the matter there. For, as he records in his autobiography, "whenever Rankin entered the Chamber, I followed after him, sitting next to him or as close as I could. One day the press reported that he moved five times. Finally, on January 15 after a Party caucus, he had to shut up."

Throughout his congressional career Powell cherished his political independence. He sensed early that deference to the political codes of Congress, no less than those of Tammany Hall, would jeopardize his autonomy. Pliant congressmen, Powell well knew, were ensured re-election or at least the resources with which to run a campaign. He had good evidence of this in the case of Dawson who, having surrendered ethnic militancy for the pliant style, seemed capable of indefinite re-election to Congress. But never mind. Powell, aided no doubt by the independent resources of his church and its communicants, was willing to forego the benefits of compliance. He alone in the years before siz-able black representation in Congress used national politics as a plat-form for articulating a form of black ethnic militancy—a militancy that was sometimes anti-white, always pro-black in form if not in sub-stance, and always at war with white supremacists.

The political costs of this course of action were often greater than Powell expected. Perhaps his biggest crisis (before the one that re-sulted in loss of his seat in 1967) occurred in the mid-1950s following his endorsement of Dwight D. Eisenhower for president. Unhappy with Democrat Adlai Stevenson, who was not as forceful on civil rights as Powell wished, and faced with a tax investigation by the Internal Reve-nue Service, Powell put his enormous influence among Afro-Americans to the service of the Republican party. And for the first time since 1936 more than one-third of Afro-American voters backed a Republican. The aftermath of this was a bitter attempt by New York Democrats to remove Powell from the party. But the Democrats were nursing a greater fissure than their one with Powell, one between re-formers, led by Mayor Robert Wagner, and the Tammany old guard, led by Carmine DeSapio. Though loathing liberals for the compro-mises they made at the federal level with racism in the South and with southern congressmen, Powell sided with the reformers, placing the clout of Harlem's voters behind them and thereby securing his party status. The only loss he sustained was the allegiance of his longtime Harlem peer, J. Raymond Jones who, by siding with DeSapio, became the first black to secure an executive position in Tammany Hall. Competition among blacks, all else equal, can augment political rewards.

Through Powell's congressional career he discovered frequently that liberalism was a problematic approach for advancing the status of Afro-Americans. The willingness of liberal congressmen to sacrifice the interest of blacks when the decisive power formations in Congress considered these interests expendable annoyed Powell profoundly. And his annoyance revealed itself in his seemingly erratic legislative behavior. For example, during his first session in Congress, Powell voted with Rankin to defeat a liberal-backed Fair Employment Practices bill; Powell opposed the bill because of its weaknesses, preferring no bill to a bad one; Rankin opposed the bill out of his racist principles. In 1959 Powell, now joined by Dawson and two new black Democratic congressmen, Charles Diggs of Michigan and Robert Nix of Pennsylvania, voted against a civil rights amendment to the Housing Act because the amendment, initiated by Republicans, was designed to defeat the Housing Act by making it unacceptable to southern congressmen. Earlier in the same session, however, Powell had initiated another civil rights amendment to the Education Act that the House adopted; when the Education Act was voted as a whole, however, the amendment was defeated. In this maneuver, Powell preferred no legislation to one that denied equality of allocations to blacks.

This mode of managing federal legislation in regard to blacks' needs was developed in earnest by Powell following his elevation in 1961 to the chairmanship of the House of Education and Labor Committee. He periodically attached a pro-black or pro–civil rights amendment—eventually they were called "Powell Amendments"—to crucial legislation emanating from his committee. This invariably caused serious delay in enacting such legislation, often requiring major modification or producing outright defeat of the legislation. In this Powell was keeping faith with both his character and his basic commitment to advancing Afro-Americans' claim for equality. Perhaps Powell as a legislator could behave in no other way.

Powell reached the peak of his legislative career in the years after his elevation to the chairmanship of the House Committee on Education and Labor. For the first time in his political life, Powell appeared to surmount certain personality deficiencies that restricted his legislative effectiveness. Now that real power was at hand, his for the asking, he seemed to grasp more fully the conditions required for its effective exercise.

Thus he was able to reach out for votes from congressmen outside both his party and ideology, trading benefits to serve the needs of Afro-Americans. For the first time, he put together a professional congressional staff, organized around the legislative functions of the important committee he chaired. Comprising twenty-four members, Powell's staff was thoroughly integrated—more than any other in Congress—with twelve black members. His most important ally in the House was not his black peers but House Speaker Sam Rayburn (Democrat, Texas), who first initiated bargaining with Powell in 1959 pursuant to Powell's succession to the committee chair. Powell backed Rayburn's protégé, Senator Lyndon Baines Johnson, for the Democratic presidential nomination in return for Rayburn's favor for the chairmanship. And Powell kept his bargain, supporting Johnson in 1960—an action that, three years later when Vice-President Johnson succeeded to the presidency after President John F. Kennedy's assassination, rebounded in legislative benefits for Afro-Americans. Powell even amended some of his behavior, reducing his absenteeism on the House floor and keeping his voting participation well over 50 percent throughout the 1960s. (For a while in the 1950s Powell's voting record was usually under 50 percent; Dawson's, on the other hand, was much higher.) Real power can usually exact the appropriate behavior for its effective management.

Powell's committee produced significant public policies beneficial to blacks, the aged, the handicapped, women, poor whites, and Hispanic-Americans. During his first five years (1961-66) Powell's committee generated nearly sixty pieces of significant social legislation, forty-nine of which were bedrock bills and eleven were amending bills. These bills covered such crucial areas of social legislation as fair employment practices, elementary and secondary school aid, manpower development and training, vocational rehabilitation, school lunch program, war on poverty, federal aid to libraries, barring discrimination in wages for women, and increasing the minimum wage.

It was not, of course, coincidental that Powell's greatest legislative success overlapped with Johnson's presidency. Johnson had owed much to Powell for supporting his presidential bid in 1960, and though it failed, Johnson gained the vice-presidency and ultimately succeeded Kennedy. Blacks joined other Democratic forces in giving Johnson a landslide victory in 1964—blacks were nearly 100 percent for Johnson—and following this even Johnson displayed a veritable reformist conversion, utilizing his tremendous legislative skills to back the

272

broadest range of social and civil rights policies ever to emanate from the U.S. Congress.

Curiously enough, just as Johnson declined in both health and political efficacy during the last years of the 1960s, so did Powell undergo a reversal of fortune, both physical and political. Powell's change in political fortune was mainly of his own making; Johnson's emanated from the profound cultural and societal changes among America's youth and young adults, precipitated by the Vietnam war. Powell seemed never able to suppress the egotistical and flamboyant elements in his personality. Thus, trips to Europe and the Caribbean with his female staff members—black and white—subjected him to criticism from anti-black elements of the press. Powell brought further criticism and notoriety on himself by charging a New York woman in 1960 with being a "bag woman" who carried bribes to New York City policemen. Mrs. Esther James sued Powell, but he escaped paying $200,000 by not visiting New York City for several years. A settlement was finally reached in 1967, when Powell paid her $46,500.

Meanwhile, anti-black elements in the House moved against Powell and in August 1966 charged him with receiving checks meant for members of his staff, particularly his wife. An investigation by an ad hoc committee, chaired by Democrat Wayne Hays of Ohio (who was himself investigated a decade later for paying staff for sexual favors), found Powell guilty. But this did not satisfy Powell's enemies: the House stripped him of his chairmanship and denied him his seat when the 90th Congress opened on January 10, 1967. Though another ad hoc committee, this one chaired by Powell's friend and fellow New York Democrat Emanuel Celler, voted to reinstate Powell after he paid a fine, the House rejected this proposal. Powell was reelected in April 1967 by a massive majority, but again Congress denied him his seat.

Powell took the fight to the U.S. Supreme Court, which ruled that he should be reinstated. Meanwhile, opposition to him emerged in Harlem, producing a viable black candidate. Just as the changes in the political demography of Harlem produced by the 1940 census aided Powell's initial election to Congress in 1944, so did the 1970 census figures contribute to Powell's defeat. Powell himself influenced some of the changes in the ethnic composition of his congressional district in 1970 by excluding some working-class whites and Puerto Ricans and adding a segment of middle-class Jews. It was the latter who, ironically, helped Charles Rangel, a half-black, half-Puerto Rican state assemblyman, defeat Powell in the 1970 primary; the margin was 205 votes: Rangel, 7,804, and Powell, 7,599. Rangel remarked, "It seems like it falls short of an overwhelming mandate." Rangel won the November election by 44,000 votes.

At the end of his autobiography, Powell offered no serious reflection on his defeat. Instead he indulged in a self-serving account of how in 1968–70 he joined forces with the black power militants in black urban communities throughout the country, basking in the celebration that all types of black militants bestowed on him. In this Powell was as true to history as to his ego. For he did indeed pioneer at the national level the political style of black solidarity. Both Powell's successes and failures during his political lifetime were outgrowths of his political style—two sides of a coin that historians cannot ignore.

Powell concluded his autobiography with a rather candid and flippant account of his last days as a womanizer. In one sense both Powell's political style and social exploits were fundamental to this character. In both, it is not incorrect to think of Powell as did the Harlem drunk who, responding to attacks on Powell's luxuriant lifestyle by a campaign opponent, shouted, "Quit your wailing, Jack. . . . The Cat's only living." Somewhere between "only living" and harnessing power for useful ends, a keen biographer will one day capture the fulsome character of Adam Clayton Powell, Jr.

Note on Sources

The context of urban America during the first three decades of the twentieth century and of the status of blacks there in is presented in three books: W. Lloyd Warner and Paul S. Lunt, *The Social Life of a Modern Community* (New Haven, Conn.: Yale University Press, 1941); W. E. B. Du Bois, *The Philadelphia Negro: A Social Survey* (Philadelphia: University of Pennsylvania Press, 1899); and Elliott Rudwick, *Race Riot at East St. Louis, July 2, 1917* (Carbondale: Southern Illinois University Press, 1964).

The formative experience of Afro-Americans with white-controlled urban party machines is treated brilliantly in Harold F. Gosnell, *Negro Politicians: The Rise of Negro Politics in Chicago* (Chicago: The University of Chicago Press, 1935). An overview of this experience is found in Martin Kilson, "Political Change in the Negro Ghetto, 1900–1940's" in Nathan Huggins et al., eds., *Key Issues in the Afro-American Experience* (New York: Harcourt Brace Jovanovich, 1971). The rise of black party machine politicians in early twentieth-century New York City is traced in Gilbert Osofsky, *Harlem: The Making of a Ghetto* (New York: Harper and Row, 1966). Valuable material on this is also found in John Morsell, "The Political Behavior of Negroes in New York City" (Ph.D. diss., Columbia University, 1950), a study that still deserves to be published.

Some of the best biographical material on Powell is in two accounts by Powell himself: *Marching Blacks: An Interpretive History of the Rise of the Black Common Man,* rev. ed. (New York: Dial Press, 1973 [orig. publ. 1945]), and *Adam by Adam: The Autobiography of Adam Clayton Powell, Jr.* (New York: Dial Press, 1971). These personal accounts, always vivid and candid, offer excellent material on Powell's political career as well. The context out of which Powell entered politics is provided by Roi Ottley, *'New World A-Coming': Inside Black America* (Boston: Houghton-Mifflin Co., 1943) and Henry Lee Moon, *Balance of Power: The Negro Vote* (Garden City, N.Y.: Doubleday, 1948). Also useful is Edmund Cronon, *Black Moses: Marcus Garvey and the Universal Negro Improvement Association* (Madison: University of Wisconsin Press, 1960).

The best general study of Powell's political style is Neil Hickey and E. Edwin, *Adam Clayton Powell and the Politics of Race* (New York: Fleet Publishing Corp., 1965). An excellent theoretical analysis of Powell's use of ethnic militancy, contrasting it with the pragmatic political style, is James Q. Wilson, "Two Negro Politicians: An Interpretation," *Midwest Journal of Political Science,* 4 (Nov. 1960): 346–69. Powell's break with New York Democrats is treated in David Hapgood, *The Purge that Failed: Tammany against Powell* (New York: Holt, 1959). Data on Powell's legislative experience, his successes, especially, are found in the *Congressional Record.* Powell's tactics as a legislator are evaluated by his former staff member, Chuck Stone, in *Black Political Power in America* (Indianapolis, Ind.: Bobbs-Merrill, 1968 [rev. ed., New York, 1970]).

David Levering Lewis 13

Martin Luther King, Jr., and the Promise of Nonviolent Populism

In the late eighteenth and nineteenth centuries ministers had often played important roles as black leaders, both in politics and civic life. But the turn of the century, with the ascendency of Booker T. Washington and later of W. E. B. Du Bois, marked the transition both to greater specialization of function among Negro leaders and the ascendancy of secular national spokesmen in civic and political affairs. (Adam Clayton Powell, Jr., in this as in other ways, was unusual.) In the South churchmen did retain a more influential role, often as intermediaries between blacks and influential whites. Martin Luther King, Jr., therefore, presents a fresh departure—a militant black protest leader with his base in the masses of southern black Baptists who played a critical role on the national stage in the battle for Afro-American freedom. Moreover, he not only symbolized the spread of militant black protest from the North to the South, but he was unique among black leaders in the way in which he became an important spokesman for broader social and economic concerns as well.

King's career was directly connected with the continued escalation of black expectations and the rising tide of Afro-American protest that followed World War II and that flowered in the early 1960s. The tactics of "nonviolent direct action" that he and his followers employed—mass marches, boycotts, sit-ins, filling the jails rather than paying bails or fines—were not new. Pioneering work in these tactics had been carried on by both A. Philip Randolph and the interracial Congress of Racial Equality, founded in 1942, but King crystallized a growing dissatisfaction with the limited changes effected by the strategies of the National Association for the Advancement of Colored People. He captured the imagination of black Americans—and many whites as well—and paved the way for the temporary ascendancy of militant demonstrations that swept the country in the early 1960s.

THE CIVIL RIGHTS CAREER of Martin Luther King, Jr., can be divided into two major periods—before Selma and after. The first begins with the December 1955 Montgomery bus boycott and ends with the march from Selma to Montgomery, Alabama, in late March 1965. The second begins with the Chicago demonstrations for jobs and housing during

1966 and ends with the assassination of King in Memphis, Tennessee, on April 4, 1968. The first period is characterized by a decade of innovative protest tactics employed to achieve traditional citizenship rights for Afro-Americans. The second—less than three turbulent years—was a time of nontraditional tactics in pursuit of increasingly radical goals for the larger society. The first was partially successful, but its relative success accentuated what yet remained to be done before the poor, the powerless, and the racially disadvantaged could begin to achieve equality of opportunity in America. The second period was marked by relative failure, and its legacy was the vision of political power and economic well-being devolving increasingly upon the poor, the powerless, and the racially disadvantaged. In the first period King and his allies brought about the beginning of the desegregated community. In the second the remote prospect of their "beloved community" vanished at Memphis. The greatness of the decade ending with Selma was in the nobility of the protesters; that of the times after Selma was in the far-reaching implications of the protest.

When Mrs. Rosa Parks, a seamstress at a downtown Montgomery, Alabama, department store, a loyal member of the National Association for the Advancement of Colored People, and a model of personal industry and propriety, defied the city's segregated transportation ordinance by refusing to surrender her bus seat to a white person on the first day of December 1955, she inaugurated an era in the struggle for civil rights. Her deed made King possible. The twenty-five-year-old Atlanta-born pastor of Dexter Avenue Baptist Church, in Montgomery less than a year and not well known in its Afro-American community, found himself at the head of a bus boycott movement before there had been time to weigh the full significance of the honor. Others had been more active and for far longer in the local civil rights activity. Others (the Pullman porter E. D. Nixon was clearly one) might have been more plausible leaders, but the city's Afro-American leadership, divided, contentious, and apprehensive, chose the newcomer to lead the Montgomery Improvement Association (MIA). It happened so quickly, King recalled, "that I did not even have time to think it through." Montgomery's Afro-American citizenry selected, almost by chance, not only the best person to lead their boycott but the person best suited to become the leader of the larger struggle for racial rights. And as the inevitable worked its purpose circumstantially in the choice of leader, the tactics by which the leader's strategy was achieved were similarly determined. If the concept of nonviolent passive resistance was as old as Christianity, with Thoreau and Gandhi as illustrious practitioners, and as recent as philosopher A. J. Muste's Fellowship of Reconciliation (FOR), its adoption by the MIA was more a matter of circumstance than of philosophy. Montgomery's Afro-Americans *had* to be nonviolent and passive in order to resist successfully.

Parks had been arrested December 1, 1955. On December 21, 1956, King, accompanied by several allies, boarded a public bus in front of his house. The MIA had won. Victory had come about through community solidarity (largely inspired by King's superb oratory and equally superb personal courage), despite jeopardized jobs, intimidation by the Ku Klux Klan, and harassment by police—and bombs. One night, as his wife, Coretta, rushed to the rear with their infant daughter, the front of the King home was shattered by dynamite. For a brief period, the Reverend King even carried a pistol. Once he was arrested on a trumped-up charge of speeding, and denied bail until his loyal lieutenant, Reverend Ralph David Abernathy, arrived at the head of hundreds of followers. A city ordinance was invoked to prohibit organized taxi transport of bus boycotters. With money raised locally and from steadily rising contributions from national labor, libertarian, and religious organizations, from benefit performances and compassionate individuals the world over, the MIA purchased a fleet of vehicles. The city sought and won an indictment of King, Abernathy, and more than eighty other MIA members for conspiracy to interfere with normal business activity. Conviction by the Montgomery court and appeal to the federal courts followed, and in the interim the city pressed the attack, belatedly seeking a local injunction of the MIA car pool. Then, just as MIA leaders awaited the inevitable adverse decision from the municipal court on November 13, the U.S. Supreme Court decreed Alabama's state and local laws enforcing segregation on buses unconstitutional.

The formula for nonviolent civil rights campaigns was perfected in Montgomery: unsuccessful presentation of elementary grievances; mounting of increasingly provocative peaceful demonstrations; gross acts of violence by white citizens and outrageous misconduct by local law enforcement and judicial bodies, relentlessly reported by the national media; infusion of money and talent from national liberal organizations and increasing participation of nonresident whites (clergy, labor, students) in nonviolent demonstrations; single or multiple atrocities perpetrated by local whites, leading to direct or indirect federal intervention and negotiated settlement with chastened or cowed white officials. King's pulpit rhetoric, electric presence in the community and at the head of singing columns, his internationally reported sojourns in jail, fund-raising prowess in the North, and unyielding enforcement of nonviolent discipline in the South, and his consistent reasonableness at the negotiating table were (more often than not) highly effective.

In retrospect, the combination of King's personal assets and nonviolent tactics have a far more formidable appearance than in reality they often did at the time. In fact, he and his movement were continually menaced by the cruel paradox that unless they triggered savage reactions from their opponents, the nation (white and black) tended to impugn his organization's motives and reproach King for disrupting what was perceived as slow yet orderly racial progress in a given community. There was also a second paradox that tended over time to undercut the performance of King and his organization: the young Afro-American and white students enrolled in the other two nonviolent direct action organizations, the recently formed Student Nonviolent Coordinating Committee (SNCC) and the older Congress of Racial Equality (CORE), were at first uneasy with and then hostile to King's "conservative" role as race leader. Despite the ink spilled over matters of doctrine both by historians and the participants themselves, what increasingly divided the SNCC and CORE "militants" from King and his followers was not so much "genuine" versus "tactical" nonviolent passive resistance, but King's leadership credibility. Thus, this critical pool of leadership and manpower—SNCC, CORE, and their less permanent analogues—was available to King often on a qualified basis and sometimes even a hostile one.

Complications arising from this second paradox were largely avoided for a time. When King left Montgomery permanently for Atlanta at the end of 1959, the doctrine of nonviolent passive resistance and the vehicle to advance it were firmly in place. By then, King had traveled widely (Europe, Ghana, India), written his first book (*Stride Toward Freedom*), lobbied nationally for civil rights, indirectly contributed to the large Afro-American vote that gave candidate John F. Kennedy a slim presidential victory, and presided over the birth of the Atlanta-based Southern Christian Leadership Conference (SCLC). In April 1960 he was present for the founding of what was to become SNCC, at Shaw University in Raleigh, North Carolina. He fully endorsed the spreading student sit-in movement, carefully participated in it when it reached conservative Atlanta, and had SCLC advance small sums to SNCC for its Freedom Rides throughout the South during spring and summer 1961 (probes into the South by interracial cadres to test compliance with federal regulations governing interstate travel). Even so, many SNCC rank and file were suspicious of King and SCLC, and the uneasiness of many SNCC leaders developed into aversion when their organization split over the debate of whether to escalate the nonviolent, direct action campaign or to shift emphasis, as the new Kennedy Administration and many northern philanthropies urged, to a voter education and registration campaign. SCLC, by encouraging SNCC to adopt the voting rights project and by serving as a conduit for funds from the Field and Taconic foundations, confirmed the worst suspicions of many in SNCC that King and his movement were too moderate. For Attorney General Robert Kennedy, Senator Hubert Humphrey, New York Governor Nelson Rockefeller, and many other concerned politicians, however, the SCLC leader was the best promise for steering Afro-American anger into what they regarded as safe channels.

Albany, Georgia, a rigidly segregated town, was King's first major setback. The initial objectives were modest: integration of interstate bus and rail facilities (the municipal bus company was added later) and formation of a permanent biracial civic committee. But three fundamental elements were amiss in Albany: (1) SCLC planned poorly; (2) local white opposition was resolute and intelligent; and (3) the federal government withheld active support. Each of these elements operated synergistically, so that the conduct of one rapidly determined that of the others. Had Albany been studied carefully rather than plunged into enthusiastically at the end of 1961, King would not have been surprised to find himself at the center of an internecine Afro-American struggle of maddening complexity. There were the SNCC operatives who, after spending months overcoming local derision of their clothes, hairstyles, youthfulness, and "crazy ideas," had only recently won the confidence of the NAACP Youth League and the Albany State College students in order to maneuver the solid church people and professionals into opposing the white community. There were the local NAACP dignitaries, middle-aged pillars of the community, who were still as resentful of being shunted aside as they were hostile to SNCC's confrontational policies. There were the Afro-American businessmen, highly successful but also highly vulnerable, who courageously advocated racial progress, but not at any price. There were the local preachers, never more given to homiletics than when action was required, whose outstanding egos made collaborative efforts difficult. There was the strong sense of local pride shared across warring generations and personalities. When SCLC's leader and his lieutenants accepted the December 15th summons from the president of the Albany

Movement, extended without prior consultation of the membership, they walked into a situation of intolerable unpredictability.

Planning would have helped in Albany, yet there was little the SCLC could have done to undercut the determination of its white adversaries. The leader of the white business community, James Gray, owner-editor of the Albany *Herald*, was an intransigent racist whose newspaper regularly inflamed white public opinion, contributing to a climate in which the political risks to city officials of meaningful biracial negotiations were prohibitive. Counting on firm support from Senator Herman Talmadge's machine in Atlanta, local white leadership drew up plans to close some public facilities and to "sell" parks, pools, playgrounds, and libraries to a group of businessmen headed by Gray, which was eventually done. When the municipal bus company, reeling from a boycott, offered to desegregate service and hire one Afro-American driver, the white establishment forced it to renege on the informal promise and declare bankruptcy. Unlike white Montgomery, which had never fully recovered from shock and lurched from tactic to tactic, or white Atlanta, which was embarrassed by sit-ins and mass demonstrations, Albany was never shocked or embarrassed. During the eight-month period of active SCLC involvement, with headlines such as "Keep on Fighting for Albany," the *Herald* spoke for businessmen and politicians determined to make their city a symbol of uncompromising racial separatism.

But what made Albany even more formidable was the form taken by its intransigence. In Sheriff Laurie Pritchett, King met a travestied image of himself—a nonviolent segregationist law officer. Off camera and especially in temporary prisons set up outside the city limits to handle the swelling population of demonstrators, there were frequent acts of police brutality. But Sheriff Pritchett was always an efficient, correct—even humane—custodian of order while the news camera rolled. "It's not a matter of whether I'm a segregationist or an integrationist," he told the press. "I'm a duly constituted law enforcement officer, dedicated to the enforcement of the law." As demonstrators marched to Albany's court house to press demands that escalated over the months to end all segregation ordinances and cause adoption of a fair hiring and employment policy for the city and its businesses, Pritchett and his men, after issuing polite orders to disperse, patiently arrested and assembled the demonstrators for transport to jails. "He tried to be decent," no less an authority than Coretta King concedes in her autobiography. "He would allow the protestors to demonstrate up to a point. He would bow his head with them while they prayed. Then, of course, he would arrest them." When violence finally erupted on the night of July 24, 1962, the perpetrators were not, as the nation was learning to expect from the South, red-faced, overweight policemen wielding clubs, they were 2,000 rampaging Afro-American teenagers. King's embarrassment was so great that he adjourned demonstrations and called for a "day of penance." It is highly likely that if Pritchett's nonviolent law enforcement technique had been followed in other southern cities, civil rights advancement would have been greatly retarded. City officials elsewhere would have been able to boast, as one in Albany did to the New York *Herald Tribune*, "We killed them with kindness. Apparently, it was a condition M. L. King and the other outsiders had never encountered before."

King's trump card, played elsewhere with perfect timing and devastating consequences—jail until an agreement to negotiate—failed in Albany. His first arrest, with Abernathy and the Albany Movement president at the head of 250 singing, praying demonstrators on December 17, 1961, was followed by refusal to post bond and a vow he knew the world would notice: "If convicted, I will refuse to pay the fine. I expect to spend Christmas in jail. I hope thousands will join me." But the next day King and Abernathy surprised the world by leaving Pritchett's jail. With the New York *Herald Tribune* calling his performance "one of the most stunning defeats of his career," the Pittsburgh *Courier* deciding that little had been achieved, and much of the Afro-American community dismayed, King eventually offered *Time* magazine an explanation: "We thought the victory had been won. When we got out, we discovered it was all a hoax." The SCLC leader was the victim of a hoax by his own allies. The fractious leadership of the Albany Movement chafed at what it regarded as high-handed behavior by several SCLC officers, resented the almost exclusive attention the media paid King and the SCLC, was suspicious of the use made of the large outside donations flowing mainly to the SCLC, unconvinced of the wisdom of SCLC's national call to Albany of volunteer demonstrators, and, finally, preferred no settlement at all to one negotiated by King and the SCLC. "There was constant war between us as to strategy," a prominent SNCC leader confessed. SNCC feared King would be too moderate at the negotiating table. Others in the Albany Movement were simply jealous of King's getting the credit.

King's second prison stay occurred on July 10, when, after a five-month delay, he and Abernathy returned to be sentenced for the December 17 infraction, refusing to pay the $178 fine and choosing instead forty-five days at hard labor. Again the media sizzled, donations arrived at SCLC headquarters, northern students and activists (mostly white) headed for Albany, Governor Rockefeller, prominent members of Congress and labor leaders urged President Kennedy to take action, while downtown Albany resounded to the strains of "We Shall Overcome." Three days later, King's jailers released him and Abernathy, explaining that his fine had been paid by an unidentified Afro-American. "Never before have I been thrown out of jail," Abernathy told a puzzled church gathering. On July 17, King, Abernathy, and the Albany Movement president were rearrested for demonstrating, again vowing not to leave their cells. Again, press and television coverage put King at the center of the nation's business. A group of ministers and rabbis conferred with Kennedy about the outrage. Others motored to Albany. Finally, the president found it politically wise to wonder aloud why the people of Albany were unable to negotiate their differences. Meanwhile, the Sunday New York *Times* (August 5) carried King's morally compelling article, "The Case against Tokenism," which praised the Kennedy administration for its international diplomacy but roundly lambasted its inaction on civil rights. Kennedy's New Frontier was "unfortunately not new enough," he charged. "And the Frontier is set too close to the rear." Five days later King and his fellow offenders were found guilty by the local court and given suspended sentences. King promptly announced his belief (encouraged by the Justice Department and local white leadership) that, if he departed for Atlanta, the city and the Albany Movement would reach an accord.

Instead, race relations deteriorated in Albany. This time, as with his second incarceration, the hoax was engineered by the whites who finally understood, as southern whites elsewhere never did, that to keep King in jail was to guarantee their own defeat. After three abortive attempts to remain imprisoned long enough to humble his adversaries through the power of national and international condemnation, King left Albany for good in late August 1962. Had he offered himself for arrest a fourth time, it is very likely that the response of northern opinion and Albany's Afro-American citizenry would have been distinctly lukewarm. Writing in a southern journal, SCLC leader Wyatt Tee Walker conceded that things had gone badly, but he thought that valuable lessons had been learned: "Albany is a milepost in the early stage of the nonviolent revolution. Our nonviolent revolution is not yet full-grown. I do not know if it will ever reach adulthood, but I pray that it will."

Birmingham, Alabama, in spring of 1963, answered the Reverend

Walker's prayers. It was a magnificent triumph for King and his movement, as well as a considerable moment in the evolution of democracy
in America. The objectives were to desegregate schools, public facilities, and commercial institutions, initiate hiring and promotion of
Afro-American personnel in downtown retail stores, and establish a
biracial committee to monitor racial progress. Here the three fundamental elements were propitious: (1) SCLC planned well; (2) local
white opposition was divided and part of it ideally intemperate; and (3)
the federal government intervened decisively on the side of equity.
Much preparation went into the Birmingham venture. In the first week
in January 1963, King, Abernathy, and Walker visited Anniston,
Gadsden, Talladega, Montgomery, Birmingham, and the rural areas
around Selma as part of SCLC's People-to-People tour to stiffen the
resolve of Alabama Afro-Americans to place their names on voter
rolls (thirty-seven teachers had recently been fired for trying) and to
garner needed area support and national publicity for the campaign.
Additionally, there was a highly successful Los Angeles fund-raising
rally organized by singer Harry Belafonte and a subsequent secret
meeting in Belafonte's New York apartment of seventy-five influential
friends of civil rights and members of the press (representatives of New
York's Mayor Robert Wagner and Governor Rockefeller and members of the business, literary, film, and religious community). King's
message was clear. Despite numerous U.S. Supreme Court rulings and
federal directives, racial desegregation continued to proceed, if at all,
at a snail's pace throughout most of the South. The Kennedy White
House and Justice Department demonstrated little inclination to risk a
slim electoral margin by angering the white South. To ameliorate the
condition of Birmingham's Afro-Americans would constitute a major
victory over Jim Crow, the repercussions of which would be felt
throughout the South. The mobilization of thousands of Afro-
American citizens in the city (using children for the first time) and the
brutal white counterreaction would compel the federal government to
implement vigorously the decision of the Supreme Court. "We've got
to have a crisis to bargain with," the Reverend Walker explained. "To
take a moderate approach, hoping to get help from whites, doesn't
work. They nail you to the cross." After two false starts (postponed
because of mayoral elections in early March and a runoff between
"progressive" candidate Albert Boutwell and racist Eugene "Bull"
Connor in early April), demonstrations began in Birmingham on
April 3.

Birmingham fixed the moral stature of King in the national consciousness. In three documents coming at the beginning, middle, and immediate aftermath of the campaign, the SCLC leader became, for a time, the embodiment of civil rights. The *Birmingham Manifesto* spelled out the circumstances that had driven the people of that city to active defiance and the moral basis of that defiance: "We act today in full concert with our Hebraic-Christian tradition, the law of morality, and the Constitution of our nation. The absence of justice and progress in Birmingham demands that we make a moral witness to give our community a chance to survive." Pledged to the Ten Commandments of Nonviolence (e.g., 1. MEDITATE daily on teachings and life of Jesus. 8. REFRAIN from violence of fist, tongue, or heart), drilled in nonviolent techniques by members of the Alabama Christian Movement for Human Rights (ACMHR) and SCLC, and fired by King's oratory, Birmingham's Afro-Americans filled Sheriff Connor's cells day after song-filled day.

King's arrest and solitary confinement resulted in the second document, the magisterial "Letter from Birmingham Jail," written in the margins of newspaper and on scraps of paper. Refuting several white southern preachers and rabbis who condemned his conduct as unworthy of a man of God, the imprisoned author wrote that he had come to bring the gospel of freedom to a city of injustice. Like the prophets of the eighth century B.C., like the Apostle Paul, he felt the urge to carry the gospel far beyond his own home. "Like Paul," he wrote of the need to "respond to the Macedonian call for aid." What had Jesus meant, King asked rhetorically, in saying "I have not come to bring peace, but a sword?" King answered that "positive peace" entailed wrathful social dislocation by the just. Citing examples from the lives and principles of Socrates and Gandhi, he justified his and his followers' "lawlessness" by arguing that only just laws need be obeyed, that, to be just, a law made by people had to correspond to God's law, and that any law that degraded people was bad. "Letter" ended on a high civic and religious note: "One day the South will know that when these disinherited children of God sat down at lunch counters, they were in reality standing up for what is best in the American dream and for the most sacred values in our Judeo-Christian heritage."

At first Sheriff Connor, in agreement with Mayor-elect Boutwell, had adopted the restrained tactics of Albany's Chief Pritchett, but when the demonstrations escalated and the incumbent city administration (seizing a technicality in the charter) decided not to leave office for another two years, Connor's police turned violent. The evening television news carried scenes of shocking brutality—dogs attacking children, police clubbing women, firemen stripping backs bare with hoses, tear gas strangling demonstrators and press alike. Burke Marshall, assistant U.S. attorney general in charge of civil rights, arrived to negotiate with 125 white civic leaders at the Birmingham chamber of commerce. Secretary of Treasury Douglas Dillon contacted the chairman of Royal Crown Cola, the president of Birmingham Trust National Bank, and the board chairman of the city's largest real estate mortgage company. Secretary of Defense Robert McNamara used his influence as former director of the Ford Motor Corporation. Eugene Rostow, dean of Yale University Law School, urged Yale graduate and U.S. Steel board chairman Roger Blough to intercede with the president of his corporation's Birmingham subsidiary. Attorney General Kennedy telephoned city officials. Nearly $300,000 in bail money was quickly raised by the United Automobile Workers (UAW) and the National Maritime Union. On May 15, 1963, what King called a "bold new design for a new South"—the Birmingham Pact (opening up schools, stores, jobs, and transportation)—was struck. The Alabama Supreme Court ruled the old city government and Connor out of office, and the U.S. Supreme Court declared sit-in demonstrations legal in cities that enforced segregation ordinances. Segregation began to end in Birmingham.

With the March on Washington at the end of August, King and other civil rights leaders hoped to inaugurate an era of racial integration and social justice on a national scale. The September 22nd bomb killing four little Afro-American girls attending Sunday school in a Birmingham church cruelly underscored a few weeks later how distant was the reality from the dream. Yet the dream of racial equality was probably never more powerfully evoked than it was by King on the steps of the Lincoln Memorial on August 28, 1963. The 250,000-strong crowd on the mall was saluted that hot day by statesmen, celebrities, writers, and actors, and addressed by John Lewis of SNCC (whose speech had been toned down before delivery), Whitney Young, Jr., of the Urban League, Walter Reuther of the UAW, Roy Wilkins of the NAACP, and A. Philip Randolph, who deserved credit for the original idea of the march. But nothing—not even the singing of Odetta or Mahalia Jackson—electrified the interracial crowd as much as King's "I Have A Dream" speech, the third great document of the Birmingham period.

King declared that despite bitter temporary setbacks and frustrations he held fast to a dream, a profoundly American dream that one day the nation would really practice its creed that "all men are created equal"; that the children of slaves and of slaveowners would one day live in brotherhood. He had a dream that one day his four little children would be judged not by their color but by their character. The day would come, he cried in closing, "when all God's children, black and white men, Jews and Gentiles, Protestants and Catholics, will be able to join hands and sing in the words of that old Negro spiritual, 'Free at last! Thank God almighty, we are free at last!' " To make the dream come true, the leaders of the March on Washington met with President Kennedy after the speeches and left a forest of specific demands: a comprehensive civil rights law; a Fair Employment Practices Act to bar federal, state, city, and private employers, unions, and contractors from job discrimination; extension of the Federal Fair Labor Standards Act to employment not covered and establishment of a national minimum wage of not less than two dollars an hour; desegregation of all public schools by the end of 1963; a massive federal program to train and place unemployed workers; withholding of federal funds from all institutions guilty of discrimination; greater power to the attorney general to provide injunctive relief for persons denied constitutional rights; a federal order prohibiting housing discrimination in all enterprises using federal funds; and reduction of congressional representation in states disfranchising minority groups.

The White House had originally tried to discourage the March on Washington, warning leaders of the civil rights movement not only of the far-reaching ramifications of possible violence in the nation's capital but of the more likely immediate damage to civil rights legislation pending before Congress. King had been impressed by the merits of the argument, but he had also been impressed by the considerable personal and organization risks involved in open defiance of the Kennedy administration. Neither the Urban League nor the NAACP had endorsed the idea of the march when it had first been presented by Randolph. For a time King restricted his collaboration to formal approval while doing little to assist the march organizers. As plans for the demonstration developed (pushed by Randolph, CORE, and SNCC), it became clear that the Kennedy administration was divided. Apparently, the president and his advisors decided on an all-out effort in June to insure the success of the March on Washington. Stephen Currier, husband of a Mellon heiress, president of the Taconic Foundation, and an unofficial Kennedy advisor, assembled nearly one hundred chairmen of the most powerful corporations at New York's Hotel Carlyle to raise a civil rights war chest. Three days later, Currier, along with King, Randolph, Wilkins, Young, and James Farmer of CORE, attended the crucial White House meeting at which the general objectives of the March on Washington were agreed upon. King now argued that, rather than being ill-timed and counterproductive, the march was the best means of "dramatizing the issues and mobilizing support in parts of the country which don't know the problem at first hand." Vice-President Lyndon Johnson and Attorney General Kennedy concurred.

In light of his historic speech and the vast enhancement of his national prestige and influence, there is irony in King's initial reluctance to be a participant in the March on Washington—a reluctance that was seen by some leaders and careful students of the civil rights movement as conclusive evidence of his readiness to move only as boldly and rapidly as his various and powerful white allies were willing to condone. Both established spokesmen in the movement as well as young militants alleged that the March on Washington had been co-opted and deradicalized by agents of the White House and the business community—that King had been used. The SCLC leader began to be regarded as an accommodationist, a leader walking a slender tightrope between those forces (mainly and significantly white) that supported him financially and politically because King appeared to them as the most "responsible" and "effective" Afro-American leader—and those forces (younger and mainly Afro-American) that believed the speed and scope of racial advancement were threatened by moderation. Increasingly, as a prominent civil rights historian wrote of this general phase, King was a leader who occupied the "vital center." The question was, how long could the center hold?

The year 1964 was the best and worst of times for King, Afro-America, and the country. *Time* magazine chose him as its Man of the Year in January, the first Afro-American selected. President Johnson, taking great pains to reassure the civil rights leadership, pushed hard for passage of the long-stalled civil rights bill. After eighty-three days of Senate debate and a historic two-thirds cloture vote, the legislation passed on June 19 and was signed into law as the Civil Rights Act of 1964 in early July with King and other civil rights leaders present. Yet, less than three weeks later, race riots swept through the North, beginning in Rochester, New York, and spreading to New York City, Chicago, and, by early August, Jersey City, New Jersey. There would now be a steady discharge of northern riots for almost the balance of the decade. Violence of a very different sort increased in the South, where the Mississippi Freedom Summer campaign (largely a SNCC and local NAACP operation) to register Afro-Americans to vote was attracting large numbers of mostly white college-student volunteers from the

North. On August 4, the nation was horrified when the bodies of three murdered young SNCC volunteers from the North were exhumed from a Philadelphia, Mississippi, cattle pond in which local whites had hidden them. Four days later, President Johnson signed his billion-dollar poverty program into law. Meanwhile, King, appalled by the compounding violence and deeply worried that Republican Senator Barry Goldwater might win the presidency, joined other civil rights leaders in calling for a moratorium on all civil rights demonstrations until after the elections. Significantly, CORE and SNCC rejected the moratorium. The year ended on a high note for King with a trip to Norway to receive the Nobel Peace Prize, the second Afro-American so honored. Speaking with eloquent modesty on this occasion, King represented himself as merely the "trustee" of a people's struggle, placing his own achievements within the context of collective heroism and the rightness of a cause. He was no longer a southern pastor fighting against regional racism; the Nobel Prize was the outward emblem of a larger sense of mission that had already begun to tug at his thinking.

The watershed in King's career occurred between early March and mid-August 1965. After enactment of the 1964 Civil Rights Act, federal legislation was badly needed to facilitate the right to vote for Afro-Americans in the South. SCLC had targeted Selma, Alabama, for its major voter registration campaign at the end of 1964. The federal government was disposed to help. Selma's white leadership was divided. The young major, Joseph T. Smitherton, was a timid moderate; the chief of police, Wilson Baker, was a disciple of Albany's Pritchett; and the county sheriff, James "Jim" Clark, was an out-of-control racist. But Selma was not to be another Birmingham. It was more like Albany. In Albany the cost of losing had been too high; in Selma, the cost of winning was too high—in both cases, largely due to poor generalship. On Sunday, March 7, as thousands of singing demonstrators marched across Selma's Pettus Bridge on their way to petition the right of ballot of Governor George Wallace in Montgomery, they were savagely repulsed and chased by state troopers and Sheriff Clark's deputies. Some demonstrators retaliated with rocks and bottles. A massacre was probably averted by the determined intervention of Police Chief Baker. King and Abernathy were in Atlanta, ostensibly to preach to their congregations but most probably to avoid a second Selma arrest in order to raise funds for the campaign. They promised to lead a second march to Montgomery. Volunteers came to Selma in all colors, classes, and faiths from every section of the country.

On March 10, SCLC attorneys asked a federal judge to enjoin Selma officials from interfering with the march; instead, Judge Frank M. Johnson, Jr., enjoined both sides from activities. "We've gone too far to turn back now," King told the demonstrators. The next afternoon he exhorted 3,000 people in a Methodist church: "I have got to march. I do not know what lies ahead of us. There may be beatings, jailings, tear gas. But I would rather die on the highways of Alabama than make a butchery of my conscience." But when the demonstrators had crossed the bridge, King knelt in prayer, then rose, and led them back into Selma (even though Alabama state troopers left the highway open). SNCC militants had never favored the Selma-Montgomery march, but they regarded King's turnabout on the bridge as an incredible waste of morale and opportunity. When they heard rumors of a secret pact between SCLC and President Johnson's special emissary, the head of the new Community Relations Service of the Justice Department, to march only a distance beyond the Pettus Bridge, thus not violating the federal injunction, dismay turned to outrage.

Had King violated a federal court injunction (something he had never done) and led his nonviolent resisters down U.S. Highway 80 to Montgomery, they might have been attacked by state troopers (also violating the injunction). Snipers, rumored to have been positioned by the Klan along the highway, might have decimated their ranks before federal officers could act. Although Johnson's Justice Department might have asked for severe penalties against King, student militants believed that the national shock and furor of any or all of these consequences would have ultimately greatly advanced the civil rights struggle. They observed, cynically, the vigorous public reaction of the White House when one of three white clergymen, the Reverend James Reeb, died of a crushed skull two days after being attacked at the conclusion of the Selma march. On March 15, Johnson brought Congress to its feet with his call for a voting rights act in a speech ending, stirringly, "And we shall overcome." The federal injunction against the Selma-Montgomery march had already been lifted. On Sunday, March 21, the momentous walk to Montgomery began under protection of federal marshals and military units. It reached the Alabama capital the following Thursday, where, after many of the nation's most famous entertainers and actors had performed, King stirred the great crowd with one of his finest speeches.

But what should have been a triumph only made King and his lieutenants more aware of the partial and fleeting nature of their accomplishments. Passage of the Civil Rights Act of 1964 and the Voting Rights Act of 1965 only caused many whites to wonder whether demonstrations any longer served a positive purpose. Such whites found powerful confirmation of their apprehensions in the explosion of the Los Angeles ghetto, Watts, in August 1965. The nation was also now well into a foreign war that would drain away resources to improve social conditions. There was a growing national sentiment, shared by Afro-American supporters of the NAACP and Urban League, that the times were right for pause and consolidation. Had King and SCLC conceded the wisdom of caution, it is certain that neither could have continued to function. NAACP and Urban League leaders, however egocentric, were organization men, and their organizations depended for survival neither upon charisma nor improvisation. SCLC, by contrast, was an improvisation surviving because of the leader's charisma, rather than because of organizational structure.

Cynics explained away SCLC's decision to fight discrimination in the North as merely expedient. If it is unlikely that this decision was wholly devoid of expediency, it is far more significant that it announced a broader and more sophisticated SCLC awareness of fundamental causes of racism. Moving to Chicago in early 1966, demanding housing, jobs, and genuine public school integration, tangling with the city's hard-nosed mayor, and gradually losing the active support of many white allies, King's foray into the North was far from successful. Many northern white supporters—labor leaders, various liberals, and prelates—called the Chicago activities inflammatory, counterproductive, and at best premature. Many Afro-Americans still loyal to SCLC were disappointed with the August 1966 truce between King and Chicago Mayor Richard Daley known as the Summit Agreement, a catalogue of extremely ambitious, loose concessions hastily conceived a few days before thousands of Afro-Americans were to march into white suburban enclaves. Finally, if young and militant Afro-Americans were now openly contemptuous of King (calling him "De Lawd"), the federal government had clearly begun to distance itself from the civil rights leader. At the White House Conference on Civil Rights (June 1966), Johnson's desire to have the issues important to King ignored was respected by the participating white businessmen and numerous Afro-American notables.

Weighing the significance of these reverses, King concluded that after years of laboring with the idea of "reforming the existing institutions of the society, a little change here, a little change there," it was time for major changes. "I think you've got to have a reconstruction of the entire society, a revolution of values," *Harper's* quoted him as saying. The cities of America must be rebuilt so that the poor could live

292

decently and work productively in them. "Some of the nation's industries must be nationalized," and a guaranteed annual wage enacted. The country's foreign investments must be reviewed. The civil rights leader, whose career had been launched by circumstance and whose success, until then, had been due largely to pushing at the boundaries of racism rather than to an assault upon its fundamental causes, was no more. Having been "bogged down in the paralysis of analysis" in the past, King in late 1966 was preparing for political and economic activity on a scale and of a nature sufficient to outrage, alienate, and even alarm the federal government, the business community, much of organized labor, and most of the senior Afro-American civil rights leadership. What he had begun to perceive was that both religion and society tended to confine their compassion and indignation to injustice and misery susceptible of attenuation without imperiling fundamental economic relationships. When Afro-Americans began to make demands that could lead to full equality, King wrote, "They found that many of their white allies had quietly disappeared."

What might best be described as the "lunch-counter" phase of the civil rights movement (King himself later called it the "Selma and Voting Rights Act phase") had been a period of straightforward moral choices between minority rights of access to public facilities and commercial establishments and the barbarous defense by jowly sheriffs and howling dogs of the southern way of life. The right of Afro-Americans to travel, eat, and vote like white American citizens was not generally construed as unreasonable outside the Deep South. But once in the North—in Chicago, Cleveland, and Detroit—bearing a list of racial grievances greatly enlarged by demands for jobs, open housing, citizen review of police and real estate boards, and economic boycott of racially unresponsive businesses, King's civil rights movement suddenly developed from a regional drama centered on racial segregation into a crusade exposing socioeconomic imbalances in the national structure itself.

A decade earlier King's ideas on the economic uplift of his race had been vintage Booker T. Washington. To succeed, he wrote in his first book, the Afro-American "must develop habits of thrift and techniques of wise investment. He must not wait for the end of the segregation that lies at the basis of his economic deprivation; he must act now to lift himself up by his own bootstraps." As late as summer 1966, he told a church packed with poor Chicagoans that they had to "face the fact" that most would be "living in the ghetto five, ten years from now." But that was no reason not to "get some things straightened out right away. I'm not going to wait a month to get the roaches out of my house." The prophecy was accurate and the summons to household hygiene and responsibility commendable, but neither quite squared with the recent now-or-never rhetoric and goals of his abortive Chicago campaign. Yet Chicago was the cradle for much of SCLC's new economic thought. In the past the formula for SCLC success depended upon arousing what King called the "moral self-interest of the nation." But SCLC quickly discovered the limits of moral self-interest in the cities of the North. If King and his movement were to find a new lease on life after the Chicago Summit Agreement, new tactics were in order. Racial compassion had to be reinforced by old-fashioned American political quid pro quo.

The potential for such a quid pro quo existed in the growing opposition to the Vietnam war and the comprehensive issue of national priorities gone awry. One way to the schools, decent jobs, decent neighborhoods, and heftier federal subsidies was as an active participant in an interracial chorus denouncing the $30,000,000,000 spent for Vietnam while the shame of poverty remained in America. King's first tentative foray into international politics (spring 1965) had raised such a firestorm in the civil rights community that the Nobel Peace laureate had quickly dropped the Vietnam war issue for the time being. When Young had attacked King's antiwar views during the White House Conference on Civil Rights in June 1966, Young correctly stated that the "Negro was more concerned about the rat at night and the job in the morning." Senator Edward Brooke, sole Afro-American in that chamber, and Urban League director Young pleaded, each after a 1968 fact-finding mission to Vietnam, that King and other critics give their government the patriotic benefit of the doubt and leave the war to the experts and the president. King replied that American "integrity" was no longer credible. Civil rights leaders and white advisors also pleaded with him to soften his antiwar statements because of the much feared and reported white backlash sweeping the nation.

Opposition caused him to falter on the war issue, but ultimately King's choice of new direction turned on the central point of his moral conception of his role. Racism and poverty were evils; if it meant embracing controversial positions and allies to eradicate them, conscience left him no other choice. War was wrong; if he lost support because he spoke out against the war in Indochina, conscience left no other choice. "Our loyalties must transcend our race, our tribe, our class, our nation," the Nobel laureate told his Atlanta congregation. "This means we must develop a world perspective." "It should be incandescently clear," he proclaimed in New York City's Riverside Church exactly one year to the day before his death, "that no one who has any concern for the integrity and life of America today can ignore the present war. If America's soul becomes totally poisoned, part of the autopsy must read 'Vietnam.' " This was the time when King told a worried financial advisor, "I don't care if we don't get another five cents in the mail, I'm going to keep on preaching my message." In fact, SCLC revenues increased.

Based on the political parochialism of his black followers, the limited allegiance of white liberals and much of the labor movement, and the certainty of federal animosity, King appeared to make all the wrong decisions in this last stage. It is now clear that another consideration, only guessed at then by a few, should have dissuaded him from his path: the malevolence of J. Edgar Hoover's Federal Bureau of Investigation. King was almost certainly aware, moreover, of rumors that a price had been put on his head by unidentified southern businessmen. Instead, he chose to merge civil rights with the larger, institutionally destabilizing crusade for human rights, to turn his back on the safer course of reducing direct action to another prominent libertarian lobby. The post-Chicago phase was not a complete leap into the unknown, of course; the militancy of the students and financial resources of the antiwar forces were becoming rapidly stronger. There was an effective presidential peace candidate prospect in Senator Eugene McCarthy, and it was credibly rumored that Senator Robert Kennedy might break with President Johnson over the war. But it was a measure of the moral steadfastness and intellectual growth of King that he was prepared to risk so much for the "reconstruction of the entire society."

A case can be made for residual influences on King of the socialism inherent in theologian Walter Rauschenbusch's Social Gospel, and a weaker case for a vague, moderate Marxism acquired at university and in the milieux of protest. Insofar as Marxism exposed the "weaknesses of traditional capitalism, contributed to the growth of a definite self-consciousness in the masses, and challenged the social conscience of the Christian churches," King wrote in *Stride Toward Freedom*, he found Marxism useful. The promptings of Gandhian principles— *satyagraha*—much refurbished by discourse and travel in India, were of major importance, but largely for the global resonance and millenarian gravity they imparted to King's own civil rights campaigns. In the final analysis, his seemingly rapid shift leftward was grounded in Christian morality and common sense. "Any religion," he emphatically stated in *Stride Toward Freedom*, "that professes to be concerned

295

with the souls of men and is not concerned with the slums that damn them, the economic conditions that strangle them and the social conditions that cripple them is a dry-as-dust religion." In what were virtually his last words on the subject, King warned in *Where Do We Go from Here* of the awesome challenges ahead for him in his post-Chicago phase: "The real cost lies ahead. The stiffening of white resistance is a recognition of that fact. The discount education given to Negroes will in the future have to be purchased at full price if quality education is to be realized. Jobs are harder and costlier to create than voting rolls. The eradication of slums housing millions is complex far beyond integrating buses and lunch counters."

In retrospect the logic of his position now seems to have had the force of inevitability. The battle against racial segregation led to the larger assault on discrimination, leading in turn to the final struggle against economic exploitation. No civil rights victory—not even the most complete ones of Montgomery and Birmingham—could be intrinsically conclusive because of the economic nature of the war for equality of opportunity, with each skirmish and battle clarifying further for King and his followers the ultimate objectives. If the Afro-American was the most visible and most vocal victim of social inequality, his plight was neither unique nor, in the final analysis, totally racial. As some of the most perceptive intellectuals, such as W. E. B. Du Bois and A. Philip Randolph, had discerned, any substantive improvement in the condition of the Afro-American necessarily entailed an at least minimal redistribution of national wealth through government intervention.

" 'The poor can stop being poor,' " King quoted approvingly an atypically candid assistant director of the Office of Economic Opportunity, " 'if the rich are willing to become even richer at a slower rate.' " In *Where Do We Go from Here*, he criticized the black separatists because they gave "priority to race precisely at a time when the impact of automation and other forces have made the economic question fundamental for blacks and whites alike." Because the struggle for rights was "at bottom a struggle for opportunities," King now moved beyond even the vast scale of his 1963 Bill of Rights for the Disadvantaged to the macroeconomics of "total, direct and immediate abolition of poverty." It could be done; it must be done, he said. There was nothing "except shortsightedness to prevent us from guaranteeing an annual minimum—and livable—income for every American family. There is nothing, except a tragic death wish, to prevent us from reordering our priorities, so that the pursuit of peace will take precedence over the pursuit of war. There is nothing to keep us from remolding a recalcitrant status quo with bruised hands until we have fashioned it into a brotherhood."

The appeal grew stronger of coalition with a new army of whites (as well as browns and reds) who could be as useful to King as the liberal-clerical-labor alliance of the past that was now unraveling. Essentially, these were the white antiwar students, the affluent white liberals far more alarmed about the Vietnam war than extremisms on the campus or in the ghetto, the forgotten Native Americans stirring on reservations, the Hispanic-Americans filling up the Southwest, and the ignored of Appalachia. A coalition such as this (of the disenchanted, disinherited, and *déclassés*) appeared, according to one's perspective, to be the vanguard of a splendid new order, an insignificant or potentially influential force for disorder and sedition, or little more than fodder for prime time televiewing.

In any case King now became the principal architect of this coalition, speaking out against the war his government insisted had to be won, calling for an end to poverty, and a "reconstruction of the entire society, a revolution of values." Participating in the huge Spring Mobilization rally in April 1967 in New York's Central Park and the United Nations Plaza, he deplored the burden upon the Afro-American poor imposed by the Asian war, drawing a moving word-picture of indiscriminate American devastation of life and property in Vietnam. Yet he withheld his signature from the Spring Mobilization manifesto because of its charge against the U.S. government of genocide; similarly, he refused to sanction the burning of draft cards. He did approve the manifesto's call for a "Vietnam Summer," a massive, peaceful, solid three-month saturation of antiwar protest and propaganda. To the leadership of the older civil rights organizations, King's position was believed to be personally suicidal and racially calamitous. The NAACP and Urban League made their disagreement unmistakably clear. There were persistent reports, vigorously denied by the parties, of an acrimonious face-to-face exchange between the Urban League's Young and King. Former ambassador and leading Afro-American columnist Carl T. Rowan attacked King in *Reader's Digest* for the unwisdom of mixing civil rights with foreign policy. Within the ranks of the SCLC itself were many who agreed that opposing the war would bankrupt the organization and turn President Johnson's Justice Department from an already lukewarm friend into a lethal foe. An unrelated but unmistakably premonitory decision by the U.S. Supreme Court in June 1967 strengthened such arguments: King and eight SCLC associates saw the Court uphold by a five to four margin their April 1963 Birmingham conviction for demonstrating without a valid municipal permit. "Terribly saddened by the ruling," King probably correctly interpreted it as the court's signal to "go slow," for as Barry Mahoney and Alan Westin observe in *The Trial of Martin Luther King*, "many black and white leaders . . . felt that the court's ruling was predestined by the flow of events on the racial front during 1965–67."

When King proclaimed for the first time, on March 25, 1967, at the Chicago coliseum that "we must combine the fervor of the civil rights movement with the peace movement," the outlines of nonviolent populism were clear. During the following months he strove to address a larger, more varied audience than ever before, driving home statistics on poverty, repeating that the numerical majority of those living below the poverty line was white, that the whites of Appalachia were worse off materially (and more powerless) than inner city Afro-Americans. He summoned the politically weak, the economically deprived, the angry young of all races, and the disenchanted liberals to form together a community of action sufficiently powerful to force the enlightened attention of Washington and Wall Street. His rhetoric and statistics promised the bare probability of a biracial front. A basic historic reality common to the white and black poor, however, was that they tended to define their worth and prospects in opposition to each other. In the main, the black and white poor also tended to have conflicting expectations of the federal government. Prospects for collaboration between Afro-Americans and other ethnics were no more promising, if for different reasons: reservation Native Americans, enveloped by their culture and traditions, not prone to share their thoughts, wanted considerably less rather than more to do with the U.S. government; Hispanic-Americans, perceived as racially ambivalent and as relentlessly occupying Afro-American urban living space, were growing politically powerful in the Southwest and were demographically projected as *the* American minority. It was difficult to believe that church-going farmers, factory workers, and domestics could successfully join with white college students whose presumptively radical politics were financed by affluent parents. It was already difficult enough maintaining a working relationship with Afro-American students and community people, angry at "whitey," supposedly alienated from The Establishment, and demanding billions in reparations from businesses, the churches, government, and quotas in education and hiring. Moreover, many of these young people gave voice to the crude anti-

Semitism found in black ghettos, further distressing libertarian and philanthropic Jews who were already alarmed by the call for quotas.

This was populist politics at its most venturesome, bringing together the ethnically, economically, culturally, and geographically disparate for long-term objectives. "Our challenge," King wrote in *Look* in 1968, "is to organize the power we already have in our midsts." It was to be a force "powerful enough, dramatic enough, morally appealing enough, so that people of goodwill, the churches, labor, liberals, intellectuals, students, poor people themselves" would begin to "put pressure on congressmen." Meanwhile, plans for the Poor People's Campaign were completed by SCLC's staff in mid-February 1968. Initial cadres were to be drawn from ten cities and five rural districts located in the East, Midwest, South, and Appalachia. From Roxbury (Boston's Afro-American ghetto), Chicago's Lawndale community, Mississippi, and West Virginia, 3,000 volunteers would travel in caravan to a shanty town erected in the capital. From there they would make daily sorties over a three-month period to press their demands at the Senate, House of Representatives, and the departments of Housing and Urban Development, Health, Education and Welfare (now Health and Human Services), and Agriculture. The core of this Poor People's Campaign was SCLC's $12,000,000,000 Economic Bill of Rights (originally proposed by A. Philip Randolph), guaranteeing employment to the able-bodied, viable incomes to all legitimately unemployed, a federal open-housing act, and vigorous enforcement of integrated education. An unfavorable response by Capitol Hill would result in thousands more converging on the capital as well as simultaneous demonstrations of the poor on the West Coast. Essentially it was a strategy substituting Washington for Birmingham, forcing even liberal senators and representatives to play parts as economic Bull Connors and hawkish George Wallaces.

If the logic and grand strategy of the Poor People's Campaign make sense today, this was not the case for most Afro-Americans in 1968. King knew that middle-class Afro-Americans and many of the simple church people would recoil at the prospect of an occupation of Washington. Orations at the Lincoln Memorial and a day of interracial songs and processionals were a different order of protest from saturating the capital with an army of potentially unruly—even riotous—unemployed, underemployed, juvenile militant, and politically unsophisticated for three months, if necessary. Opposition of Johnson to the campaign and the president's reportedly fierce dislike of King could only distress, if not alarm, such civil rights leaders as Wilkins, Young, and Farmer, who were fearful of the much reported white backlash sweeping the nation.

King professed to discount the depth and duration of the white backlash. The reality was that King dreaded the backlash and believed that nothing short of luck and quick, decisive, "creative" action could preclude it. But it was not the backlash then being recorded in the polls and reflected by articles in national publications that distressed King. What little truth was contained in NAACP charges that SCLC's Chicago campaign had cost liberal Illinois Senator Paul Douglas his seat undoubtedly troubled the Nobel laureate, as did the desertion of his traditional white allies and sympathizers, who warned that the pace of civil rights had become improvidently rapid. But the SCLC leader saw beyond these concerns to the graver racial and national peril. To slow the pace of racial progress now was, he believed, to make certain that the exhortations of young racial extremists, like H. Rap Brown, Stokely Carmichael, and Floyd McKissick and the Black Panthers, would be translated into reality. "The white liberal must escalate his support for the struggle for racial justice," King pleaded in *Where Do We Go from Here*. "This would be a tragic time to forsake and withdraw from the struggle." But, instead, many white allies succumbed to "radical chic," finding, as did most of the national media, much more to be fascinated by in the fiery demands and threats of the rising Black Power movement. "Dr. King's faith was draining," Andrew Young said of this period, speaking to a New York *Times* reporter, "because even people inside the organization were running around the country spouting talk about violence." Meanwhile, derisory articles such as that in the *New York Review of Books* dismissing *Where Do We Go from Here* as warmed-over middle-class reflections and alleging that the author had been "outstripped by his times" made it clear that even professional white liberals had not grasped his message. In July 1967, three months after the publication of the book, race riots engulfed Newark and Detroit—the Detroit riot was one of the worst in American history. King's verdict, quoted in the April 1968 edition of *Look*—"The flash point of Negro rage is close at hand"—seemed beyond dispute.

Disappointed and deserted as 1968 unfolded, King was still absolutely certain that his was not only the more viable politics but the sole politics possessing authentically reformist socioeconomic potential. Black Power—retaliatory violence, inverted racism—was not the path to social revolution but to racial backlash and official repression. In 1964 King had with arresting candor placed the civil disobedience and

300

demonstrations of the civil rights movement in the perspective of public policy: "White Americans must be made to understand the basic motives underlying Negro demonstrations. . . . It is not a threat but a fact of history that if an oppressed people's pent-up emotions are not nonviolently released, they will be violently released. So let the Negro march. Let him make pilgrimages to city hall. Let him go on freedom rides. And above all, make an effort to understand why he must do this. For if his frustrations and despair are allowed to continue piling up, millions of Negroes will seek solace and security in black-nationalist ideologies." In the years since this lecture, King had repeatedly warned the nation that a rhythm of legal and political and, later, socioeconomic concessions had to be maintained in order to avoid Afro-American violence and permanent alienation. With the rhythm of concessions almost arrested by 1968, he expected the data of the unfinished Kerner Commission on Civil Disorders to fulfill James Baldwin's terrible predictions in *The Fire Next Time.* He expected much worse, for, although he usually left it unsaid, King knew that after the fires were extinguished, the arsonists would pay a fearful price. What he feared most was the backlash that would surely come after the explosion of "black rage" he was racing to head off.

It is a signal irony of recent history that the leader who had become the most hard-headed realist with a plan and a vehicle to alter the course of national events in a positive, humanitarian direction was widely portrayed in his final months as a fuzzy-minded moralist, disappointing to liberals and held in contempt by Black Power enthusiasts. King's new approach—a Popular Front of the racially abused, economically deprived, and politically outraged, cutting across race and class—was prospectively potent. It was also an approach that revealed King at his imaginative best as a leader and demonstrated the pragmatist who calibrates his swing leftward the better to construct a basis for civilized, moderated, genuine social progress.

King went to Memphis on March 28, 1968, to lead a demonstration in support of striking municipal sanitation workers. There was violence. Afro-American teenagers known as the Invaders clashed with police, lightly damaged some commercial property, and one of them was fatally shot by an officer. A deeply disturbed King left the city, promising to return to organize and lead a proper nonviolent march within a few days. Before this fateful return to Memphis, there were astonishing developments that portended great success for the SCLC leader. Johnson announced that he would not seek reelection. With Kennedy already campaigning for the Democratic nomination on a peace and poverty platform satisfactory to King (and McCarthy still a strong contender), the SCLC leader could reasonably anticipate a Democratic national convention much more than ceremoniously interested in what he had to say. The Economic Bill of Rights and a presidency capable and willing to push it through Congress were imminent possibilities. King's assassination produced literally overnight the political climate and consequences he had devoted his feverish final days trying to prevent.

During his twelve years on the national scene King pursued a policy of conciliatory confrontation that depended for success upon the perception by controlling forces in the larger society (namely, labor, religious, business, government) that, however premature, costly, or destabilizing his demands, the probable consequences of hostile or ineffective response would be much graver than the crisis created by such demands. When the immediate scope of objectives was mainly constitutional and regional—desegregation and voting rights in the South—King's allies (willing and reluctant) more often than not came effectively to his assistance. The minimal demands of integrated schools, open public facilities, and access to the ballot were always recognized as legitimate in principle by a majority of Americans. King used the same tactics of conciliatory confrontation when the scope of his objectives was enlarged as he moved northward. The specter of terrible social and economic upheaval was put forward as inevitable, unless swift and profound national advances were achieved in the area of human rights and economic opportunity. This time, however, resistance was far greater; many of King's powerful Establishment supporters came to regard him as a major contributor to rather than the antidote for intolerable socioeconomic disorder. Among many Afro-Americans—leaders and citizens—there was honest confusion about the role King was forging for himself in the final months. They believed that the combination of civil rights with other issues (e.g., the peace movement) would detract from the former. Whether he could have constructed the effective new coalition symbolized by the Poor People's Campaign is far from certain.

Note on Sources

PRIMARY SOURCES

Coretta Scott King. *My Life with Martin Luther King, Jr.* New York: Holt, Rinehart & Winston, 1969.

Martin Luther King, Jr. "A Comparison of the Conceptions of God in the Thinking of Paul Tillich and Henry Nelson Wieman." Ph.D. diss., Boston University, 1955.

———. *The Measure of a Man.* Philadelphia: United Church Press, 1968.

———. *Strength to Love.* New York: Harper & Row, 1963.

———. *Stride Toward Freedom: The Montgomery Story.* New York: Harper & Row, 1958.

———. *Trumpet of Conscience.* New York: Harper & Row, 1968.

———. *Where Do We Go from Here: Chaos or Community?* New York: Harper & Row, 1967.

———. *The Wisdom of Martin Luther King in His Own Words*, ed. by Bill Adler. New York: Lancer Books, 1968.

———. *Why We Can't Wait.* New York: Harper & Row, 1964.

SECONDARY SOURCES

Lerone Bennett. *What Manner of Man*, 3rd rev. ed. Chicago: Johnson Publishing, 1968.

Jim Bishop. *The Days of Martin Luther King, Jr.* New York: G. P. Putnam's Sons, 1971.

Charles E. Fager. *Selma, 1965.* New York: Charles Scribner's Sons, 1974.

David Garrow. *The FBI and Martin Luther King: From 'Solo' to Memphis.* New York: W.W. Norton, 1981.

———. *Protest at Selma.* New Haven, Conn.: Yale University Press, 1978.

David Levering Lewis. *King: A Biography*, 2nd ed. rev. Urbana: University of Illinois Press, 1978.

August Meier. "On the Role of Martin Luther King" in Meier and Elliott Rudwick, *Along the Color Line: Explorations in the Black Experience.* Urbana: University of Illinois Press, 1976. Reprinted from *New Politics*, 4 (Winter 1965).

William Robert Miller. *Martin Luther King, Jr.: His Life, Martyrdom, and Meaning for the World.* New York: Weybright & Talley, 1968.

Lawrence Reddick. *Crusader without Violence.* New York: Harper & Row, 1959.

Hanes Walton, Jr. *The Political Philosophy of Martin Luther King, Jr.* Westport, Conn.: Greenwood Publishing, 1971.

Alan F. Westin and Barry Mahoney. *The Trial of Martin Luther King.* New York: Thomas Y. Crowell, 1974.

Harris Wofford. *Of Kennedys and Kings.* New York: Farrar, Straus and Giroux, 1980.

Peter Goldman   **14**

Malcolm X:
Witness for the Prosecution

*Blacks experienced pride in the victories of the late 1950s and early
1960s, and the level of black expectations consequently far outpaced the
rate of social change, especially in the North, where the problems of the
urban slumdwellers proved far more impervious to attack than had the
segregation and disfranchisement of the South. Accordingly, there was
considerable disillusionment, especially among younger Negroes. The
middle and late 1960s witnessed a growing skepticism about the worth of
integrating into the mainstream of white American society, an increase
in support for the use of violent tactics, and a surge of nationalist sentiment unmatched since Marcus Garvey's days. In this context the doctrines of a small, lower-class nationalist sect, the Nation of Islam,
achieved unusual salience. The fiery speeches of its most noted public
spokesman, Malcolm X, resonated widely throughout black America,
and they proved particularly appealing to militants, who were coming to
perceive less and less validity in the goals of social integration and cultural assimilation and who, in their alienation, were using an increasing
revolutionary rhetoric. At the height of his career in 1962–64, before he
was assassinated, Malcolm X stood as the direct antithesis to the nonviolent activism and faith in an integrated society that were the hallmarks of
Martin Luther King, Jr.*

FOR THE THIRTEEN impassioned years of his ministry, Malcolm X was
a witness for the prosecution against white America—a "field nigger,"
he called himself, giving incendiary voice to the discontents of our urban black underclass. Everything about Malcolm was an accusation:
his Muslim faith, his militant politics, his self-made manhood, even the
name he took in token of his renunciation of white society and his embrace of black Islam. He was a dissonant and mostly misunderstood
figure in his own public lifetime, a bitter and cynical counterpoint to
the orthodox civil rights movement in its romantic high of the 1950s
and 1960s; he stood apart, dimly perceived as a racist and demagogue
inflaming the black lumpenproletariat to revenge its grievances in
blood. Only with his death and the movement's discouraged exhaus-
tion could Malcolm be seen more nearly as he was: a revolutionary of

the soul who, by word and charismatic example, helped awaken a proud and assertive new black consciousness among the grandsons and granddaughters of slaves.

Even then, Malcolm has had to survive his admirers—to pass, that is, through a kind of posthumous canonization that caricatured him almost as unrecognizably as his prior media image as a hate-monger. He was neither thinker nor planner nor tactician but rather, by his own definition, a "black Billy Graham"—a revivalist calling souls to Allah and blackness as Graham summoned them to Christ. He made his fiery witness for a dozen years in the ministry of the late Messenger Elijah Muhammad and his Lost-Found Nation of Islam in the Wilderness of North America, the then anti-white doomsday sect better known to us as the Black Muslims; only slowly and with intense pain did he cast off its trammeling dogmas and strike out for a single year on his own, searching America, Africa, and the Middle East for the uncreated conscience of a race. The search was still unfinished at his death, at age thirty-nine, as El-Hajj Malik El-Shabazz, an accredited minister of orthodox Sunni Islam and a happily unconstrained agitator against the way things were. He passed in that quest from the belief on faith that all white people are devils to the conviction on the available evidence that American white society is irremediably racist. But the shadings of gray that stole into his black-and-white world view in his last year of life never softened the bleak landscape of his politics. Malcolm was, before anything else, a public moralist—a scold whose private manner was gentlemanly, even priestly, but whose aspect to the world was one of implacable and uncompromising fury.

As moralist, he was a voice of quite another sort than his contemporary, Martin Luther King, Jr.—a voice of that estranged backstreet black community where the churchly southern style has not traveled well. He spoke a fluent, downtown English when he needed to, but his first language was a slurred and cynical ghetto black, and his first source of authority was that the ghetto recognized so much of itself in him. His life was, as he wrote in his *Autobiography*, a "chronology of changes"—a series of provisional identities that he did not live to complete. He began it, in 1925, as Malcolm Little, the fourth of eight children of a fragile West Indian woman and a fiery black preacher devoted with equal heat to the Baptist gospels and the secular teachings of the nationalist Marcus Garvey. Malcolm was born the year Garvey went to prison for mail fraud, and his boyhood was a casualty of the Garvey movement's subsequent rout; white vigilantes harried the Littles out of Omaha, Nebraska, burned their home in Lansing, Michigan, and finally mobbed Malcolm's father, beating him nearly lifeless and leaving him to die under the wheels of a streetcar. The family disintegrated thereafter, and Malcolm, stormy and rebellious, wound up in the foster care of a white couple—a beneficence that was the beginning of his education in white folkways and, later, the object of his unsparing rage. He described the interlude in a televised debate with black journalist Louis Lomax in 1964:

> *Lomax*: Are all white men immoral, Minister Malcolm? Is there not one good one?
> *Malcolm*: I haven't met all of them. Those whom I have met are the type I would say are insincere. Now if there are some sincere whites somewhere, it's those that I haven't met yet.
> *Lomax*: How about the woman . . . that took you in when you were a little boy and put you on the road to learning something?
> *Malcolm*: . . . My presence in that home was like a cat or a parrot or any type of pet that they had. You know how you'll be around whites and they'll discuss things just like you're not there. I think [Ralph] Ellison calls it the *Invisible Man* and [James] Baldwin calls it *Nobody Knows My Name*. My presence in that home was not the presence of a human being.
> *Lomax*: But she did feed you.
> *Malcolm*: You feed your cat.
> *Lomax*: She clothed you.
> *Malcolm*: You clothe any kind of pet that you might have.
> *Lomax*: And you impute to her no humanitarian motivation?
> *Malcolm*: No. Not today.

That pitiless wrath had been Malcolm's personal salvation, once Elijah Muhammad and his little nation in the wilderness taught him what it was and how to use it. His life till then had been a descent into hell. He dropped out of school as soon as he finished the eighth grade, ran away east to Boston and later Harlem, and drifted through a series of menial jobs into the zoot-suited, bop-gaited life of a street hustler. Malcolm Little became Detroit Red, then Big Red, dealing (and using) drugs, running numbers slips and bootleg whiskey, steering white customers to black brothels, burglarizing homes, and sticking up stores. "I loved the devil," he said later. "I was trying as hard as I could to be white." There is some evidence that he tended to inflate his size in the hustler underground for pedagogical effect; he is only dimly remembered by old-timers on the street, and then principally as having been a "john-walker"—a curbside shill for a Harlem whorehouse. But his degradation was complete and was ultimately certified by the Commonwealth of Massachusetts with an eight-to-ten-year sentence for burglary—a severe penalty then thought commensurate with the fact that one of his accomplices was his white mistress.

His redemption began in prison with his exposure to Muhammad's ghetto theology and its Damascene central revelation: that white people were a race of devils created for the torment of the black sons and daughters of Allah. Muhammad said he had this on the word of God Himself, who had appeared in the black slums of Detroit in 1930 in the person of a silk peddler named Wallace D. Fard and announced himself as "the one the world has been expecting for the past two thousand years." His teachings took root in a little communion of country southern blacks flung north, like Muhammad himself, in the great black diaspora of the 1920s. He found Muhammad, then Elijah Poole, a particularly apt and willing pupil—a fragile man whose sleepy eyes and faltering speech masked a keen native wit and a certain genius for the main chance. When Fard disappeared in 1934—or, as believers prefer, when he returned to Mecca to prepare for the end of the world—Muhammad stood first in the line of succession; the fountainhead of the extraordinary authority he held for forty years thereafter was that he had known Allah and been personally ordained his last Messenger, "missioned" by him to lead his people out of bondage to their white slavemasters and back to their lost Zion "in the East."

Outsiders commonly found Muhammad's cultish scriptures rather quaint; even believers in the parting of the Red Sea or the miracle of the loaves and fishes smiled at the revelation that whites were a bleached-out, blue-eyed mutant race created by a dissident black scientist named Yacub and set loose to subjugate black people to its satanic pleasure. But, as James Baldwin once wrote, Muhammad's theology was "no more indigestible than the more familiar brand asserting that there is a curse on the sons of Ham," and for some fraction of black America, as for Malcolm himself, it had the force of empirical truth. Stripped of its exotica and its hyperbole, Muhammad's message was that white slavers had destroyed the black civilizations of Africa and reduced black men and women to chattel; had stripped them of their culture, their religion, even their names; had taught them to speak a foreign tongue, worship a "spook" Christian God, and call themselves Smith, Jones, Powell, Bunche, and King; had reduced them from African blacks to "so-called American Negroes," wallowing in the white man's vices and obedient to the white man's unthreatening Negro leaders; had, in sum, murdered them spiritually, emotionally, and morally. What Muhammad asked, and what Malcolm demanded in his name, was that blacks understand what they had in common—the color of their skins and the enmity it provoked against them. "You don't catch hell because you're a Methodist or a Baptist," Malcolm told a black audience in 1963. "You don't catch hell because you're a Democrat or a Republican; you don't catch hell because you're a Mason or an Elk, and you sure don't catch hell because you're an American, because if you were an American you wouldn't catch no hell. You catch hell because you are a black man."

What the Muslims thus offered black people was an alternative to the religious positions then available to them: to accept the fallen state of one's people as the judgment of God or to extrapolate from it that God does not exist. The message was much misunderstood by white people, who heard only the Nation's imprecations against the devil and saw only the scowling, paramilitary face it turned outward to the world; the Muslims were accordingly deemed a threat to the peace and good order of our society and were already under surveillance by the Federal Bureau of Investigation, among other police agencies, when Malcolm left prison and joined the ministry in 1952. It was a case of mistaken identity. The Muslims belonged more nearly to the tradition of Booker T. Washington than of Nat Turner; they practiced a kind of quietist withdrawal from the black struggle, leading peaceful and abstemious lives, tithing to the Nation and the Messenger, building a business empire once valued at $70,000,000 on a base of small retail stores and streetcorner newspaper sales.

But Malcolm saw and exploited the uses of rage as an organizing principle akin in force, for example, to the divinity of Christ or the labor theory of value; he promoted it brilliantly and, once the mass media discovered his extraordinary star quality, made the Nation a force in our national life far beyond its enrolled membership of around 10,000. At his dazzling peak, it was easy to forget that he was a prison-educated man schooled in the language by copying words out of a dictionary and introduced to wisdom by the revelations of Fard; he became a regular on the talk shows, a lecturer on the university tour—only Barry Goldwater had more bookings in Malcolm's day—and a figure in the diplomatic lounge of the United Nations. He praised Elijah Muhammad second only to Allah for his success, and for years he meant it; in private, he spoke of himself as "a little Charlie McCarthy sitting on the Messenger's knee"; in public, he dropped the old man's name so often—once a minute, by his own accurate count—that it sometimes came out "the Honorbubble Elijah Muhammad." But he was in the process creating a style of leadership and a pitch of demand all his own—a politics in which demagoguery was a legitimate means of struggle and "responsibility" a form of treason. The responsible leaders, he said, were responsible to whites, not blacks. "They controlled you, but they have never incited you or excited you," he said at a rally in 1963. "They controlled you. They contained you. They have kept you on the plantation."

The Malcolm style was finally too successful; his militance agitated the calm of Muhammad's courtiers, who saw it as bad for business, and his gifts for and easy access to the media excited their jealousies. With their encouragement, what had been a father-and-son relationship between the Messenger and Malcolm stretched thin and finally snapped; Malcolm was set down from the ministry late in 1963, officially because he had cheered the assassination of John F. Kennedy as a case of "the chickens coming home to roost," actually because he had begun trying to secure his own threatened position by spreading tales about Muhammad's indulgent private life. Malcolm's keen and free-running intelligence had always been a subversive force in the Nation and had been driving him toward the exit for years before even he realized it. Still, when he made his break in March 1964, it was an act of temple politics more than a breach of faith; his stated purpose was to go right on preaching Muhammad's apocalyptic gospels on his own.

His resolve did not last out the single year left to him—or even the first spring of his freedom. He took tutorials in orthodox Islam and in April made his *hajj* to Mecca—a transforming exposure to the company of white Muslims, whose existence he had known about but denied, and to a leveling spiritual brotherhood with them, which he had never before imagined possible. The pilgrimage, he said, "broadened my scope probably more in twelve days than my previous experience during my 39 years on this earth"—deepened his faith, ventilated his politics, and reduced the American white man in his sight from the devil to a fallible human enemy. His development thereafter was an explosive rush from the certitudes of the Black Muslims through a conventional streetcorner black nationalism to a world view of more subtle weave—a shifting and uncompleted blend of orthodox Islam, African socialism, Third World anticolonialism, and that doctrine of racial solidarity known later as Black Power. His destination was no clearer to him then than to us now, in the tangle of contending words and ideas he left us; he was still searching America and Africa for it when he died.

Malcolm was a casualty of our bloodied 1960s, assassinated by black men at a rally of his fledgling Organization of Afro-American Unity in uptown Manhattan in February 1965. Three Black Muslims were arrested, tried and convicted of his murder, and sentenced to life in prison. A considerable body of folklore and published speculation has it that the real culprit was the state—that, whether Muslims pulled the triggers, the assassination was fomented by the Central Intelligence Agency or the Federal Bureau of Investigation and at least passively abetted by the New York City police. My own detailed examination of the evidence does not support this view. There are persuasive grounds for belief that two of the three men imprisoned for killing Malcolm were in fact innocent; there is equally suggestive evidence that the agencies of our justice foresaw an attempt on Malcolm's life and kept a distance long and disinterested enough to let it happen. But the record taken objectively and whole points to the conclusion that the police *theory* of the case was correct—that Malcolm's death was plotted and executed by Muslims in revenge for his blasphemies against Muhammad and that the real miscarriage of justice is that the wrong Muslims were imprisoned for it.

Malcolm could fairly be judged a failure by the conventional measures of leadership; he left behind no concrete program for the deliverance of black Americans, no disciplined following to carry on for him, no organization sturdy enough to survive his death. It does not diminish him at all to say that none of these was his particular gift. He belongs instead to what the political scientist Charles Hamilton has identified as the tradition of spokesmanship in the black struggle; he was an artist of the spoken word, and his contributions cannot be adequately judged by the normal standards of success or failure, as King's could, or Roy Wilkins's, or Whitney Young's. Malcolm, as the movement strategist Bayard Rustin told me in an interview,

> has to be seen over and above the pull and tug of struggle for concrete objectives. King had to be measured by his victories. But what King did, what the NAACP did, what the March on Washington did, what Whitney Young did, what Roy Wilkins did, all that was for the benefit of the Southern Negro. There were no obtainable, immediate results for the Northern ghettoized black, whose housing is getting worse; who is unable to find work; whose schools are deteriorating; who sees constantly more rats and roaches and more garbage in the streets. He, because he is human, must find victory somewhere, and he finds his victory within. He needed Malcolm, who brought him an internal victory, precisely because the external victory was beyond his reach. What can bring satisfaction is the feeling that he is black, he is a man, he is internally free. King had to win victories in the real world. Malcolm's were the kind you can create yourself.

311

Malcolm's victories, that is, were private victories; and yet they were no less consequential for having been won in the soul instead of in that world of legislation and negotiation and compromise—the world of affairs—that most of us think of as real. He was a force for the liberation of black people, both by the example of his triumph over the degradation of his own young manhood and by the furious war he waged on the myths, manners, and polite hypocrisies of race in America. That he contributed to the education of some few whites in the process was a fact largely lost to him—the explosion of interest in Malcolm began after his death and the publication of his *Autobiography*—and was of secondary concern to him in any case. What interested Malcolm first was the decolonization of the black mind—the wakening of a proud, bold, demanding new consciousness of color and everything color means in white America.

Malcolm pursued this end with utter recklessness of the settled rules of debate and of his own reputation. His genius was attack, for which he offered no apology beyond the argument that a program was pointless until the slumbering black masses were wakened to their need for one. Within range of a camera or a microphone, his marvelous private civility gave way to a wintry public wrath and occasionally to the kind of thoughtless cruelty that moved him to cheer earthquakes and plane crashes—anything that caused white men pain or grief. "This is the thing—whatever I say, I'm justified," he told the black journalist Claude Lewis late in his life. "If I say that Negroes should get out here right tomorrow and go to war, I'm justified." His objectives, when he excoriated the white devils or called for the formation of an American Mau Mau, were precisely to frighten whites and embolden blacks.

> He was always challenging the white man, always debunking the white man [the sociologist C. Eric Lincoln said in an interview]. I don't think he was ever under any illusion that a powerless black minority could mount a physical challenge to a powerful white majority and survive. But they could mount a psychological challenge, and if they were persistent, they might at least produce some erosion in the attitudes and the strategies by which the white man has always protected himself and his interests. His challenge was to prove that you are as great as you say you are, that you are as moral as you say you are, that you are as kind as you say you are, that you are as loving as you say you are, that you are as altruistic as you say you are, that you are as *superior* as you say you are.

Malcolm saw his life as combat and words as his weapon. It has been said of him that he had no other strategy—that he stood talking on the sidelines through the most momentous years in our race relations since the Civil War. He was denouncing intermarriage on a radio talk show the night James Meredith and 5,000 soldiers "integrated" the University of Mississippi in 1962; he watched the police dogs and fire hoses of Birmingham on television in New York in 1963; he was off in Cairo pursuing a dream alliance with black Africa when the first of the big-city ghetto insurrections exploded out of the alleys of Harlem in 1964. He was always somewhere else, it was said, with a lavaliere microphone or a little knot of reporters, hooting, heckling, scolding, accusing, but never participating.

All of this was true, and probably beside the point. If Malcolm lived at the margins of our national life, he was rarely out of sight. He was a dark presence, angry, cynical, implacable; a man whose goodwill or forgiveness or even pity we could neither earn nor buy. He meant to haunt us—to play on our fears, quicken our guilts, and deflate our dreams that everything was getting better—and he did. "America's problem is *us*," he said in a speech in 1963. Others had been telling us that politely for years, and since his death a blue-ribbon presidential commission on the ghetto riots has subscribed to his once heretical view that we are a society decisively shaped by our racism. The difference was that most of the others held out the hope that matters could be put right with enough conscience, will, and money. Malcolm did not.

He did not even accept that America *had* a conscience; he offered as proof the tragic past of the blacks beginning the day the first trader took the first slave out of Africa. He therefore did not accept the formulation that there is an American dilemma—a constant tension between the ideals of the American creed and the realities of caste and color. Our creed and our Constitution were never meant to include black people, Malcolm told us, and if we argued that the sins of the past ought not to be visited on us, he replied: "Your father isn't here to pay his debts. My father isn't here to collect. But I'm here to collect, and you're here to pay."

Malcolm may never have hated all white people with that uncritical religious passion he brought to his ministry in the Nation of Islam; in his last months he renounced Muhammad's teachings as a racist "straitjacket" and apologized to black America for having repeated them. He absolved white Americans in that period from the blanket judgment that they were all devils and announced that he would thereafter hold them accountable only for their behavior, not for their color or their genes. But he never altered the fundamental terms of his in-

313

dictment: that American whites collectively were the enemy of American blacks collectively until their actions proved them otherwise. "I'm not blanketly condemning all whites," he told a Harlem rally in the days after his pilgrimage to Mecca accomplished his personal emancipation from hatred. "All of them don't oppress. All of them aren't in a position to. But most of them are, and most of them do."

Even at his most feral in the Black Muslim years, hate was less visceral than a point of principle for Malcolm. He saw rage as a potential liberating force for the retrieval of blacks from what he perceived as the worst crime whites had done them: teaching them to hate themselves. Malcolm himself had been dragged low by self-hatred; had pimped and hustled and sniffed cocaine and had finally done time; had pegged his pants, processed his hair, and pursued white women in what he imagined then to be an accurate imitation of the master class. He understood self-hatred, that is, because he had been there and seen it. "We hated our head, we hated the shape of our nose—we wanted one of the long, *dog*-like noses, you know," he said in a speech in 1964. "Yeah. We hated the color of our skin. We hated the blood of Africa that was in our veins. And in hating our features and our skin and our blood, why, we had to end up hating ourselves."

Malcolm achieved his own liberation and invited black Americans to follow him by creating a new life whole out of the ashes of his past and theirs. He became in his own eyes neither a Negro nor an American but a spiritual refugee, an African Muslim in forced exile from the mother country. "I'm not going to sit at your table and watch you eat, with nothing on my plate, and call myself a diner," he said in a speech in 1964. He was appalled by the degradations of ghetto life and, even more, by the acquiescence of black men and women in them. The original sin in his eyes was the white man's, for having severed the blacks from their past and reduced them to property, but he insisted that the responsibility for their salvation was their own. To Malcolm, this meant getting up out of the mud—out from under the charity as well as the tyranny of white America. It meant renouncing integration, which was only a further denial of the worth of black people, and nonviolence, which was only a newer, subtler form of humiliation before the slavemaster. It meant embracing the African past, till then a source of shame; it meant identifying not with the white majority in America and the West but with the dark majority of the world. It meant the discovery of what Eric Lincoln has termed "a negotiable identity" as black men and women, deserving of the world's respect and their own.

And it meant standing up to "the man." One of the worst humiliations of all, in Malcolm's eyes, was that paralytic silence, that head-bobbing surrender, that seemed to him to afflict so many blacks in the presence of whites. The ghetto had been cursing whitey for years in its own back streets, but seldom to his face; so seldom, indeed, that a black man who did so seemed to whites presumptively insane—a *crazy nigger*—and so was accorded a kind of gingerly safe-conduct against reprisal. Malcolm was the crazy nigger gone public; he undertook to carry Harlem's fury downtown, to tell white people to their faces, in their own mass media, what ordinary blacks had been saying about them backstairs for all those years. He did not "teach" hate, or need to; he exploited a vein of hate that was there already and to which few black Americans were totally immune. He saw himself as waging war—a war of words whose objective was to outrage an enemy to whom black people could not otherwise cause pain.

He could be quite conscienceless doing battle; he believed (and once defended in a debate at Oxford) the Goldwater homily that moderation in the pursuit of justice is no virtue, and, because he believed it, he quite literally did not care what he said. Once, in a debate in New York in 1962, Rustin accused him of engaging in emotionalism, to which Malcolm hotly replied:

> When a man is hanging on a tree and he cries out, should he cry out unemotionally? When a man is sitting on a hot stove and he tells you how it feels to be there, is he supposed to speak without emotion? This is what you tell black people in this country when they begin to cry out against the injustices that they're suffering. As long as they describe these injustices in a way that makes you believe you have another 100 years to rectify the situation, then you don't call that emotion. But when a man is on a hot stove, he says, "I'm coming up. I'm getting up. Violently or nonviolently doesn't even enter into the picture—I'm coming up, do you understand?"

By the measure of a society that meters applause, Malcolm nearly always won these encounters, partly because he ignored the niceties and partly because he preempted a kind of moral high ground for himself. To respond that he overstated the indictment was to quibble with details; the condition of the blacks in America was proof enough for him of his basic claims. To oppose him by arguing the necessity of programs and alliances with whites was to throw in with the enemy, since programs and alliances implied the goodwill or at least the tractability of the enemy. And to contend that there had after all been some progress was to deny the continuing pain of the great masses of blacks.

315

"You don't stick a knife in a man's back nine inches and then pull it out six inches and say you're making progress," Malcolm said on a radio talk show in 1963. "It's dangerous to even make the white man *think* we're making progress while the knife is still in our backs, or while the wound is still there, or while even the intention that he had is still there."

Malcolm's war challenged the leaders and the orthodoxies of the civil rights movement in the midst of its glory days, and he paid for it; the cost was a kind of quarantine that lifted only with his death. Alive, he made the leaders of the movement uncomfortable, like an unquiet conscience or an unhappy memory. They thought him a genuine danger to the cause of racial comity; they resented his running attacks on them; they envied his easy access to radio and television; they were embarrassed by his claim to the allegiance of a ghetto lumpenproletariat they had talked about but had never reached. So Malcolm found himself isolated from the front-line struggle, even after he had broken with Elijah Muhammad and wanted to join it. He was isolated from respect as well; the movement—even the radical movement—kept him in a kind of moral Coventry and saw him not as a comrade-in-arms but as a hobgoblin to be held up to whites for a certain scare effect. Malcolm at once acquiesced in this role and was wounded by it. He hungered for legitimacy, for a place among the recognized black leadership; he found himself obliged instead to play bogeyman—to make King's life easier by playing on white America's fantasies of a bloody black revenge. "I don't know why they hate me," he told the actor, Ossie Davis, a friend with mainstream connections. "I raise hell in the back yard and they run out front and 'the man' puts money in their hands."

King's celebrity particularly pained him. It has been argued since their deaths that the two men had been moving inexorably together in what might have been a single, irresistible mass movement against racism, poverty, and the war in Vietnam—that they may even have been assassinated to keep their alliance from happening. The dream is beguiling but finally unpersuasive. Malcolm and King were not so much Manichaean opposites as halves in a yin-yang duality deep in the black soul. But there was too much unhappy history between the two men, too many irreconcilable differences of politics, principle, and style. King's moral authority was that he asked black people to transcend their humanity; Malcolm proposed that they embrace it—that they reserve their love for one another and address white people as people have always addressed their enemies. King's politics was insistently

316

multiracial, Malcolm's insistently black; King's means were nonviolent, which Malcolm considered beggarly; King's ends were assimilationist, which Malcolm derided as a fantasy for all but a token few "acceptable" middle-class blacks. The distance between them was the distance between utility and morality; between the street and the seminary; between the American reality and the American dream. When Harlem honored King on his receipt of the Nobel Peace Prize late in 1964, Malcolm and a few followers watched in moody silence from a back row. "He got the peace prize, we got the problem," he told Claude Lewis a few days later. "I don't want the white man giving me medals. If I'm following a general and he's leading me into battle, and the enemy tends to give him rewards, or awards, I get suspicious of him. Especially if he gets a peace award before the war is over."

Malcolm was wounded as well by his outlaw reputation in the press, particularly after he left the Nation of Islam with its iron anti-white certitudes and entered on the extraordinary personal transformations of the last months of his life. He hoped in that period to come into "a new regard by the public," he wrote in the *Autobiography*, but it eluded him during his lifetime; he remained, in print and on camera, a cartoon Black Muslim inciting an otherwise pacific black underclass to insurrection. Malcolm came to understand that he shared the blame for this with the media—that he had been perhaps too willing to pay the price for their attention, which was to say something outrageous. His image, he told a newspaper interviewer in his last days, "was created by them and by me. . . . They were looking for sensationalism, for something that would sell papers, and I gave it to them."

Malcolm gave it to them with a prolixity that troubled his friends, armed his enemies, and deepened his isolation from that respect he sought—gave it to them because there was so little else within his power to give. He had been our Frantz Fanon; the natives in America have neither the numbers nor the guns to do to whites that gratifying violence perceived by Fanon at the heart of the Algerian terror, but at least for a time in the 1960s they could make white people jump when they said *boo!* and that was something. Malcolm discovered this early—discovered, that is, how close the specter of the black revenge lies to the surface of the white American consciousness—and, having discovered it, he could rarely resist its pleasures.

Only in his last months did Malcolm understand the damaging degree to which he was imprisoned by the common expectations of the media and the ghetto that he would scandalize whites—and by his own unfailingly willing response. At the press conference at which he formally declared his independence of Elijah Muhammad in March 1964, he argued that black people ought to get guns and organize to use them in their own defense wherever the government failed in its duty to protect them. It was not an unreasonable position, given the run of unpunished and unrequited acts of violence against blacks in the South and the then rather distant interest of the federal government in protecting them; it was, moreover, only one of several themes Malcolm struck in announcing his breakaway. But, precisely as he anticipated, it dominated the evening newscasts and the morning headlines. "I bet they pass a bill to outlaw the sale of rifles," he told me with visible enjoyment that afternoon, "and it won't be filibustered either." The problem, as he learned later, was that his talk of guns—and the attendant suggestion of violence—took on an inflated priority that he was stuck with and obliged to defend for the rest of his life. Sometimes, seen through the filter of our mass media, he seemed to stand for nothing else.

His dalliance with the politics of armed struggle never progressed beyond rhetoric; the only weapon he was carrying at the moment of his death was a tear-gas pen. But he understood the uses of verbal violence as an outlet for black America's helpless fury and as an instrument of assault on white America's unbudging resistance. "You have to walk in with a hand grenade and tell the man, 'Listen, you give us what we've got coming or nobody is going to get anything,' " he said at a Harlem rally in July 1964. "Then he might listen to you. But if you go in there polite and acting responsible and sane, why, you're wasting your time, you have to be *insane*." He spoke regularly of riot and revolution and of the necessity for "reciprocal bloodshed" as against the one-way flow then running in the South. "I am the man you think you are," he announced to white people; he meant that he would respond as rudely and as dangerously as individuals historically have to the systematic ruin of one's people.

Malcolm's objective in these flights of rhetoric was the liberation of the *invisible man* from his invisibility—from that vast physical and psychological distance white middle-class society has placed between itself and the ghetto poor. It was a favorite formulation of his—a statement of his own past as busboy, bootblack, and hustler—that the servant sees the master, but the master does not see the servant. The serving class, he told a newspaper interviewer in early 1965, had to change that—had to "make them see that we are the enemy. That the black man is a greater threat to this country than Vietnam or Berlin. So let them turn the money for defense in our direction and either destroy us or cure the conditions that brought our people to this point." He saw no way to make white power move except violence—or, as he pointedly added, "a real threat of it." Yet even then the violence in his rhetoric had less to do with guns than with manhood. "I don't believe we're going to overcome [by] singing," he said at a Harlem rally late in 1964. "If you're going to get yourself a .45 and start singing 'We Shall Overcome,' I'm with you." Malcolm himself kept the only guns he owned at home, for the protection of his family; he talked about .45s because he wanted black and white Americans alike to understand that the .45 may be the last resort of people for whom there is no other redress.

Malcolm saw no possibility of redress whatever in the alternative posed by King and the mainstream movement—nonviolent actions whose unspoken objective was precisely to provoke white violence against unresisting black demonstrators. He saw nonviolence as degrading and beggarly—the rough equivalent, as he once said, of the sheep reminding the wolf that it was time for dinner. He contended that whites themselves had never practiced "this little passive resistance or wait-until-you-change-your-mind-and-then-let-me-up philosophy" but had conjured it up to unman the blacks when they began getting restless. "When the Japanese attacked Pearl Harbor," Malcolm told me in an interview in 1962, "Uncle Sam didn't say, 'Forget Pearl Harbor.' No—he said, '*Remember* Pearl Harbor.' Uncle Sam said, 'Praise the Lord and pass the ammunition.' "

Malcolm accordingly derided the notion that the movement of the 1960s could accurately be called a revolution. In his "Message to the Grassroots," recorded in 1963 and perhaps his most influential single public utterance, he reminded his black audience that *all* revolutions—the American, the French, the Russian, the Chinese, the Mau Mau—have spilled blood. There "was no love lost, was no compromise, was no negotiation. I'm telling you, you don't know what a revolution is, because when you find out what it is, you'll get back in the alley. You'll get out of the way. . . . Only kind of revolution that is nonviolent is the Negro revolution. The only revolution based on loving your enemy is the Negro revolution. The only revolution in which the goal is a desegregated lunch counter, a desegregated theater, a desegregated park, and a desegregated toilet. You can sit down next to white folks—on the toilet." No, he went on, revolution was bloody and destructive, not polite and nonviolent and psalm-singing, and not trusting in the conscience of its enemy. What the mainstream leadership called a revolution, Malcolm said, was more nearly like a shot of Novocain at the dentist's: "You sit there and 'cause you got all that Novocain in your

319

jaw, you suffer—peacefully." He chuckled. "Blood runnin' all down your jaw and you don't know what's happening, 'cause someone has taught you to suffer—peacefully."

For most of his public life, Malcolm's alternative to nonviolence was not violence but abstention. He was, for his dozen years in the service of the Nation of Islam, a doomsday fundamentalist; he taught and by every evidence believed that the time of the white devil was at hand and that Allah would shortly visit a terrible vengeance on him. Malcolm's increasing worldliness drew him to the edges of the struggle and to a kind of itchy restiveness to make himself and the Muslims part of it. "The Messenger [Muhammad] has seen God," he told Lomax during his last days as a Black Muslim. "He was with Allah and was given divine patience to deal with the devil. He is willing to wait for Allah to deal with this devil. Well, sir, the rest of us Black Muslims have not seen God, we don't have this gift of divine patience with the devil. The younger Black Muslims want to see some action."

The action they were taught to await was the apocalypse—the descent from space of a Mother Plane piloted by Allah; the release in turn of 1,500 "baby planes," each armed with high explosives and piloted by a black man so devoted to revenge that he had never smiled; a firestorm that would set the atmosphere ablaze for 310 years and destroy white life forever. The vision permitted the faithful a certain vicarious pleasure in natural and man-made catastrophes, which were taken to be harbingers of Allah's wrath; once, chafing under Muhammad's restraints, Malcolm announced the crash of a jetload of whites as "a very beautiful thing that has happened. . . . We call on our God and He gets rid of 120 of them at one whop." Otherwise, he lived with a policy of abstention so strict that Muhammad's Muslims were discouraged even from voting. It was a measure of the schizoid tensions this caused him that he could not join the great civil rights March on Washington of summer 1963 and yet could not stay away; he stood at the edge of the event, a bitter black chorus of one deriding it as a circus and a picnic—and acknowledging by his presence that it was locus of black America's heart and soul for a day.

The tug of the struggle drew Malcolm away from Muhammad, dangerously so, for his faith, and so did his discovery that the man he had revered for a decade as the Last Messenger of Allah had turned his pool of nubile young secretaries into a private harem. The erosion of his belief in Muhammad's moral authority quickened the secularization of his ministry even before he left the fold—turned his devotions to the Messenger into mechanical asides in a politics moving toward black nationalism and straining for action. "The Black Muslim movement has nothing within its mechanism that's designed to deal with things on this earth right now," he told Claude Lewis long after his departure. "Most of the Black Muslim movement's objectives are similar to those of the church, the only difference being that the church says you're going to die and go to the Promised Land, and in the Black Muslims I was taught that we get to the Promised Land when God comes and takes us there. Now, I believe in the Promised Land, and I believe in God. But I believe that we should be doing something toward trying to get to it right now. And if God wants to get into the act, good. But if He's not ready yet, we at least won't be sitting around here waiting."

Once on his own, Malcolm spent what little time was left him trying to create a new fighting faith on the wreckage of the old. He began by founding his own Muslim Mosque Inc. and pledging his continuing allegiance to the gospels according to Muhammad, partly out of belief, partly out of obligation to the Old Muslims who followed him out of the Nation; he continued briefly to preach that whites were devils, that coexistence was impossible, and that the only course of deliverance for blacks was to separate to the African motherland or to a partitioned section of the United States. But his pilgrimage to Mecca and his electrifying exposure to the color-blind democracy of the *hajj* transformed his politics as certainly and as radically as his theology. He did not fall in love with white people, as some black cynics imagined then and some white liberals imagine now; he argued, on the contrary, that the racial climate in the United States remained poisoned against black people—irremediably poisoned, short of the mass conversion of white America to Islam. All he conceded was the humanity of white people—an admission that seemed, to him and to us, to be revolutionary.

Malcolm's ideological development thereafter was free-running, improvisational, and incomplete. Admirers of every tendency from integrationist to nationalist to revolutionary socialist recognized passages of their own beliefs in his speeches and laid posthumous claim to possession of the True Malcolm. Their contention, as his friend and lawyer Percy Sutton observed to me, was rather like the ancient fable of the blind men and the elephant: "One feels the ear, one feels the trunk, one feels the tail and so on, and each of them thinks he can describe the whole animal." The truth, as Malcolm himself kept telling us, was that he did not know where he was going or what he wanted to be, except *flexible*. He thought of himself as a teacher, a minister, a Muslim, an African, an internationalist, and in the most general terms a revolutionary—and, before any of these things, as black. The details were vague and fluid, subject to change *extempore* from speech to speech or talk show to talk show. He was searching (some said groping) for his bearings; in the meantime, he said straight out, he would ride with the wind, changing his mind and his course as circumstance changed around him. Where was he headed? "I have no idea. I can capsulize how I feel—I'm for the freedom of the 22 million Afro-Americans by any means necessary. *By any means necessary.* I'm for a society in which our people are recognized and respected as human beings, and I believe that we have the right to resort to *any means necessary* to bring that about. So when you ask me where I'm headed, what can I say? I'm headed in any direction that will bring us some immediate results. Isn't anything wrong with that."

By any means necessary: the words of Malcolm were program enough, slogan enough, ideology enough. They carried a little edge of menace, which troubled him not at all; they gave him enormous political maneuvering room, which pleased him greatly. He had trusted in fixed answers for most of his adult life and now saw that they had betrayed him. He said, "I'm not dogmatic about anything any more."

What ideology and program he had in his last months took form out of the slow agglomeration of all those words he spilled forth so extravagantly. On two long journeys to the Middle East and Africa and in his regular rounds at the United Nations, he made it his first priority to "internationalize" the struggle—to form an alliance of interest and soul between black Americans and the nonwhite world and to bring the United States to book before the United Nations for its racist crimes. His international politics ebbed and flowed between pan-Africanism—the unity of black people everywhere around their color and common origin in Africa—and a wider identification with the entire Third World from Cuba to Vietnam against the colonialist and capitalist white West. Which label more nearly fit him was not nearly so important as his underlying therapeutic purpose—making black and white Americans alike see themselves on a larger stage, where the old majority-minority arithmetic was reversed and the future, if not the present, belonged to the dark peoples. Late in his life, the Student Nonviolent Coordinating Committee brought a group of teenagers from McComb, Mississippi, to see Malcolm in Harlem—black children for whom even Jackson was a great and distant place—and Malcolm spent an afternoon telling them that there were men of power who looked like them and cared about them in Dar-es-Salaam and Accra and Conakry. "It is important," he told them, "for you to know that when you're in Mississippi, you're not alone."

The formal objective of Malcolm's diplomacy—his effort to bring a human rights case against America in the United Nations—was doomed by the realities of international politics and the dependence of the Third World on American foreign aid. Malcolm was brilliantly received on his travels down the corridors of African power; he met with heads of state, addressed the Ghanaian parliament, and was admitted with semi-official status to the second summit conference of the Organization of African Unity in Cairo—an occasion for which the certified representatives of the U.S. Department of State were largely outsiders looking in. "Our problems are your problems," Malcolm wrote in an impassioned memorandum to the conferees. ". . . We pray that our African brothers have not freed themselves of European colonialism only to be overcome and held in check now by American dollarism. Don't let American racism be 'legalized' by American dollarism." His lobbying was rewarded by the conference with a resolution—a rather guarded affair, praising the United States on the one hand for having passed the Civil Rights Act of 1964, worrying on the other about the continuing evidence of racial oppression, and concluding with the wish that Washington intensify its efforts against color discrimination. The sentiments were disappointingly tame for Malcolm and were substantially identical in thought and tone to a resolution passed without his help at the first all-African summit the year before. What was extraordinary was that he got anything at all; the reach and restraining power of American dollars were even more formidable than he had imagined, and the hedged little bill of reproof from the Africans was the only tangible victory his diplomacy ever won.

A strand of leftist rhetoric crept into Malcolm's public vocabulary in his last days, inspired by his encounters with African socialism and encouraged by Trotskyist and Maoist admirers back home. He continued to see color as central but not necessarily the single motivating force in his world; he began arguing that nonwhite people around the globe had not only their nonwhiteness in common but their exploitation by the West. Occasionally he identified capitalism straight out as an enemy—"You show me a capitalist, I'll show you a bloodsucker," he said—and socialism as the almost universal system among the new Third World nations coming into independence. "Instead of you running downtown picketing city hall," he told a Harlem audience, "you should stop and find out what they do over there to solve their problems. This is why the man doesn't want you and me to look beyond Harlem or beyond the shores of America . . . I mean, what they use to solve their problem is not capitalism."

But the politics of the Left has never sold well in the ghetto; Malcolm's public flirtation with its ideas and its vocabulary was an affair largely conducted downtown, not in Harlem, and it disappeared almost without a trace from his last interviews and speeches. He seemed then to be moving away from Marx and back to Allah—to the mosque as his real base of operations. Friends concluded that he was withdrawing from a system of thought and a society of people that had grown claustrophobic for him—a straitjacket as constricting as the one he had only just shucked off. "He had been moving with a number of people who thought they could use him," one close associate told me. "They didn't think Malcolm was as bright as he was. At the end, he was looking at where he would be the leader and where he would be the victim. . . . He wanted to detach from the Left and reassert himself as a Muslim. He wanted to really compete with Elijah Muhammad. He wanted to be his own man." Old friends who had always regretted his new comrades encouraged this trend—told him that he could use the pulpit as an instrument for social change, just as King had, and that he would be free to create whatever political theology he wanted. These friends believed, with some evidence, that they were winning; Malcolm in his last days had been certified in Cairo as a Sunni Muslim minister, had brought home an African imam as his spiritual adviser, had laid in a supply of orthodox Islamic literature, and was actively shopping for a mosque the day he died.

The shape that ministry might have taken is rather more difficult to define. Its value was precisely that it would have permitted him to say whatever he wanted and so would have suited his real genius. Malcolm was never as much a politician as a moral commentator on politics, and the Sunni mosque he sought would have given him an unencumbered pulpit of his own for the first time—a theater in which to assert his claim to recognition as an authentic man of God *and* as a legitimate political leader.

That recognition reached him only posthumously. Malcolm was perceived in his lifetime as a demonic presence at the edges of our field of sight—an angel of darkness contending with the angels of light for possession of the black soul. It was King who occupied center stage then and eclipsed everyone else in polls of black and white public opinion. Malcolm's day came later, out of the ruin of the riots and the desperation they revealed in the black casbahs of the urban North. T-shirts bearing his likeness appeared in the streets of Watts while the ashes of the rioting there in 1965 were still warm. King could not even go there; he attempted one peace-making speech near the end of the uprising, was heckled mercilessly, and shortly thereafter left town. The streets were Malcolm's; he had lived there; he belonged. The destruction of the rioting would have appalled him, not because it was illegitimate in his eyes but because it wasted black lives and spoiled neighborhoods where black people lived. But he once guessed that if he had been home during the Harlem insurrection of 1964, he would have died fighting. It was the established leaders who referred to the street people as "they." To Malcolm, there was no such distance; they were always "you and me."

His vision of events was street vision, cynical and mocking, sometimes even cruel, and it held him back from participation in the movement even when he began gingerly to seek it. He helped energize the established leaders, helped force them into a quickening militancy, but he wounded them, too. "With Malcolm," Wilkins once told me, "the only way you could judge things was whether you did the thing that was *manly*, no matter if it was suicidal or not. A prosecutor like Malcolm has to be able to put himself in the shoes of people who did the best they could under the circumstances." Malcolm had no such gift of toleration. For all his sense of history, he felt no empathy for the heroes and heroines of that long middle passage in the black American past when the National Association for the Advancement of Colored People and the Urban League were all there was and you petitioned and sued and even swallowed your pride and begged at the back door if you had to. Malcolm assumed that what was middle class was venal and that what was polite was cowardly. The mainstream leaders neither forgot nor forgave what he said about them; even the younger radicals rather wished, nearly to the end of Malcolm's life, that he would go away. The movement people reciprocated insult for insult, but their answer to him finally was that *they* had the bodies and the motion and the pulse of the times; *they* were out in the rush of history, where the real battles were fought and the real risks run, and he was not.

The older leaders never quit believing that. But the radical young did cool off; they went into the 1960s as King's children and came out Malcolm's. The process of disenchantment was a broken one, not a revelation but a series of painful recognitions. It came out of too many beatings and nights in jail and too many funerals; out of the gathering suspicion that the federal government saw the events of the day not as a moral struggle but as a contention of interests to be balanced; out of the political, social, and sexual tensions between the northern white youngsters who summered in the movement and the southern black youngsters who would still be there when the whites went home; out of the great compromise at the Democratic national convention in 1964, at which the higher necessity of electing Lyndon Johnson took precedence over the claims to justice of the disfranchised blacks of Mississippi; out of the creeping paralysis of the old liberal audience when the struggle moved North and got abrasive and when ghettos started burning down; out of the discovery that integration was a delusive hope for the black poor, since they did not have the money to be mobile, and, anyway, the liberals talking integration were not talking about integration with *them*.

Only then did Malcolm's path and that of the radical movement intersect, and with his death and the publication of the *Autobiography*, a process something like beatification began. He left his heirs little that was tangible beyond a legacy of words—his speeches became gospels of the new movement along with Fanon, and, later, Eldridge Cleaver—and an uncompleted set of priorities. It was the stresses that endured—the beauty, and the worth, of blackness; the racism endemic in American society; the legitimacy of defending oneself by any means, including violence; the irrelevance of integration for the black poor and the self-loathing implied in begging for it; the futility of appeals to conscience in the conscienceless; the necessity of connecting with Africa and with the African past; the central importance of confronting power with power, not supplication; the recognition that the separation of the races was not a program but a fact and that blacks ought therefore to control the life and politics of the black community. Malcolm otherwise left no strategy or platform for change; he was to have announced his program for the redemption of the blacks at his last rally, but the committee composing it for him brought it in late and heavy with the commonplaces of black nationalism, and he felt it was unready for publication. His bequest instead was a style of thought; it came back to us beginning in the summer of 1966 codified under a new name—Black Power—and the sayings of Minister Malcolm became the orthodoxies of a black generation.

He was most important as a prophetic figure in our race relations. He could be, as prophets often are, unreasonable; he could stretch, color, heighten, rearrange, distort, and grossly oversimplify the truth; he could contradict himself from speech to speech, or sentence to sentence. Garvey anticipated some of his vision, and Muhammad taught him a lot of it. But Malcolm transmuted the message and combined it with his intuitive genius for modern communications, and it was he in catalytic chemistry with his time who really began the difficult passage from Negro to black consciousness. Semantics was rather a vice of Malcolm's; he placed enormous importance, probably too much, on terminology, as though by redrawing the map one could alter the territory. He argued that the name "Negro" was itself a prison—that it disconnected black people from their land and their history and turned them into denatured, deracinated objects rather than men and women. He advanced this view when it was still a conscious political act to call oneself black—an affirmation of a word and a color that had been matters of shame in the past.

The central objcct of Malcolm's public life was to reverse that—to reveal to black people their worth as men and women and their competence to find their own way. The point was self-esteem, an assertion of size and place and what King called *somebodyness*; everything else in his politics and his theology was an elaboration of this inner purpose. The success or failure of his particular enterprises—his inability to organize the unorganized, or cobble up a platform, or bring America to justice before the nations of the world—was almost beside the point. He was dealing in symbolic action—attempting the liberation of black people by altering the terms in which they thought and the scale by which they measured themselves.

Malcolm's gift finally was not policy but polemic; he said things that black people had been afraid to say or even to think for years; he forced us to respond to him—forced whites to examine their consciences and blacks to confront their color. The beginning of his appeal for blacks was that he dared identify whites as the devil, and the continuing source of his authority was that he never quit thinking of them in the large as the enemy. Where King appealed to the higher instincts of black people, Malcolm addressed their viscera; he asked them not to sublimate their resentments but to recognize and express them, to turn their hatreds outward against their oppressors instead of inward against themselves. "He was a kind of alter ego for people who were too vulnerable and too insecure to say what they really felt regarding our situation in America," Eric Lincoln said in an interview. "He was trying to strip the white man of his mystique, and that made him a demagogue for most white people."

It made Malcolm an authentic folk hero for blacks, and it was they to whom he primarily addressed himself. His supreme gift to them was that he loved them, that he believed in their possibilities and tried to make them believe, too. His real legacy was his example, his bearing,

327

his affirmation of blackness—his understanding that one is paralyzed for just as long as one believes one cannot move.

His collateral purpose was to educate whites as well—to expose them to the depths of black grievance against them. His message was that whites could neither define nor control black leadership by inviting those who most closely resembled them to the White House; that the goal of integration was a delusion when the sprawl of suburbia testified to the distance even liberal whites wanted to put between themselves and ordinary blacks; that the requirement that blacks address their demands to whites nonviolently was incongruent with our own violent history, from Lexington and Concord to Seoul and Saigon; that the ruin white America had visited on the blacks was about to be returned, out of the explosive anger of the inner cities; that in the back alleys of white consciousness, there were black people who hated whites in direct proportion as whites despised them, and who would rejoice in their deaths; that, for men and women so desperate, parades and pageants and marches on Washington were not an adequate surrogate experience. Whites called him irresponsible for saying so; Malcolm left us the burnt-out ruins of Watts and Newark and Detroit as his evidence. We protested that we were making progress; he responded by quoting what Patrice Lumumba had told the king of Belgium—*we can never forget these scars.*

The sad last irony for Malcolm was that his own martyrdom was a part of the price he had to pay for the legitimacy he had always wanted. The assassination and the *Autobiography* were bracketing events in a year that transformed our understanding of race in America by revealing the explosive furies just beneath the skin—the furies Malcolm had warned us so prophetically against. It was the winter of his death; the spring of the last of the great civil rights parades, from Selma to Montgomery, and the last of the great civil rights victories, the Voting Rights Act of 1965; the summer of the riot in Watts and the attending first signs of the collapse of the ad hoc American majority for racial justice. When Malcolm's memoirs were published that autumn, America was only just getting ready to listen to him, without the intervening scare image that he and the media had created together.

The celebration of Malcolm followed, with a fervor and an ecumenism that would have astonished him. It was an epiphany of his passage from manhood to myth that Imamu Amiri Baraka, then still LeRoi Jones, sent Young a greeting card bearing Malcolm's likeness one Christmas season; the card was meant as a token of unity, which Malcolm would have approved, but the fact that a nationalist like

328

Baraka chose his image and an assimilationist like Young showed it around with pleasure suggested how little was left of Malcolm except his blackness and his sentimentalized legend. The process was carried out by blacks of every tendency—by those who had loved him and those who had been terrified by him; by nationalists and integrationists; by black Marxists and black capitalists; by scholars and street-gang children with nothing but the dimmest sense that Malcolm had been the *baddest*; even, *mirabile dictu*, by white people.(Schoolboys from Harlem to Watts wore buttons proclaiming Malcolm Our Shining Black Prince. Black students put on festivals on his birthday. A publicly funded college in Chicago was named after him; so were a Democratic club in Harlem and a black enlisted men's association in the military. The Nebraska Historical Society authorized a marker near his birthplace in Omaha. A black woman officeholder in Washington waved away the Bible at her swearing-in and substituted a copy of the *Autobiography*. Two plays, a movie, a book of poems, and even a ballet were done about him. His memoir and his speeches sold in the hundreds of thousands and were required reading at dozens of universities.)

The consecration in the end nearly drained Malcolm's public life of real meaning; his gifts and flaws, his public passion and his private ironies, were smoothed flat and stylized, like the holy men burning coolly in a Byzantine icon. By the mid-1970s, with the death of Muhammad and the gentling succession of his son Wallace to the leadership of the old Lost-Found Nation, even the Muslim mosque in Harlem was named for him; a temple that had once been a center of revanchist incitement against him thus became our most imposing brick-and-mortar monument to his memory. In the streets his memory has receded into a kind of gauzy half-light. A black psychologist mentioned Malcolm's name to a class of teen-aged street youngsters in Harlem and got only the dimmest show of recognition; he displayed Malcolm's photograph, narrow-tied and Ivy-tailored, and was asked, "Why the dude dress so funny?" But the young blacks in that classroom, who were in diapers when Malcolm died, were raised by parents who knew who Malcolm was and were touched by him. Malcolm survives to the extent that they see themselves as he saw them: as men and women of worth, beauty, and untested possibility in white America.

Note on Sources

The Malcolm literature, sizable and still growing, begins indispensably with *The Autobiography of Malcolm X* (New York: Grove Press, 1965), written in collaboration with Alex Haley and accompanied by Haley's own affecting and perceptive memoir of Malcolm. My own *The Death and Life of Malcolm X* (New York: Harper & Row, 1973; rev. 2nd ed., Urbana: University of Illinois Press, 1979), from which this essay was adapted, is a biography focused heavily on Malcolm's last years, his assassination, and his place in our recent past; it is based on my three-year acquaintance with him, on wide interviewing with his associates, and on extensive documentary sources, published and unpublished. George Breitman's *The Last Year of Malcolm X* (New York: Merit, 1967) is a Trotskyist analysis, arguing on a selective reading of the evidence that Malcolm was becoming a revolutionary socialist—a conclusion rejected by his family and his closest friends and advisers.

Malcolm speaks eloquently for himself in several volumes of speeches, of which the most important by far are one edited by his close associate Benjamin Goodman, *The End of White World Supremacy* (New York: Merit, 1971), drawn from Malcolm's last year as a Black Muslim, and two edited by Breitman, *Malcolm X Speaks* (New York: Merit, 1965) and *By Any Means Necessary* (New York: Pathfinder, 1967, 1970), both culled almost entirely from the year between his break with the Nation of Islam and his death. A number of recorded speeches convey Malcolm's style even more vividly and flavorfully—none more so than the brilliant *Message to the Grass Roots* (Afro-American Broadcasting Co., 1965).

There is, lamentably, no serious biography yet of the late Elijah Muhammad, but his extraordinary ministry—and Malcolm's Black Muslim years—are treated in two excellent volumes on the Nation, C. Eric Lincoln's seminal *The Black Muslims in America* (Boston: Beacon, 1961; rev. ed., 1973), and E. U. Essien-Udom's *Black Nationalism* (Chicago: University of Chicago Press, 1962). The most important collections of Muhammad's own rambly theological meditations are *The Supreme Wisdom* (Chicago: The University of Islam, n. d.) and *Message to the Blackman in America* (Chicago: Muhammad Mosque of Islam No. 2, 1965).

In *The Assassination of Malcolm X* (New York: Pathfinder, 1976), Breitman, Herman Porter, and Baxter Smith advance various state-conspiracy theories of Malcolm's murder—all finally speculative and none convincingly supported by the real evidence, old or new. More extensive bibliographical entries appear in my book; in Breitman's *The Last Year*; and in John Henrik Clarke, ed., *Malcolm X: The Man and His Times* (New York: Macmillan, 1969), a largely elegiac collection otherwise useful mostly for a selection of Malcolm's speeches and interviews.

Nancy J. Weiss   **15**

Whitney M. Young, Jr.:
Committing the Power Structure
to the Cause of Civil Rights

The National Urban League, founded about the same time as the Na-tional Association for the Advancement of Colored People, and dedi-cated especially to improving employment opportunities for Negro workers, had been the most conservative of the race advancement orga-nizations. Financed mainly by employers and wealthy philanthropists, the League and its local affiliates typically followed a strategy of persua-sion rather than engaging in militant offensives (though there were, of course, exceptions, with certain local Urban Leagues boldly attacking a wide range of discriminatory practices). With the coming of the civil rights revolution of the 1960s the National Urban League was in a posi-tion to revamp its strategy, and no one was better equipped to do this than its new executive director, Whitney M. Young, Jr. Though he died prematurely, it was he who transformed the Urban League into a truly effective instrument of social reform.

"CERTAINLY if any one can drag the Urban League screamingly into the 20th century you can!" a friend wrote Whitney M. Young, Jr., when she learned of his appointment as executive director of the Na-tional Urban League in 1961. "You've certainly got your work cut out for you and that's for sure! Trying to make rich white folks pay for a program to make them do something they aren't too keen about doing in the first place—oh brother!"

Making "rich white folks" pay for racial progress proved to be Young's particular forte. Consummate politician, salesman, inter-preter, and ebullient personality, he bridged the gulf between the ghetto and the power structure. The "inside man" of the black revolu-tion, he brought the white establishment to the support of civil rights. The National Urban League gave him a platform. The civil rights movement gave him the establishment's ear. What he would do with them was a function of his own imagination and style. This essay exam-ines Young's roles as head of the National Urban League and as civil rights leader, with particular emphasis on his relationships with corporations, foundations, and presidential administrations, and on the ways he functioned with different groups of blacks.

By the late 1950s the National Urban League was in the doldrums. The executive director, Lester B. Granger, already past sixty, had been on the job for almost two decades. In earlier years Granger had been a capable leader. But in the judgment of many Urban Leaguers, he had become excessively cautious: unwilling to identify the League with the emerging civil rights movement, reluctant to speak out on major public issues, and resistant to pressures from local executives and board members who called for greater activism. The organization could barely raise a modest budget of $300,000 a year. Some weeks it could not even meet its payroll.

The League's condition was cause for concern on the part of its supporters. One of them was a new board member, Lindsley Kimball, executive vice president of the Rockefeller Foundation and a philanthropic counselor to the Rockefeller family. Looking after the Urban League was a family tradition; in its earliest years, John D. Rockefeller, Jr., had been the largest single contributor; in the 1940s, his son Winthrop, a trustee, shaped its major fund-raising efforts. A personal gift from Winthrop enabled the League in 1956 to acquire its first permanent headquarters building on East 48th Street in New York. With the League in difficulty in the late 1950s, the Rockefellers suggested that Kimball go on the board and see what he could do to invigorate the organization.

The major task was to give the League some fresh leadership. In 1959 Kimball found his man. He heard Young address the annual meeting of the National Urban League in Washington, D.C. The substance of Young's speech had faded two decades later, but Kimball's impression of Young's qualities was still sharp. "He had courage, forthrightness, understanding, intellectual honesty—a rare combination." Kimball sent for him to talk about his future. Was Young satisfied at Atlanta? What were his hopes for his career? "He said he was bumping his head against the ceiling at Atlanta. I told him that he belonged in the active arena rather than the halls of academe."

Young's life had been a blend of "the active arena" and "the halls of academe." Born in 1921 in Lincoln Ridge, Kentucky, he spent his childhood on the campus of Lincoln Institute, which had been founded in 1912 by the trustees of Berea College to provide academic and industrial education for blacks who were excluded from Berea by state law. Young's father, Whitney Moore Young, Sr., was a member of the Lincoln Institute's faculty and subsequently its president. His mother, Laura Ray Young, was the local postmistress. Young grew up in a warm, loving, close-knit family that gave him a security and a self-confidence that would clearly mark his adult life. From his parents, he later wrote, he gained an "inbred belief in the ultimate power of decency over bigotry, of intelligence over ignorance, of truth over fear," which "sustained [him] in [his] life and life's work."

Graduating from Lincoln Institute at the age of fourteen, Young enrolled in a premedical course at the all-black Kentucky State College, where he played forward on the basketball team and was elected president of his senior class. He graduated in 1941. Lacking the means to enter medical school, he took a teaching job at a high school in Madisonville, Kentucky. Following Pearl Harbor, he joined the Army Specialized Training Program in the hope of being sent to medical school. Instead, the Army sent him to study engineering at the Massachusetts Institute of Technology. When the Army program was disbanded, Young was assigned to the 369th Regiment, Anti-Aircraft Artillery Group, a black company with white officers. "Most of our combat was building roads," he later commented, "but we did get into the Battle of the Bulge when they ran out of infantry." Once they were in Europe, strong racial tensions surfaced. Young, a first sergeant, became the "mediator between the alienated, bitter, black troops and their white officers."

Those experiences gave Young a new direction. Instead of medicine, he would make race relations his life's work. In 1946, after his discharge from the service, he went to Minneapolis, where his wife, the former Margaret Buckner, whom he had married before he went overseas, was a graduate student in educational psychology at the University of Minnesota. Young enrolled immediately in the School of Social Work.

Young wrote his thesis on the St. Paul Urban League. In 1947, master's degree in hand, he joined the St. Paul Urban League as director of industrial relations and vocational guidance. In 1950 he became executive director of the Omaha Urban League. He also taught part-time—at the College of St. Catherine in St. Paul and at the University of Nebraska School of Social Work and Creighton University in Omaha. In 1954 he became dean of the Atlanta University School of Social Work.

The deanship at Atlanta gave Young a laboratory in which to develop his ideas about social work training. He thought that social workers tended to be "ivory towerish," Margaret Young said. He wanted to make them "more action-oriented." Young promoted the integration of the faculty and student body, doubled the school's budget, substantially increased faculty salaries, and arranged field work assignments for his students in leading social service institutions. In 1959 in recognition of his leadership the National Conference on Social Welfare gave him the Florina Lasker Award for outstanding achievement.

Moving to the South in 1954 also brought Young to the threshold of the emerging civil rights movement. He later commented on the move: "Many Negroes had stayed South to help me get educated. I felt that I owed it to them, and to others, to be there during the change." The years in Atlanta gave Young a chance to work actively for social change. He was a board member of the Atlanta chapter of the National Association for the Advancement of Colored People and a founder of the Atlanta Committee for Cooperative Action, an organization of young black professionals and businessmen, who provided research and technical assistance to support the struggle for civil rights. When the Atlanta student movement began, Young was one of the few faculty from the Atlanta University Center who worked closely with the protesters.

Young had never intended to remain permanently in Atlanta. His meeting with Kimball provided the impetus for his departure. Kimball arranged for him to spend the academic year 1960–61 at Harvard University on a fellowship provided by the Rockefeller Foundation. The $15,000 grant was "an investment in a man," the Foundation told him. There was no set program, no advanced degree to pursue; the purpose, as Kimball later described it, was for Young "to think and study and read and get to know people."

In retrospect, it is clear that Young was being groomed to succeed Granger. At the time Young's future course was not yet obvious to his family; when they went to Harvard, Margaret Young said, they did not know that they would be going to the National Urban League. When a committee of Urban League trustees began looking for a successor to Granger, however, Young's name was on the list. In January 1961 the board announced his appointment, effective that October.

Young's arrival at the National Urban League was like "a fresh breeze," one of his staff remarked. Immediately the pace quickened: "We don't work this fast," a longtime Urban Leaguer protested.

"From now on, we will," Young told him. "We've got to, or we'll be left behind." Young restructured the national headquarters, tightened the national organization's control over its affiliates, and expanded the scope of the agency's program. No longer would the League focus on "pilot" job placements and vocational guidance; no longer would it simply dispense social services. It undertook new projects to improve employment opportunities: the National Skills Bank, for example, matched unemployed or underemployed blacks who had marketable skills with positions that utilized their talents; On-the-Job-Training (under contract from the Department of Labor) placed unskilled workers in training slots in private industry; the Broadcast Skills Bank sought jobs for blacks in television and radio; the Secretarial Training Project prepared women for secretarial employment. The numbers of people whose economic fortunes the Urban League affected changed significantly. When Young took over the League, annual reports still commented on token successes: twenty jobs for black sales people in large food chains in Richmond; the first black teacher in a Westchester school. On-the-Job-Training alone trained 50,000 workers in seven years. By the late 1960s, the League reported 40,000 to 50,000 placements annually in new or upgraded jobs.

The National Urban League developed new efforts to improve the quality of black education and to motivate young blacks to stay in school: individual tutoring for ghetto youngsters; street academies to prepare high school dropouts for college; summer fellowships in industry for black college teachers and administrators; short-term teaching assignments for black executives at black colleges; transfer plans to bring gifted southern blacks to finish their high school education at first-rate schools in the North. The agency's traditional housing, health, and welfare services took on new dimensions: assistance to black veterans; campaigns for open housing; consumer protection; efforts to find adoptive families for hard-to-place black children; group parent counseling to strengthen family life.

Finally, the League undertook new programs to give blacks a stronger voice in public affairs: for example, voter education and registration; leadership development; and, with the "New Thrust" of the late 1960s, community organizing.

By most objective measurements, Young's executive directorship was a period of remarkable expansion for the National Urban League. Not only did its programs multiply; in the decade of Young's leadership the League grew from sixty-three affiliates to ninety-eight; its professional staff grew from 300 to over 1,200; its budget increased ten-fold.* Yet, despite these accomplishments, managing the Urban League was never Young's special strength. For all his success in moti-vating a dedicated staff, he was more tolerant than he might have been of inadequate performance. He could not bear to hurt anyone; he hated to tell staff members that they were not doing a good job. He carried people who failed to pull their weight; instead of firing them, he transferred them to other positions.

In part Young's limitations as an administrator were a function of his personal style. He was impatient with detail. Desk work bored him. Sitting in an office, shuffling papers, giving orders, supervising their execution—none of that engaged his interest.

In part, too, it was hard to be a good administrator when he spent so little time in the office. Simply staying on top of the varied, far-flung activities of a growing national organization kept him traveling much of the time. Even beyond that, however, there were unending de-mands on him: too many invitations to speak, too many dinners to at-tend, too many committees to join. So much of minority leadership in the 1960s was "built around the attraction of one personality that it was very difficult for anyone to be your deputy or stand in for you," Marga-ret Young pointed out. After a while, the pace became a reflex—two, three cities in one day, endless meetings, press conferences, recep-tions. Young took on too much; what was surprising was not that he was, on occasion, less than thoroughly prepared, spread too thin, but that he did it all as well as he did.

Despite Young's limitations in handling day-to-day business inside the National Urban League, he clearly stretched and strengthened the organization through the roles he played outside. The early 1960s were a propitious time to take the helm of a racial advancement organiza-tion; the civil rights movement and the growing federal involvement in social welfare gave the Urban League a chance to "make its greatest contribution." "The stage [was] uniquely set," Young felt, for the League "to play a major role in making true integration a reality in all aspects of American life."

Toward that end, in two dramatic ways, early in his tenure, Young broke from the mold he had inherited and charted new directions: on the one hand, by making the Urban League an influential voice in the

---

* These figures refer to the national office and the affiliates. The income of the Na-tional Urban League alone grew from $340,000 in 1961 to $14,749,000 in 1970.

formation of public policy; on the other, by identifying it with activism in behalf of civil rights.

Speaking out on issues was Young's style. He took a highly visible public posture: through his books (*To Be Equal* [1964] and *Beyond Racism* [1969]), weekly newspaper column, radio commentaries, television appearances, and frequent speeches, he set forth his vision of American society and his prescriptions for racial progress. He spoke often about the complexities of civil rights: blacks needed not just political and legal rights, but jobs, a good education, adequate health care, and decent housing. The civil rights movement, as it was commonly understood, strove to open the doors of opportunity; the Urban League's role was to equip blacks to walk through them. Young looked forward to an "impossible dream": a world of equality and justice, free from want, in which blacks and whites would live harmoniously with recognition and respect for each other's individuality and common bonds. Probably his most original contribution to discussions of public policy came in the method he suggested for the dream's achievement— that is, in his arguments for compensatory action.

The term "affirmative action" had first entered the public vocabulary in 1961, when the executive order creating the President's Committee on Equal Employment Opportunity required government contractors to take affirmative action in hiring. But at that point its meaning was vague. Contractors were expected to make positive efforts to employ members of minority groups but exactly what these efforts should entail was never made specific. For practical purposes, affirmative action meant avoidance of discrimination. In this sense, it was consistent with the main thrust of the civil rights movement toward equality of opportunity.

Young's ideas were more advanced. Equality of opportunity was not enough. Almost immediately after he assumed the executive directorship, in speeches and in discussions with staff, he began articulating a case for *compensatory* action to help blacks move toward full and equal participation in American life. In June 1963, in a major policy statement, Young called for a decade of "special effort" in employment, education, health and welfare services, and housing to compensate blacks for past discrimination. Three centuries of discrimination, segregation, and deprivation, he later explained, had "burdened the Negro with a handicap that will not automatically slip from his shoulders as discriminatory laws and practices are abandoned." It was time for some discrimination in favor of black Americans. Blacks needed "more than equal rights"—they needed a period of extra attention and

337

extra opportunities to make up for past discrimination, to enable them to "compete equally for, or share in, the full rewards and responsibilities of our society." Whereas historically blacks had been consciously *ex*cluded, now they needed to be consciously *in*cluded. "Special effort" meant a massive investment by government and the private sector in crash programs to close the economic, social, and educational gap between blacks and whites, to end poverty and revitalize urban life. Young called it a Domestic Marshall Plan.

While the federal government never directly embraced the Urban League's Domestic Marshall Plan, the social programs of the New Frontier and the Great Society (for example, Manpower Development and Training, the War on Poverty, Head Start, and Model Cities) picked up some of its major themes. Young was not the architect of these efforts, but by repeatedly communicating his vision to policymakers (in private memoranda, in meetings with John F. Kennedy and Lyndon B. Johnson and other members of their administrations, as an expert witness in congressional hearings, as an adviser to the poverty program, among other ways), he helped to shape the results. By 1965 Johnson had begun to speak publicly of the need not only for equality of opportunity for blacks, but for equality of results. By the late 1960s, "affirmative action" had come to be understood in terms of the "special effort" or compensatory activity that Young had described.

The call for a Domestic Marshall Plan thrust the Urban League into the public policy arena. At the same time, Young moved the organization into the cauldron of civil rights.

Early in 1962 Young began meeting regularly with other civil rights leaders—A. Philip Randolph of the Brotherhood of Sleeping Car Porters, Roy Wilkins of the NAACP, Martin Luther King, Jr., of the Southern Christian Leadership Conference (SCLC), James Farmer of the Congress of Racial Equality (CORE), James Forman of the Student Nonviolent Coordinating Committee (SNCC), Dorothy Height of the National Council of Negro Women, and Jack Greenberg of the NAACP Legal Defense and Educational Fund—under the aegis of philanthropist Stephen Currier. Currier had called the group together to discuss the racial situation and to develop ideas for practical programs that his Taconic Foundation might fund. The meetings quickly began to serve a broader purpose. They acquainted the leaders with the purposes and activities of the other organizations. They afforded them a chance for reflection and thoughtful analysis, an opportunity to step back from the day-to-day preoccupations of each one's own organization to look at the broad civil rights picture and to examine aspects of the race problem in greater depth and from new perspectives.

Following the assassination of Medgar Evers in June 1963, the group constituted itself as a formal organization: the Council of United Civil Rights Leadership (CUCRL). It served two functions: raising money for the constituent organizations and providing a forum for the leaders to share ideas and coordinate strategy. Currier and Young became co-chairmen.

Within the Urban League Young was also moving to establish civil rights connections. In a memorandum to local executives that June he spelled out the agency's stance. With demonstrations occurring throughout the country, the Urban League could not remain quietly on the sidelines. Affiliates ought not to participate actively in picketing and boycotting, but they needed to be visible and to communicate effectively with the protesters. Urban Leagues had important roles to play: fact-finding, mediating, and negotiating between the demonstrators and the power structure.

With the March on Washington in August 1963, the National Urban League's new involvement in civil rights became a matter of public record. When Randolph first approached the Urban League about the proposed march in the spring of 1963, the League hung back. The executive committee was skittish: protest was not the Urban League's way. A responsible social service organization had no place in a mass demonstration. As a tax-exempt agency, it was barred from lobbying the Congress. Besides, the National Urban League had made real progress in opening communications with administration officials in Washington; participation in the march might jeopardize those ties.

Despite the executive committee's reluctance, Young himself was certain that the Urban League ought to be involved. Through his own discussions in CUCRL and through the participation of his aides in planning sessions for the march, the League helped to shape the forthcoming demonstration. At the same time, Young brought his troops into line. "We have to make a decision," he told his staff. "We must keep the respect of the Negro people and provide some leadership. The revolution is here. Should we divorce ourselves and let it go as it [is], or intervene and try to bring our experience to bear in these matters? Unless we are in communication with the people we are not in a position to advise those who give us money on matters of the Negro." Ultimately he won a consensus that the League would join the group.

339

It was "a beautiful example of how successful Whitney was," Guichard Parris, his public relations director, observed. He got the board and staff to understand "that even though we'd never done a thing like this before, it was very important for this organization to be part of it." Once the decision was taken, local executives and their boards had to be brought along as well; only at that point, well into the summer, was the League's commitment as a sponsoring organization made public.

The Urban League's presence, Young declared in his speech at the march, "says, and I hope loud and clear, that while intelligence, maturity, and strategy dictate that as Civil Rights agencies we use different methods, we are all united as never before on the goal of securing first class citizenship for all Americans—NOW." The march was a watershed for the League. From that point forward, Young later reflected, it was no longer possible for people to "think of civil rights agencies without considering the Urban League."

As the civil rights movement heated up, Young kept the Urban League involved. While the National Urban League itself never embraced demonstrations or protests, by February 1964 the board had modified its standoffish posture. The agency, it declared, would be willing to lend "moral support" to nonviolent direct action as long as it was undertaken by "responsible groups" in situations "where inequities are clearly obvious and attempts at persuasion and negotiation have failed to produce any results."

Young never got himself arrested as a civil rights demonstrator ("I do not see," he once said, "why I should have to go to jail to prove my leadership"), but at critical junctures in the history of the protests the Urban League was there. When Martin Luther King led the dramatic civil rights march from Selma to Montgomery in March 1965, Young was among the black leaders who spoke from the steps of the Alabama State Capitol. When James Meredith was shot en route from Memphis, Tennessee, to Jackson, Mississippi, in June 1966, and civil rights groups rallied to complete his march, Young went to Jackson to address the crowd. He had argued to the Urban League's executive committee that he ought to go (he would not use regular League funds to pay his expenses); the committee gave its "cautious approval."

As the executive committee's caution makes clear, Young had to walk a tightrope on such occasions. A press release issued before the Meredith march pointed up the delicacy of his position. He emphasized that the League's participation did not mean abandoning the principles that set it apart from other civil rights agencies. Each organization had "its own unique role to fulfill within the movement":

340

While others march in the streets and the highways to galvanize support for broad measures, the Urban League marches its people to job training centers, neighborhood development centers and the like. Each organization does what it can do best.

These different activities undertaken by the various civil rights agencies complement each other. Jointly we are working toward the same goals—to close the shocking economic and cultural gap which exists between Negroes and other citizens.

Young knew, in Urban League executive Alexander J. Allen's words, that "being able to identify with the growing protest" was essential to "the League's effectiveness." He also knew its costs. As SCLC's Andrew Young wrote at the time of Whitney Young's death, any move in the direction of protest required "an agonizing appraisal of every action," for the League's affiliates "would feel in their budgets the reverberation of any miscalculation."

In public Young claimed a role for the Urban League in civil rights activism. In private he functioned as peacemaker among the civil rights leadership. When tempers flared, he was the one to interject a note of humor to break up the tension. When divisions arose, he was the one to find some middle ground where the leaders could reunite.

In functioning as a mediator, Young benefited from his position as head of the Urban League. Always minor tensions festered among the leaders: Who had gotten the most attention in the media? Who had done the most effective job of mustering demonstrators? Who deserved credit for the victories? Young was not immune to the competition of egos, but since the Urban League was not involved in direct action, he was somewhat removed from the jealousies and rivalries among the NAACP, CORE, SCLC, and SNCC.

More important, Young's personal qualities fitted him for the peacemaker's role. Due in part to his training as a social worker, he knew how to listen, to understand where someone else was coming from, to avoid being judgmental, and to build bridges to link different poles. He was "the kind of fellow," Parris observed, "who would say, 'Look, let's get together, fellows . . . we don't agree, but let's get together as rational men and find out how we can achieve our end.'" And he did it with a warmth, a graciousness, and a sense of humor that were positively infectious.

Two examples illustrate Young's ability to preserve harmony among the leaders: the matter of the leadership of the March on Washington and the issue of the civil rights leaders' stand on the war in Vietnam.

As the leader of the proposed March on Washington in 1941, Randolph was the logical person to call his colleagues together in 1963. But the seventy-four-year old Randolph expected to vest responsibility for the day-to-day planning and direction of the march in the hands of Bayard Rustin. Wilkins objected. Rustin was an experienced organizer, but he was also a radical: a socialist, a one-time member of the Young Communist League, a conscientious objector in World War II. The civil rights movement had enough problems of its own, Wilkins argued; why saddle the march with unnecessary liabilities?

Young engineered the compromise. Before the group met, as Rustin tells the story, "Whitney got ahold of Dr. King and explained the situation to him. Whitney said, 'Well, you know, Martin, Bayard's worked with you all this time. Were there any real problems?' " " 'No,' " King responded. " 'Well, then,' " Young rejoined, " 'whatever Randolph proposes, I hope you'll vote for.' "

"Then he went to Jim Farmer and repeated it. Then he went down the line to the others." To Randolph, Rustin recalled, laughing aloud at the memory, Young proposed a way to settle the dispute: " 'Randolph, *you* be the leader of the March, but you insist that Bayard be your deputy.' "

When the group convened, the script went according to plan. Randolph insisted on Rustin leading the march, and Wilkins objected. "So Whitney looked at Randolph as if to say, 'The time has come,' and Randolph said, 'Well, Roy, if you feel that way, *I* will be the director, but I want full powers of directorship, which means I have the right to select my deputy.'' Roy looked over at Mr. Randolph and said, 'O.K., Phil, I've warned you, but if you want him, you take him, and it's *your* responsibility.' " " 'I'm telling you, black boy, you'd better behave yourself,' " Young admonished Rustin, patting him on the back and laughing as they left the room.

In April 1967 King came out against the war in Vietnam. Other civil rights leaders—most notably Young and Wilkins—declined to follow King's lead. As a matter of strategy, they disputed the commingling of civil rights with the antiwar movement; with resources and supporters limited, with so much remaining to be accomplished in civil rights, it was a mistake to divert precious energy to another cause. Tempers became heated, and there were reports of public squabbling among the leaders.

The distinguished black psychologist, Kenneth B. Clark, called a meeting at his home to air the issue and to try to restore some unity among the leadership. The talk lasted all day. It was "the first time I'd ever seen Martin angry," Clark recalled. Wilkins "had made some disparaging public statements about Martin"; there were "charges and countercharges," and the meeting could have degenerated into "a totally non-productive donnybrook." Then "Whitney stepped in at the appropriate moment and was masterful in bringing these two men around, modifying his own position, understanding Martin, understanding Roy." Young probed for common ground, reminding them "that underneath the differences" over Vietnam, they still shared common goals of overriding importance. "I accused [Whitney] of bringing his social work background and training into those discussions," Clark said. "It was Whitney's victory that these two men came together."

Young's talent as a mediator made him more successful than many of his colleagues in understanding and relating to the militants. He believed in communicating—at the very least, it was important to find out what the other fellow was talking about. They might not convince each other, might not agree, but it was essential to sit down and talk. The approach applied equally to young militants and to his colleagues in the civil rights leadership. He believed that if he could talk to anyone long enough, then he had a chance of making him see his position, perhaps even of changing his mind.

Young understood the anger and impatience of young militants, and he took pains to hear them out. When protesters disrupted an Urban League meeting, he brought them to the podium to speak. When another group insisted on a confrontation, he invited them to his hotel suite for a drink. He acknowledged their grievances and welcomed their suggestions and criticisms. "We're working for the same thing," he told them, but working through the power structure was more effective than "raising hell." Despite the fact that some black audiences heckled him, he continued to address even the most hostile gatherings, never shrinking from explaining his position, sometimes turning boos into applause, as he did during his address to the Congress of African Peoples in Atlanta in September 1970.

For all of Young's insistence on the ineffectiveness of simply raising hell, his training as a social scientist equipped him to appreciate the militants' role in effecting change. Dorothy Height spoke about his ability to recognize the interdependence of different approaches, the value of "different roles": "He used to have a way of saying, 'Well, you see, the more they pound on the table, then the readier other people are to sit at the table and talk to me.' " In Rustin's judgment, Young "got along with [the radicals] much better than almost all the other civil rights leaders, including King."

"You can holler, protest, march, picket, demonstrate," Young declared, "but somebody must be able to sit in on the strategy conferences and plot a course. There must be the strategists, the researchers and the professionals able to carry out a program." Each civil rights organization, each leader, had a distinct strength, a particular role. Young's was clear. "Someone," he often explained, "has to work within the system to try to change it." He had the access to the power structure. He was the bridge, the interpreter, to the rich and the powerful. It was his role to bring the establishment to the support of civil rights. In understanding that process, one needs to begin, again, with the human qualities of Young.

Above all, the people who knew him remember the attractiveness of the man. The sheer physical presence: a big, imposing, bear of a man; energy, electricity, bound up in a 6'2", 200-pound frame. The style: exuberant, ebullient, eager to take on the challenges and pleasures of life; aggressive, indefatigable, a study in perpetual motion; frank, open, without pretense, almost boyish; self-confident, personally secure, at ease professionally and socially; a man's man, a magnet for women, delightful company, easy with a drink, adept on the dance floor, a talented raconteur. Fun to be with, fun to work with. Perhaps most striking, the warmth, the charm, the wit. A man who loved people, a man whom people loved.

The personal attractiveness, the ability to accept and relate to difference, and the skill at dealing with other people equipped Young to move easily across barriers of race, wealth, and social standing. A black journalist described him: "He was urbane enough to talk with the fat cats downtown and hip enough to talk with the tough cats uptown and he never seemed out of place doing either." He was at home in a black community center in Georgia or in a Harlem bar. He spoke easily in the idiom of the street. Still, his friends and associates claim that he was most effective in one-on-one situations, or in small groups, making his case to the white corporate establishment.

"Whitney did as much as any other single individual," former National Urban League President James A. Linen said, "to sell American industry on the advantages of being a good corporate citizen." His message was simple: the business community had a vital interest in eradicating poverty and racism and in "preserv[ing] a stable, orderly, democratic society." Businessmen had a choice: either they could give blacks a stake in society by employing them, "by helping [them] to become productive consumers and producers of goods and services," or

344

they could leave blacks outside the system "as producers of violence and consumers of taxes." Either they could back the efforts of responsible racial advancement organizations, or "the extremists and the irresponsibles" would hold sway.

Young presented his case in a variety of settings. He might ask a business leader to invite some friends to lunch to learn about the Urban League. Or he might meet with the top management of a single company to discuss the training and hiring of black employees. As the years went by, opportunities for getting to know leading businessmen multiplied—they served together on presidential commissions, attended the same conferences, met each other on social occasions, sat on the same boards.* Young made it his business to establish ties with the principal executives of hundreds of the nation's largest corporations.

The *Time* tour of Eastern Europe in November 1966 illustrates Young's dealings with the corporate establishment. The twelve-day trip was one of the tours *Time* magazine sponsored to introduce American businessmen to political and economic leaders and circumstances in different regions of the world. The Eastern European tour included two dozen chairmen and chief executive officers of such companies as North American Aviation, Goodyear Tire & Rubber, Alcoa, Mobil Oil, Borg-Warner, and Ford Motor Company. Young stood out; not only was he from outside the corporate sector, but he was the only black person in the group.[†]

Armed with information about each company's employment of blacks and contributions to the Urban League, Young was ready to give each of his fellow tour members "the treatment." "I never saw a man work a crowd as hard as Whitney did," recalled Time chairman Andrew Heiskell. "He just went after one guy after the other to drum up support for the Urban League." Mixing tough talk and charm, he made his case: corporate America had a responsibility to play a positive role in racial progress. Get involved, he exhorted; do better, try

---

* For example, Young served on the boards of the Rockefeller Foundation, the National Urban Coalition, Urban America, Inc., the Massachusetts Institute of Technology, the New York Federal Reserve Bank. He declined invitations to join corporate boards in order to preserve his impartialilty and freedom to criticize.

† The Urban League had close ties to Time, Inc.; Time president Linen headed the League's corporate support committee and would, in 1968, become the National Urban League's president. League board member W. J. Trent, Jr., who arranged the invitation to Young, was the top black executive at Time.

harder. He knew when to stop, when to change his tack and soften his approach, how to use a joke or a story to turn his listener around. "He had the ability," Heiskell noted, ". . . to push you right up against the wall, and you're about to get mad, and at that point he smiles and laughs and you smile and laugh and you're the greatest buddies in the world." The technique was irresistible. "By the end of the trip," Heiskell remembered, "there wasn't a person who didn't think that Whitney Young was one of the great guys they'd ever met."

The Young treatment paid off. He came back from the trip with promises of jobs for blacks (on the basis of his conversations, he expected 50,000 new positions, he later told a reporter; "I'd be very surprised and disappointed if we didn't get that") and financial support for the Urban League. (He also had offers of corporate vice-presidencies for himself, which he declined.) The most dramatic result was a Christmas letter from Henry Ford II, enclosing a check for $100,000. The $100,000 gift continued each year until Young's death.

It is difficult to say how many jobs for blacks Young won over the years from the corporate establishment, but it is easy to measure his success in gaining corporate support for the National Urban League. In 1961 the Urban League's income from commerce and industry totaled $70,000; in 1970, the last full year of Young's directorship, it received $1,973,000.

Several factors accounted for Young's success in courting corporate America. He approached donors whom the League had never previously asked for money, and he set his sights high. His technique was disarming. As he wrote to the chairman of the board of National Cash Register after the *Time* tour, "This letter comes to fulfill a promise: To stop discriminating against your company by denying it an opportunity to contribute to the work of the National Urban League." In telephone calls and personal visits, Young argued and shamed corporations into raising their donations. Looking over the list of contributors, he would exclaim to his administrative assistant, Enid Baird, "So and so only gives us $1,000? That's crazy—get him on the phone!" In a typical incident, he went to call on the head of a major corporation, who offered the company's usual gift of $5,000. Young said he would not take it. "I can't take it because it is not befitting the size and dignity and stature of your company to give us just $5,000. In fact, I won't take less than $50,000." The man agreed to make the gift.

In addition, corporate leaders responded favorably to Young because they felt comfortable with him. Not only was he personally at-

tractive, but he talked their language and to a great extent shared their outlook and values. And he made a compelling case. He had the ability, in banker Morris D. Crawford, Jr.,'s words, to "tell it like it was" without offending anyone, to tell it "with a kind of grace and sense of humor, and yet with force, that was kind of unique." The result, Time, Inc., president James R. Shepley said, was that he "sold damn near everyone that I've ever seen him work on with the idea that there weren't any conflicting causes that were superior to the one he supported."

Moreover, the times were on Young's side. The 1964 Civil Rights Act made equal employment the law of the land. The riots frightened segments of white America (at least in the short run) into constructive action. Industrial leaders knew they had to do something about the race problem, and the Urban League could be of tangible, constructive assistance. Amid the militance and violence of the 1960s, the League—safe, respectable—looked especially attractive. In Shepley's words, "I don't think there's any doubt that the average establishmentarian American white would have certainly considered Whitney Young's alternative the best of all possible alternatives that confronted him." The racial ferment of the decade made businessmen more receptive to racial concerns; Young knew how to capitalize on that receptivity.

The qualities that enabled Young to move comfortably in the board rooms of corporate America also gave him entree to other sectors of the white establishment. He established close ties with the major foundations. Again, as in the case of corporations, the Young appeal translated into tangible gains for his organization: foundation support for the National Urban League rose from $62,000 in 1961 to $5,054,000 in 1970.

While the Rockefeller Foundation, the Rockefeller Brothers Fund, the Carnegie Corporation, and the Taconic Foundation were all important benefactors of the Urban League in the 1960s, the new relationship that Young forged with the Ford Foundation proved most lucrative for the organization. When McGeorge Bundy became president of Ford in March 1966, Young was the first black leader to come to call. In August, at Young's invitation, Bundy made his first major public address as president of Ford at the Urban League's annual conference. There he announced the new commitment of the Foundation to major programming in the area of civil rights and minority problems. Henceforth, the race question would be the Foundation's primary domestic concern.

The activities of the Urban League and the strength and effectiveness of Young made the organization a logical vehicle for Ford's support. Without the Urban League, Bundy later explained, Ford would have been unable at that time to undertake urban projects "through someone respected and respectable." In the first year of Bundy's presidency, Ford gave the Urban League $1,500,000 for a fair housing project as well as $430,000 for general support. In 1968 and 1969 Ford contributed $4,700,000 to support the League's "New Thrust," a multifaceted effort to improve the quality of life in the ghettos.

The various Ford grants were less an endorsement of a particular set of programs than an investment in the continuing strength of the National Urban League. "It was really a vote of confidence in Whitney Young," Ford vice-president Mitchell Sviridoff explained. Investing in Young meant supporting "a powerfully effective national leader." It was a way of "strengthening . . . the center," Sviridoff observed; "if that center ever came apart, I think there would be unholy chaos in the civil rights community."

The corporations and the foundations were Young's special province. Alone among the civil rights leadership, he had the contacts, the privileged access, the close ties that enabled him to function persuasively as an interpreter for black America. In Washington it was different. There were blacks in government, black advisers in the White House, and established black lobbyists. The civil rights leaders often counseled with the president as a body; in addition, the individual leaders had their own channels of communication with the president and his advisers.

Always there were reasons for Young to go to Washington. Meetings at the White House. Conferences with cabinet officials. Testimony before congressional committees. Personal lobbying on Capitol Hill. "There were times when I'd say to Whitney," his wife recalled, laughing, "we'd be better off if we had moved to Washington instead of New York; we'd see more of you."

The pattern of close communication with the administration began in the Kennedy years: good contacts with administration officials in social welfare, employment, and housing; occasionally, meetings with the president; more frequently, memoranda and telephone calls from Young to the president, making recommendations for programs, commenting on racial conditions, endorsing blacks for appointment to government committees, or urging substantive action on civil rights. But the actual access to the White House was limited, and Kennedy fell short of Young's expectations. The president's civil rights program was too timid, he thought; his actions were much too influenced by political caution. When would Kennedy throw the power of his office behind the cause of civil rights, Young wondered; when would he show "the kind of guts" he had written about in *Profiles in Courage*?

In the Johnson administration, the atmosphere was different. As vice-president, Johnson had been well acquainted with the leaders of the racial advancement organizations through his chairmanship of the President's Committee on Equal Employment Opportunity. As president, deliberately distancing himself from the racial conservatism of his southern heritage, Johnson actively embraced the cause of civil rights.

Among the civil rights leadership, the president's closest ties were to Wilkins, but Young came in a close second. From the first Young was publicly complimentary toward the new president. He wrote Johnson frequently, praising speeches, commenting on legislation, and recommending people for government jobs. Johnson, in turn, often telephoned Young to ask advice and test ideas. At critical junctures, he turned to him for help on Capitol Hill. Young was one of the people Johnson mobilized in the successful effort to persuade Senate Minority Leader Everett Dirksen to help break the filibuster that was holding up the 1964 civil rights bill. ("When are you going to get down here and start civil-righting?" he cajoled over the phone.)

Access to the White House was heady stuff. Young "liked being able to pick up the phone and talk to Lyndon Johnson," Enid Baird said. He was in and out of the executive mansion—for ceremonies, social occasions, and meetings on civil rights and other issues. Johnson appointed Young to numerous advisory panels and presidential commissions ("many of which," Young later commented, "I didn't want"). There was talk of Young joining the administration—the position of deputy director of the poverty program was offered in 1964, but refused; later speculation centered on a cabinet post (Young's name was often mentioned as a possibility for Health, Education, and Welfare; indeed, King telephoned Johnson in January 1965 to advance the suggestion), although it apparently never reached the stage of a concrete offer.

Most of the time, the visibility served Young's purposes as well as the president's. When it did not, the president's purposes took precedence. Johnson's designation of Young as one of a team of observers for the South Vietnamese elections in 1967 is a case in point. Young had already been to Vietnam once on his own initiative in 1966, to investigate the situation of black servicemen. He was publicly committed to supporting the president's policy in Vietnam,* but he was not eager to go as an election observer. In typical Johnson fashion the president left him no choice. The call came in the midst of the Urban League's annual conference. Young explained that he had conflicting commitments. "Well, Whitney," Johnson said, "I'm going to announce you as one of the team, and if you feel you can't serve your country, you explain it to the press."

The Vietnam assignment notwithstanding, the two men remained entirely cordial. In the late autumn of 1968 Johnson made an unexpected appearance at the Urban League's Equal Opportunity Day Dinner in New York. Young later described the occasion: "It was really a beautiful gesture on his part. . . . There was a room of 2000 people and there was hardly a dry eye in the place . . . there was nothing but enthusiastic cheers. It gave us a real opportunity to say 'Thanks' to what we all feel has been the greatest leadership job in civil rights done by any President." Young announced that the League was establishing a scholarship fund in Johnson's name to enable blacks to study public affairs at the University of Texas. Johnson, he wrote in his newspaper column in January 1969, would "go down as a great President whose domestic accomplishments far outweighed the international policies that divided the nation." Later that month, just before he left office, Johnson awarded Young the Medal of Freedom.

The departure of the Democratic administration from Washington raised questions about the future of the gains accomplished through the Great Society. With Richard Nixon in the White House, what would happen to the federal commitment to civil rights and social justice?

At a private meeting following the election, the president-elect talked with Young about joining the cabinet. (There was much speculation at the time that Nixon had offered Young a position, but Young denied that a direct offer had been made; in Nixon's eulogy at Young's burial service in Lexington, Kentucky, in 1971, the president said that they had "discussed the possibility" of such an appointment.) "He told me," the president later recounted, "that he could do more of the things he believed in outside of Government than he could inside." Margaret Young put it this way: "Whitney could not have stood the bureaucracy of Washington, except for being President."

---

* Young finally came out against the war in October 1969, after Johnson had left the White House.

Outside the administration, Young took a pragmatic approach. Nixon was president; "he's the only one we've got." Trying to work with him was the only practical choice. But working with Nixon proved to be difficult. The access to the president that Young had previously enjoyed no longer obtained. In the absence of direct communication, one had to judge Nixon's intentions from administration actions. And there it was hard to avoid the conclusion that he meant to roll back the gains that had been realized in civil rights.

Like other black leaders, Young soon began publicly to criticize the administration for failing to face up to "the urban-racial problems that should be at the top of the list of priorities" and for encouraging a national mood of polarization, "indifference and repression." At the same time he engaged in private discussions with some of the more sympathetic administration officials to try to get some action on the pressing social and economic needs of black Americans. At the end of June 1970 the criticism reached a crescendo when NAACP board chairman Stephen G. Spottswood charged that there was "a calculated policy to work against the needs and aspirations" of black Americans. A Gallup poll published in early July revealed widespread black dissatisfaction with Nixon. Dismayed, White House moderates sought ways of redeeming the administration's standing. It had been (and would continue to be) common for Leonard Garment and others privately to encourage people like Young to see the administration in a more favorable light. (Indeed, Garment had some discussions with Young about joining the administration.) Now, in the early summer, a more explicit suggestion came through intermediaries: if, in his forthcoming speech to the Urban League's annual conference, Young would moderate his criticism, if he would say that he believed that the president might be willing to make some accommodation with black America, the administration would be prepared to provide substantial programs to benefit blacks.

Where the suggestion originated within the administration, and on what authority it was communicated, remains unclear. Nor is it known how Young responded to the idea. But the July 19 speech can easily be interpreted to contain a signal. "As critical as I have been of Administration actions," Young declared, "I do admit that there are some signs that elements of this Administration are moving forward to bring about change. . . . It would be a mistake for us to fail to recognize that within every Administration there are contending forces." Within the context of an otherwise critical speech, it was no great departure from what Young had said before; indeed, he had made precisely the same point in private Urban League gatherings in late spring and early summer. But in the wake of Spottswood's attack, Young drew public criticism from blacks for being soft on Nixon. What negotiations may have ensued cannot be ascertained, but it seems clear that the signal failed to elicit the positive response for which Young may have hoped.* In late August, at a press conference, Young delivered a stinging attack on the administration for its "indecisiveness" and "flabbiness" on civil rights. Nixon's record was "sort of like Jell-O," he said. "You can't really get ahold of it. . . . it's what I call white magic, you know, now you see it, now you don't." As for the public mood, "I've never seen the black community quite as universally disillusioned and lacking in confidence about an Administration as I have this one."

While Young continued to be sharply critical throughout the fall, again, privately, he made another attempt to come to terms with the administration. This time his efforts bore fruit. The arrangement was made through Garment: Young would meet with the president and cabinet and subcabinet officials who were concerned with urban affairs. At the meeting at the White House on December 22, Young spoke about the crushing impact on blacks of unemployment and poverty and the desperate need for intensified efforts to alleviate the urban crisis. He proposed a partnership between the government and nonprofit social agencies: instead of establishing its own machinery to administer social programs, the government should subcontract them to established agencies that had the experience to run them.

Nixon directed the cabinet to develop cooperative arrangements along the lines Young suggested. The result of the meeting was a federal commitment of $28,000,000 to the Urban League for social and economic programs to be implemented by League affiliates and other agencies. In February 1971 the Urban League board ratified the League's new "Federal Thrust," setting the pattern for the massive infusion of federal money into the organization in the next decade.

Any assessment of Young's relationships with the white establishment must take account of the varied perspectives from which blacks evaluated him. To many blacks, Young pulled off a delicate, difficult balancing act. In Rustin's words, he had a "unique talent for dealing with the white power structure without losing touch with the grass-

---

* Young's close associates were apparently unaware of the overture from the administration, and some of them find the story improbable. But Linen, who as president of the National Urban League would have been in position to know about it, confirms this interpretation.

roots movements in the black community." "He managed to be militant," the former mayor of Cleveland, Carl Stokes, reflected, "but not to the point of identification with militants that would jeopardize his relations with white corporate America. . . . That takes a skill that there haven't been many around to do."

But not all blacks saw Young that way. To some, his easy access to the power structure meant that he had sold out to the white establishment. "Moderate" was a polite way to characterize him; less restrained critics coined derisive forms of description—"Oreo cookie," "Uncle" Whitney, "Whitey" Young.

At issue behind the name-calling were two fundamental charges: first, that in the methods he used and the goals to which he aspired, Young was a moderate instead of a militant; second, that in values, attitudes, and life-style, he was too much at home in white America. Each deserves consideration.

Insofar as Young eschewed black separatism and deplored racial violence, "moderate" was an appropriate label. He was committed to integration, and he believed in the democratic process. He sought to work within the system to change it, not to opt out of it or overturn it. But the way the white media used the term "moderate," it carried misleading connotations. Just because someone "doesn't shout and scream or throw bricks and Molotov cocktails" did not mean that he was a moderate, Young insisted. In his own writings, in interviews, and in responses to repeated questioning, he explained his position: "There are no moderates in the civil rights movement; . . . we are all militant when it comes to demanding our full rights." The Urban League was "just as angry" at racial injustice "as anybody else." The proper distinction was not between "moderate" and "militant," but between "burners and builders, between insane and sane leadership."

In fact, both the National Urban League and its leader became more militant as the racial crisis grew more intense. The explosion of the ghettos and the assassination of King provided the catalyst for a reorientation in the Urban League's emphases. In an emergency meeting in April 1968 the League announced a "New Thrust" to bring the organization more directly into the ghetto. While the Urban League never abandoned its historic commitment to integration, it was clear that genuine integration was a distant dream; for the foreseeable future, most blacks would continue to live in segregated communities. The "New Thrust" committed the League "to sink [its] roots deep in the ghetto"—to build economic and political power where most blacks were concentrated. The emphasis would be on community organizing, on bolstering indigenous leadership, on creating self-sufficient economic institutions, and on gaining community control. The Urban League would provide technical assistance and professional expertise to facilitate confrontations between ghetto dwellers and the power structure. Instead of acting as spokesman for blacks, the League would help them to speak effectively for themselves. Instead of merely providing social services, it would function as a direct agent of social change.

By the summer of 1968 Young, too, was moving toward a different stance. His basic thinking had not changed dramatically, but there was a sufficient change in emphasis, a sufficient reorientation of perspective, to betoken something new. He began to couch his vision in terms of an "open," not an integrated society—a pluralistic society that permitted the healthy persistence of "ethnic and cultural differences"; a world in which blacks would "have their fair share of the power, the wealth, and the comforts of the total society," but would be free to choose between integrated and segregated living.

Similarly, while Young never gave up his commitment to nonviolent strategies and interracial cooperation, he seemed increasingly to empathize with the frustrations of blacks who were impatient with the capacity of the system to deliver social change. Addressing the annual convention of CORE in July 1968, he spoke favorably of Black Power. "The Urban League," he declared, "believes strongly in that interpretation of Black Power that emphasizes self-determination, pride, self-respect, participation and control of one's destiny and community affairs." It brought the delegates to their feet, shouting, "The brother has come home!" "I had to make a rather basic decision," Young explained in an interview the following year. "One is of no value to a society or to institutions as a leader unless he has the respect of his people, his constituency, the people he would lead." He could have condemned Black Power, he said, or he "could try to reinterpret it, redefine it, sanitize it a bit if you will, and give it a positive connotation." He "chose the latter route."

"The test of what makes a Negro leader," Young insisted, ". . . is not who shouts the loudest or gets the angriest but who *gets the most results.*" Young's success in getting results depended on his ability to win concessions from the establishment. Of course he kept company with white corporate chiefs; as he put it, "They've got the jobs. *Somebody's* got to talk to the people who have something to give." To use the establishment as an instrument of change, he had to be compatible with it.

354

When blacks criticized Young's life-style, he confronted the issue head-on. He often told black audiences the story of the train ride between his home in New Rochelle and his office in Manhattan. "I think to myself," he said, "should I get off this morning and stand on 125th Street cussing out Whitey to show I'm tough? Or should I go downtown and talk to an executive of General Motors about 2,000 jobs for unemployed Negroes?" To those who were skeptical of his decision to live in a predominantly white, middle-class suburb, he responded, "I never promised to live in the ghetto with you. I said I would work to ensure every one of you the right to live in decent housing wherever you choose. The solution isn't for me to come and join you and the rats; it's for you to come on out here and join me and these white folks."

Young's white friends sometimes twitted him about his establishment ways. Johnson once tracked him down at lunch at the 21 Club in New York. Young picked up the phone and heard the familiar Texas voice: "You're a hell of a leader of the poor blacks, having lunch at 21." When Young was relaxing one summer afternoon in Morris Crawford's backyard swimming pool, floating lazily, Scotch and soda in hand, Crawford snapped a picture and later gave him a copy. "Now, Whitney, you behave yourself," he joked, "because I'm gonna show that picture all around Harlem."

Young got a kick out of conferring with corporate chieftains and counseling presidents, and he had a healthy ego. "Sometimes he was excited by the aura of the power structure," Margaret Young reflected. "Whitney wasn't beneath being intrigued with being able to manipulate [it]." But enjoying his foothold in the power structure did not mean forgetting why he was there. Social contacts had constructive uses. A woman he met at a party might be asked to take two tables at a future Urban League function. An elegant dinner with another couple might be a chance for argumentation and persuasion. "I don't get so flattered by floating around on some yacht," he once said, "that I lose sight of my goal." The point of his entree was to facilitate social change.

After nearly a decade at the helm of the National Urban League, Young was ready to move on to something else. It had not reached the stage of any public announcement, but those who were closest to him knew that he was eager for a change. He had accomplished his major objectives—reorganizing the League, making it financially sound, bringing it into the mainstream of civil rights. The job had lost its challenge, and he was tired. "He really wanted to take a year off," Margaret Young said, "and just travel and think, read, and kind of retool, kind of just get it back together."

What would have come next? There was no plan in place. One job he would have liked fell beyond his reach. J. George Harrar would be retiring as president of the Rockefeller Foundation. Young, a trustee of the Foundation, hoped to succeed him. When he learned that he was not among the final candidates,* it was a real disappointment. "I don't think they're ready for a black man to handle that much money," he confided to a colleague.

Young's intimates disagree over the direction he would have chosen. A corporate post? Unlikely. Politics? Some say he had his eye on a Senate seat; others believe that he would eagerly have accepted a cabinet position—HEW, most likely, perhaps Housing and Urban Development. He used to joke about his political prospects, but beneath the jest, friends discerned a serious intent.

There had not yet been much chance for black leaders to move beyond the racial arena to assume significant leadership positions on the broader national scene. Young was "uniquely situated to do that," Vernon Jordan said; he would have been able "to transform, to parlay all of his Urban League experiences of ten years into something bigger and better that would have impacted the nation and the world."

The chance never came. In March 1971 Young went to Nigeria to participate in the African-American Dialogue. He drowned while swimming off the coast of Lagos.

He wished to be remembered, Young had often said, as "an effective voice of the voiceless, an effective hope of the hopeless." Certainly he succeeded in bringing the voiceless and the hopeless to the attention of the power structure. He communicated the needs and aspiration of black Americans to the white establishment. He goaded, challenged, and prodded white businessmen and professionals to pay attention to racial problems. (His own profession was no exception; as president of the National Conference on Social Welfare and the National Association of Social Workers, he pushed successfully for greater involvement in social and political action.) At the very least, he neutralized strong white voices that might otherwise have been raised as real obstacles to racial progress. At best, he won jobs and money, and he played a critical role in motivating white leaders to act. Andrew

---

* In September 1971 the Foundation announced that the job would go to Dr. John H. Knowles of Massachusetts General Hospital. The search for Harrar's successor, however, had begun well before Young's death.

356

Heiskell put it succinctly: "I started the Urban Coalition. Would I have done it if I hadn't known Whitney? Probably not." Ford, who headed the National Alliance of Businessmen, made the same point: "Knowing Whitney Young got me more interested in [urban and racial problems] and doing more [about them] than I would have done otherwise."

Of course, there were instances where he failed to get results. There were still too many prominent whites whose social consciences lay dormant, too many businesses that took refuge in tokenism, and too few effective federal efforts to wipe out racism and poverty. No one black leader, no matter how skillful an interpreter, no matter how strong a bridge, could dramatically change the face of American race relations.

But Young had made a significant dent. He excelled as a mediator at a time when mediators were in short supply. He understood the power structure, and he knew the processes of social change. He depended more on personality than ideology, and he was pragmatic enough to work with anyone who could help him reach his goals. When others set change in motion by marching in the streets, Young, in the words of black journalist Chuck Stone, "helped to guide it and orchestrate it . . . to give it direction, shape, and a certain stability." In a time of intense passion and upheaval, he was a steady source of reason and calm.

Ironically, the role that Young played deprived him of much popular adulation from blacks during his lifetime. What he did best, he accomplished quietly. In an age of dramatic gestures and strident voices, his deeds and his message were usually overshadowed. Popular convention made it unfashionable for contemporary blacks to applaud his role. And yet, when his funeral procession made its way through Harlem, throngs of grieving people lined 125th Street, pressing into the roadway, hands outstretched to touch the passing hearse. Whitney Young had made a striking impact on those for whom he strove to speak.

Note on Sources

The principal sources for a study of Whitney M. Young, Jr., are Young's own papers, deposited in the Rare Book and Manuscript Library at Columbia University, New York City, and the National Urban League Papers, Part II, Manuscript Division, Library of Congress, Washington, D.C.

For an introduction to Young's views see his books, *To Be Equal* (New York: McGraw-Hill Book Co., 1964), and *Beyond Racism* (New York: Mc-

Graw-Hill Book Co., 1969). Guichard Parris and Lester Brooks, *Blacks in the City* (Boston: Little, Brown and Co., 1971), cover the history of the National Urban League during the bulk of Young's executive directorship.

Useful brief accounts include: *Current Biography*, 1965, pp. 476–78; Allan Morrison, " 'New Look' for the Urban League," *Ebony*, 21 (Nov. 1965): 164ff.; "Races," *Time*, 90 (Aug. 11, 1967): 12–17; Irwin Ross, "The Black Power of Whitney Young," *Reader's Digest*, 94 (Jan. 1969): 117–21; Carl T. Rowan and Dreda K. Ford, "In Memory of Whitney Young," *Reader's Digest,* 100 (Apr. 1972): 121–25; Robert Penn Warren, *Who Speaks for the Negro?* (New York: Random House, 1965), 157–71; "Whitney Young, Power Player," *Newsweek* (May 15, 1967): 28-29; "Whitney Young: He Was a Doer," *Newsweek* (Mar. 22, 1971): 29. Tom Buckley, "Whitney Young: Black Leader or 'Oreo Cookie'?" *New York Times Magazine*, Sept. 20, 1970, pp. 33ff., while controversial, ought to be consulted.

The foregoing essay is based to a large extent on interviews with family, friends, and associates of Whitney Young: Alexander J. Allen, Enid Baird, Arnita Young Boswell, Wiley A. Branton, McGeorge Bundy, Kenneth B. Clark, Clarence D. Coleman, Morris D. Crawford, Jr., Joseph F. Cullman III, Daniel S. Davis, James R. Dumpson, Marvin Feldman, Henry Ford II, Leonard Garment, Mitchell I. Ginsberg, Jack Greenberg, J. George Harrar, Dorothy Height, Andrew Heiskell, M. Carl Holman, Vernon E. Jordan, Jr., Theodore W. Kheel, Lindsley F. Kimball, James A. Linen III, Louis Martin, Clarence M. Mitchell, Jr., Guichard Parris, Donald Rumsfeld, Bayard Rustin, Edwin F. Shelley, Florence D. Shelley, James R. Shepley, William B. Simms, Harold R. Sims, Henry Steeger, Carl Stokes, Chuck Stone, Mitchell Sviridoff, Ann Tanneyhill, W. J. Trent, Jr., Sterling Tucker, Robert C. Weaver, Betti S. Whaley, and Margaret B. Young.

Notes on Contributors

JOHN HOPE FRANKLIN has been at the University of Chicago since 1964 and in 1969 was named John Matthews Manly Distinguished Service Professor of History. In 1980 he was appointed a Senior Mellon Fellow at the National Humanities Center. His books include: *From Slavery to Freedom: A History of Negro Americans* (5th ed., 1980); *A Southern Odyssey: Travelers in the Antebellum North* (1976), and *Racial Equality in America* (1976).

PETER GOLDMAN is a senior editor at *Newsweek*, specializing in national affairs. He is the author of three books on aspects of the black situation in America, including, most recently, *The Death and Life of Malcolm X* (1973, rev. ed. 1979).

LOUIS R. HARLAN is professor of History at the University of Maryland, College Park. He is the author of *Separate and Unequal* (1958) and *Booker T. Washington: The Making of a Black Leader* (1972); he is the co-editor of *The Booker T. Washington Papers* (1972–   ).

DARLENE CLARK HINE is an associate professor of History and assistant provost at Purdue University, West Lafayette, Indiana. She is the author of *Black Victory: The Rise and Fall of the White Primary in Texas* (1978).

THOMAS C. HOLT is a member of the department of History at the University of Michigan, Ann Arbor. He is the author of *Black over White: Negro Political Leadership in South Carolina during Reconstruction* (1977).

MARTIN KILSON is professor of Government at Harvard University, Cambridge, Massachusetts. He is the author of *Political Change in a West African State* (1966), and he has co-edited *New States in the Modern World* (1975).

LAWRENCE LEVINE is professor of History at the University of California, Berkeley. His latest book is *Black Culture and Black Consciousness: Afro-American Folk Thought from Slavery to Freedom* (1977).

359

EUGENE LEVY is an associate professor of History at Carnegie-Mellon University, Pittsburgh. He is the author of *James Weldon Johnson: Black Leader, Black Voice* (1973).

DAVID LEVERING LEWIS is professor of History at the University of California, San Diego. His books include *King: A Critical Biography* (1970) and *When Harlem Was in Vogue* (1981).

GENNA RAE MCNEIL is the project archivist for the Phelps-Stokes Fund Archival Project of the New York Public Library at the Schomburg Center for Research in Black Culture. Her doctoral dissertation was a biography of Charles Hamilton Houston.

AUGUST MEIER is University Professor of History at Kent State University, Kent, Ohio. He is the author of *Negro Thought in America, 1800–1915* (1963) and co-author, with Elliott Rudwick, of several books, including *From Plantation to Ghetto* (3d ed., 1976).

BENJAMIN QUARLES is emeritus professor of History at Morgan State University, Baltimore. He is the author of several books on black history, among them *Frederick Douglass* (1948), *The Negro in the Civil War* (1953), *The Negro in the American Revolution* (1961), and *Black Abolitionists* (1969).

B. JOYCE ROSS taught at Kent State University, Kent, Ohio, and Stanford University. She is the author of *J. E. Spingarn and the Rise of the N.A.A.C.P.* (1972).

ELLIOTT RUDWICK is professor of History and Sociology at Kent State University, Kent, Ohio. He is the author of *W. E. B. Du Bois: A Study in Minority Group Leadership* (1960) and *Race Riot at East St. Louis* (1964), and he has co-authored, with August Meier, several volumes, most recently, *Black Detroit and the Rise of the UAW* (1979).

EMMA LOU THORNBROUGH is McGregor Professor of American History at Butler University, Indianapolis, Indiana. Her publications in Afro-American history include *The Negro in Indiana before 1900: A Study of a Minority* (1957) and *T. Thomas Fortune: Militant Journalist* (1972).

WALTER WEARE is professor of History at the University of Wisconsin-Milwaukee. He is the author of *Black Business in the New South: A Social History of the North Carolina Mutual Life Insurance Company* (1973).

NANCY WEISS is associate professor of History at Princeton University. She is the author of, among other works, *The National Urban League, 1910–1940* (1974).

Index

Abbott, Robert S., 55
Abernathy, Ralph David, 279; and Albany, Ga., 283, 284
Abrams, Charles, 192-93
Abstention: and Malcolm X, 320
Abyssinian Baptist Church, 263, 264
Adam by Adam, 267
Addams, Jane, 44, 46, 54, 55
Affirmative Action, 337
AFL: and Brotherhood of Sleeping Car Porters, 151; and Randolph, 160
AFL-CIO: and Randolph, 160-61
Africa: and Garvey, 128-31
African Blood Brotherhood, 134
African Legionnaires, 125
African Methodist Episcopal Church, 24; and Wells-Barnett, 58
African Orthodox Church, 126
African Times and Orient Review, 109
"Afro-American": and Fortune, 24
Afro-American Council, 4, 13, 49, 50; and Fortune, 27, 31, 33; and Wells-Barnett, 46, 50-51
Afro-American League, 19, 33; and Fortune, 26-27, 35; and Wells-Barnett, 41
Afro-American Press Association, 41
Agnew, W. J. C., 253, 254
Akridge, Garth, 214
Albany, Ga., 281-84
Albany *Herald*, 282
Allen, Alexander J., 341
Along This Way, 102
A.M.E. Church Review, 22
An American Dilemma, 93
American Fund for Public Service, 94
American Negro Academy, 23
American Negro Labor Congress, 152
American Nurses' Association: and black nurses, 255-56
American Red Cross Nursing Service, 246, 247, 248, 252
American Tobacco Co., 171, 177
Amsterdam *News*, 35, 249
Anderson, Charles W., 72, 87, 88, 261
Anderson, Thomas W., 125

Anna T. Jeanes Foundation, 10
Anti-lynching legislation: and F. Roosevelt, 192
Apocalypse: and Black Muslims, 320
"Appeal to Racial Pride," 137
Arline, Charles, 94
Armed forces: segregation in and Randolph, 158-59
Army Nurse Corps, 246, 248
Association of Colored Railway Trainmen, 226, 232
Atlanta Baptist College, 169
Atlanta Compromise, 3, 4, 16
Atlanta *Constitution*, 22
Atlanta Cotton States Exposition, 175
Atlanta Exposition speech, 49
Atlanta University, 7
Austin, Louis, 180, 186
Autobiography (Malcolm X), 306, 312, 317, 326, 328
The Autobiography of an Ex-Colored Man, 87, 101

Bagnall, Robert, 91
Bailey, Alonzo, 13
Bailey, Josiah W., 186
Baird, Enid, 346, 349
Baker, Wilson, 290
Baldwin, James, 301; on Muhammad, 308
Banjo, 115
Baptists: and Washington, 4; and Spaulding, 179
Barber, J. Max, 14
Barnes, Gerald, 206, 213
Barnett, Claude, 241, 246
Barnett, Ferdinand L., 43
Beard, Mary, 246, 252
Belafonte, Harry, 285
Belgarnie, Florence, 56
Bennet, William S., 268
Bennett, John J., 268
Bentley, Charles E., 52, 54, 55
Bethune-Cookman College, 182, 191
Bethune, Mary McLeod, 189, 191-219;

and NACW, 57; and Spaulding, 182, 183; and biracial groups, 195; and racial equality, 196; and M. Johnson, 197-98, 214; racial philosophy of, 198; administrative assistants of, 198-201; and segregation, 201
Beyond Racism, 337
Bilbo, Theodore, 16, 132
Birmingham, Ala.: King in, 284-87
Birmingham Manifesto, 286
Birth of a Nation, 53
Black and White, 21, 30
Black Belt Diamonds, 31
Black business: and Washington, 15
Black cabinet: of F. Roosevelt, 191-219
Black capitalists: and Du Bois, 64
Black Cross Nurses, 120, 125
Black leadership: and Randolph, 152
Black Man, 136, 137
Black Manhattan, 101
Black Muslims, 306, 310, 314, 320
Black newspapers: and Brotherhood of Sleeping Car Porters, 148
Black nurses: and World War II, 241-57
Black Panthers, 300
Black Power, 300, 326; and Randolph, 162-63; and Young, 354
Black press: and Washington, 6; and Niagara Movement, 69-70; and Spaulding, 180-81; and Staupers, 245
Blacks: and World War I, 112-13; and Communist party, 154; and New Deal, 192; and World War II, 193; and city machines, 261
Black separatism: and Randolph, 162-63
Black Star Steamship Line, 80, 127-28, 134
Black teachers, 185
Black women's clubs, 191; and Wells-Barnett, 56-57
Black Worker, 149, 153
Black workers: and Houston, 232-36
Blaine, James G., 25
Blough, Robert, 287
Blyden, Edward Wilmot, 24
Bolling v. *Sharpe*, 221
Bolton, Frances Payne, 245, 255
The Book of American Negro Poetry, 101
The Book of American Negro Spirituals, 101
Borah, William, 97
Boston *Guardian*, 6, 34, 39, 51, 71; and nurses, 253
Boston riot, 7, 14
Boston *Transcript*, 21, 30

Bousfield, M. A., 249
Boutwell, Albert, 285
Boycotts: and Powell, 264-65
Briggs, Cyril, 134
British Anti-Lynching Society, 51, 56
Broadcast Skills Bank, 335
Brooke, Edward, 294
Brooklyn *Eagle*, 23
Brotherhood of Sleeping Car Porters, 139, 147-52, 234, 241
Brown, H. Rap, 300
Brown, Richard R., 203, 207, 208, 210
Brown v. *Board of Education*, 221
Browning, Charles P., 198
Brownsville, Tex., 70, 71
Bruce, Herbert, 268
Bullock, Ralph W., 199, 206, 214
Bunche, Ralph, ix, 82, 93
Bundy, LeRoy, 261
Bundy, McGeorge, 347, 348
Burkett, Randall, 125
Burns, James MacGregor, 86
Burrowes, Mr.: and Garvey, 107
Business, white: and Young, 344-47
Byrnes, James, 76, 144

Calder, William, 98
Capper, Arthur, 98
Carmichael, Stokely, 300
Carnegie, Andrew: and Washington, 4, 10
Carnegie Corporation, 347
Carnegie Hall Conference, 7, 67
Carolina Times, 180, 186
Carver, George Washington, 2
Celler, Emanuel, 273
Chaney, James, 60
Chesapeake, Ohio and Southwestern Railroad, 42, 58
Chicago: Wells-Barnett work in, 43-45
Chicago *Conservator*, 43
Chicago *Defender*, 55, 249
Chicago Summit Agreement, 294
Chicago *Tribune*, 46
Chisum, Melvin J., 14
CIA: and Malcolm X, 311
Civilian Conservation Corps, 183
Civil rights: and Fortune, 23; and Houston, 221-40; and Young, 338-42; movement and Malcolm X, 316
Civil Rights Act, 1964, 289, 291, 323
"Civil Rights and Social Privileges," 23
Civil Rights Committee, AFL-CIO, 161
Clansman, 70
Clark, James, 290

Clark, Kenneth B., 342-43
Clark, Samuel, 232
Cleaver, Eldridge, 326
Clergy: and Garvey, 125; and Brother-
hood of Sleeping Car Porters, 148
Cleveland, Grover, 25
Colored American Magazine, 34
Commission on the Interracial Coopera-
tion, 188
Committee Against Jim Crow in Military
Service and Training, 158
Committee of 40, 52
Committee on Fair Employment Prac-
tices (FEPC), 156-57
Communists: and Randolph, 152-54; and
National Negro Congress, 153; and
blacks, 154
Compromise of 1877, 25
Congress of African Peoples, 343
Congress of Racial Equality (CORE),
157, 241, 277, 280, 354
Connor, Eugene "Bull," 285, 299
"The Conservation of Races," 77
Conservator, 49, 50
Consolidated Edison, 266
Constitution League, 52
Coolidge, Calvin, 135
Cooperative stores: and DuBois, 78
Corrigan v. *Buckley*, 236, 237
Cosgrove, R. H., 125
Cosmopolitan Club, 14
Council of United Civil Rights Leader-
ship, 339
Crawford, Morris D., Jr., 347, 355
Crisis, 91; and Du Bois, 73-78, 80; and
Pullman Co., 149; and discrimination
in education, 229
Crummell, Alexander, 23
Cullen, Countee, 100
Cummins, Albert, 98
Currier, Stephen, 288, 338

Dailey, Phyllis, 254
Daily Commercial, 43
Daily News, 55
Daley, Richard, 292
Darrow, Clarence, 93
Dauser, Sue S., 251
Davis, Ossie, 316
Dawson, William, x, 259, 263, 269, 271,
272
Defender, 148
Dent, Albert W., 249
Department of Housing and Urban De-
velopment, 191

DePriest, Oscar, x, 269
DeSapio, Carmine, 270
Dewey, Thomas E., 268
Diagne, Blaise, 79-80
Diggs, Charles, 271
Dillon, Douglas, 287
Dirksen, Everett, 349
Discrimination: and Fortune, 28
Divine, Father, x
Dixon, Russel, 249
Dixon, Thomas, 16
Domestic Marshall Plan, 338
Douglas, Paul, 300
Douglas, William O.: on Houston, 239
Douglass, Frederick, 17, 25, 28, 153, 182;
and Republican party, 112
Du Bois, W. E. B., 49, 50, 59, 63-83, 142,
171, 277, 296; and Washington, 6, 7, 9,
15-16, 39, 64-70; and Fortune, 32, 35;
and Wells-Barnett, 44; and NAACP,
52, 73-77, 80-82; as propagandist, 63-
64; quoted, 64; personality of, 64;
background of, 65; and higher educa-
tion, 65; and *Crisis*, 73-78; and Pan-
Africanism, 77, 78-79; and Garvey,
77, 80, 116; and Walter White, 81-82;
as symbol, 83; and Johnson, 88, 91,
102; on Garvey, 120, 133-34; and Pullman Co., 149, 150; and National Negro Business League, 169; and Durham, 173
Duke Endowment, 182
Duke family, 183
Duke University, 177, 183
Duke, Washington, 172, 173
Dunbar, Virginia, 246
Dunjee, Roscoe, 201, 204
Durham Committee on Negro Affairs,
185-87
Durham, N.C., 167, 172, 173, 175, 176
Dusk of Dawn, 63
Dyer bill, 59, 96-99
Dyer, L. C., 96

East St. Louis, Ill.: riot in 1917, 117
Ebony, 182
Economic Bill of Rights, 299, 302
Economic independence: and Garvey,
126-28
"The Editor's Mission," 21
Education: and Fortune, 30; and Du
Bois, 65-66; industrial and Washing-
ton, 66; discrimination in and Hous-
ton, 227-31; and Urban League, 335

Eisenhower, Dwight D., 270
Embree, Edwin R., 142
Emotionalism: and Malcolm X, 315
England: and Garvey, 109-10, 136
Espy, Henry, 229, 230
Evening Scimitar, 43
Evening Star, 41
Evers, Medgar, 60, 339
Executive Order 8802 (FEPC), 156, 158, 235, 242
Executive Order 9981 (armed forces), 159
Expatriation: and Fortune, 24

Fairbanks, Gen., 249
Fair employment practices: and F. Roosevelt, 156
Fair Employment Practices Act, 192
Fair Employment Practices Committee, 235, 242
Famous Negroes, 182
Fanon, Frantz, 317, 326
Fard, Wallace D., 308, 309
Farmer, James, 241, 288, 300, 342; and Young, 338
Federal Bureau of Investigation: and King, 295; and Muslims, 309; and Malcolm X, 311
Fellowship of Reconciliation, 154, 279
Field Foundation, 281
"Fifty Years," 101
"Fifty Years of Negro Progress," 175
The Fire Next Time, 301
Fisher, Miles Mark, 179
Fisher, Rudolph, 101
Fisk University, 65, 188
Flikke, Julia O., 248
Florida A & M College: and NYA, 204
Florina Lasker Award, 334
Ford Foundation, 347, 348
Ford, Henry II, 357; and Young, 346
Forman, James, 338
Fortune, Carrie, 20, 34
Fortune, Emanuel, 20
Fortune, Timothy Thomas, 19-37; and Washington, 4, 26, 28-31; early life of, 19-20; career as journalist, 19-24; and civil rights, 23; and interracial marriage, 23-24; and expatriation, 24; and term Afro-American, 24; and politics, 24-26; as orator, 26; and discrimination, 28; and education, 30; and T. Roosevelt, 31-32; last years of, 33-36; and Du Bois, 35; and Garvey, 35; and Wells-Barnett, 41, 49

Foundations: and Young, 347-48
France, Joseph, 129
Frankfurter, Felix, 222
Frazier, E. Franklin, 82; on Durham, 167, 172
Frederick Douglass Center, 52, 55
Freedmen's Bureau, 20
Freeman, 26, 34
Free Speech and Headlight, 42, 43, 45
Friends of Negro Freedom, 145

Gaines, Lloyd Lionel, 229-31
Gandhi, 159, 278
Garfinkel, Herbert, 155
Garment, Leonard, 351, 352
Garvey, Amy Jacques, 126, 130, 135
Garvey, Indiana, 106, 109
Garvey, Marcus, x, 105-38, 326; and Fortune, 35; and Wells-Barnett, 40; and Du Bois, 77, 80, 116; and Johnson, 102; early life and family, 106-8; in England, 109-10; and Washington, 109-10, 111; and doctrine of revitalization, 114-16; in the United States, 114-36; and Washington's philosophy, 118; philosophy of, 118-19; and the masses, 119-22; and pageantry, 120-21; and religion, 122-26; and the clergy, 125; and economic independence, 126-28; and Black Star Line, 127-28; and Africa, 128-31; and whites, 131; racial ideology of, 131-33; and other black leaders, 133-34; exile of, 135-37; and Randolph, 163; and Durham, 175; and Powell, 263, 264; and Malcolm X, 306
Garvey Movement, 262
"The Gentlemen's Agreement and the Negro Vote," 99
George, Henry, 29
Gillett, Frederick, 97
Globe, 20, 22, 23, 25, 30
God's Trombones, 101
Goldwater, Barry, 290, 309
Gompers, Samuel, 11
Goodman, Andrew, 60
Grace, Daddy, ix
Grady, Henry W., 22, 23, 28, 41
Graham, Billy, 306
Granger, Lester, 241, 246, 332
Grant, Dr. Richard, 201
Graves, William, 55
Gray, James, 282
Great Britain: and Wells-Barnett, 46-47
Greater New York Coordinating Committee for Employment, 266

Great Men of Color, 182
Greenberg, Jack, 338
Green, William, 151

"Hail! United States of Africa!," 128
Hall, Grover Cleveland, 55
Hamilton, Charles, 311
Hampton Institute, 2
Harding, Warren G., 96, 97, 98, 132
Harlem Hospital, 265
Harlem Renaissance, 115, 172, 176, 262; and Du Bois, 78; and Johnson, 100-102
Harlem riot, 1935, 266
Harper, Conrad, 237
Harrar, J. George, 356
Harris, Abraham, 148
Harvard Law Review, 222
Harvard Law School, 222
Hastie, William H., ix, 185, 191, 193, 231, 249, 250-51; and Houston, 225; and Staupers, 244, 246; and Stimson, 247
Hawkins, Augustus, 204
Hayes, Wayne, 273
Hays, Arthur Garfield, 93
Headwaiters and Sidewaiters Society of New York, 145
Hedgeman, Anna Arnold, 157, 252
Heflin, J. Thomas, 16
Height, Dorothy, 338, 343
Heiskell, Andrew, 345, 357
Henry, Stephen G., 253
Hershaw, L. M., 71
Hill, James, 40
Hill, Oliver, 227
Hill, T. Arnold, 55, 155, 198
Hillquit, Morris, 145
Hitler, Adolf, 136
Hocutt, Thomas, 184
Hocutt v. *North Carolina*, 184-85
Hodges v. *United States*, 233
Hollins v. *State of Oklahoma*, 226
Hoover, Herbert, 175
Hoover, J. Edgar: and Randolph, 144; and King, 295
Hope, John, ix, 169
Horizon, 71, 72
Horne, Frank, 191, 193, 198
House Committee on Education and Labor, 271
Housing: and NAACP, 236-38
Houston, Charles Hamilton, 184, 221-40; and Howard University Law School,

222, 223-25; early life of, 222; and Hastie, 225; as activist, 225-26; and NAACP, 226-39; appearance of, 227; and discrimination in education, 227-31; and black workers, 232-36; and FEPC, 235; and equal housing opportunities, 236-38
Houston, Henrietta, 236
Houston, William L., 223
Howard, Perry, 148
Howard University, 20, 182; Law School and Houston, 222, 223-25
Hughes, Charles Evans: and Gaines case, 230
Hughes, Langston, 100, 101, 182; quoted, 115
Hull House, 44, 46, 54
Human rights: and King, 295
Humphrey, Hubert: and King, 281
Hunt, H. A., 193
Hunter, Jane Edna, 254
Hurd v. *Hodge*, 236, 238
Hurst, John, 113
Hurston, Zora Neale, 100
Hylan, John, 261

Ickes, Harold, 183
"I Have a Dream" speech, 287-88
Improved and Benevolent Order of Elks of the World, 149
Indritz, Phineas, 237
Institute of Negro Literature and Art, 77-78
Integration: and Saddler, 200; and Malcolm X, 314
International Association of Railway Employees, 226, 232-33
International Labor Defense, 226
Interracial marriage: and Fortune, 23-24
Iola, pseud. *See* Wells-Barnett, Ida

Jacks, James, 56
Jackson, Alexander L., 55
Jackson, Mahalia, 287
Jamaica: Garvey in, 110-11
James, Esther, 273
Jamestown Tercentennial, 175
Jews: and Washington, 10
Jobs: and Urban League, 335
Johnson, Charles S., 100, 188
Johnson, Edward A., 261
Johnson, Frank M., Jr., 291
Johnson, Guy Benton, 176, 188
Johnson, Henry Lincoln, 128

Johnson, Jack, 188
Johnson, James Weldon, 67, 85-103, 171; and Du Bois, 82, 91, 102; early life of, 86-87; and New York *Age*, 88; as NAACP field secretary, 88-90; as head of NAACP, 90-100; and legal attacks, 92; and publicity, 92; and anti-lynching bill, 96-99; and Harlem Renaissance, 100-102; and art, 102; and Garvey, 102; and UNIA, 124; and Brotherhood of Sleeping Car Porters, 149
Johnson, Lyndon B., 191, 326; and Saddler, 200; and integration, 202; and Powell, 272; and 1963 March, 289; and Young, 338, 349-50, 355
Johnson, Mordecai W., ix, 209; and Bethune, 197-98, 214; and Howard University Law School, 223
Johnson, Rosamond, 87, 101
Joint Committee Investigating Seditious Activities, 144
Jones, Eugene Kinckle, 55
Jones, J. Raymond, 270
Jones, LeRoi, 328
Jordan, Vernon, 356
Julius Rosenwald Fund, 142, 182, 243

Kennedy, John F., 272, 280; and Albany, Ga., 284; and 1963 March, 288; and Malcolm X, 310; and Young, 338, 349
Kennedy, Robert, 295; and King, 281; and Birmingham, 287; and 1963 March, 289
Kenyatta, Jomo, 120
Kerner Commission on Civil Disorders, 301
Kilson, Martin, 187
Kimball, Lindsley, 332
King, Coretta, 279, 282-83
King, Martin Luther, 17, 171, 189, 277-303; and Randolph, 161; career before Selma, 277-89; and Albany, Ga., 281-84; in Birmingham, 284-87; and 1963 March on Washington, 287-89; and Nobel Prize, 290; and Selma, 290-91, 340; and discrimination in North, 291-94; and Vietnam, 294-95, 342-43; and human rights, 295; and Malcolm X, 306, 311, 316-17, 319, 324-25; and Young, 338
Kirk, Norman T., 253, 254
Knowles, Dr. John H., 356
Ku Klux Klan, 20, 132

Labor unions: and Washington, 10-11
Ladd, Everett C., Jr., 186
LaGuardia, Fiorello, 156, 268
Laura Spelman Rockefeller Memorial, 223
Lawson, Victor F., 55
Leadership, 86
League for Non-Violent Civil Disobedience Against Military Segregation, 159
League of Nations, 130
"Letter from Birmingham Jail," 286
Lewis, Claude, 312, 317, 321
Lewis, John, 287
Lewis, William H., 5-6
Liberia, 130
Liberty Hall, 120
Liggett and Myers, 183
Lincoln, C. Eric: on Malcolm X, 312, 313, 325
Lincoln Hospital, 180, 183
Linen, James A., 344, 345, 352
Little, Malcolm. *See* Malcolm X
Locke, Alain, 100
Lodge Federal Elections bill, 22
Lodge, Henry Cabot, 98, 99
Lomax, Louis, 307, 320
Longworth, Nicholas, 97
Lorimer, William E., 58
Louis, Joe, 188
Louisiana grandfather clause, 13
Love, Col., 248, 249
Lovett, Eddie, 227, 230
Lull, George F., 248
Lumumba, Patrice, 328
Lynching, 9; and Washington, 12; and Wells-Barnett, 40, 47-48; motives for, 47-48; and NAACP, 59, 95-99

McCarthy, Eugene, 295
McCown, Ira, 264-65
McDowell, Calvin, 42, 45
McGuire, George Alexander, 125-26
McKay, Claude, 100, 101, 115
McKinley, William, 25
McKissick, Floyd, 300
McNamara, Robert, 287
Madden, Martin, 96-97
Magee, James C., 250; and War Dept., 247-48
Mahoney, Barry, 298
Malcolm X, x, 305-30; early life of, 306-8; militance of, 310; assassination of, 310-11; and whites, 313-14; and emotionalism, 315; and civil rights move-

ment, 316; and King, 316-17, 319, 324-25; and violence, 318-19; and abstention, 320; break with Muhammad, 320-21; last months of, 321-26; and United Nations, 322-23; and politics, 324; and NAACP and Urban League, 325; as folk hero, 327-29
March on Washington, 1941, 140, 154-55
March on Washington, 1963, 287-89; and Randolph, 159-60, 162; and Urban League, 339-42; and Young, 341-42
March on Washington Movement, 241
Marshall, Burke, 287
Marshall, George C., 251, 253
Marshall, Louis, 225
Marshall, Thurgood, 230, 238; on Houston, 221-22
Marxism: and Du Bois, 64
Masses: and Garvey, 119-22
Mass protest: and Randolph, 140
Masterson, William Edward, 230
May, Andrew J., 254
Meany, George: and Randolph, 161
The Mechanics and Farmers Bank, 174
Meier, August, 161
Meredith, James, 313, 340
Merrick, John, 170-71, 172, 173, 183
"Message to the Grassroots," 319
Messenger, 77, 134, 143-45, 146, 149
Micheaux, Elder Solomon Lightfoot, ix
Migration to North, 140, 260
Milholland, John, 52, 59
Militants: and Young, 343-44
Miller, Kelly, 8-9
Mississippi Freedom Summer, 289-90
Mitchell, Arthur, x, 269
Montgomery Improvement Association, 278-79
Moon, 71
Moore, Aaron McDuffie, 170, 171, 177, 183
Moore, Fred R., 34, 88
Mortgage Company of Durham, 174
Morton, Ferdinand Q., 261-62
Moss, Thomas, 42, 45
Moton, Robert, 175
Muhammad, Elijah, 306, 308, 309, 316, 318, 326; Malcolm's break with, 320-21
Mulzac, Hugh, 128
Murphy, Charles Francis, 268
Murray, F. H. M., 71
Muslim Mosque, Inc., 321
Muslims: and blacks, 309
Mussolini, Benito, 136

Muste, A. J., 154, 279
Myrdal, Gunnar, 93

NAACP, ix, x, 195; and Washington, 14; and Wells-Barnett, 40, 50-54; and Du Bois, 52, 63, 73-77, 80-82; first decade of, 53; and lynching, 59, 95-99, 192; and Pan-African Movement, 79; and Johnson, 85-103; and Garvey, 116; and working class, 141; and *Messenger*, 143; and Brotherhood of Sleeping Car Porters, 149; and 1941 March on Washington, 155; and Hocutt case, 184-85; and black teachers, 185; and segregation, 201; and Houston, 226-39; and equal housing opportunities, 236-38; and Powell, 263-64; and 1963 March on Washington, 288; and Vietnam, 297; and Malcolm X, 325
NAACP Legal Defense and Educational Fund, 231
La Nacionale, 108
Nash, Roy, 88
National Afro-American Council. *See* Afro-American Council
National Afro-American League. *See* Afro-American League
National Association for the Promotion of Labor Unionism, 145
National Association of Colored Graduate Nurses, 242-43, 245
National Association of Social Workers, 356
National Brotherhood Workers of America, 145
National Cash Register, 346
National Conference on Social Welfare, 356
National Council for a Permanent Fair Employment Practice Committee, 252
National Council of Negro Women, 191
National Defense Council. Subcommittee on Negro Health, 249
National Equal Rights League, 58
National Federation of Afro-American Women, 28, 56
National Negro Bar Association, 262
National Negro Business League, 4, 7, 15, 34, 49-50, 70, 169; and Fortune, 31
National Negro Congress: and Communists, 153
National Negro Finance Corporation, 174
National Negro Medical Association, 262
National Negro Press Association, 148

367

National News, 57
National Nursing Council for War Service, 245, 252
National Recovery Administration, 183
National Skills Bank, 335
National Urban League. *See* Urban League
National Youth Administration, 191-219; Division of Negro Affairs, 195, 207-10, 212; National Advisory Committee, 196; in the South, 203-5, 211; and segregation, 204; and salaries for blacks, 206; regional Negro affairs representatives, 212
Nation of Islam, 305, 320
Navy Nurse Corps, 246, 251
Negro American Labor Council, 161
Negro Americans, What Now?, 102
Negro Cooperative Guild, 78
Negro Factories Corporation, 126
Negro Fellowship League, 54, 58
The Negro in Business, 31
The Negro in Politics, 25
Negro Slave Songs in the United States, 179
Negro World, 35, 120, 127
Nelson, William Stuart, 201
New Deal: and Spaulding, 183; and blacks, 192-93
A New Negro for a New Century, 31
New South, 172
New York *Age*, 4, 41, 49, 169; and Fortune, 21, 30, 32, 34; and Wells-Barnett, 28, 43; and Niagara Movement, 70; and Johnson, 88; and Staupers, 249
New York City Council: and Powell, 266-67
New York *Commoner*, 113
New York *Evening Post*, 68
New York *Freeman*, 20-21
New York *Herald Tribune*: and Albany, Ga., 283
New York Review of Books, 300
New York *Sun*, 21
New York Telephone and Telegraph Co., 266
New York *Times*, 300; and Albany, Ga., 284
Niagara Movement, 8, 33, 68-73; and Washington, 14; and Wells-Barnett, 50
Nigeria, 356
Nix, Robert, 271
Nixon, E. D., 278

Nixon, Richard: and Young, 350-52
Nixon v. *Herndon*, 93-94
Nobel Peace Prize, 290, 317
Nonviolent civil disobedience: and Randolph, 157-58
Nonviolent civil rights campaigns: formula for, 279-80
Nonviolent direct action, 277
Norfolk *Journal and Guide*, 35, 235, 249
North Carolina College, 176; and Spaulding, 181, 182
North Carolina Mutual Life Insurance Company, 167-90
Nurses. *See* Black nurses

"O Black and Unknown Bards," 101
Odetta, 287
Odum, Howard, 188
Office of Economic Opportunity, 296
Ogden, Robert C., 10
Oklahoma *Black Dispatch*, 201
Omnibus Corporation, 266
Opportunity, 146
Organization of Afro-American Unity, 310
Osborne-Marsh, Vivian, 204
Outlook, 70
Ovington, Mary White, 52-53, 54, 58, 59, 92
Owen, Chandler, 143-45
Oxley, Lawrence, 193

Pageantry: and Garvey, 120-21
Pan-Africanism: and Du Bois, 63, 77, 78-79
Parks, Rosa, 278-79
Parris, Guichard, 340, 341
Parsons, Talcott, 267
Patterson, John N., 214
Patterson, Robert P., 250
People's Advocate, 20
People's Grocery, 42
The People's Voice, 268
Peterson, Jerome, 32
The Philadelphia Negro, 65
Pickens, William, 91
Picketing: and Powell, 264-65
Pittsburgh *Courier*, 155, 249, 283
Plessy v. *Ferguson*, 228, 229, 230
Politics: and Washington, 5, 15-16; and Fortune, 24-26; and Spaulding, 176, 183-84, 185-86; and blacks, 261; and Malcolm X, 324
Poole, Elijah. *See* Muhammad, Elijah
Poor People's Campaign, 299, 302
Pound, Dean Roscoe, 222

Poverty: and King, 296

Powell, Adam Clayton, Jr., 169, 179, 259-75, 277; and black solidarity, 263, 274; early life of, 263; and boycotts and picketing, 264-65; and N.Y. City Council, 266-67; character of, 267; in Congress, 269-73; as womanizer, 274

Powell, Adam Clayton, Sr., 263

Powell, John, 132

La Prensa, 108

President's Committee on Equal Employment Opportunity, 337, 349

Prince, Joseph C., 27

Pritchett, Laurie, 282

Profiles in Courage, 349

Propagandist: Du Bois as, 63-64

Publicity: and Johnson, 94-95

Pullman Company, 141, 147-52

"The Quick and the Dead," 29, 35-36

Railway Labor Act of 1934, 150

Randolph, A. Philip, 139-65, 189, 234, 241, 252, 277, 296; and Du Bois, 76; and Garvey, 134, 163; and Brotherhood of Sleeping Car Porters, 139; and mass protest, 140; and black working class, 140-41; early life of, 140-41; character and personality of, 141-42; as orator, 142; as Socialist, 142-47; and Russia, 144; as administrator, 149-50; and AFL, 151, 160; and black leadership, 152; and Communists, 152-54; and lynching, 155; and other organizations, 155; and nonviolent civil disobedience, 157-58; and segregation in armed forces, 158-59; and 1963 March on Washington, 159-60, 162, 287, 288, 342; and black power, 162-63; and black separatism, 162-63; and Economic Bill of Rights, 299; and Young, 338, 339

Randolph, Lucille, 140

Rangel, Charles, 273-74

Rankin, John E., 269

Ransom, Leon, 230

Rape: and lynching, 47-48

Rauschenbusch, Walter, 295

Rayburn, Sam, 272

Reader's Digest, 182

Redmond, Sidney, 229, 230

A Red Record, 43

Reeb, James, 291

Reeding, J. Saunders, 73-74

"Relation of the Division of Negro Af-

fairs to the General Program of the National Youth Association," 210

Religion: and UNIA, 122-26; and Durham, 176

"Reply to Congressman James F. Byrnes of South Carolina," 144

Republican Party: and Fortune, 24-25

"Returning Soldiers," 76-77

Reuther, Walter, 287

Revitalization, doctrine of: and Garvey, 114-16

Reynolds, Grant, 158

Reynolds, J. A., 232

Rhoads, Joseph J., 202

Riddle, Estelle Massey, 243, 245, 255

Robeson, Paul, ix, 189

Robinson, Spottswood III, 237, 238

Rockefeller Brothers Fund, 347

Rockefeller family, 172

Rockefeller Foundation, 243, 332, 347, 356

Rockefeller, John D.: and Washington, 10

Rockefeller, John D., Jr., 332

Rockefeller, Nelson, 285; and King, 281, 284

Rockefeller, Winthrop, 332

Rogers, Dan: case, 13

Rogers, Henry H., 10

Rogers, J. A., 182

Roosevelt, Eleanor, 156, 183; and Staupers, 245, 252-53; and black nurses, 252

Roosevelt, Franklin Delano, 155, 156; and fair employment practices, 140; and Spaulding, 176; black cabinet of, 191-219; and anti-lynching legislation, 192; and NYA, 209; and FEPC, 235, 242; and nurses, 253

Roosevelt, Theodore: and Washington, 5; and Fortune, 25-26, 31-32; and Niagara Movement, 71

Rosenwald, Julius, 54; and Washington, 10; and Urban League, 55. *See also* Julius Rosenwald Fund

Ross, Malcolm, 157

Rostow, Eugene, 287

Rowan, Carl T., 297

Ruffin, Josephine, 56, 57

Russia: and Randolph, 144

Rustin, Bayard, 157, 241; on Randolph, 142, 164; and 1963 March on Washington, 159, 162, 342; on Malcolm X, 311, 315; on Young, 343; on Young and whites, 352

Saddler, Juanita, 204; and NYA, 198-201, 202; and integration, 200; career of, 215-16
Saturday Evening Post, 182
Schiff, Jacob, 10
School of African Philosophy, 136
Schuyler, George S., 141
Schwerner, Michael, 60
Scott, Emmett, 13, 29, 32, 35, 76; and Johnson, 88
Scottsboro case, 185; and Houston, 225
Secretary Training Project, 335
Segregation: and Bethune, 201; and NYA, 204
Seligmann, Herbert, 94
Selma, Ala., 290-91; and Young, 340
Seymour, Marion B., 248
Shaw University, 40-41, 182
Shelley v. *Kraemer*, 236, 238
Shepard, James E., 181, 186
Shepley, James R., 347
Sherril, William L., 122
Shillady, John R., 90
Shores, Arthur, 234
Simmons, Furnifold, 186
Slater Fund, 182
Smitherton, Joseph T., 290
Social Gospel, 295
Socialism: and Randolph, 142-47
Socialist party: and blacks, 146-47
The Souls of Black Folk, 7, 65, 83
South: NYA in, 203-5, 211
Southern Christian Leadership Conference, 280; in Albany, Ga., 281; in Birmingham, 285; and Selma, 290-91
Southern Education Board, 10
Southern Horrors, 43, 45
Southern Women for the Prevention of Lynching, 60
Spaulding, Charles Clinton, 167-90; and Washington, 168, 189; early life of, 169-71; character and personality of, 171-72; and politics, 176, 183-84, 185-86; influence and power of, 177-89; and the church, 179-80; and black press, 180-81; and North Carolina College, 181, 182; fame of, 182; and Hocutt case, 184-85; and NAACP, 185; and race relations, 188-89
Spero, Sterling D., 148
Spingarn, Arthur, 92
Spingarn, Joel, 74, 75, 82; and Johnson, 88
Spingarn Medal, 256
Spottswood, Stephan G., 351

Spring Mobilization, 1967, 297
Staupers, Mabel K., ix, 241-57; early life of, 243-44; and E. Roosevelt, 252-53; leadership style of, 256
Steele, Bester William, 234
Steele v. *Louisville & Nashville*, 233
Stevenson, Adlai, 270
Stewart, William, 42, 45
Stimson, Henry, 247, 252, 253
St. Luke Herald, 175
Stokes, Carl, 353
Stone, Chuck, 357
Storey, Moorfield, 59, 94, 96, 225
Stoute, Herman, 266
Stride Toward Freedom, 280, 295
Student Nonviolent Coordinating Committee (SNCC), 163, 280, 281; in Albany, Ga., 281; and Mississippi Freedom Summer, 289-90; and Malcolm X, 322
Sunni Islam, 306
Sunni Muslim, 324
Sutton, Percy, 321
Sviridoff, Mitchell, 348
Sweet, Ossian, 93

Taconic Foundation, 281, 288, 347
Taft, William Howard: and Washington, 5; and Brownsville, 71
Talented Tenth, 6, 8, 15, 16, 64, 66, 79, 82, 187
Talmadge, Herman, 282
Tammany Hall, 261, 268
Tennessee Valley Authority, 183
Terrell, Mary Church, ix, 56-57
Terrell, Robert, 57
Texas, 200, 202
30 Years of Lynching in the United States, 1889-1919, 95
Thompson, William, 56
Thurman, Wallace, 115
Tillman, Benjamin, 16
Time magazine, 345; and Albany, Ga., 283; and King, 289
To Be Equal, 337
Tobias, Channing H., 256, 266
Torrens, James, 268
Townsend, Charles, 98
Townsend, Willard S., 160
The Trial of Martin Luther King, 298
Trent, W. J., Jr., 345
Trotter, William Monroe, ix, 49, 51; and Washington, 6-7, 39; and Du Bois, 8, 71; and Fortune, 32; and Wells-Barnett, 58-59

Truman, Harry: and equality in armed forces, 158; and FEPC, 235
Truth, Sojourner, 153
Tubman, Harriet, 153
Tunstall, Tom, 234
Tunstall v. *Brotherhood of Locomotive Firemen*, 232
Turner, Henry M., 24
Turner, Nat, 153, 309
Tuskegee Machine, 4-5, 16, 169; and Du Bois, 68
Tuskegee Normal and Industrial Institute, 2, 3, 12, 13, 116; and NYA, 204

United Brotherhood of Elevator and Switchboard Operators, 145
United Colored Democracy, 261
United Nations: and Malcolm X, 322-23
United Negro Trades, 145
Universal Negro Catechism, 125
Universal Negro Improvement Association, 35, 80, 105; in Jamaica, 110-11; New York division, 117; Conventions, 1920 and 1921, 120-21; and religion, 122-26; and economic independence, 126-28; and KKK, 132; and Garvey's exile, 135; and Powell, 263
Universal Negro Ritual, 125
University of Missouri: and Gaines, 229-31
University of North Carolina, 184
"The Upbuilding of Black Durham," 173
Up From Slavery, 3, 109
Urban League, 195, 331; and Washington, 55; and Wells-Barnett, 55-56; and working class, 141; and *Messenger*, 143; and Brotherhood of Sleeping Car Porters, 149; and 1941 March on Washington, 155; and Spaulding, 183; and 1963 March on Washington, 288, 339-42; and Vietnam, 297; and Malcolm X, 325; and Young, 334-58; and ghetto, 353-54

Valien, Preston, 148
Vardaman, James, 16
Vaughn, A. N., 249
Vesey, Denmark, 153
Vesey, Gabriel, 153
Vietnam War: and King, 294-95; and Young, 342-43
"Views and Reviews," 88
Villard, Oswald Garrison, 51, 52, 53, 59, 68, 74; and Johnson, 88
Violence: and Malcolm X, 318-19

Voting rights: and Washington, 12; Act, 1965, 291, 328

Waddy, Joseph, 233, 234, 238
Wagner-Costigan bill, 59
Wagner, Robert, 270, 285
Walker, Jimmy, 268
Walker, Wyatt Tee, 284, 285
Wallace, Anthony F. C., 113-14
Wallace, George, 299
Warner, Lloyd, 260
Washington, Booker T., 1-18, 112, 116, 143, 277; early life of, 2; approach to black-white relations, 3; as machine boss, 3; and white philanthropists, 4; and politics, 5, 15-16; and black press, 6; critics of, 6-9; and Du Bois, 7, 9, 15-16, 64-70; and whites, 9-11; and Jews, 10; and working class, 10-11; and lynching, 12; and voting rights, 12; and espionage, 13-14; secret actions of, 13-14; and Niagara Movement, 14, 68-70; character of, 14; and black business, 15; and Fortune, 26, 28-31; and Wells-Barnett, 39, 44, 48-50, 54, 59; Birmingham speech, 49; and Urban League, 55; and NACW, 57; and education, 66; and Garvey, 109-10, 118; and Spaulding, 168, 181, 189; and Durham, 173; and King, 293; and Muslims, 309
Washington Colored American, 26
Washington, Margaret, 57
Washington Sun, 35
Watson, James, 99
Watts riot, 292
Weaver, Robert C., 183, 191, 194
Webster, Milton P., 150, 156
Wells-Barnett, Ida B., 39-61; and Fortune, 28, 32, 49; and Washington, 39, 48-50, 54, 59; and lynching, 40, 47-48; early life of, 40-43; and Garvey, 40; journalistic career of, 41-43; in Chicago, 43-45; and accommodation, 44; and economic power, 44, 45; and whites, 45-47; and Niagara Movement, 50; and NAACP, 50-54; and Urban League, 55-56; and black women's clubs, 56-57; lack of black support for, 58-59; and organizations, 58-59; and Trotter, 58-59; and Fisher, 179
Wells, Ida. *See* Wells-Barnett, Ida B.
Wells, Jim, 40
Westin, Alan, 298

Where Do We Go From Here, 296, 300
Whip, 148
White, George, 58
White House Conference on Civil Rights, 292
Whites: and Washington, 4, 9-11; and Wells-Barnett, 45-47; and Johnson, 94-95; and Garvey, 131; in Durham, 173; and Bethune, 195; and Malcolm X, 313-14; and civil rights, 331; and Young, 352-53
White, Walter, ix, 85, 155, 184, 238, 241, 249; and Du Bois, 81-82; and Johnson, 91, 92; and Houston, 227; on World War II, 242
Wickenden, Elmira B., 252
Wilkins, Roy, 83, 238, 300, 311; and Houston, 227; and 1963 March on Washington, 287, 288, 342; on Malcolm X, 325; and Young, 338; and Vietnam War, 342-43
Williams, Aubrey, 207, 209
Williams, Fannie Barrier, 57
Williams, S. Laing, 49, 50, 57
Wilson, Woodrow, 87, 144
Women's Era, 56
Woodson, Carter G., 180
Woodward, C. Vann, 172
Woolley, Celia, 52, 55

Working class: and Washington, 10-11
Works Progress Administration, 183, 213
World War I: and blacks, 112-13
World War II: and black history, 241; and black nurses, 241-57
Wright, R. R., 179

Yarmouth (ship), 128
Yergan, Dr. Max, 266
Young, Andrew, 300, 341
Young, Laura Ray, 333
Young, Margaret Buckner, 333, 334, 336, 350, 355, 356
Young, Whitney M., Jr., 162, 300, 311, 331-58; and 1963 March on Washington, 287, 288; and Vietnam, 294, 342-43; and Malcolm X, 328-29; early life of, 332-34; and Urban League, 334-58; and activism, 337-38; and public policy, 338; and civil rights, 338-42; as peacemaker among civil rights leaders, 341-43; personal qualities of, 341-43; and militants, 343-44; appearance and personality of, 344; and white business, 344-47; and foundations, 347-48; and the government, 348-52; and whites, 352-53; as moderate, 353; life-style of, 355
Young, Whitney Moore, Sr., 333

BOOKS IN THE SERIES

Before the Ghetto: Black Detroit in the Nineteenth Century   *David M. Katzman*

Black Business in the New South: A Social History of the North Carolina Mutual Life Insurance Company   *Walter B. Weare*

The Search for a Black Nationality: Black Colonization and Emigration, 1787–1863   *Floyd J. Miller*

Black Americans and the White Man's Burden, 1898–1903   *Willard B. Gatewood, Jr.*

Slavery and the Numbers Game: A Critique of *Time on the Cross*   *Herbert G. Gutman*

A Ghetto Takes Shape: Black Cleveland, 1870–1930   *Kenneth L. Kusmer*

Freemen, Philanthropy, and Fraud: A History of the Freedman's Savings Bank   *Carl R. Osthaus*

The Democratic Party and the Negro: Northern and National Politics, 1868–92   *Lawrence Grossman*

Black Ohio and the Color Line, 1860–1915   *David A. Gerber*

Along the Color Line: Explorations in the Black Experience   *August Meier and Elliott Rudwick*

Black over White: Negro Political Leadership in South Carolina during Reconstruction   *Thomas Holt*

Keeping the Faith: A. Philip Randolph, Milton P. Webster, and the Brotherhood of Sleeping Car Porters, 1925–37   *William H. Harris*

Abolitionism: The Brazilian Antislavery Struggle   *Joaquim Nabuco, translated and edited by Robert Conrad*

Black Georgia in the Progressive Era, 1900–1920   *John Dittmer*

Medicine and Slavery: Health Care of Blacks in Antebellum Virginia   *Todd L. Savitt*

Alley Life in Washington: Family, Community, Religion, and Folklife in the City, 1850–1970   *James Borchert*

Human Cargoes: The British Slave Trade to Spanish America, 1700–1739   *Colin A. Palmer*

Southern Black Leaders of the Reconstruction Era   *Edited by Howard N. Rabinowitz*

Black Leaders of the Twentieth Century   *Edited by John Hope Franklin and August Meier*

REPRINT EDITIONS

King: A Biography   *David Levering Lewis*   Second Edition

The Death and Life of Malcolm X   *Peter Goldman*   Second edition

Race Relations in the Urban South, 1865-1890   *Howard N. Rabinowitz,* with a Foreword by C. Vann Woodward

Race Riot at East St. Louis, July 2, 1971   *Elliott Rudwick*

W. E. B. Du Bois: A study in Minority Group Leadership   *Elliott Rudwick*